A CENTURY OF PLAYS

BY AMERICAN WOMEN

A CENTURY OF PLAYS
BY AMERICAN WOMEN

Edited with an Introduction
by

Rachel France

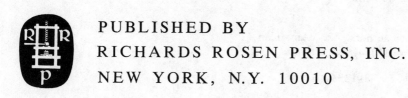

PUBLISHED BY
RICHARDS ROSEN PRESS, INC.
NEW YORK, N.Y. 10010

Published in 1979 by Richards Rosen Press, Inc.
29 East 21st Street, New York, N.Y. 10010

Copyright 1979 by Rachel France

First Edition

Library of Congress Cataloging in Publication Data
Main entry under title:

A Century of plays by American women.

  Bibliography: p.
  1. American drama—Women authors. 2. American
drama—20th century. 3. One-act plays, American.
I. France, Rachel, 1936–
PS628.W6C4   812′.041   78–12347
ISBN 0–8239–0472–5

Manufactured in the United States of America

for Sarah
and Harry Sellin

ABOUT THE EDITOR

Born on May 26, 1936, in New York City, Rachel Mehr France was graduated from the High School of Music and Art before going on to earn a B.A. in Drama and Art History from Vassar College, an M.F.A. in Stage Design from the Yale School of Drama, and a Ph.D. in Dramatic Theory and Literature from Carnegie-Mellon University. The work of Dr. France, a member of the United Scenic Artists, has appeared Off-Broadway and on television, and she has served as resident designer at the Cecilwood Summer Theatre in Fishkill, N.Y.; Cincinnati's Playhouse-in-the-Park; and the Washington (D.C.) Theatre Club.

She has taught at the State University of New York–Geneseo and is presently on the faculty of Lawrence University in Appleton, Wisconsin. Her articles and reviews have appeared in such publications as *Film* and the *Educational Theatre Journal.* She is the author of the critical study *The Drama of Sex: Apropos of Women and the American Theatre,* and she is in the process of completing her first novel.

Dr. France is married to playwright-scholar Richard France. They have two daughters, Miriam and Rebecca.

PHOTO BY RICHARD S. DAVIS

EDITOR'S NOTE

The one-act play was synonymous with the Little Theatre movement. That, plus the resurgence of the one-act form in recent years, was a major influence in the selections that I made for this anthology.

Moreover, many of the authors who are represented here—among them, the most famous—wrote only short plays. Those others who did not are ably represented by their shorter works.

In examining the spectrum of 20th-century drama we find that, thanks to the gift of hindsight, one-act plays have often been the best and certainly the most interesting works that have appeared on the American stage.

ACKNOWLEDGMENTS

The idea for this book was conceived by my husband, Richard. Likewise, its final form owes its existence to this most beloved of collaborators.

I owe a debt of profound gratitude to my Uncle Harry, without whose avuncular supervision there would be no younger generation of scholars in our family.

The staff of the Seeley G. Mudd Library at Lawrence University—Harriet Tippet and Kathy Isaacson in particular—were invaluable in helping me to track down many of the plays and their authors.

Gayle Counts and Richard Shelden of the Ford Foundation were kind enough to provide me with a travel and research grant.

Last, but hardly least, I would like to thank Rebecca Foster France and Miriam Sellin France for constantly inspiring me to become an appropriate role model.

CONTENTS

SUPPLEMENTAL READINGS

By the middle of the 19th century, American women had conquered the literary marketplace, even if their efforts did not always result in works of lasting artistic significance. For example, Louisa May Alcott, who described her teary novels as "moral pap for the young," recognized that in literature she and her sister writers had a field that could provide them with a substantial livelihood. This did not apply to dramatic writing. Indeed, it was not until shortly before the turn of the century, the "Gilded Age," that women began to write for the stage in any numbers. From then on, no examination of America's dramatic tradition can be complete without discussing the work of its women playwrights.

More often than not, however, these women have been altogether neglected. It is an omission that stems in part from the fact that the history of the American theatre has been concerned primarily with plays that were successful on Broadway. With the resurgence of interest in noncommercial theatre, however, this omission will surely be corrected.

In his essay "Realism in the American Theatre," John Gassner voiced the belief that realism has all too often been equated with what is modern in the American theatre. This critical confusion originates in the assumption that American realism is a 20th-century—or, more specifically, post- World War I—phenomenon. In an attempt to correct this judgment, Gassner points to James Herne, Clyde Fitch, and Augustus Thomas as writers who departed from the strictures of Victorian conventions. Their studies in psychological and character drama point up the growing, if flawed, influence of Henrik Ibsen in America. The defect in early American realism was, according to Gassner, a kind of forced optimism, which he regards as characteristic of American society. This optimism encouraged "happy endings." Even well into the 20th century he found American realism, in the main, still suffering from this same sort of defect.

If we include the work of our women dramatists, however, we find some startling exceptions to this analysis. Mary Burrill's *Aftermath* first appeared in *The Liberator* in April, 1919. This brutally realistic play depicts the reactions of a black World War I veteran to the lynching of his father.

Despite the importance of realism in the development of American drama, it constitutes only one aspect of our modern tradition, which is more closely linked to the aesthetic ideals of the European art theatre movement of the last century. That, in turn, had developed as a reaction to the dictates of realism and its most extreme counterpart, naturalism. The symbolism of Maurice Maeterlinck and the expressionism of August Strindberg were fundamental to the growth of the American avant garde. This led, over the years, to a fusion of realism with poetic imagery, a category that is usually set aside for Eugene O'Neill and Clifford Odets, but which is just as appropriate for Carson McCullers and Lillian Hellman.

Critical debates about playwriting from O'Neill to the present day often center on one important issue—whether the author has succeeded in blending the realistic elements of the play with its poetry. Even those works long considered basic to any discussion of American drama are still frequently judged to be "too arty" or "lacking in poetic sense."

Hallie Flanagan's and Margaret Clifford's *Can You Hear Their Voices* (1931) was a victim of "artiness." Susan Glaspell's *The Outside* (1917) similarly lends itself to such discussion. Whether these plays succeed in fusing their various elements is an open question. It is not the purpose of this anthology to resolve such issues. My objective, simply, is to bring women authors into the critical mainstream of American drama.

Response to the avant garde, not only of critics but of the general public as well, is rarely favorable at first, even to well-established playwrights. Despite its often dubious results, the tendency has always been to place particular emphasis on the importance of realism in the theatre.

Women dramatists are our latest avant garde. Yet, for all the great number and variety of plays written by them in the past decade, few have received favorable or wide attention. Their efforts have succeeded with only a select and highly sophisticated audience. Accordingly, the playwrights of the 1970's, men and women alike, have turned to simpler and more popular techniques. In other words, they have retreated to a more clearly recognizable reality.

Realism, however, can be more than verisimilitude or the artificial inflation of a subject through poetic language. In the same way antirealism is more than disguised realism. Critics are confronted with a different dramatic equation in each play that they see or read. The plays in this volume are worthy of such critical confrontation. They comprise an important part of our dramatic tradition; the fact that they were written by women gives them added current appeal.

In assembling this anthology, I have a further point to make. American women dramatists share a unique history. Relatively few women wrote plays before the turn of the century. After that, they quickly became an integral part of the avant-garde movement, as well as braving the rigors and constraints of Broadway. As a result, cultural factors must be applied to them that do not apply to other dramatists.

I refuse to accept the notion that women, as a group, have a unique point of view, or special sensibilities. It would require a larger volume than this one merely to articulate the various points of view and differing sensibilities of each of the authors represented in this anthology—to say nothing of how they differed from male playwrights individually or in the aggregate. I leave it to psychologists and sociologists to assign differences (whatever they may be) on the basis of sex. The role that interests me most in these women is that of playwright. I cannot even say that their observations of other women are more cogent because they too are women. Except in special cases, women wrote for the very same audience that men did; an understanding of that audience is more to the point than any analysis of the playwrights' own personal histories.

The cultural developments that fostered the success of the Woman's Movement also made it possible for women to write for the stage. It must be understood that in the early days, as today, this refers only to a small body of women who are both talented and usually affluent.

Although women were to figure prominently in the founding of the Little Theatre movement, women dramatists in sizable numbers first became evident when they began to write for the Broadway stage. This was explained by Harry J. W. Dam in *The Sunday Magazine* of April 10, 1904:

There have been produced in this country since 1890 the most numerous group of women dramatists known to history. This is primarily a result of social conditions, the emancipation of women from the practical domestic servitude which prevails in other countries, and the feminine sphere of activity. It is further due to the fact that women, with their superiority in tact, in sensitiveness of perception and in closeness of observation, are, up to a certain point, more at home in dramatic expression than men.

We may well question Dam's analysis in attributing special qualities to women. As it happens, however, he was only voicing public opinion as shaped by the Woman's Movement, which represented a powerful pressure group even in his day.

An organized, articulated Woman's Movement led by Elizabeth Cady Stanton and Susan B. Anthony first came to fruition in the 1890's. Anthony was a septuagenarian and something of a sacred cow when, in 1893, she took her seat in the magnificent three-story colonnaded Women's Pavilion of the World's Columbian Exposition in Chicago. The Movement had become respectable. Delegates from suffrage organizations, temperance societies, and missionary groups assembled to expound on the "woman question" and its social, political, aesthetic, and philosophical implications. No coherent idea of feminism was to emerge from their many, varied, and often contradictory pronouncements. Nor can anything of the sort be deduced from the record left by the Exposition's Congress of Women. What resulted was not so much an assemblage uniting in the struggle for its rights, as the triumph of Victorian womanhood.

President Chester A. Arthur, in a speech at about the time of the Exposition, referred to "our cultured and enlightened womanhood." What he had in mind were the wives and daughters of America's aristocracy. Robert G. Ingersoll, echoing these words, spoke of the "nobility of womanhood." From their own pronouncements, it is clear that the Congress of Women felt that these natural virtues empowered them to begin the reform of the manners and morals of society. They were adamantly in favor of "social purity," which, of course, meant the suppression of vice. The "nobility of democracy" must be preserved, and women's inevitable enfranchisement would ensure it.

Morals were confused with manners; aesthetics was made synonymous with purity and beauty; and temperance became the cure for society's ills. Voices blended in the chorus that was to determine social behavior for years to come. The Movement asserted itself. Changes in property rights and the liberalization of divorce laws demonstrated its influence. The issue of the double standard was taken up by the Congress of Women, but only by implication: the rigid standards of morality, which already existed for women, ought to be applied to men as well.

The women who turned to the Broadway stage around the turn of the century wrote for an audience that subscribed to Victorian morality. Their social ideals were not to be offended. Organized womanhood held to the belief that women should expand their sphere of activities and at the same time increase social pressure to conform strictly to existing moral standards.

Burns Mantle, in his retrospective volume *The Best Plays of 1894–1899,* shows the names of women playwrights appearing with frequency beginning as early as 1890. Such was their impression that Augustin Daly, at the end of his long and illustrious career as a producer and playwright for the Broadway stage, was impelled to remark that "the theatre in America is made by women for women." This conclusion was echoed by Harry Dam, who noted that while Germany had produced a Hermann Sudermann, Norway an Ibsen, and England a G. B. Shaw, none of these was a writer for the masses. That is to say, they could not be relied upon to furnish a play that was certain to profit the author or his producer. For Dam, the future of the Broadway stage lay in the hands of a new crop of women playwrights who, like Martha Morton and Madeline Lucette Ryley, were able to generate in abundance the kind of sure-fire commercial properties that all too often eluded more noteworthy dramatists. Critical attention began to be paid to those "Women Who Have Written Successful Plays" and to the rise of the woman playwright.

Without a doubt, much of the sensation was caused by the sheer novelty of having women write for the stage. By 1908, however, William Bullock and others were already discussing why women fail as playwrights. The reason most often cited was their inability to create "genuine" women characters. Ryley's *Mice and Men* (1909), which is reminiscent of Molière's *The School for Wives* and Morton's *Her Lord and Master* (1902), tend, unfortunately, to confirm this judgment. (It is worth noting that Rachel Crothers was the only woman playwright to meet with Bullock's approval.)

But the fact is that women who wrote for the Broadway stage achieved a level of commercial success out of all proportion to their numbers. Crothers' work was outstanding because she was a dramatist of genuine ability. The others, one can fairly speculate, were on the level of most Broadway hacks, depending more on theatrical trends than on the innate merits of their work. The same, of course, is true of the many male authors now in oblivion. The wonder is not that Broadway rejected the work of so many women playwrights, but that it recognized the genius of the Crotherses and produced their plays.

Clearly, the Broadway stage does not reveal the depth and breadth of our dramatic tradition. Many women, finding it a hindrance to their own personal freedoms and defeating to the growth of progressive drama, rebelled against the constraints of Broadway's Victorian morality and commercialism.

The suffrage play was one of the earliest forms of dramatic activity to be taken up by women writing for the noncommercial theatre. In its report for 1911, the Dramatic Committee of the College Equal Suffrage League of Northern California describes the selection of the English farce *How the Vote Was Won*. It was for them "so much more amusing than any other play we know." Ethel Moore, head of the Dramatic Committee, noted that people were unwilling to pay to be converted to suffrage, so the play was usually performed free of charge "in order to present our sugar-coated pill before as large an audience as possible." Although written by two Englishwomen, Cicely Hamilton and Christopher St. John, *How the Vote Was Won* (1909) is included in this anthology because it played such a substantial role in our own suffrage activity, and because the American suffrage movement often emulated the work of Emmeline Pankhurst and her Women's Political and Social Union, in support of which it was written. There were, of course, a great many suffrage plays written by American women, Selina Solomon's *The Girl from Colorado* (1906) being among the best of them; but they lack the historical significance of *How the Vote Was Won*.

By the time of World War I, the Independent Theatre movement had crossed the Atlantic to take root in America. Before the decade was over, Little Theatre, as it came to be known in this country, was being heralded as the archfoe of commercialism. So rapidly did the movement take hold that by 1924 nearly 2,000 Little Theatres had sprung up in cities and towns across America. Among the first to be established were the Little Theatre of Chicago, the Toy Theatre in Boston, the New York groups, and the Wisconsin Dramatic Society. Women were integral and coequal partners in the founding and creative life of these organizations.

The one-act play, normally not feasible for Broadway, emerged as a necessary concomitant of the Little Theatre movement. The sheer number of plays, full-length as well as one-act, produced by and for Little Theatres before 1929 is overwhelming. While producing much of the same fare as their European counterparts, the Little Theatre movement also provided a place where native playwrights could come into their own.

It is important that Little Theatre should not be confused with amateur theatricals, which, in the words of Constance D'Arcy Mackay, "only invite lenience." The aim of the Little Theatre movement was to be judged by theatrical, not social, standards; rather than showing off local dilettantes, they sought to exhibit potential artists.

By 1929 many Little Theatres had attracted groups of subscribers, who, in effect, underwrote their activities by purchasing season tickets or making outright contributions. With the collapse of the stock market the affluence upon which these theatres depended for much of their financial support ended.

Some of the most famous Little Theatres were to be found in New York. That is not to say that they were the particular province of native New Yorkers, but rather that New York, as the center of American cultural life, attracted artists and writers from everywhere.

The Provincetown Players, one of the earliest and most successful groups, divided their time between Greenwich Village and Provincetown, Massachusetts. They quickly had many subscribers, who were attracted by the low rates and eager to become "associate members" of the company. The Provincetown Players are especially notable for being the only Little Theatre whose main interest was to produce plays by living American authors. This ran counter to many other companies, which preferred to exhibit the work of European playwrights over our own.

During the winter of 1916–17, 30 new one-act plays were introduced on the Provincetown stage. Although O'Neill is clearly the Players' best remembered dramatist, Susan Glaspell, Djuna Barnes, Neith Boyce, and Edna St. Vincent Millay also numbered among its ranks. The Provincetown Playhouse, the group's home in New York, is still in operation.

The Little Theatre movement tended to serve its own membership. However, places like the Neighborhood Playhouse, founded in 1915 by Alice and Irene Lewisohn, functioned in still another capacity. The Neighborhood Playhouse's stated intention was "to set before the people of its thronging tenement district plays they would not otherwise see." Affiliated, as it was, with the Henry Street Settlement, the Neighborhood Playhouse attracted guest artists such as Ellen Terry and Ethel Barrymore, who were eager to join in its service to the community.

Little Theatre has frequently been equated with radical politics. One example is the Negro Players. In forming this company, Emilie Hapgood flew in the face of established tradition. Under her aegis, blacks, for the first time in New York, appeared in plays about people of their own race, although most were written by white authors. By the mid-1920's, however, nearly a dozen Negro Little Theatres had been organized across the country. *Opportunity: A Journal of Negro Life,* the official publication of the National Urban League, initiated annual play contests for black authors. The 1927 award went to Georgia Douglas Johnson for *Plumes,* which bears a striking resemblance in its mood to the Irish play *Riders to the Sea.*

The authors who wrote for the Little Theatre movement did not share Broadway's predisposition for "happy endings," often scuttling such popular notions as salvation through romantic love. Its women dramatists turned to writing about other women whose lives had been blighted by society and by their families. *Winter's Night* (1928) by Neith Boyce portrays a woman who dreams of a free life in the era of the New Woman. The women in *Plumes* are damaged by their poverty and by the position of the Negro in the South.

The combined effect of the works of Karl Marx and Sigmund Freud, as they were understood in the 1920's, provided the rhetorical ammunition for the New Woman. Freud, through his American disciple, A. A. Brill, revealed the means for ridding the psyche of its Victorian-inspired neuroses. Once freed, a person could then go on to participate in social or political revolution. Playwrights of the 1920's examined the idea of liberation for the individual, rather than of women as an organized group. For the New Woman, personal liberation and freedom for the individual were the main concern. The idea of liberation for the masses became popular only toward the end of the decade, and it ushered in a new era of radicalism. Women who now enjoyed personal emancipation turned to the problems of other depressed groups.

Women were major contributors to the dramatic activity of the 1930's. Their plays are neglected today for the same reason that so much of the drama of that period is: they bear the label of "politically subversive."

At first glance, plays dealing with poverty (be it of farmers or industrial workers) and an impending war would hardly seem anti-American; however, the connection between plays about social ills and Marxism was inevitable. Although only a very few such works and their productions could be considered "leftist" in any precise sense, the label of leftist, in time, came to be attached to all serious-minded theatre. (The irony is that, in its day, this label had a vaguely complimentary air to it, associated, as it was, with proponents of libertarian ideals.)

We can thus understand why so much of the drama of this period is unknown to us. It would serve little purpose to dwell on the damage that political repression has done to the American theatre. The point is that many playwrights, men as well as women, are unknown today because of it.

If there appear to have been fewer women writing at this time, it is because so many of their plays depicted such harsh realities. Sada Cowan's *Auf Wiedersehen* (1937) is about the horrors of Nazism; *Take My Stand* (1935) by Elizabeth England takes us through the birth pangs of the labor movement in America; and Ann Seymour wrote *Lawd, Does You Undahstan'* (1937) to aid the efforts of the Association of Southern Women for the Prevention of Lynching. Broadway authors such as Rachel Crothers and Edna Ferber and Clare Kummer wrote mostly romantic comedies. Even more serious-minded Broadway efforts, such as Clare Boothe's *The Women* (1936) and Zoë Akins' *The Old Maid* (1934), while purporting to be about unpleasant truths, reveal none of the despair of the poor and struggling masses of Americans caught up in the Depression.

Change was in the air. Little Theatres were made to feel the need to be something more than merely "centers of experimentation." Because of the radical intellectual climate in New York during the 1930's, those few theatres that were not politically committed found themselves in an especially sensitive position—that of having to take stock lest their work become known as devoid of social meaning. Years before, Emma Goldman, leader of the anarchist movement, had made clear the direction that she thought modern drama must take. Because it mirrors every phase of life and embraces all strata of society, the drama is forced to join in the process of social unrest or be left behind. In *The Social Significance of the Drama* (1914), she stated the essence of her doctrine. "This is the significance which differentiates modern dramatic art from art-for-art's-sake. It is the dynamite which undermines superstition, shakes the social pillars and prepares men and women for the reconstruction."

Even those who were not in sympathy with Goldman's political views could at least agree that art-for-art's-sake represented a thing of the past. It smacked of Victorian notions that seemed to endorse a certain prudery and to embrace the beliefs of social reactionaries. The intellectual climate in New York, even when not directed toward a specific ideology, was still progressive and libertarian.

The always-cautious Broadway stage responded to the changing social and political situation, much to the sorrow of many of its authors. Plays of social significance ceased being presented with our entry into World War II. Thereafter, serious drama, unless politically neutral, all but disappeared. For the remainder of the 1940's and much of the 1950's, the drama conformed to established social and political opinions.

A hostile Congress ended the Federal Theatre Project in 1939. Largely an amalgam of the remnants of the Little Theatre movement and, in New York, elements of the left-wing workers' theatres, the project had been in operation for little more than four years. By design, only a small percentage of the plays produced by the Federal Theatre were to be of socially meaningful content. Many more productions were either revivals or European in origin—and 19th-century European, at that. Although any number of plays were written under subsidy by the project, and many of them by women, comparatively few were in fact produced.

The 1920's and 1930's gave us many women playwrights. They were, by virtue of being playwrights alone, emancipated to some extent. Popular psychology, such as Florence Guertin Tuttle's *The Awakening of Women* (1915), equated emancipation with sexual liberation. Even before that Edward Carpenter had, in *Love's Coming of Age* (1911), presented the notion that sexual liberation was the key to all human freedoms. Few plays written between the wars reflected these views of sexual behavior. Society at large remained staunchly conservative, but playwrights such as Djuna Barnes and Edith Ellis were able to live and work as they pleased. The individual freedom they enjoyed within the intellectual community provided a congenial working atmosphere.

In 1944 Helene Deutsch, a student of Freud's, published *The Psychology of Women*. She insisted that there was indeed a difference between masculine and feminine attributes. The source of women's genius was, for Deutsch, "the treasure of intuition."

Deutsch and the other members of her school harken back fully 100 years to "The Cult of True Womanhood," a notion that purity, domesticity, and submissiveness are a woman's cardinal virtues. This was given wide circulation among ladies' magazines, sentimental novels, newspaper columnists, and religious literature. Such ideas probably would have been rejected out of hand had they not come with an aura of scientific truth. Works like the Deutsch book allowed all those women who had not ventured into the social and intellectual life of the time to feel superior in having maintained the more traditional constraints of Victorian morality. As a result the emancipation movement was superseded in the 1940's by the concept of adjustment. Middle-class women came to believe that their primary role in life was to aid in the proper adjustment of the family to the postwar world.

The broader climate of political and intellectual repression that set in after World War II strengthened these ideas. Women playwrights were in a double bind. Not only were they repressed as writers, but their active participation in anything outside of the home was considered symptomatic of their maladjustment.

The noncommercial theatre was slower to recover from the results of the political activism of the 1930's than was Broadway. After its treatment of the Federal Theatre Project, government sponsorship of the arts was looked upon as most unlikely. Thanks to the support of private foundations, however, regional theatres began to appear in the late 1940's and multiplied in number during the 1950's. Like the Off-Broadway movement, which also dates from about this time, regional theatres tended to favor revivals or adaptations over original work. Still, some were done: Goldie Lake's *Glory Day* (1952) at the Karamu Theatre in Cleveland was among the new plays.

At this time, also, another outlet for playwrights appeared. They could and did turn to the medium of television. Hedda Rosten's *The Happy Housewife* (1952), originally written for CBS's "Studio One," shows the advantages (financial) and limitations (subject matter) of this new commercial outlet.

With the rise of Off-Off-Broadway in the 1960's, there was, once again, ample opportunity for women playwrights, and they appeared in greater numbers than at almost any other time in the history of the American theatre. A new avant garde emerged with them in the persons of Megan Terry, Rochelle Owens, Rosalyn Drexler, Adrienne Kennedy, and Maria Irene Fornes, to name a few of the most prominent. Their reception as playwrights (rather than women) gave no indication of the divisiveness that was to come in the next decade. Yet a few years later, some of their plays were to be called feminist or women's drama.

The driving ideology of today's Woman's Movement is, to put it simply, that women have traditionally been deprived both of their economic rights and of full participation in the cultural life of this country. Therefore, it is necessary for women to discard the stereotypes and develop a new image for themselves. Their hope is that this will lead to the formulation or rediscovery of a truly female culture.

In her book *Apropos of Women and Theatres* Olive Logan wrote, "There are certainly two branches of industry in this world where women stand on an absolutely equal plane in the matter of cash reward. These are literature and the drama." Logan's remarks date from 1869. The plays in this anthology are evidence of the correctness of her observation. They establish that there is a long and consistent, if little-known, tradition of American women who have written for the stage.

At present, a network of regional feminist theatres is eager to find plays by women, and long-established theatres, which had heretofore ignored them, are now vying for the attention of women authors. There is a growing demand among women for a literature that will provide a new image of themselves. The Movement has led to a fuller exploration of women's lives. There are little-studied facets of their existence that women now want to see revealed. The plays from the 1970's that are included here all express a longing for fulfillment.

Joan Holden's widely produced *The Independent Female* (1970) is, as she frankly states, a propaganda piece of behalf of the Bay Area Women's Liberation Movement. *A Lament for Three Women* (1975) is Karen Malpede's impression of the sorts of grief that all women must learn to bear throughout their lifetimes.

Although plays are meant to be staged, they can and should be read as literature. Eugene O'Neill, our greatest playwright, may well be quoted at this time. "I hardly ever go to the theatre . . . although I read all the plays I can get. Acting, except when rarely inspired, simply gets between me and the play" [New York *Herald-Tribune,* November 10, 1924].

In *The Changing World in Plays and Theatres* (1935), Anita Block makes the point that the social meaning of the drama can be properly understood only through "play-consciousness," which is derived from the printed page. Mere "theatre-consciousness," she intimates, only makes hits out of theatrical claptrap.

We may not share Block's disdain of "theatre-consciousness," but her point is well taken in reference to a volume of plays, many of which cannot be classified as "hits." There is much about the plays in this anthology that reveals aspects of our cultural identity beyond the theatre itself—much from which we can learn about our past and our present, both as women and as Americans.

A CENTURY OF PLAYS

BY AMERICAN WOMEN

CRISS CROSS

by **Rachel Crothers**

CHARACTERS

ANN CHADWICK, *a writer of stories*
CECIL CHADWICK, *her cousin*
JACK ALLISTER, *an artist*

PLACE.—New York City. PERIOD.—The present.

SCENE: *The apartment of the Misses Chadwick. A tastefully furnished sitting room with door leading to hall, fireplace and mantel with mirror, bookshelves against wall by windows. There is a couch near the fireplace, with chair at the foot of it; writing-table with chairs; a smaller table with a chair; a piano and stool by the wall. There are curtains or hangings at the door and both windows. Old portraits of two young men hang over the bookshelves. On the piano are a vase of flowers and a lot of sheet music. The writing table is covered with books, papers, writing-materials, etc. On the couch are pillows, two books and a handkerchief. Lamps on both tables, the one on writing table being lighted. Time, 8.30 P.M.*

Discover, as curtain rises, ANN seated at table, writing; CECIL at piano, singing.

CECIL (*at piano, singing softly*):
"For some must watch, and some must wait,
And some will find their love too late.
For some must watch, and some must wait,
But, ah! for the love that comes too late."

ANN (*after listening, much moved, resumes her writing. Irritably*). Don't, don't, *don't!* For goodness sake, don't!

CECIL (*stops singing; after a pause*). Are you tired tonight, Ann dear?

ANN. No, no more so than usual. (CECIL *sighs, crosses to the window, then to bookshelves, taking out a book, lets it fall.*) Oh, I

say! If you *could* be quiet for just *one* minute. I *might* be able to finish this copy.

CECIL. Oh, I beg your pardon, dear. I didn't know. I—I'll go away—

ANN. No, stay where you are. (*After a pause.*) We might have a little more light.

CECIL. Oh, Ann, this is so perfectly sweet and dreamy.

ANN. Don't be so absurdly sentimental. Light the other lamp—do. (CECIL *lights lamp on the table, and draws the curtains regretfully.* ANN *finishes her writing and throws herself upon the couch.*) Thank Heaven, that's done.

CECIL. What is it, Ann, your last story?

ANN. Um!

CECIL. Oh, I hope it's going to be the greatest success you've had.

ANN. Your sarcasm is supreme.

CECIL. I'm not sarcastic. You know you are successful. Everybody says so. Jack was saying only yesterday that for a girl it is—

ANN. Yes, yes, I know. Let's change the subject, if you don't mind.

CECIL (*standing, with one knee on chair, at foot of couch*). But I do mind. You never let me talk about your work. Jack says—

ANN. Turn 'round; you're looking uncommonly well tonight.

CECIL. Am I? (*Walking off.*) I'm awfully glad. Am I, really?

ANN. Why?

CECIL. Jack's coming, you know.

ANN. Oh, to be sure; I quite forgot.

CECIL (*before the mirror*). Aren't you going to dress, dear? I mean, put on something special for Jack?

ANN. Oh, you are very considerate, but I think I shall do quite as well in this—as in anything else—for—for that—gentleman.

CECIL. Why, Jack likes to see you look well, too; he's really very fond of you. A little bit afraid, of course; but then, so are we all.

RACHEL CROTHERS (1878–1958)

Few people have been blessed with a keener eye for the drama than was Rachel Crothers. For nearly 35 years she was one of the most successful of our playwrights. Moreover, Joseph Wood Krutch voiced the consensus of critical opinion when he praised her unique ability as a comic artist and master of dramatic form.

Almost all of Crothers' plays dealt with some theme of importance to contemporary women. One of her staunchest supporters, *The Woman's Journal,* noted that Crothers' work was "worldly enough for the sophisticated and moral enough for the famous old lady from Dubuque." Crothers herself considered it most unusual that someone from so deeply religious and conservative a background as hers should have been interested in the stage at all.

Both of her parents were physicians in Bloomington, Indiana, where Rachel grew up. Her mother, who began her medical training only after the age of forty, was one of the first women doctors in the state. By the time she was twelve years old, Rachel had written her first play, and thereafter she singlemindedly devoted herself to the theatre.

Upon graduation from college, Crothers enrolled in the Wheatcroft School of Acting. This was followed by further study in Boston and New York and by three years on the stage.

In 1902 her play *The Rector* opened at the Madison Square Theater in New York. It was her first professional production. Beginning with *The Three of Us* in 1906, her first major Broadway success, until *Susan and God* in 1937, Crothers was to exercise almost total control over each of her 27 New York productions. In her case this usually meant serving as producer and director and even overseeing the design and construction of the costumes and scenery.

Rachel Crothers the actress was not idle

Rachel Crothers (left) rehearsing A Man's World.

either. For example, she appeared as Ann Herford, the leading part, in her own 1911 production of *He and She.*

Crothers' failures were few and far between. Even those plays that had only marginal runs on Broadway were repeatedly performed throughout the Little Theatre movement. In fact, she received more productions of her plays by these so-called art theatres than did any other American author.

Crothers' only published work other than plays appears to have been, appropriately enough, "The Construction of a Play," a paper she delivered at the University of Pennsylvania in 1928.

ANN. Thank you—

CECIL (*running to sit beside* ANN *on the couch*). I didn't mean that!

ANN. Never mind what you meant. See here, what are you going to do with yourself? (*She still lies on couch with her arms above her head, watching* CECIL *closely.*)

CECIL. What do you mean?

ANN. You know what I mean.

CECIL. It isn't my fault.

ANN. Whose is it, then?

CECIL. Oh, Ann, I have a horrible fear—

ANN. Go on!

CECIL. That Jack doesn't—doesn't—(*crying a little*).

ANN. Oh, if you are going to weep—

CECIL. Oh, no, I'm not. There! That Jack doesn't care for me as he used to.

ANN. Oh, no, no—

CECIL. You needn't laugh. I mean it. I've been wanting to tell you for a long time. It—it frightens me to death.

ANN. You are a silly child!

CECIL (*up*). I'm not; I wish I were. But I'm a woman, with this awful thing staring me in the face. I've been putting it off, and saying it isn't so—it can't be so—but it comes back. I can't tell how nor where it began, nor why it is —but there is a difference. It isn't that he isn't kind (*goes to* ANN)—he's always that; but he seems so far away from me—so—you see how late he is now—absorbed in something else. I don't seem a part of his life at all. I'd rather he'd quarrel with me, as he does with you. Anything but this horrible suspense. And oh, Ann, there is that fearful thought that he's too honorable to break it all off—but still that he's waiting and hoping for something to happen. He—he doesn't ask me to set our wedding day.

ANN. Give him time.

CECIL. Time! Haven't we known each other five years, and been engaged, oh, ever so long? What shall I do, Ann? Tell me, tell me! You're so strong, and sure of things. You've made everything easy for me all my life—help me now. Sometimes I think I will go to him and release him—and then—

ANN. Why don't you?

CECIL. Oh, you don't know what you're saying. I think it would kill me. Of course, it's all very well for you to say that—you've never loved anyone. I can see you throwing him over without a pang, because of an idea.

ANN. But what are you going to do? You're entirely wrong, of course. You know that Jack loves you devotedly, with his whole heart, as he has done all these years.

CECIL (*seizing* ANN's *hands*). Are you sure, dear? Are you sure? It helps me, just to hear you say it.

ANN. But suppose he didn't—just suppose —are you going to let him drift away from you? Suppose there were—another—girl?

CECIL. Oh!

ANN. Would you sit meekly by and let her take him from you?

CECIL. No—I'd—I'd—Oh, I don't know what I'd do. What could I do?

ANN. Why don't you bring him back, if you think he has wandered? You haven't anything else in this wide world to do. What are you doing with your charms and the wonderful sweetness the gods have lavished upon you? (*Raising herself on her elbow.*) Why doesn't he love you? You're never disagreeable. Always pretty, always ready to amuse and please. Make him love you. You've left him to—anyone who may come along. You don't appreciate him—his mind, his talent, his power.

CECIL. Why Ann, I do—I do! I love him better than anything in this world. (*Bell rings outside. Both rise.*)

ANN. There he is. Go tell him—

CECIL. No, no, no; my eyes are all red. He'd see that I've been crying, and I wouldn't have him know it for the world—not for the world. You must talk to him. I'll come back as soon as I can. (*Exit, hastily*)

ANN (*standing before fireplace*). "Without a pang! Because of an idea!"

(*Enter* JACK ALLISTER. *He pauses in doorway and smiles at* ANN.)

JACK. Oh, good evening!

ANN (*at fireplace, with back toward* JACK). Oh, how do you do! How do you do! My cousin will be back directly. She's putting some extra powder on her nose, which is very flattering to you, isn't it?

JACK (*advancing*). Is it?

ANN (*half turning*). Well, isn't it? Make yourself comfortable. There's a chair full of new books.

JACK (*turning away*). Thank you.

ANN. Oh, don't mention it. (*fussing with things on mantel*).

JACK. I had something to tell you.

ANN. Oh? (*A pause.*) Well? (*Turns to face him.*)

JACK (*turning to her*). My picture is sold.

ANN (*eagerly*). "Shadows"?

JACK. Yes.

ANN (*checking herself*). How much?

JACK. Seven hundred.

ANN (*indifferently*). That isn't bad. (JACK *stands in front of couch, hands in pockets, then he walks about restlessly.*)

JACK. But that isn't the point. I changed the figure in the foreground. (ANN *listens breathlessly.*) The girl's face—do you remember? It was your idea. You made the picture! (*He turns to her.*)

ANN (*turning away*). Did I? I don't seem to remember.

JACK (*going to the chair full of books*). Oh, of course, you don't care a fig.

ANN. Of course I don't care—only for one thing.

JACK. Is it possible there *is one* thing you *do* care for?

ANN. You won't mind if I make myself disagreeable?

JACK. Ahem!

ANN. That is—I mean—even more so than usual?

JACK (*throwing down book and turning to her*). Oh, no, not in the least.

ANN. I want to say something to you.

JACK (*sitting in chair at end of couch*). I'm flattered—beyond measure.

ANN. It's this: I think you're a fool.

JACK. But you've said that so often. (*Shrugs his shoulders.*)

ANN. You can't think me presuming nor indelicate, because you know that I have your best interests at heart—yours and Cecil's (JACK *looks at her*)—and that there is no one but me to look after her.

JACK. You seem to forget me.

ANN. But you're not doing it!

JACK. What do you mean?

ANN (*crosses to sit on the couch*). Just this. You're making her awfully unhappy.

JACK. Well, really—

ANN. Now you're going to be angry, and there isn't time. Besides, it won't do any good. Turn 'round here and listen. (JACK *turns chair to her.*) I don't think you realize it, that's why I speak. But she has confessed—to me—the fear—that you don't care for her as you—used to.

JACK. Why, I—

ANN. And you've allowed her to fear it. What are you doing? If you are ever going to marry her, why don't you marry her now? (*A pause.*)

JACK. Why, there is—

ANN. Oh, yes, there is—there is—what is there? There is your work, which you are not getting half enough out of. (JACK *protests.*) Oh, you know it. (*She rises.*) You know you have never done what you might. To be a mild success is not living up to your best self. Paint, paint, paint; work, work, work. Everything is in your own hands. Seize it, and realize the highest.

JACK. But there's something lacking—a man's got to have inspiration. I don't think—what if—what if I couldn't make Cecil happy?

ANN. Oh, but you can! She said to me only just now, "I love him better than anything in this world," and that's a great deal for a woman to say, isn't it? Why, you've made her love you! You found her a careless, happy child; you've made her an unhappy woman, humiliated in her own eyes; she's so alone! I can't go on protecting her all my life. I—I may die, my next story may not be a success, and then where is the bread and butter to come from?

JACK. Oh, don't.

ANN. I know that doesn't sound well—you're not going to let her starve, and all that; but that isn't it! Make her happy! She might have been so with somebody else, if you hadn't thrown yourself in her way, and taken her life into your hands. What is it? Why do you hesitate? Do you care for some one else? Does anyone else care for you? (JACK *walks away.*) Here come back; I haven't finished. So like a man; he runs away from uncomfortable truths. But some one must say it, and it always seems to have been my province to be disagreeable. Isn't it strange how we've been left alone together—Cecil and I? It was just so with our fathers. (*Points to portraits above bookshelves.*) My father was the older, stronger brother, and when he lay dying he made me promise that I would always be to my cousin Cecil what he had been to his brother. If I were a man, now, it would be so easy. So easy to take her up in my arms and shield her against the whole world. There's such an honest, trusting light in the girlish eyes she raises to me. Pray Heaven that light may never be shadowed, and that I may always look honestly back, and say that I have been true.

(CECIL *is heard singing without, "For Some Must Love," etc.*)

JACK (*softly, eagerly*). I did not know you could be so exquisitely sweet. I've never even had a glimpse of your heart before. I thought you were all brain and nerves. What couldn't you do if you'd only always let us see and feel that sweetness? And yet—(*seizing her hands*)—I can't bear to think of you showing it to anyone else. Ann, why don't you let me understand you, dear?

(CECIL's *voice swells out, "And Some Will Find Their Love Too Late."*)

ANN (*controlling herself*). As if you could—(*rising, with a sneer*). You flatter yourself.

(*Jack leans suddenly forward, elbows on knees.* ANN *turns to the fire.*)

(*Re-enter* CECIL.)

CECIL. Well? What are you two doing, quarreling, as usual?

ANN. On the contrary, we're very good friends. Jack has just been making me promise that I'd let you marry him at once, and I have said—well, not tomorrow. (JACK *rises and stands watching* CECIL, *then goes slowly to her as* ANN *speaks. Takes both her hands.*) This troublesome book is taking me away (*fumbling with books on table*).

CECIL. Why, Ann!

ANN. Just for a little while, you know; the business is most important, or I shouldn't be so inconsiderate. But I'll be back in plenty of time (*hurries into outer room, off.*) to marry you off with all the necessary laces and frills. There'll be a Paris gown or two (*coming out with wraps for* CECIL), and if the story's a go we can manage that. (*Putting her into them.*) Just enough to start you off, you know, for when you are Mrs. Jack Allister (*dropping a courtesy*) I shall expect to be quite overcome with your foreign finery.

CECIL. Oh, Ann! (*Laughs happily.*)

ANN. Here are your gloves; he's going to take you out to supper, just to talk it over, for I can't give up my den.

CECIL (*looking at* JACK). Is he?

ANN (*going to her writing*). He is, indeed.

JACK. I am, indeed (*buttoning* CECIL's *gloves*).

ANN. Now clear out, clear out. I've already wasted a lot of time on you youngsters. Good-night! (*Writing*). Good-night!

CECIL (*crossing to* ANN; *puts her hand on her shoulder*). Good-night, Ann, dear.

ANN (*reaching up to touch her hand*). Good-night, little girl. (*She hesitates, then draws* CECIL *down and kisses her tenderly. Puts out left hand to* JACK, *who stands back of her chair.*) Good-night, Jack—and good-by, just for a little, you know—

CECIL (*as they go out.*) Oh, my key! No, here it is. Isn't she dear? I never knew her to be so charming before. Good-night, Ann, good-night!

(*A door closes heavily and the sound of the voices gradually dies away.* ANN *rises and goes quickly to the window. She waves her hand gaily and blesses them in pantomime. Then goes slowly back to her table.*)

ANN. If I could only tell it to somebody—only say it aloud to myself—just once—it would not be quite so hard! (*Sinks with head upon table.*)

(*Soft music.*)

CURTAIN

HOW THE VOTE WAS WON

by Cicely Hamilton and Christopher St. John

CHARACTERS

HORACE COLE, *a clerk, about 30*
ETHEL, *his wife, 22*
WINIFRED, *her sister*
AGATHA COLE, *Horace's sister*
MOLLY, *his niece*
MADAME CHRISTINE, *his distant relation*
MAUDIE SPARK, *his first cousin*
MISS LIZZIE WILKINS, *his aunt*
LILY, *his maid-of-all-work*
GERALD WILLIAMS, *his neighbour*

SCENE: *Sitting-room in* HORACE COLE'S *house at Brixton. The room is cheaply furnished in genteel style. The window looks out on a row of little houses, all of the Cole pattern. The door leads into a narrow passage communicating at once with the front door. The fireplace has a fancy mantel border, and over it is an overmantel, decorated with many photographs and cheap ornaments. The sideboard, a small bookcase, a table, and a comfortable armchair, are the chief articles of furniture. The whole effect is modest, and quite unpleasing.*

TIME: *Late afternoon on a spring day in any year in the future.*

When the curtain rises, MRS. HORACE COLE *is sitting in the comfortable armchair putting a button onto her husband's coat. She is a pretty, fluffy little woman who could never be bad-tempered, but might be fretful. At this minute she is smiling indulgently, and rather irritatingly, at her sister* WINIFRED, *who is sitting by the fire when the curtain rises, but gets up almost immediately to leave.* WINIFRED *is a tall and distinguished-looking young woman with a cheerful, capable manner and an emphatic diction which betrays the public speaker. She wears the colours of the N.W.S.P.U.*

WINIFRED. Well, good-bye, Ethel. It's a pity you won't believe me. I wanted to let you and Horace down gently, or I shouldn't be here.

ETHEL. But you're always prophesying these dreadful things, Winnie, and nothing ever happens. Do you remember the day when you tried to invade the House of Commons from submarine boats? Oh, Horace did laugh when he saw in the papers that you had all been landed on the Hovis wharf by mistake! "By accident, on purpose!" Horace said. He couldn't stop laughing all the evening. "What price your sister Winifred," he said. "She asked for a vote, and they gave her bread." He kept on—you can't think how funny he was about it!

WINIFRED. Oh, but I can! I know my dear brother-in-law's sense of humor is his strong point. Well, we must hope it will bear the strain that is going to be put on it today. Of course, when his female relations invade his house—all with the same story, "I've come to be supported"—he may think it excruciatingly funny. One never knows.

ETHEL. Winnie, you're only teasing me. They would never do such a thing. They must know we have only one spare bedroom, and that's to be for a paying guest when we can afford to furnish it.

WINIFRED. The servants' bedroom will be empty. Don't forget that all the domestic servants have joined the League and are going to strike, too.

ETHEL. Not ours, Winnie. Martha is simply devoted to me, and poor little Lily *couldn't* leave. She has no home to go to. She would have to go to the workhouse.

WINIFRED. Exactly where she will go. All those women who have no male relatives, or are refused help by those they have, have instructions to go to the relieving officer. The number of female paupers who will pour through the workhouse gates tonight all over England will frighten the Guardians into blue fits.

CICELY HAMILTON (1872–1952)

After a harsh childhood spent, for the most part, in boarding schools and foster homes, Cicely Hamilton set about to establish herself and her sister in London. She would earn their living, she decided, by the "art of the theatre."

Hamilton had her heart set on becoming an actress, but, lacking the sort of looks that would have immediate appeal to agents and managers, she spent many months just hanging around their offices. Her "big break" came in the form of an offer to tour in a play by Henry Arthur Jones. Thus began ten years of life in the provinces.

She found that she could supplement her still meager income as an actress by writing "sensation" stories for pulp magazines. When she concluded that the stage belonged more to its authors than to the actors, Hamilton turned her already practiced pen to playwriting.

As it happens, her reputation as a dramatist was secured even before she finally became a successful London character actress. The first production of a play by Cicely Hamilton was memorable only because its producer, Ortho Stuart, advised her to list herself as "C. Hamilton" on the program— at least until the notices came out. With the success of *Diana of Dobson's* in 1908, however, there was no longer any need for Hamilton to disguise the fact that she was a woman.

Hamilton credits this change in attitude toward women playwrights to the efforts of the suffragist movement in England. *How the Vote Was Won* (1909) was written in support of the militant Women's Political and Social Union. Eventually, Hamilton became disenchanted with the methods and leadership of this organization, and, with Christopher St. John (among others), founded the Writers' Franchise League.

While noting that "beneath its fun there is a great deal of propaganda," the London critics were by and large quite taken with *How the Vote Was Won,* and it enjoyed a successful engagement. Both its fun and its propaganda made the play appealing to American suffragists. The College Equal Suffrage League of Northern California sent out a troupe of actors who performed *How the Vote Was Won* in and around the San Francisco Bay Area during that state's suf-

Cicely Hamilton dressed as George Eliot, and Christopher St. John as George Sand.

frage campaign of 1911. Afterwards, the play was recommended to other suffrage organizations for use in their own campaigns.

Hamilton wrote a number of other plays, from *Just to Get Married* in 1910 to *The Beggar Prince* in 1929. She also continued as a character actress through about the time of World War I, appearing in such plays as *The Twelve Pound Look* by J. M. Barrie and *Fanny's First Play* by George Bernard Shaw. Her autobiography, *Life Errant,* was published in 1935. Three years later, Cicely Hamilton was awarded a Civil List Pension in recognition of her services to literature.

CHRISTOPHER ST. JOHN

Her dramatic output included some 18 plays, many of them—from *The Good Hope* in 1903 to *The Rising Sun* in 1929 —adaptations. In addition, she wrote two novels and a steady stream of articles on music and the drama. Her translation of *Paphnutius* by the 10th-century German playwright-nun Hrotsvitha appeared in The Medieval Library series.

The life and work of Ellen Terry was one of St. John's major interests. Between 1931 and 1933 she edited Terry's correspondence with George Bernard Shaw, as well as the volume *Four Lectures on Shakespeare by Ellen Terry,* and, with Edith Craig, prepared a new edition of *Ellen Terry's Memoirs.*

For all her activity, there is far less information available today about Christopher St. John than about her contemporary and collaborator on *How the Vote Was Won,* Cicely Hamilton. They are known to have written one other play together, *The Pot and the Kettle,* also in 1909.

In that same year St. John made her only recorded stage appearance—as Hannah Snell in *The Pageant of Great Women* by Cicely Hamilton.

ETHEL. Horace says you'll never *frighten* the Government into giving you the vote.

WINIFRED. It's your husband, your dear Horace, and a million other dear Horaces who are going to do the frightening this time. By tomorrow, perhaps before, Horace will be marching to Westminster shouting out "Votes for Women!"

ETHEL. Winnie, how absurd you are! You know how often you've tried to convert Horace and failed. Is it likely that he will become a Suffragette just because—

WINIFRED. Just because—? Go on, Ethel.

ETHEL. Well, you know—all this you've been telling me about his relations coming here and asking him to support them. Of course I don't believe it. Agatha, for instance, would never dream of giving up her situation. But if they did come Horace would just tell them he *couldn't* keep them. How could he on £4 a week?

WINIFRED. How could he! That's the point! He couldn't, of course. That's why he'll want to get rid of them at any cost—even the cost of letting women have the Vote. That's why he and the majority of men in this country shouldn't for years have kept alive the foolish superstition that all women are supported by men. For years we have told them it was a delusion, but they could not take our arguments seriously. Their method of answering us was exactly that of the little boy in the street who cries "Yah—Suffragette!" when he sees my ribbon.

ETHEL. I always wish you wouldn't wear it when you come here. . . . Horace does so dislike it. He thinks its unwomanly.

WINIFRED. Oh! does he? Tomorrow he may want to borrow it—when he and the others have had their object-lesson. They wouldn't listen to argument . . . so we had to expose their pious fraud about woman's place in the world in a very practical and sensible way. At this very minute working women of every grade in every part of England are ceasing work, and going to demand support and the necessities of life from their nearest male relatives, however distant the nearest relative may be. I hope, for your sake, Ethel, that Horace's relatives aren't an exacting lot!

ETHEL. There wasn't a word about it in the *Daily Mail* this morning.

WINIFRED. Never mind. The evening papers will make up for it.

ETHEL. What male relative are you going to, Winnie? Uncle Joseph?

WINIFRED. Oh, I'm in the fighting line, as usual, so our dear uncle will be spared. My work is with the great army of women who have no male belongings of any kind! I shall be busy till midnight marshalling them to the workhouse. . . . This is perhaps the most important part of the strike. By this we shall hit men as ratepayers even when they have escaped us as relatives! Every man, either in a public capacity or a private one, will find himself face to face with the appalling problem of maintaining millions of women in idleness. Will the men take up the burden, d'ye think? Not they! (*Looks at her watch.*) Good heavens! The strike began ages ago. I must be off. I've wasted too much time here already.

ETHEL (*looking at the clock*). I had no idea it was so late. I must see about Horace's tea. He may be home any minute. (*Rings the bell* L.)

WINIFRED. Poor Horace!

ETHEL (*annoyed*). Why "poor Horace"? I don't think he has anything to complain of. (*Rings again.*)

WINIFRED. I feel some pity at this minute for all the men.

ETHEL. What can have happened to Martha?

WINIFRED. She's gone, my dear, that's all.

ETHEL. Nonsense. She's been with me ever since I was married, and I pay her very good wages.

(*Enter* LILY, *a shabby little maid-of-all-work, dressed for walking, the chief effect of the toilette being a very cheap and very smart hat.*)

ETHEL. Where's Martha, Lily?

LILY. She's left, m'm.

ETHEL. Left! She never gave me notice.

LILY. No, m'm, we wasn't to give no notice, but at three o'clock we was to quit.

ETHEL. But why? Don't be a silly little girl. And you mustn't come in here in your hat.

LILY. I was just goin' when you rang. That's what I've got me 'at on for.

ETHEL. Going! Where? It's not your afternoon out.

LILY. I'm goin' back to the Union. There's dozens of others goin' with me.

ETHEL. But why—

LILY. Miss Christabel—she told us. She says to us: "Now look 'ere, all of yer—you who've got no men to go to on Thursday—yer've got to go to the Union," she says; "and the one who 'angs back"—and she looked at me, she did—"may be the person 'oo the 'ole strain of the movement is restin' on, the traitor 'oo's sailin' under the 'ostile flag," she says; and I says, "That won't be me—not much!"

(*During this speech* WINIFRED *puts on a sandwich board which bears the inscription: "This way to the Work-*

WINIFRED. Well, Ethel, are you beginning to believe?

ETHEL. Oh, I think it's very unkind—very wicked. How am I to get Horace anything to eat with no servants?

WINIFRED. Cheer up, my dear. Horace and the others can end the strike when they choose. But they're going to have a jolly bad time first. Good-bye.

(*Exit* WINNIE, *singing the "Marseillaise."*)

LILY. Wait a bit, Miss. I'm comin' with yer (*sings the "Marseillaise" too*).

ETHEL. No, no. Oh, Lily, please don't go, or at any rate bring up the kettle first, and the chops, and the frying-pan. Please! Then I think I can manage.

LILY. (*coming back into the room and speaking impressively*). There's no ill-feeling. It's an objick lesson—that's all.

(*Exit* LILY. ETHEL *begins to cry weakly; then lays the table; gets bread, cruet, tea, cups, etc., from the cupboard.* LILY *re-enters with a frying-pan, a kettle, and two raw chops.*)

LILY. 'Ere you are—it's the best I can do. You see, mum, I've got to be recognized by the State. I don't think I'm a criminal nor a lunatic, and I oughtn't to be treated as sich.

ETHEL. You poor little simpleton. Do you suppose that, even if this absurd plan succeeds, *you* will get a vote?

LILY. I may—you never know your luck; but that's not why I'm giving up work. It's so as I shan't stop them as ought to 'ave it. The 'ole strain's on me, and I'm goin' to the Union—so good-bye, mum.

(*Exit* LILY.)

ETHEL. And I've always been so kind to you! Oh, you little brute! What *will* Horace say? (*looking out of the window*). It can't be true. Everything looks the same as usual. [HORACE'S *voice outside*): We must have at least sixteen Dreadnoughts this year. (WILLIAMS' *voice*): You can't get 'em, old chap, unless you expect the blooming colonies to pay for 'em.] Ah, here is Horace, and Gerald Williams with him. Oh, I hope Horace hasn't asked him to tea! (*She powders her nose at the glass, then pretends to be busy with the kettle.*)

(*Enter* HORACE COLE—*an English master in his own house—and* GERALD WILLIAMS, *a smug young man stiff with self-consciousness.*)

ETHEL. You're back early, aren't you, Horry? How do you do, Mr. Williams?

GERALD WILLIAMS. How do you do, Mrs. Cole? I just dropped in to fetch a book your husband's promised to lend me.

(HORACE *rummages in book-shelves.*)

ETHEL. Had a good day, Horry?

HORACE. Oh, much as usual. Ah, here it is—(*reading out the title*)—"Where's the

Wash-tub now?" with a preface by Lord Curzon of Kedleston, published by the Men's League for Opposing Women's Suffrage. If that doesn't settle your missus, nothing will.

ETHEL. Is Mrs. Williams a Suffragette?

GERALD. Rather; and whenever I say anything, all she can answer is, "You know nothing about it." Thank you, old man. I'll read it to her after tea. So long. Good-bye, Mrs. Cole.

ETHEL. Did Mrs. Williams tell you anything this morning . . . before you went to the City? . . .

GERALD. About Votes for Women, do you mean? Oh, no. Not allowed at breakfast. In fact, not allowed at all. I tried to stop her going to these meetings where they fill the women's heads with all sorts of rubbish, and she said she'd give 'em up if I'd give up my footer matches; so we agreed to disagree. See you tomorrow, old chap. Good-bye, Mrs. Cole.

(*Exit* GERALD WILLIAMS.)

HORACE. You might have asked him to stop to tea. You made him very welcome— I don't think.

ETHEL. I'm sorry; but I don't think he'd have stayed if I *had* asked him.

HORACE. Very likely not, but one should always be hospitable. Tea ready?

ETHEL. Not quite, dear. It will be in a minute.

HORACE. What on earth is all this!

ETHEL. Oh, nothing. I only thought I would cook your chop for you up here today —just for fun.

HORACE. I really think, Ethel, that so long as we can afford a servant, it's rather unnecessary.

ETHEL. You know you're always complaining of Martha's cooking. I thought you would like me to try.

HORACE. My dear child! It's very nice of you. But why not cook in the kitchen? Raw meat in the sitting-room!

ETHEL. Oh, Horry, don't!

(*She puts her arms round his neck and sobs. The chop at the end of the toasting fork in her hand dangles in his face.*)

HORACE. What on earth's the matter? Ethel, dear, don't be hysterical. If you knew what it was to come home fagged to death and be worried like this. . . . I'll ring for Martha and tell her to take away these beastly chops. They're getting on my nerves.

ETHEL. Martha's gone.

HORACE. When? Why? Did you have a row? I suppose you had to give her a month's wages. I can't afford that sort of thing, you know.

ETHEL (*sobbing*). It's not you who afford it, anyhow. Don't I pay Martha out of my own money?

HORACE. Do you call it ladylike to throw that in my face. . . .

ETHEL (*incoherently*). I'm not throwing it in your face . . . but as it happens I didn't pay her anything. She went off without a word . . . and Lily's gone, too.

(*She puts her head down on the table and cries.*)

HORACE. Well, that's a good riddance. I'm sick of her dirty face and slovenly ways. If she ever does clean my boots, she makes them look worse than when I took them off. We must try and get a charwoman.

ETHEL. We shan't be able to. Isn't it in the papers?

HORACE. What *are* you talking about?

ETHEL. Winifred said it would be in the evening papers.

HORACE. Winifred! She's been here, has she? That accounts for everything. How that woman comes to be your sister I can't imagine. Of course she's mixed up with this wildcat scheme.

ETHEL. Then you know about it!

HORACE. Oh, I saw something about "Suffragettes on Strike" on the posters on my way home. Who cares if they do strike? They're no use to anyone. Look at Winifred. What does she ever do except go round making speeches, and kicking up a row outside the House of Commons until she forces the police to arrest her. Then she goes to prison and poses as a martyr. Martyr! We all know she could go home at once if she would promise the magistrate to behave herself. What they ought to do is to try all these hysterical women in camera and sentence them to be ducked— privately. Then they'd soon give up advertising themselves.

ETHEL. Winnie has a splendid answer to that, but I forget what it is. Oh, Horry, was there anything on the posters about the nearest male relative?

HORACE. Ethel, my dear, you haven't gone

dotty, have you? When you have quite done with my chair, I—— (*He helps her out of the chair and sits down.*) Thank you.

ETHEL. Winnie said that not only are all the working women going to strike, but they are going to make their nearest male relatives support them.

HORACE. Rot!

ETHEL. I thought how dreadful it would be if Agatha came, or that cousin of yours on the stage whom you won't let me know, or your Aunt Lizzie! Martha and Lily have gone to *their* male relatives; at least, Lily's gone to the workhouse—it's all the same thing. Why shouldn't it be true? Oh, look, Horace, there's a cab—with luggage. Oh, what shall we do?

HORACE. Don't fuss! It's stopping next door, not here at all.

ETHEL. No, no; it's here. (*She rushes out.*)

HORACE (*calling after her*). Come back! You can't open the door yourself. It looks as if we didn't keep a servant.

(*Re-enter* ETHEL, *followed after a few seconds by* AGATHA. AGATHA *is a weary-looking woman of about thirty-five. She wears the National Union colours, and is dowdily dressed.*)

ETHEL. It *is* Agatha—and such a big box. Where *can* we put it?

AGATHA (*mildly*). How do you do, Horace. (*Kisses him.*) Dear Ethel! (*Kisses her.*) You're not looking so well as usual. Would you mind paying the cabman two shillings, Horace, and helping him with my box? It's rather heavy, but then it contains all my worldly belongings.

HORACE. Agatha—you haven't lost your situation! You haven't left the Lewises?

AGATHA. Yes, Horace; I left at three o'clock.

HORACE. My dear Agatha—I'm extremely sorry—but we can't put you up here.

AGATHA. Hadn't you better pay the cab? Two shillings so soon becomes two-and-six. (*Exit* HORACE.) I am afraid my brother doesn't realize that I have some claim on him.

ETHEL. We thought you were so happy with the Lewises.

AGATHA. So were the slaves in America when they had kind masters. They didn't want to be free.

ETHEL. Horace said you always had late dinner with them when they had no company.

AGATHA. Oh, I have no complaint against my late employers. In fact, I was sorry to inconvenience them by leaving so suddenly. But I had a higher duty to perform than my duty to them.

ETHEL. I don't know what to do. It will worry Horace dreadfully.

(*Re-enter* HORACE.)

HORACE. The cab *was* two-and-six, and I had to give a man twopence to help me in with that Noah's ark. Now, Agatha, what does this mean? Surely in your position it was very unwise to leave the Lewises. You can't stay here. We must make some arrangement.

AGATHA. Any arrangement you like, dear, provided you support me.

HORACE. I support you!

AGATHA. As my nearest male relative, I think you are obliged to do so. If you refuse, I must go to the workhouse.

HORACE. But why can't you support yourself? You've done it for years.

AGATHA. Yes—ever since I was eighteen. Now I am going to give up work, until my work is recognized. Either my proper place is the home—the home provided for me by some dear father, brother, husband, cousin or uncle—or I am a self-supporting member of the State who ought not to be shut out from the rights of citizenship.

HORACE. All this sounds as if you had become a Suffragette! Oh, Agatha, I always thought you were a lady.

AGATHA. Yes, I *was* a lady—such a lady that at eighteen I was thrown upon the world, penniless, with no training whatever which fitted me to earn my own living. When women become citizens I believe that daughters will be given the same chances as sons, and such a life as mine will be impossible.

HORACE. Women are so illogical. What on earth has all this to do with your planting yourself on me in this inconsiderate way? You put me in a most unpleasant position. You must see, Agatha, that I haven't the means to support a sister as well as a wife. Couldn't you go to some friends until you find another situation?

AGATHA. No, Horace. I'm going to stay with you.

HORACE (*changing his tone and turning nasty*). Oh, indeed! And for how long—if I may ask?

AGATHA. Until the Bill for the removal of the sex disability is passed.

HORACE (*impotently angry*). Nonsense. I can't keep you, and I won't. I have always tried to do my duty by you. I think hardly a week passes that I don't write to you. But now that you have deliberately thrown up an excellent situation as a governess and come here and threatened me—yes, threatened me—I think it's time to say that, sister or no sister, I will be master in my own house!

(*Enter* MOLLY, *a good-looking young girl of about twenty. She is dressed in well-cut, tailor-made clothes, wears a neat little hat, and carries some golf-clubs and a few books.*)

MOLLY. How are you, Uncle Horace? Is that Aunt Aggie? How d'ye do? I haven't seen you since I was a kid.

HORACE. Well, what have you come for?

MOLLY. There's a charming welcome to give your only niece!

HORACE. You know perfectly well, Molly, that I disapprove of you in every way. I hear —I have never read it, of course—but I hear that you have written a most scandalous book. You live in lodgings by yourself, when if you chose you could afford some really nice and refined boarding-house. You have most undesirable acquaintances, and altogether——

MOLLY. Cheer up, Uncle. Now's your chance of reforming me. I've come to live with you. You can support me and improve me at the same time.

HORACE. I never heard such impertinence! I have always understood from you that you earn more than I do.

MOLLY. Ah, yes; but you never *liked* my writing for money, did you? You called me "sexless" once because I said that as long as I could support myself I didn't feel an irresistible temptation to marry that awful little bounder Weekes.

ETHEL. Reginald Weekes! How can you call him a bounder! He was at Oxford.

MOLLY. Hullo, Auntie Ethel! I didn't notice you. You'll be glad to hear I haven't brought much luggage—only a night-gown and some golf-clubs.

HORACE. I suppose this is a joke!

MOLLY. Well, of course that's one way of looking at it. I'm not going to support myself any longer. I'm going to be a perfect lady and depend on my Uncle Horace—my nearest male relative—for the necessities of life. (*A motor horn is heard outside.*) Aren't you

glad that I am not going to write another scandalous book, or live in lodgings by myself!

ETHEL (*at the window*). Horace! Horace! There's someone getting out of a motor—a grand motor. Who can it be? And there's no one to answer the door.

MOLLY. That doesn't matter. I found it open, and left it open to save trouble.

ETHEL. She's got luggage, too! The chauffeur's bringing in a dressing-case.

HORACE. I'll turn her into the street—and the dressing-case, too.

(*He goes fussily to the door and meets* MADAME CHRISTINE *on the threshold. The lady is dressed smartly and tastefully. Age about forty, manners elegant, smile charming, speech resolute. She carries a jewel-case, and consults a legal document during her first remarks.*)

MADAME C.. You are Mr. Cole?

HORACE. No! Certainly not! (*wavering*). At least, I was this morning, but—

MADAME C.. Horace Cole, son of John Hay Cole, formerly of Streatham, where he carried on the business of a—

(*A motor horn sounds outside.*)

HORACE. I beg your pardon, but my late father's business has really nothing to do with this matter, and to a professional man it's rather trying to have these things raked up against him. Excuse me, but do you want your motor to go?

MADAME C.. It's not my motor any longer; and—yes, I do want it to go, for I may be staying here some time. I think you had one sister Agatha, and one brother Samuel, now dead. Samuel was much older than you—

AGATHA. Why don't you answer, Horace? Yes, that's perfectly correct. I am Agatha.

MADAME C.. Oh, are you? How d'ye do?

MOLLY. And Samuel Cole was my father.

MADAME C.. I'm very glad to meet you. I didn't know I had such charming relations. Well, Mr. Cole, my father was John Hay Cole's first cousin; so you, I think, are my second cousin, and my nearest male relative.

HORACE (*distractedly*). If anyone calls me that again I shall go mad.

MADAME C.. I am afraid you aren't quite pleased with the relationship!

HORACE. You must excuse me—but I don't consider a second cousin exactly a relation.

MADAME C.. Oh, it answers the purpose. I suddenly find myself destitute, and I want you to support me. I am sure you would not like a Cole to go to the workhouse.

HORACE. I don't care a damn where any of 'em go.

ETHEL (*shocked*). Horry! How can you!

MADAME C.. That's frank, at any rate; but I am sure, Cousin Horace, that in spite of your manners, your heart's in the right place. You won't refuse me board and lodging, until Parliament makes it possible for me to resume my work?

HORACE. My dear madam, do you realize that my salary is £3 10s. a week—and that my house will hardly hold your luggage, much less you?

MADAME C.. Then you must agitate. Your female relatives have supported themselves up till now, and asked nothing from you. I myself, dear cousin, was, until this morning, running a profitable dressmaking business in Hanover Square. In my public capacity I am Madame Christine.

MOLLY. I know! I've never been able to afford you.

HORACE. And do you think, Madame Christine—

MADAME C.. Cousin Susan, please.

HORACE. Do you think that you are justified in coming to a poor clerk and asking him to support you—you could probably turn over my yearly income in a single week! Didn't you come here in your own motor?

MADAME C.. At three o'clock that motor became the property of the Women's Social and Political Union. All the rest of my property and all available cash have been divided equally between the National Union and the Women's Freedom League. Money is the sinews of war, you know.

HORACE. Do you mean to tell me that you've given all your money to the Suffragettes! It's a pity you haven't a husband. He'd very soon stop your doing such foolish things.

MADAME C.. I had a husband once. He liked me to do foolish things—for instance, to support him. After that unfortunate experience, Cousin Horace, you may imagine how glad I am to find a man who really is a man, and will support me instead. By the way, I should *so* much like some tea. Is the kettle boiling?

ETHEL (*feebly*). There aren't enough cups! Oh, what *shall* I do?

HORACE. Never mind, Ethel; I shan't want any. I am going to dine in town and go to the theatre. I shall hope to find you all gone when I come back. If not, I shall send for the police.

(*Enter* MAUDIE SPARK, *a young woman with an aggressively cheerful manner, a voice raucous from much bellowing of music-hall songs, a hat of huge size, and a heart of gold.*)

MAUDIE. 'Ullo! 'ullo! who's talking about the police? Not my dear cousin Horry!

HORACE. How dare you come here?

MAUDIE. Necessity, old dear. If I had a livelier male relative, you may bet I'd have gone to him! But you, Horace, are the only first cousin of this poor orphan. What are you in such a hurry for?

HORACE. Let me pass! I'm going to the theatre.

MAUDIE. Silly jay! the theatres are all closed—and the halls too. The actresses have gone on strike—resting indefinitely. I've done my little bit towards that. They won't get any more work out of Maudie Spark, Queen of Comédiennes, until the women have got the vote. Ladies and fellow-relatives, you'll be pleased to hear the strike's going fine. The big drapers can't open tomorrow. One man can't fill the place of fifteen young ladies at once, you see. The duchesses are out in the streets begging people to come in and wash their kids. The City men are trying to get taxi-men in to do their typewriting. Every man, like Horry here, has his house full of females. Most of 'em thought, like Horry, that they'd go to the theatre to escape. But there's not a blessed theatre to go to! Oh, what a song it'll make. "A woman's place is the home—I don't think, I don't think, I don't think."

HORACE. Even if this is not a plot against me personally, even if there are other women in London at this minute disgracing their sex—

MAUDIE. Here stop it—come off it! If it comes to that, what are *you* doing—threatening your womankind with the police and the workhouse.

HORACE. I was not addressing myself to you.

AGATHA. Why not, Horace? She's your cousin. She needs your protection just as much as we do.

HORACE. I regard that woman as the skeleton in the cupboard of a respectable family; but that's neither here nor there. I address myself to the more lady-like portion of this gathering, and I say that whatever is going on, the men will know what to do, and will do it with dignity and firmness. (*The impressiveness of this statement is marred by the fact that* HORACE'S *hand, in emphasizing it, comes down heavily on the loaf of bread on the table.*) A few exhibitions of this kind won't frighten them.

MAUDIE. Oh, won't it! I like that! They're being so firm and so dignified that they're running down to the House of Commons like lunatics, and blackguarding the Government for not having given us the vote before! (*Shouts outside of newsboys in the distance.*)

MOLLY. Splendid! Have they begun already?

MADAME C.. Get a paper, Cousin Horace. I know some men never believe anything till they see it in the paper.

ETHEL. The boys are shouting out something now. Listen.

> (*Shouts outside. "Extry special. Great strike of women. Women's strike. Theatres closed. Extry special edition. Star! News! 6.30 edition!"*)

MOLLY. You see. Since this morning Suffragettes have become women!

ETHEL (*at window*). Here, boy, paper!

> (*Cries go on. "Extry special Star. Men petition the Government. Votes for Women. Extry special."*)

Oh, heavens, here's Aunt Lizzie!

> (*As* ETHEL *pronounces the name* HORACE *dives under the table. Enter* AUNT LIZZIE *leading a fat spaniel and carrying a birdcage with a parrot in it.* MISS ELIZABETH WILKINS *is a comfortable, middle-aged body of a type well known to those who live in the less fashionable quarter of Bloomsbury. She looks as if she kept lodgers, and her looks do not belie her. She is not very well educated, but has a good deal of native intelligence. Her features are homely and her clothes about thirty years behind the times.*)

AUNT L.. Well, dears, all here? That's right. Where's Horace? Out? Just as well; we can talk more freely. I'm sorry I'm late, but animals do so hate a move. It took a long time to make them understand the strike. But I think they will be very comfortable here. You love dogs, don't you, Ethel?

ETHEL. Not Ponto. He always growls at me.

AUNT L.. Clever dog! he knows you don't sympathize with the cause.

ETHEL. But I do, Aunt; only I have always said that as I was happily married I thought it had very little to do with me.

AUNT L.. You've changed your mind about that today, I should think! What a day it's been! We never expected everything would go so smoothly. They say the Bill's to be rushed through at once. No more broken promises, no more talking out; deeds, not words, at last! Seen the papers? The press are not boycotting us today, my dears. (MADAME C., MOLLY, *and* MAUDIE *each take a paper.*) The boy who sold them to me put the money back into Ponto's collecting box. That dog must have made five pounds for the cause since this morning.

> (HORACE *puts his head out and says "Liar!"*)

MOLLY. Oh, do listen to this. It's too splendid! (*Reading from the paper*) "Women's Strike—Latest: Messrs. Lyons and Co. announce that by special arrangement with the War Office the places of their defaulting waitresses will be filled by the non-commissioned officers and men of the 2nd Battalion Coldstream Guards. Business will therefore be carried on as usual."

MADAME C.. What do you think of this? (*Reading*) "Latest Intelligence.—It is understood that the Naval Volunteers have been approached by the authorities with the object of inducing them to act as charwomen to the House of Commons."

AUNT L. (*to* ETHEL). Well, my dear! Read, then, what the *Star* says.

ETHEL (*tremulously reading*). "The queue of women waiting for admission to Westminster workhouse is already a mile and a half in length. As the entire police force are occupied in dealing with the men's processions, Lord Esher has been approached with a view to ascertaining if the Territorials can be sworn in as special constables."

MAUDIE (*laughing*). This is a little bit of all right. (*Reading*) "Our special representative, on calling upon the Prime Minister with the object of ascertaining his views on the situation, was informed that the Right Honourable gentleman was unable to receive him, as he was actively engaged in making his bed with the assistance of the boot-boy and a Foreign Office messenger."

AUNT L.. Always unwilling to receive people, you see! Well, he must be feeling sorry now that he never received us. Everyone's putting the blame on to him. It's extraordinary how many men—and newspapers, too—have suddenly found out that they have always been in favour of woman's suffrage! That's the sensible attitude, of course. It would be humiliating for them to confess that it was not until we held a pistol to their heads that they changed their minds. Well, at this minute I would rather be the man who has been our ally all along than the one who has been our enemy. It's not the popular thing to be an "anti" any more. Any man who tries to oppose us today is likely to be slung up to the nearest lamp-post.

ETHEL (rushing wildly to the table). Oh, Horry! my Horry! (HORACE comes out from under the table.)

AUNT L.. Why, bless the boy, what are you doing there?

HORACE. Oh, nothing. I merely thought I might be less in the way here, that's all.

AUNT L.. You didn't hide when I came in by any chance!

HORACE. I hide from you! Aren't you always welcome in this house?

AUNT L.. Well, I haven't noticed it particularly; and I'm not calling today, you understand, I've come to stay. (HORACE, dashed and beaten, begins to walk up and down the room, and consults ETHEL.) Well, well! I won't deny it was a wrench to leave 118a, Upper Montagu Place, where I've done my best for boarders, old and young, gents and ladies, for twenty-five years—and no complaints! A home from home, they call it. All my ladies had left before I started out, on the same business as all of us—but what those poor boys will do for their dinner tonight I don't know. They're a helpless lot! Well, it's all over; I've given up my boarding-house, and I depend on you, Horace, to keep me until I am admitted to citizenship. It may take a long time.

HORACE. It must not take a long time. I shan't allow it. It shall be done at once. Well, you needn't all look so surprised. I know I've

been against it, but I didn't realize things. I thought only a few howling dervishes wanted the vote; but when I find that you—Aunt —— Fancy a woman of your firmness of character, one who has always been so careful with her money, being declared incapable of voting! The thing is absurd.

MAUDIE. Bravo! Our Horry's waking up.

HORACE (looking at her scornfully). If there are a few women here and there who are incapable—I mention no names, mind—it doesn't affect the position. What's going to be done? Who's going to do it? If this rotten Government think we're going to maintain millions of women in idleness just because they don't like the idea of my Aunt Lizzie making a scratch on a bit of paper and shoving it into a ballot-box once every five years, this Government have reckoned without the men—— (General cheering.) I'll show 'em what I've got a vote for! What do they expect? You can't all marry. There aren't enough men to go round, and if you're earning your own living and paying taxes you ought to have a say; it's only fair. (General cheering and a specially emphatic "Hear, hear" from MADAME CHRISTINE.) The Government are narrow-minded idiots! (MADAME C.: Hear! hear!) They talk as if all the women ought to stay at home washing and ironing. Well, before a woman has a wash-tub, she must have a home to put it in, mustn't she? And who's going to give it her? I'd like them to tell me that. Do they expect me to do it? (AGATHA: Yes, dear.) I say if she can do it herself and keep herself, so much the better for everyone. Anyhow, who are the Government? They're only representing me, and being paid thousands a year by me for carrying out my wishes. (MOLLY: Oh, er—what ho! HORACE turns on her angrily) I like a woman to be a woman—that's the way I was brought up; but if she insists on having a vote—and apparently she does [ALL: She does! she does!]—I don't see why she shouldn't have it. Many a woman came in here at the last election and tried to wheedle me into voting for her particular candidate. If she has time to do that—and I never heard the member say then that she ought to be at home washing the baby—I don't see why she hasn't time to vote. It's never taken up much of my time, or interfered with my work. I've only voted once in my life—but that's neither here nor there. I know what the vote does for me. It gives me a status; that's what you women want—a status. (ALL: Yes, yes; a status.) I might even call it a *locus standi*. If I go now and tell these rotten Cabinet Ministers what I think of them, it's my *locus standi* —[MAUDIE: That's a good word.]—that will force them to listen to me. Oh, I know. And, by gum! I'll give them a bit of my mind. They shall hear a few home truths for once. "Gentlemen," I shall say—well, that won't be true of all of them to start with, but one must give 'em the benefit of the doubt—"gentlemen, the men of England are sick and tired of your policy. Who's driven the women of England into this? *You—*(*he turns round on* ETHEL, *who jumps violently*)—because you were too stupid to know that they meant business— because you couldn't read the writing on the wall. (*Hear, hear.*) It may be nothing to you, gentlemen, that every industry in this country is paralyzed and every Englishman's home turned into a howling wilderness—(MOLLY: Draw it mild, Uncle. HORACE: A howling wilderness, I repeat)—by your refusal to see what's as plain as the nose on your face; but I would have you know, gentlemen, that it *is* something to us. We aren't slaves. We never will be slaves—(AGATHA: Never, never!)—and we insist on reform. Gentlemen, conditions have changed, and women have to work. Don't men encourage them to work, *invite* them to work? (AGATHA: Make them work.) And women are placed in the battle of life on the same terms as we are, short of one thing, the *locus standi* of a vote. (MAUDIE: Good old *locus standi!*) If you aren't going to give it them, gentlemen, and if they won't go back to their occupations without it, we ask you, how they're going to live? Who's going to support them? Perhaps you're thinking of giving them all old age pensions and asking the country to pay the piper! The country will see you damned first, if, gentlemen, you'll pardon the expression. It's dawning upon us all that the women would never have taken such a step as this if they hadn't been the victims of gross injustice. (ALL: Never.) Why shouldn't they have a voice in the laws which regulate the price of food and clothes? Don't they pay for their food and clothes? (MAUDIE: Paid for mine all my life.) Why shouldn't they have a voice in the rate of wages and the hours of labour in certain industries? Aren't they working at those industries? If you had a particle of common sense or decent feeling, gentlemen——"

(*Enter* GERALD WILLIAMS *like a souvenir of Mafeking night. He shouts incoherently and in a hoarse voice. He is utterly transformed from the meek, smug being of an hour before. He is wearing several ribbons and badges and carrying a banner bearing this inscription: "The men of Brixton demand votes for women this evening."*)

WILLIAMS. Cole! Cole! Come on! come on! You'll be late. The procession's forming up at the town hall. There's no time to lose. What are you slacking here for? Perhaps this isn't good enough for you. I've got twelve of them in my drawing-room. We shall be late for the procession if we don't start at once. Hurry up! Come on! Votes for Women! Where's your banner? Where's your badge? Down with the Government! Rule Britannia! Votes for Women! D'you want to support a dozen women for the rest of your life, or don't you? . . . Every man in Brixton is going to Westminster. Borrow a ribbon and come along. Hurry up, now! Hooray! (*Rushes madly out crying "Votes for Women! Rule Britannia; Women, never, never shall be slaves! Votes for Women!"*)

(*All the women who are wearing ribbons decorate* HORACE.)

ETHEL. My hero! (*She throws her arms round him.*)

HORACE. You may depend on me—all of you—to see justice done. When you want a thing done, get a man to do it! Votes for Women!

(AGATHA *gives him a flag which he waves triumphantly.*)

(*Curtain tableau:* HORACE *marching majestically out of the door, with the women cheering him enthusiastically.*)

CURTAIN

THE MOTHERS

by Edith Ellis

CHARACTERS

MARK CROCKER, *a Cornish farmer*
SELINA CROCKER, *Mark's wife*
HANNAH BRIMMICOMB, *a widow to whom Mark is attracted*

THE SCENE *is laid in a Cornish farm kitchen. Deep window-seat. Fireplace facing audience. Door leading to road. Table under window, but well out in room, and settle at top of table by side of fireplace (cornerwise.) Usual kitchen furniture. As curtain goes up, MARK CROCKER is seen sitting on the settle finishing his dinner. SELINA, having finished hers and moved the things she has used aside, is busy making "heavy cake" for tea. MARK eats little and keeps staring at SELINA. At last he thrusts his plate, cup, and saucer impatiently on one side and folds his arms as he tilts his chair back and gazes at his wife. She goes on mixing dough—now and then looking at him in a fixed way, and after each look pounding her paste in the bowl more vigorously.*

MARK. My blessed grandfather! You might be deaf and dumb. (SELINA *smiles.*) Where be John James and Susan Annie?

SELINA. To school.

MARK. Look! (*thumping table*). Let's get at close range, I'm damned sick of beating round bushes.

(SELINA *suddenly stops her work and leans forward toward MARK.*)

SELINA. I'm hoping you are. I'm a bit sick as well as you.

(MARK'S *head lowers a moment, and he lays down his pipe, leans forward in his chair, and looks at his wife.*)

MARK. Marriage be a great frustration.

(SELINA *thumps the dough with her doubled fist and MARK puts his thumbs in his waistcoat, drumming on it impatiently with his fingers.*)

MARK. Here's the straight tip. I'm thy husband, thee 'rt my wife, and a better one no man ever had. Now, fix this up if you can. I'm madly—

(*He frowns, stops and bites his lips. SELINA comes toward him and puts her hand on his shoulder as she almost whispers.*)

SELINA. Don't say it, MARK. The children is between thy thought and thy speech. And it isn't as if I didn't know.

(MARK *frowns and closes his eyes as he mutters.*)

MARK. Thee's allus so darned reasonable, Selina. It's that as 'ave partly made me wander. A man must have flicker betimes. He can't go steady trot and never a canter. If I could have she, I'd likely love thee more.

SELINA (*with a gasp and sob*). You've gone and said it.

MARK. And mean it.

(SELINA *returns quietly to her pastry-making, and MARK begins to fill his pipe.*)

MARK. Thee's far too daft on me. Man and wife should be staid and settled in a manner of speaking.

SELINA (*very quietly*). So I do think.

MARK. Thee's more demandin' now than in our first courtship and even as a bride.

(SELINA *rolls the pastry out on her board and hits it slowly with the rolling-pin. MARK watches her sullenly.*)

MARK. Bean't I right?

SELINA. Seemly being daft over thee, if that's what you reckon I be, Mark, don't make me sure. I'm only sure about the children.

MARK. The children! You'll soon be daft over they too.

SELINA (*gently*). They won't tire. They'm fixed.

MARK. Say, you don't know. Too much be as bad as too little even in youngsters.

(SELINA *suddenly stands taut and puts*

EDITH ELLIS (1861–1916)

Edith Mary Oldham Lees Ellis wrote 16 books, most of which were concerned with her own life or with the sexual radicalism of the New Thought movement of her day. Uppermost among her many idols was the mystic philosopher-socialist Edward Carpenter.

Most of her work appeared under the name of Mrs. Havelock Ellis. They were married in 1891, which also happens to be the date of the first volume of Dr. Ellis' famous *Studies in the Psychology of Sex.* Throughout their tortured marriage, he tried unsuccessfully to accommodate his wife's view of absolute sexual freedom with his own impotence.

Edith Ellis wrote only three plays, which were published together in 1915 under the title *Love in Danger;* they were premiered by Maurice Browne at the Little Theatre in Chicago. Like *The Mothers,* they all deal with the hoped-for reconciliation between the sexual impulse and the vicissitudes of daily life.

The full extent of her views on the subject were not published until after her death. In *The New Horizon in Love and Life* (1921) and *Stories and Essays* (privately printed in 1924), she advocates sexual fulfillment through homosexual as well as heterosexual relationships.

Unstated though strongly implied in her works is a belief in the continuation of life after death. But this was by no means peculiar with Edith Ellis. If one must point to a single, unifying feature of New Thought in the early decades of the 20th century, it would most likely be a belief in the "wonders" of the occult. This notion

COURTESY SOPHIA SMITH COLLECTION

Edith Ellis

permeated many of the plays written for the Little Theatre movement, especially those by women. Broadway, on the other hand, generally adopted a more cynical attitude toward parapsychology, as evidenced by the likes of Vaughan Moody's *The Faith Healer* (1909) and Rachel Crothers' offering for 1924, *Expressing Willie.*

---

her hands behind her back and clasps them fiercely together.)

SELINA. What of she? [*She speaks bitterly.*] Is she scanty i' talk and steadfastness that she be worth while?

(*The man takes his pipe from his mouth and lays it on the table. His face softens and a smile spreads over it.*)

MARK. She? What, as you do say, of she?

SELINA. She've children, too, older than ours.

MARK. I never think upon they.

(SELINA *laughs bitterly and begins to gather up the plates and dishes.* MARK *walks restlessly about the room.*)

SELINA. What do you think would become of them and of ours if you was flighty with she? What would the neighbors say?

(MARK *stands up suddenly and looks calmly at* SELINA.)

MARK. They'd only pity thee and blame me.

SELINA (*with a gesture of impatience*). Is

that what you think I'm cut out for? Pity? Soon my own children will kiss me to comfort me because their father loves a woman who is not their mother.

(*She begins to cut some dough and fits it into a baking-tin.* MARK *watches her thoughtfully and then speaks slowly.*)

MARK. It's damned jealousy, that's all about it.

(SELINA *suddenly thrusts the knife she is holding in her hand toward* MARK.)

SELINA. What if I was drawn to another man? How then?

(MARK *laughs loudly and chucks her under the chin. They stand facing one another.*)

MARK. Don't be foolish, that's not likely.

SELINA. No. (*she speaks sneeringly*). But if it was so? Would thee come to me and urge me to leave thee?

MARK. I'm not a ninny. Women be women.

SELINA. And men men. Seein' as it's so, I'm not for argufyin' nor yet resentin'. It's like childbirth, the less noise you make and fuss the better for everybody all round. If she be daft on thee, neither me nor any other body can stop it. She will win.

MARK. It's not in nature to be otherwise. (*Thoughtfully smoking pipe.*) I be unbeknowns over this even to myself.

(SELINA *puts down the knife and places her hand a moment on her husband's shoulder.*)

SELINA. I bean't a mother for nothin', Mark. Go thy ways without thought of me. Women gets their comfort sideways, in a manner of speaking. Men gets theirs forthright. We've our whimsies and you have your big catches. A woman as knows anything do never stand in the way of a man hunting and shooting. It's his disposition same as slyness be ours.

MARK (*impatiently, smoking furiously, and pointing toward his wife with his pipe*). It's them out-of-the-way speeches, Selina, as beats me. I've no call to go out of my way to hurt thee, but I can't be tied to thy apron-strings.

SELINA (*very quietly as she puts away the things and folds the tablecloth*). Marriage bean't like no apron-string. It be most like an iron chain.

MARK. Or a jail door.   (SELINA *sighs.*)

SELINA. Thee's allus been free as a gull, Mark. Bondage would be more new-fangled for thee than liberty.

MARK. I've done my best by thee.

(SELINA *bangs a cupboard door, where she has been putting away sugar, etc. She wheels round.*)

SELINA. Is that what she's told thee, or what thee've taught she, I wonder? It might be g'eat virtue instead of love 'twixt man and wife to hear thee talk.

MARK. We do never scarcely speak of thee. It's best not. She knows I love thee, right enough.

SELINA (*bitterly*). I wonder how she found that out?

MARK. By signs, of course. A man don't never wait to take kisses if there bean't no obstacle. She knows that.

(*He jerks his head back and clasps his hands behind it.*)

MARK. But it's most beyond me now. So there! I had to say it. It's fair choking me. We'll leave it be. It's all we can do.

SELINA. Iss! We'll leave it be. Shall I make thee a savor for thy tea?

(MARK *gazes at his wife. Her whole tone and attitude have changed into tender motherliness.*)

MARK. As you've a mind to, woman. I be going out after.

(*He looks away shamefacedly as he unhooks his cap from the door.* SELINA *takes a clothesbrush from the shelf and brushes his coat.*)

SELINA (*kindly*). How be the cow and calf?

MARK. Nicely. A fine bull calf and some g'eat sucker.

(*He goes out and bangs the door.* SELINA *goes to a little mirror on the wall and gazes into it for some time. Then she sits down. She suddenly rises, wipes her eyes with her apron, and opens a drawer in the kitchen table. She takes out a bundle of children's half-dried pinafores and socks and hangs them on a little clothes-horse near the fire. Her face brightens as she does it. She suddenly takes a little sock in her hand and holds it against her cheek.*)

SELINA. They bean't lent, anyway. They belong, same as the veins in my body.

(*A knock at the door startles her. She*

opens it and faces HANNAH BRIMMI-
COMB. *The two women stand speechless before one another.* HANNAH BRIM-
MICOMB *is dressed very daintily, and
her easy movements and beautiful figure contrast with the regularity of figure
and sharpness of expression of* SELINA.
SELINA *looks bitterly at* HANNAH.)

HANNAH (*nervously*). Are you alone, Mrs.
Crocker?

SELINA (*dully*). The children are at school.
Come in and sit down. I meant to come to you
this very afternoon. It's perhaps as well it's this
way. Sit.

(HANNAH *sits and draws chair nearer as if
she expected* SELINA *to sit too.* SELINA
*draws herself to her full height and
smooths her parted hair down with
both hands for a second.*)

SELINA. I can talk better standing, though
talk won't help much. My husband be leaving
me for you. I need n't tell you what you know
already, but I want him to think of our children. It'll be a slur on they.

HANNAH (*hesitatingly*). I 'm North-Country,
as you know. I was only amongst you all for
a few months before my husband died. The
two years have been very lonely.

SELINA. Stealin' don't make things easier.

(MRS. BRIMMICOMB *stands up, puts out a
hand and withdraws it as* SELINA *ignores it. But as she sits again, she
slowly draws off her gloves, her head
bent.*)

SELINA. Mark be dazzled same as a child i'
full sunlight. When he's smoking, he be
thinkin', and when he's working, it's the same
and—and—(*she hesitates and clenches her
hands together*)—even when h'm dreaming,
he do make use of your name. (*Lowering her
eyes.*) That's how I first fell on it. (MRS.
BRIMMICOMB *looks up and gazes at* SELINA.
Iss! It is a thing to color up for. I be covered
with shame inside and out that I be forced to
sit before a stranger and beg for my children.

HANNAH (*in surprise*). Beg!—for your children?

SELINA. Iss! Beg to a woman of your make.
They'm wonderful happy and there'd be a stain
on them.

HANNAH. I've often wondered about you. To
think this is our first real talk, only nods before.

SELINA. Mark saw to that, seemly. It began
afore he ever knew. First sight, I should think.

HANNAH. So he says.

(SELINA *stamps her foot and almost hisses
and then turns to the fire and rearranges the children's clothes.* HANNAH
watches her wistfully.)

SELINA. I wish me and the children could go
and leave you both. We're best away. But
we've no money and the talk would be worse.

HANNAH. But you love him.

(SELINA *draws a chair near and kneels
with one knee on it, staring at* HAN-
NAH.)

SELINA. Love! I never make use of no such
word nowadays. It's been all suffering so long.

HANNAH. Poor dear!

SELINA. How dare you? (*Roughly.*) I want
none of your pity, considering it's been all you.

HANNAH (*meaningly*). Has it?

SELINA (*bitterly*). Iss! The woman allus
beckons and the man follows. Women don't
never uphold one the other. They as win be
covered with vanity and triumph whether they
calls theirselves bad uns or good uns.

HANNAH (*drawing her chair closer to* SE-
LINA). What would you have done in my
place?

(*She puts a hand on* SELINA'S *knee.*)

SELINA. Spit at him. Anything to save the
children even if I hated the woman.

(HANNAH *smiles and* SELINA *sits down by
her.*)

HANNAH. You seem to know very little about
men, Mrs. Crocker. I'd no wish to bind him to
me forever. Scorn would have led to scenes,
and in scenes no one can tell what might have
happened. I've always shunned them. It was
after a scene that I took my husband for better
or worse.

SELINA (*more gently*). You love mine now
and want him—that suffices. He's going to you
this very night and any time might—might—

(*She puts her face in her hands and beats
the ground with her foot.*)

HANNAH. Be the end.

SELINA. What do you mean? (*She looks up
at* HANNAH *in a bewildered way.*) You sit there
as calm and stolid as if you wasn't worse nor a
thief and a witch.

HANNAH. I'm neither. I'm just a mother, like
you.

SELINA (*in a dull, even voice*). I ain't slept

proper for weeks and every morsel I eat tastes like chaff.

HANNAH (*gently*). How you love him, and he knows it!

SELINA (*bitterly*). Ain't he by chance told you how much he do love me? It's not sufferable that I should be the only one to be supposed to care. I wouldn't have done it to you nor to no woman.

HANNAH. I've done nothing.

SELINA. That's pretty brazen, anyway.

(HANNAH *rises and walks up and down once or twice with her hands clasped behind her back, and then faces* SELINA *with her right forefinger emphasizing what she says.*)

HANNAH. I'm speaking nothing but the truth. When your husband told me he loved me, it was a greater surprise to me than it was to you. I was not prepared for such a strange thing, but I hate to see suffering, and I believed he was very wretched. I probably made up my mind why he said what he did, and at first I felt hard toward you. I thought you did not care for him and made him suffer, and I wanted badly to help.

(SELINA *pushes* HANNAH *down in her chair and rises. She puts the kettle on the fire and gets out the tea-cloth, and as she speaks leaves the table and gets out saffron cake, etc. She leans over the table toward* HANNAH *as she finishes and speaks slowly and thoughtfully.*)

SELINA. Interference between husbands and wives be never helpful. It's allus a hinderment. It would be hardly bearable if angels took it in hand, but when a woman choked with vainglory meddles, it's most past mending.

(*She makes the tea and beckons to* HANNAH. HANNAH *draws her chair to the table and speaks quietly.*)

HANNAH. If I'd only seen you together, it would have made all the difference. I was foolish enough to be afraid of meeting you. He took me by surprise, and a man's stealth and persuasion moithered me and kept me wondering and the time has flown till now. Something he said to me the other day made the truth appear to me, and now we're here and can talk. I wanted to come to you, but I'm not much at explaining. I grew to care for you in a strange, silent way because I understood.

(SELINA *stands holding the teapot in air*

and then drops it suddenly on the table. She folds her arms across her breast and laughs bitterly.)

SELINA (*with emphasis*). Care for me?

HANNAH. Yes, for you. I knew how you must be feeling and I wondered what you would have done if you'd been me.

(SELINA *sits down and wipes her lips with the corner of her apron and pours out a cup of tea.* HANNAH *draws up to the table.*)

SELINA. Kissed him, after all, I suppose. How can I tell? I ain't never been tried. Nobody ain't never wanted me but Mark, and he soon tired.

(HANNAH *takes up her cup and hands it to* SELINA.)

HANNAH. You drink first. You're tired more than I am. (SELINA *pours out another and drinks.*) He's never kissed me, and that's why he's so crazy over me. He'd soon cure if he had. He's red-hot, and that never lasts. Somehow I wouldn't let him. It's different, too, now I've seen you. He's a born hunter, but it's a vixen he's tracking, not a fox. Your cubs and mine are safe.

(SELINA *sips her tea very slowly, her eyes on the table, as if thinking deeply.*)

SELINA. I'm considerably took back.

(HANNAH *sips her tea and takes some cake* SELINA *offers.*)

HANNAH. He's quite curable, and I mean to cure him and at once. It is not me he loves the most of us three.

SELINA (*incredulously*). You don't want him?

HANNAH (*emphatically*). No. He is a child now in my eyes, and children must be cured of fevers.

SELINA (*drawing the words out slowly and gulping more tea*). Then you're *not* daft on him as he thinks?

HANNAH. Oh! I'm quite fond of him. At first I own I was taken with his way. You know what vigor he has, and how he talks and hits things and tosses his head.

SELINA (*smiling*). Iss!—like a g'eat boy with a new top.

HANNAH (*looking steadily at* SELINA *and stretching out her hand across the table*). A woman can't give her soul as a top.

SELINA. It ain't made probably for constant spinning, sure enough. I never thought of that.

HANNAH. Nor for being wound up by fits and starts, just to hear the hum.

SELINA. Not at all.

(*She leans back in her chair and watches* HANNAH *with a gradual relaxing of her features.*)

HANNAH. He drew me so strangely to you and away from himself by all the things he said and did. Do you believe me? I like you, why should I deceive you?

SELINA (*slowly*). There's a semblance of truth about it all.

HANNAH. It's gospel truth from woman to woman.

SELINA. They do generally say from man to man.

(*The two women rise simultaneously and* SELINA *puts back the clothes-horse to the fire.* HANNAH *helps her to turn the little clothes.*)

HANNAH. As far as I am concerned, your husband is as clean as your own children.

SELINA (*shakes out a pair of little cotton breeches*). And as foolish. (HANNAH *suddenly takes* SELINA'S *hand and presses it to her face.*) You've a cool hand.

HANNAH. And a grip.

SELINA. I feel a g'eat load gone from my chest.

HANNAH. You love him more than you know.

SELINA (*simply*). I'm his wife. It's nature.

HANNAH. You dear!

(*She draws* SELINA *to her and kisses her very tenderly.* SELINA *draws away slowly from the embrace.*)

SELINA. I'm real refreshed. It's like a cooling drink when any one be thirsty. I've never cottoned to girls nor women folkses. I've no chums. This be different. Seemly, it's a part of Mark.

(*She clears away all trace of the meal.*)

HANNAH. We'll mother him and all the children, too. This has taught me more than I ever knew before about what being a mother really means.

SELINA. It be right through our make-up, seemly.

HANNAH. Not to one another. That be a sister's part.

SELINA. It be a tower of strength, anyway. I feel fortified all through my system.

HANNAH. We know the secrets.

SELINA. And keep 'em.

HANNAH. Fast.

(*The two women smile into one another's faces as they hold hands and suddenly kiss.* HANNAH *moves toward the door with head lowered as if to hide her smile as she disappears.* SELINA *folds the children's aired clothes and puts them on a chair. She begins to dust the mantel-shelf and little kitchen, stopping now and again as if thinking. The door is suddenly burst open and* MARK *steps in. He takes down a pipe from the mantel-shelf, fiercely empties it, and rams tobacco into the bowl.* SELINA *flicks dust from his coat. He shakes his shoulders and says suddenly as he takes off his coat and hangs it up.*)

MARK. Matches.

(SELINA *goes to the cupboard and finds matches and hands them to her husband. He lights his pipe, smokes quickly and faces* SELINA.)

MARK. Let's have a cup of tea, sharp. My mouth be dry. Woman!—(MARK *speaks slowly and bitterly*)—You be right. She be a hussy. Damn her!

SELINA (*putting on kettle*). Have you been to see her? I thought you weren't going till night!

MARK. So *she* thought. But I met her just now. Fell on her after she's been crying or something. Her eyes had tales in 'em, and I guessed to oncet and she couldn't deny. My gosh! Selina! Thee be revenged, sure enough. I'm surely seemly in thy place now.

(*He sits down near table and leans his head on his right hand.*)

SELINA. My place! You'm dreaming.

MARK. No! I'm not. (*Roughly.*) I'm jolly well wide awake at last. I thought she a fine 'un, but sh'm a whimsy same as lots of women.

(*He suddenly tilts his chair and clasps his hands behind his head. He has dropped his pipe on the table.*)

MARK. She've left me like a bleating calf at the stable door. She had been with some one just afore I met her. She couldn't deny it. She cares for him, too.

(*He suddenly unclasps his hands and throws his pipe in the fireplace.*)

MARK. Even that has no savor. It's all like death itself.

SELINA. Death, seemly, be a finish. Perhaps this be a beginning.

MARK. Talk sense, Selina, not riddles. (*Irritably.*) Facts is facts. She've made a dashed fool of me I tell thee.

SELINA. Have you ever kissed her?

MARK. No. (*Shortly.*) I meant to make her kiss me tonight. A man be a bit pacified if he've won, even halfway.

SELINA (*looking curiously at* MARK *and holding him by one shoulder as she bends over him*). Didn't thee try just now? Thee's got a look—

(*She stops as* MARK *suddenly jumps up and paces about the kitchen. As if too hot, he flings off his waistcoat.*)

MARK. Oh! damn it! shut up. Why frenzy me with such fancies? *You'd* best start kissing me again, I reckon, according to she. I feel mad— mad. She jolly well gave me the go-by, and said as I was to go and kiss you if I wanted kisses. Flung up in my face a few out-of-the-way words I once said about you. Told me I was no man, and that she despised me. I stamped with rage at last, and she only laughed. Laughed! Do you hear? (*As* SELINA *smiled and stooped to pick up* MARK'S *pipe from the fireplace.*) Said I was like her boy Rob when he fired his popgun. At that I just marched away, but she called me back with a bit of her old manner.

SELINA. Oh!

(*Handing him his pipe which he snatches and puts in his big waistcoat pocket.*)

MARK (*pointing to a chair for* SELINA *to sit on*). She be a false, flighty woman, but there's just one thing I like in she even yet.

SELINA. Sakes! Mark! Only one! At dinner-time there wasn't one you didn't like.

MARK. At dinner-time I thought she was daft on me, too. That makes all the difference.

SELINA. What's the thing left, I wonder?

(*MARK lights his pipe and speaks slowly and almost gently.*)

MARK. She spoke of you as if she'd known what you was. She said she wished she was good like you. I'm a blasted fool, but it came over me like a soft shower of rain what you'd had to put up with in this truck and she not worth a pennord of it, and carin', seemly, for some one else all the time. Sakes alive! I'd never have let on even to thee if I wasn't in a boil of hate and rage. No man tells his wife his fooleries, and now there's another poor devil let in by a woman's eyes, whoever he be.

(*SELINA folds the children's clothes and puts the kettle right on the fire to make it boil.*)

SELINA. It mayn't be no man at all.

(*MARK flings his head back and laughs.*)

MARK. If it bean't no man, who the devil should it be? A woman? No! my patience, I do know she.

SELINA (*thoughtfully*). Perhaps nobody don't never know another.

MARK (*standing up and putting his arm around* SELINA'S *waist. His voice has lost its bitterness*). Iss! they do, my gosh! I do know thee, Selina, right through. The difference between you two be the difference between night and day. I knew that bit of gust would be over afore I came back, and you be as comfortable as possible in spite of all this flare-up.

SELINA (*gently freeing herself from his embrace*). Seems to me, Mark, women be much of a muchness. They be unlike men-folkses, and even their frenzies be things apart, seemly, and to their selves.

MARK. Thee's daft on me still, woman, in spite of all this 'ere set out. Curse her—she never cared a bit.

(*Suddenly kissing* SELINA, *who kisses him again as a mother would her child as she holds his head to her and smooths back his hair from his hot forehead.*)

MARK. Thee kisses most like mother. No fire and brimstone, but just soothey. It's a real ease to a poor devil as be tired and tormented past bearing.

CURTAIN

THE OUTSIDE

by Susan Glaspell

CHARACTERS

CAPTAIN of "The Bars" Life-Saving Station
BRADFORD, a Life-Saver
TONY, a Portuguese Life-Saver
MRS. PATRICK, who lives in the abandoned Station
ALLIE MAYO, who works for her

SCENE: *A room in a house which was once a life-saving station. Since ceasing to be that it has taken on no other character, except that of a place which no one cares either to preserve or change. It is painted the life-saving gray, but has not the life-saving freshness. This is one end of what was the big boat room, and at the ceiling is seen a part of the frame work from which the boat once swung. About two thirds of the back wall is open, because of the big sliding door, of the type of barn door, and through this open door are seen the sand dunes, and beyond them the woods. At one point the line where woods and dunes meet stands out clearly and there are indicated the rude things, vines, bushes, which form the outer uneven rim of the woods—the only things that grow in the sand. At another point a sand-hill is menacing the woods. This old life-saving station is at a point where the sea curves, so through the open door the sea also is seen. (The station is located on the outside shore of Cape Cod, at the point, near the tip of the Cape, where it makes that final curve which forms the Provincetown Harbor.) The dunes are hills and strange forms of sand on which, in places, grows the stiff beach grass —struggle; dogged growing against odds. At right of the big sliding door is a drift of sand and the top of buried beach grass is seen on* this. *There is a door left, and at right of big sliding door is a slanting wall. Door in this is ajar at rise of curtain, and through this door* BRADFORD *and* TONY, *life-savers, are seen bending over a man's body, attempting to restore respiration. The captain of the lifesavers comes into view outside the big open door, at left; he appears to have been hurrying, peers in, sees the men, goes quickly to them.*

CAPTAIN. I'll take this now, boys.
BRADFORD. No need for anybody to take it, Capt'n. He was dead when we picked him up.
CAPTAIN. Dannie Sears was dead when we picked him up. But we brought him back. I'll go on awhile.
  (*The two men who have been bending over the body rise, stretch to relax, and come into the room.*)
BRADFORD (*pushing back his arms and putting his hands on his chest*). Work,—tryin' to put life in the dead.
CAPTAIN. Where'd you find him, Joe?
BRADFORD. In front of this house. Not forty feet out.
CAPTAIN. What'd you bring him up here for?
  (*He speaks in an abstracted way, as if the working part of his mind is on something else, and in the muffled voice of one bending over.*)
BRADFORD (*with a sheepish little laugh*). Force of habit, I guess. We brought so many of 'em back up here. [*Looks around the room.*] And then it was kind of unfriendly down where he was—the wind spittin' the sea onto you till he'd have no way of knowin' he was ashore.
TONY. Lucky I was not sooner or later as I walk by from my watch.
BRADFORD. You have accommodating ways, Tony. Not sooner or later. I wouldn't say it of many Portagees. But the sea (*calling it in to the* CAPTAIN) is friendly as a kitten alongside

SUSAN GLASPELL (1882–1948)

Susan Keating Glaspell maintained a lifelong affection for the Middle America of her birth. By 1901 she had returned from Des Moines, Iowa, where she was graduated from Drake University, to Davenport, her birthplace, there to begin a career as a newspaper reporter. Soon she was also publishing short stories known for their "local color." With the encouragement of her friend Lucy Huffaker, she published the first of her ten novels, *The Glory of the Conquered,* in 1911. Throughout the remainder of her professional life, Glaspell's income was derived mainly from the sales of her novels and short stories.

The most profound influence on her life was the powerful and enigmatic personality of George Cram Cook, whose most outstanding quality would be described today as "charisma." They were introduced at a meeting of a quasi-religious group known as "The Monist Society." Cook divorced his first wife in 1913 to marry Susan Glaspell, and the two of them then left Davenport to join the "Bohemians"—writers, artists, and itinerant thinkers who spent their winters in New York's Greenwich Village and their summers in the Massachusetts retreat known as Provincetown.

Nowadays, we might accuse this group of what is referred to as "radical chic." But in the early part of this century politics and art were part of a ferment of talents and ambitions that crystallized in the New Theatre Movement. It was "Jig" Cook who founded the Provincetown Players; he was also instrumental in launching his wife's career as a dramatist.

Glaspell's earliest efforts consisted of seven one-act plays, two of which, *Suppressed Desires* (1915) and *Tickless Time* (1918), she wrote in collaboration with Cook. A third, *Trifles* (1916), has over the years become one of the most widely performed and anthologized short plays in our literature. *The Outside* (1917) is included in this volume because it anticipates her later, more serious dramatic style.

Her most characteristic plays—*Bernice*

Susan Glaspell and George Cram Cook

(1919), *The Verge,* and *Alison's House* (1930)—all center around a single, ambitiously conceived female character. On closer examination, however, these three heroines bear a striking resemblance to the biographic reflections of Cook that Glaspell published in *Road to the Temple* (1927), three years after the death of her beloved husband.

Susan Glaspell's career as a dramatist was inextricably bound to the fortunes of the Provincetown Players. The notable exception to this is *Alison's House,* for which she won a Pulitzer Prize. Modern feminists cite her concern for "women's issues"; yet, as *The Outside* introduces, Glaspell's main preoccupation as a dramatist was to be the essential affinity between the enlightened individual and the creative forces of the universe.

the women that live *here*. Allie Mayo—they're *both* crazy—had that door open (*moving his head toward the big sliding door*) sweepin' out, and when we come along she backs off and stands lookin' at us, *lookin'*—Lord, I just wanted to get him somewhere else. So I kicked this door open with my foot (*jerking his hand toward the room where the* CAPTAIN *is seen bending over the man*) and got him *away*. (*Under his voice.*) If he did have any notion of comin' back to life, he wouldn't a come if he'd seen her. (*More genially.*) *I* wouldn't.

CAPTAIN. You know who he is, Joe?

BRADFORD. I never saw him before.

CAPTAIN. Mitchell telephoned from High Head that a dory came ashore there.

BRADFORD. Last night wasn't the *best* night for a dory. (*To* TONY, *boastfully.*) Not that *I* couldn't 'a' stayed in one. Some men can stay in a dory and some can't. (*Going to the inner door.*) That boy's dead, Capt'n.

CAPTAIN. Then I'm not doing him any harm.

BRADFORD (*going over and shaking the frame where the boat once swung*). This the first time you ever been in this place, ain't it, Tony?

TONY. I never was here before.

BRADFORD. Well, *I* was here before. (*A laugh.*) And the old man—(*nodding toward the* CAPTAIN) he lived here for twenty-seven years. Lord, the things that happened *here*. There've been dead ones carried through *that* door. (*Pointing to the outside door.*) Lord—the ones *I've* carried. I carried in Bill Collins, and Lou Harvey and—huh! 'sall over now. You ain't seen no *wrecks*. Don't ever think you have. I was here the night the *Jennie Snow* was out there. (*Pointing to the sea.*) There was a *wreck*. We got the boat that stood here (*again shaking the frame*) down that bank. (*Goes to the door and looks out.*) Lord, how'd we ever do it? The sand has put this place on the blink all right. And then when it gets too God-for-saken for a life-savin' station, a lady takes it for a summer residence—and then spends the winter. She's cheerful one.

TONY. A woman—she makes things pretty. This not like a place where a woman live. On the floor there is nothing—on the wall there is nothing. Things—(*trying to express it with his hands*) do not hang on other things.

BRADFORD (*imitating* TONY's *gesture*). No

—things do not hang on other things. In my opinion the woman's crazy—sittin' over there on the sand—(*a gesture toward the dunes*) what's she *lookin'* at? There ain't nothin' to see. And I know the woman that works for her's crazy—Allie Mayo. She's a Provincetown girl. She was all right once, but—

(MRS. PATRICK *comes in from the hall at the right. She is a "city woman," a sophisticated person who has been caught into something as unlike the old life as the dunes are unlike a meadow. At the moment she is excited and angry.*)

MRS. PATRICK. You have no right here. This isn't the life-saving station any more. Just because it used to be—I don't see why you should think— This is my house! And—I want my house to myself!

CAPTAIN (*putting his head through the door. One arm of the man he is working with is raised, and the hand reaches through the doorway*). Well I must say, lady, I would think that any house could be a life-saving station when the sea had sent a man to it.

MRS. PATRICK (*who has turned away so she cannot see the hand*). I don't want him here! I—(*defiant, yet choking*) I must have my house to myself!

CAPTAIN. You'll get your house to yourself when I've made up my mind there's no more life in this man. A good many lives have been saved in this house, Mrs. Patrick I believe that's your name—and if there's any chance of bringing one more back from the dead, the fact that you own the house ain't goin' to make a damn bit of difference to me!

MRS. PATRICK (*in a thin wild way*). I must have my house to myself.

CAPTAIN. Hell with such a woman!

(*Moves the man he is working with and slams the door shut.*)

(*As the* CAPTAIN *says,* "And if there's any chance of bringing one more back from the dead," ALLIE MAYO *has appeared outside the wide door which gives on the dunes, a bleak woman, who at first seems little more than a part of the sand before which she stands. But as she listens to this conflict one suspects in her that peculiar intensity of twisted things which grow in unfavoring places.*)

MRS. PATRICK. I—I don't want them here! I must—

(*But suddenly she retreats, and is gone.*)

BRADFORD. Well, I couldn't say, Allie Mayo, that you work for any too kind-hearted a lady. What's the matter with the woman? Does she want folks to die? Appears to break her all up to see somebody trying to save a life. What d'you you work for such a fish for? A crazy fish —that's what I call the woman. I've seen her— day after day—settin' over there where the dunes meet the woods, just sittin' there, lookin'. (*Suddenly thinking of it.*) I believe she *likes* to see the sand slippin' down on the woods. Pleases her to see somethin' gettin' buried, I guess.

(ALLIE MAYO, *who has stepped inside the door and moved half across the room, toward the corridor at the right, is arrested by this last—stands a moment as if seeing through something, then slowly on, and out.*)

BRADFORD. Some coffee'd taste good. But coffee, in this house? Oh, no. It might make somebody feel better. (*Opening the door that was slammed shut.*) Want me now, Capt'n?

CAPTAIN. No.

BRADFORD. Oh, that boy's dead, Capt'n.

CAPTAIN (*snarling*). Dannie Sears was dead, too. Shut that door. I don't want to hear that woman's voice again, ever.

(*Closing the door and sitting on a bench built into that corner between the big sliding door and the room where the* CAPTAIN *is.*)

BRADFORD. They're a cheerful pair of women—livin' in this cheerful place—a place that life-savers had to turn over to the sand— huh! This Patrick woman used to be all right. She and her husband was summer folks over in town. They used to picnic over here on the outside. It was Joe Dyer—he's always talkin' to summer folks—told 'em the government was goin' to build the new station and sell this one by sealed bids. I heard them talkin' about it. They was sittin' right down there on the beach, eatin' their supper. They was goin' to put in a fire-place and they was goin' to paint it bright colors, and have parties over here—summer folk notions. Their bid won it—who'd want it? —a buried house you couldn't move.

TONY. I see no bright colors.

BRADFORD. Don't you? How astonishin'! You must be color blind. And I guess *we're* the first party. (*Laughs.*) I was in Bill Joseph's grocery store, one day last November, when in she comes—Mrs. Patrick, from New York. "I've come to take the old life-saving station," says she. "I'm going to sleep over there to-night!" Huh! Bill is used to queer ways—he deals with summer folks, but that got *him*. November—an empty house, a buried house, you might say, off here on the outside shore—way across the sand from man or beast. He got it out of her, not by what she said, but by the way she looked at what he said, that her husband had died, and she was runnin' off to hide herself, I guess. A person'd feel sorry for her if she weren't so stand-offish, and so doggon *mean*. But mean folks have got minds of their own. She slept here that night. Bill had men hauling things till after dark—bed, stove, coal. And then she wanted somebody to work for her. "Somebody," says she, "that doesn't say an unnecessary word!" Well, when Bill come to the back of the store, I said, "Looks to me as if Allie Mayo was the party she's lookin' for." Allie Mayo has got a prejudice against words. Or maybe she likes 'em so well she's savin' of 'em. She's not spoke an unnecessary word for twenty years. She's got her reasons. Women whose men go to sea ain't always talkative.

(*The* CAPTAIN *comes out. He closes door behind him and stands there beside it. He looks tired and disappointed. Both look at him. Pause.*)

CAPTAIN. Wonder who he was.

BRADFORD. Young. Guess he's not been much at sea.

CAPTAIN. I hate to leave even the dead in this house. But we can get right back for him. (*A look around.*) The old place used to be more friendly. (*Moves to outer door, hesitates, hating to leave like this.*) Well, Joe, we brought a good many of them back here.

BRADFORD. Dannie Sears is tendin' bar in Boston now.

(*The three men go; as they are going around the drift of sand* ALLIE MAYO *comes in carrying a pot of coffee; sees them leaving, puts down the coffee pot, looks to the door the* CAPTAIN *has*

closed, moves toward it, as if drawn.
MRS. PATRICK *follows her in.*)

MRS. PATRICK. They've gone?

(MRS. MAYO *nods, facing the closed door.*
MRS. PATRICK. And they're leaving—him?
(*Again the other woman nods.*) Then he's—?
(MRS. MAYO *just stands there.*) They have no
right—just because it used to be their place—!
I want my house to myself!

(*Snatches her coat and scarf from a hook
and starts through the big door toward
the dunes.*)

ALLIE MAYO. Wait.

(*When she has said it she sinks into that
corner seat—as if overwhelmed by
what she has done. The other woman is
held.*)

ALLIE MAYO (*to herself*). If I could say
that, I can say more. (*Looking at the woman
she has arrested, but speaking more to herself.*)
That boy in there—his face—uncovered something—(*Her open hand on her chest. But she
waits, as if she cannot go on; when she speaks
it is in labored way—slow, monotonous, as if
snowed in by silent years.*) For twenty years,
I did what you are doing. And I can tell you—
it's not the way. (*Her voice has fallen to a
whisper; she stops, looking ahead at something
remote and veiled.*) We had been married—
two years. (*A start, as of sudden pain. Says it
again, as if to make herself say it.*) Married—
two years. He had a chance to go north on a
whaler. Times hard. He had to go. A year and
a half—it was to be. A year and a half. Two
years we'd been married.

(*She sits silent, moving a little back and
forth.*)

The day he went away. (*Not spoken, but
breathed from pain.*) The days after he was
gone.

I heard at first. Last letter said farther north
—not another chance to write till on the way
home. (*A wait.*)

Six months. Another. I did not hear. (*Long
wait.*) Nobody ever heard.

(*After it seems she is held there, and will
not go on.*) I used to talk as much as any girl
in Provincetown. Jim used to tease me about
my talking. But they'd come in to talk to me.
They'd say—"You may hear *yet.*" They'd talk
about what must have happened. And one day
a woman who'd been my friend all my life said

—"Suppose he was to walk *in!*" I got up and
drove her from my kitchen—and from that
time till this I've not said a word I didn't have
to say. (*She has become almost wild in telling
this. That passes. In a whisper.*) The ice that
caught Jim—caught me. (*A moment as if held
in ice. Comes from it. To* MRS. PATRICK *simply.*) It's not the way. (*A sudden change.*)
You're not the only woman in the world whose
husband is dead!

MRS. PATRICK (*with the cry of the hurt*).
Dead? My husband's not *dead.*

ALLIE MAYO. He's *not?* (*Slowly understands.*) Oh.

(*The woman in the door is crying. Suddenly picks up her coat which has
fallen to the floor and steps outside.*)

ALLIE MAYO (*almost failing to do it*). Wait.

MRS. PATRCK. Wait? Don't you think you've
said enough? They told me you didn't say an
unnecessary word!

ALLIE MAYO. I don't.

MRS. PATRICK. And you can see, I should
think, that you've bungled into things you
know nothing about!

(*As she speaks, and crying under her
breath, she pushes the sand by the door
down on the half-buried grass—though
not as if knowing what she is doing.*)

ALLIE MAYO (*slowly*). When you keep still
for twenty years you know—things you didn't
know you knew. I know why you're doing that.
(*She looks up at her, startled.*) Don't bury the
only thing that will grow. Let it grow.

(*The woman outside still crying under her
breath turns abruptly and starts toward
the line where dunes and woods meet.*)

ALLIE MAYO. I know where you're going!
(MRS. PATRICK *turns, but not as if she wants
to.*) What you'll try to do. Over there. (*Pointing to the line of woods.*) Bury it. The life in
you. Bury it—watching the sand bury the
woods. But I'll tell you something! *They* fight
too. The woods! They fight for life the way
that Captain fought for life in there!

(*Pointing to the closed door.*)

MRS. PATRICK (*with a strange exultation*).
And lose the way he lost in there!

ALLIE MAYO (*sure, sombre*). They don't
lose.

MRS. PATRICK. Don't *lose?* (*Triumphant.*)
I have walked on the tops of buried trees!

ALLIE MAYO (*slow, sombre, yet large*). And vines will grow over the sand that covers the trees, and hold it. And other trees will grow above the buried trees.

MRS. PATRICK. I've watched the sand slip down on the vines that reach out farthest.

ALLIE MAYO. Another vine will reach that spot. (*Under her breath, tenderly*). Strange little things that reach out farthest!

MRS. PATRICK. And will be buried soonest!

ALLIE MAYO. And hold the sand for things behind them. They save a wood that guards a town.

MRS. PATRICK. I care nothing about a woods to guard a town. This is the outside—these dunes where only beach grass grows, this outer shore where men can't live. The Outside. You who were born here and who die here have named it that.

ALLIE MAYO. Yes, we named it that, and we had reason. He died here (*reaches her hand toward the closed door*) and many a one before him. But many another reached the harbor! (*Slowly raises her arm, bends it to make the form of the Cape. Touches the outside of her bent arm.*) The Outside. But an arm that bends to make a harbor—where men are safe.

MRS. PATRICK. I'm outside the harbor—on the dunes, land not life.

ALLIE MAYO. Dunes meet woods and woods hold dunes from a town that's shore to a harbor.

MRS. PATRICK. This is the Outside. Sand. (*Picking some of it up in her hand and letting it fall on the beach grass.*) Sand that *covers*—hills of sand that move and cover.

ALLIE MAYO. Woods. Woods to hold the moving hills from Provincetown. Provincetown—where they turn when boats can't live at sea. Did you ever see the sails come round here when the sky is dark? A line of them—swift to the harbor—where their children live. Go back! (*Pointing.*) Back to your edge of the woods that's the *edge of the dunes*.

MRS. PATRICK. The edge of life. Where life trails off to dwarfed things not worth a name.

(*Suddenly sits down in the doorway.*)

ALLIE MAYO. Not worth a name. And—meeting the Outside!

(*Big with the sense of the wonder of life.*)

MRS. PATRICK (*lifting sand and letting it drift through her hand*). They're what the sand will let them be. They take strange shapes like shapes of blown sand.

ALLIE MAYO. Meeting the Outside. (*Moving nearer; speaking more personally.*) I know why you came here. To this house that had been given up; on this shore where only savers of life try to live. I know what holds you on these dunes, and draws you over there. But other things are true beside the things you want to see.

MRS. PATRICK. How do you know they are? Where have you been for twenty years?

ALLIE MAYO. Outside. Twenty years. That's why I know how brave *they* are. (*Indicating the edge of the woods. Suddenly different.*) You'll not find peace there again! Go back and watch them *fight!*

MRS. PATRICK. (*swiftly rising*). You're a cruel woman—a hard, insolent woman! I knew what I was doing! What do you know about it? About me? I didn't *go* to the Outside. I was left there. I'm only—trying to get along. Everything that can hurt me I want buried—buried deep. Spring is here. This morning I *knew* it. Spring—coming through the storm—to take me—take me to hurt me. That's why I couldn't bear—(*she looks at the closed door*) things that made me know I feel. You haven't felt for so long you don't know what it means! But I tell you, Spring is here! And now you'd take *that* from me—(*looking now toward the edge of the woods*) the thing that made me know they would be buried in my heart—those things I can't *live* and know I feel. You're more cruel than the sea! "But other things are true beside the things you want to see!" Outside. Springs will come when I will not know that it is Spring. (*As if resentful of not more deeply believing what she says.*) What would there be for me but the Outside? What was there for you? What did you ever find after you lost the thing you wanted?

ALLIE MAYO. I found—what I find now I know. The edge of life—to hold life behind me—

(*A slight gesture toward* MRS. PATRICK.)

MRS. PATRICK (*stepping back*). You call what you are life? (*Laughs.*) Bleak as those ugly things that grow in the sand!

ALLIE MAYO (*under her breath, as one who speaks tenderly of beauty*). Ugly!

MRS. PATRCK (*passionately*). I have *known*

life. I have known *life*. You're like this Cape. A line of land way out to sea—land not life.

ALLIE MAYO. A harbor far at sea. (*Raises her arm, curves it in as if around something she loves.*) Land that encloses and gives shelter from storm.

MRS. PATRICK (*facing the sea, as if affirming what will hold all else out*). Outside sea. Outer shore. Dunes—land not life.

ALLIE MAYO. Outside sea—outer shore, dark with the wood that once was ships—dunes, strange land not life—woods, town and harbor. The line! Stunted straggly line that meets the Outside face to face—and fights for what itself can never be. Lonely line. Brave growing.

MRS. PATRICK. It loses.

ALLIE MAYO. It wins.

MRS. PATRICK. The farthest life is buried.

ALLIE MAYO. And life grows over buried life! (*Lifted into that; then, as one who states a simple truth with feeling.*) It will. And Springs will come when you will want to know that it is Spring.

(*The* CAPTAIN *and* BRADFORD *appear behind the drift of sand. They have a stretcher. To get away from them* MRS. PATRICK *steps farther into the room;* ALLIE MAYO *shrinks into her corner. The men come in, open the closed door and go in the room where they left the dead man. A moment later they are seen outside the big open door, bearing the man away.* MRS. PATRICK *watches them from sight.*)

MRS. PATRICK (*bitter, exultant*). Savers of life! (*To* ALLIE MAYO.) You savers of life! "Meeting the Outside!" Meeting—(*But she cannot say it mockingly again; in saying it, something of what it means has broken through, rises. Herself lost, feeling her way into the wonder of life.*) Meeting the Outside!

(*It grows in her as slowly.*)

CURTAIN

AFTERMATH

by **Mary Burrill**

TIME: The Present.

PLACE: The Thornton Cabin in South Carolina.

It is late afternoon of a cool day in early spring. A soft afterglow pours in at the little window of the Thornton cabin. The light falls on MILLIE, *a slender brown girl of sixteen, who stands near the window ironing. She wears a black dress and a big gingham apron. A clothes-horse weighted down with freshly ironed garments is nearby. In the rear there is a door leading out to the road. To the left, another door leading into the other room of the cabin. To the right there is a great stone hearth blackened by age. A Bible rests on the mantel over the hearth. An old armchair and a small table on which is a kerosene lamp are near the hearth. In the center of the room sits a well-scrubbed kitchen table and a substantial wooden chair. In front of the hearth, in a low rocking chair drawn close to the smouldering wood fire, sits* MAM SUE *busily sewing. The many colors in the old patchwork quilt that she is mending, together with the faded red of the bandanna on her head, contrast strangely with her black dress.* MAM SUE *is very old. Her ebony face is seamed with wrinkles; and in her bleared, watery eyes there is a world-old sorrow. A service flag containing one star hangs in the little window of the cabin.*

MAM SUE (*crooning the old melody*).
    O, yes, yonder comes mah Lawd,
        He is comin' dis way
    Wid his sword in his han'
        O, yes, yonder comes—

(*A burning log falls apart, and* MAM SUE *suddenly stops singing and gazes intently at the fire. She speaks in deep mysterious tones to* MILLIE, *who has finished her task and has come to the hearth to put up her irons.*)

See dat log dah, Millie? De one fallin' tuh de side dah wid de big flame lappin' 'round hit? Dat means big doin's 'round heah tonight!

MILLIE (*with a start*). Oh, Mam Sue, don' you go proph'sying no mo'! You seen big doin's in dat fire de night befo' them w'ite devuls come in heah an' tuk'n po' dad out and bu'nt him!

MAM SUE (*calmly*). No, Millie, Ah didn' see no big doin's dat night—Ah see'd *evul* doin's an' Ah tole yo' po' daddy to keep erway f'om town de nex' day wid his cotton. Ah jes knowed dat he wuz gwine to git in a row wid dem w'ite debbils—but he wou'd'n lis'n tuh his ole mammy—De good Lawd sen' me dese warnin's in dis fiah, jes lak He sen' His messiges in de fiah to Moses. Yo' chillun bettah lis'n to—

MILLIE (*nervously*). Oh, Mam Sue, you skeers me when you talks erbout seein' all them things in de fire—

MAM SUE. Yuh gits skeered cause yuh don' put yo' trus' in de good Lawd! He kin tek keer o' yuh no mattuh whut com'!

MILLIE (*bitterly*). Sometimes I thinks that Gawd's done fu'got us po' cullud people. Gawd didn' tek no keer o' po' dad and *he* put *his* trus' in Him! He uster set evah night by dis fire at dis here table and read his Bible an' pray—but jes look whut happen' to dad! That don' look like Gawd wuz tekin' keer—

MAM SUE (*sharply*). Heish yo' mouf, Millie! Ah ain't a-gwine to 'ave dat sinner-talk 'roun' hyeah! (*Derisively.*) Gawd don't tek no keer o' yuh? Ain't yuh bin prayin' night an' mawnin' fo' Gawd to sen' yo' brudder back f'om de war 'live an' whole? An' ain't yuh git dat lettah no longer'n yistiddy sayin' dat de fightin's all done stopp't an' dat de blessid Lawd's done brung yo' brudder thoo all dem battuls live an'

55

MARY BURRILL (1879–1946)

Many of the members of New York's two leading Little Theatres, the Provincetown Players and the Washington Square Players (which was later to become the Theatre Guild) and their friends wrote for *The Masses,* a small but politically radical publication. In 1918 the government banned *The Masses* from the mails because of its opposition to our entry into World War I. That same year, however, it was succeeded by *The Liberator,* which continued to publish many of the same authors.

The Liberator was turned over to the Communist Party in 1922; however, its early issues spoke the generalized, though often angry, rhetoric of social protest. One of the first contributors to *The Liberator* was Mary Burrill. Her play *Aftermath* appeared in April, 1919. Within a few months of its publication, *Aftermath* was being heralded as one of the hopes for a new Negro drama by *Crisis,* the literary organ of the N.A.A.C.P., then presided over by W. E. B. Du Bois.

The N.A.A.C.P. had urged blacks to enlist in the war effort in the belief that American democracy would offer greater promise than German Imperialism. *Aftermath* echoes an editorial by Du Bois in which he called for returning Negro soldiers to marshal their wartime courage to fight "the forces of hell" at home. *Aftermath* was part of a losing effort to stem the rising tide of lynchings in the South and race riots in the North that followed in the wake of World War I.

Other than her teaching English in Washington, D.C., from 1905 until her retirement in 1944 (mostly at Dunbar High School), very little is known of Mary (or Maimie P.) Burrill's personal life. She was, however, known to be active in the Harlem Renaissance, and is said to have been in wide demand as a narrator with the Howard University choir in *The Other Wise Man.* She is buried in Washington's Woodlawn Cemetery.

Burrill also took as her cause the fight for freer access to birth-control information. *They That Sit in Darkness* (1919) appeared in the *Birth Control Review.* This "one-act play of Negro life" tells the story of a young girl who is forced to give up her plans to attend college when her mother dies following the birth of her seventh child. This need not have happened had the mother been given the forbidden information.

Since Mary Burrill wrote in support of both the N.A.A.C.P. and the Birth Control League during their most difficult periods, we can reasonably assume that this playwright was also a woman of extraordinary courage.

---

whole? Don' dat look lak de Lawd's done 'membered yuh?

MILLIE (*thoughtfully*). I reckon youse right, Mam Sue. But ef anything had a-happen' to John I wuz'n evah goin' to pray no mo'!

(MILLIE *goes to the clothes-horse and folds the garments and lays them carefully into a large basket.* MAM SUE *falls again to her crooning.*)

MAM SUE.

O, yes, yonder comes mah Lawd,
He's comin' dis way-a.

MILLIE. Lonnie's so late gittin' home tonight; I guess I'd bettah tek Mis' Hart's wash home tonight myse'f.

MAM SUE. Yas, Lonnie's mighty late. Ah reckons you'd bettah slip erlon' wid hit.

(MILLIE *gets her hat from the adjoining room and is about to leave with the basket when* MAM SUE *calls significantly.*) Millie?

MILLIE. Yas, Mam Sue.

MAM SUE (*firmly*). Don' yo' fu'git to drap dat lettah fu' John in de Pos' Awfus ez yuh goes by. Whah's de lettah?

MILLIE (*reluctantly*). But, Mam Sue, please don' lets—

(*A knock is heard.* MILLIE *opens the door and* REVEREND LUKE MOSEBY *enters.* MOSEBY *is a wiry little old man with a black, kindly face, and bright, searching eyes; his woolly hair and beard are snow-white. He is dressed in a rusty black suit with a coat of clerical cut that comes to his knees. In one hand he carries a large Bible, and in the other, a stout walking stick.*)

MILLIE. Good evenin', Brother Moseby, come right in.

REV. MOSEBY. Good eben', Millie. Good eben', Mam Sue. Ah jes drap't in to see ef you-all is still trus'in' de good Lawd an'—

MAM SUE. Lor', Brudder Moseby, ain't Ah bin trus'n' de good Lawd nigh onter dese eighty yeah! Whut fu' yuh think Ah's gwine to quit w'en Ah'm in sight o' de Promis' Lan'? Millie, fetch Brudder Moseby dat cheer.

MOSEBY (*drawing his chair to the fire*). Dat's right, Mam Sue, you jes a-keep on trus'n' an' prayin' an evah thing's gwine to come aw-right. (*Observing that Millie is about to leave.*) Don' lemme 'tain yuh, Millie, but whut's all dis good news wese bin heahin' 'bout yo' brudder John? Dey say he's done won some kind o' medal ober dah in France?

MILLIE (*brightening up*). Oh, yes, we got a lettah day befo' yestiddy f'om John tellin' us all erbout it. He's won de War Cross! He fought off twenty Germuns all erlone an' saved his whole comp'ny an' the gret French Gen'rul come an' pinned de medal on him, *hisse'f!*

MOSEBY. De Lawd bles' his soul! Ah know'd dat boy wud mek good!

MILLIE (*excited by the glory of it all*). An' he's been to Paris, an' the fines' people stopp't him when they seen his medal, an' shook his han' an' smiled at him—an' he kin go evah-where, an' dey ain't nobody all the time a-lookin' down on him, an' a-sneerin' at him 'cause he's black; but evahwhere they's jes gran' to him! An' he sez it's the firs' time evah in his life he's felt lak a real, sho-nuf man!

MOSEBY. Well, honey, don't de Holy Book say, "De fust shill be las' and de las' shill be fust"?

MAM SUE (*fervently*). Dat hit do! An' de Holy Book ain't nebber tole no lie!

MOSEBY. Folks ober in Char'ston is sayin' dat some sojers is gwine to lan' dah today or tomorrer. Ah reckons day'll all be comin' 'long soon now dat de war's done stopp't.

MILLIE. I jes hates the thought of John comin' home an' hearin' 'bout dad!

MOSEBY (*in astonishment*). Whut! Yuh mean to say yuh ain't 'rite him 'bout yo' daddy, yit?

MAM SUE. Dat she ain't! Millie mus' 'ave huh way! She 'lowed huh brudder ough'n be tole, an' dat huh could keep on writin' to him jes lak huh dad wuz livin'—Millie allus done de writin'—An' Ah lets huh 'ave huh way—

MOSEBY (*shaking his head in disapproval*). Yuh mean tuh say—

MILLIE (*pleadingly*). But, Brother Moseby, I couldn't write John no bad news w'ilst he wuz way over there by hisse'f. He had 'nuf to worry him with death a-starin' him in the face evah day!

MAM SUE. Yas, Brudder Moseby, Millie's bin carryin' on dem lies in huh lettahs fu' de las' six months; but today Ah jes sez to huh —Dis war done stopp't now, an' John he gwine to be comin' home soon, an' he ain't agwine to come hyeah an' fin' me wid no lie on mah soul! An' Ah med huh set down an' tell him de whole truf. She's gwine out to pos' dat lettah dis minute.

MOSEBY (*still disapproving*). No good nebber come—

(*The door is pushed violently open, and* LONNIE, *a sturdy black boy of eighteen rushes in breathlessly.*)

LONNIE. Mam Sue! Millie! Whut'da yuh think? John's come home!

MILLIE (*speechless with astonishment*). John? Home? Where's he at?

MAM SUE (*incredulously*). Whut yuh sayin'? John done come home? Bles' de Lawd! Bles' de Lawd! Millie, didn' Ah tell yuh sumpin wuz gwine tuh happen?

LONNIE (*excitedly*). I wuz sweepin' up de sto' jes befo' leavin' an' de phone rung—it wuz John—he wuz at Char'ston—jes landid! His comp'ny's waitin' to git de ten o'clock train fu' Camp Reed, whah dey's goin' to be mustered out.

MOSEBY. But how's he gwine to get erway?

LONNIE. Oh, good evenin', Brother Moseby, Ise jes so 'cited I didn' see yuh— Why his Cap'n done give him leave to run over heah 'tell de train's ready. He ought tuh be heah now 'cause it's mos' two hours since he wuz talkin'—

MAM SUE. Whuffo yuh so long comin' home an' tellin' us?

LONNIE (*hesitatingly*). I did start right out

but when I git to Sherley's corner I seen a whole lot of them w'ite hoodlums hangin' 'round de feed sto'—I jes felt like dey wuz jes waitin' dah to start sumpin, so I dodged 'em by tekin' de long way home.

MILLIE. Po' Lonnie! He's allus dodgin' po' w'ite trash!

LONNIE (*sullenly*). Well, yuh see whut dad got by not dodgin' 'em.

MOSEBY (*rising to go*). Ah mus' be steppin' 'long now. Ah got to stop in to see ole man Hawkins; he's mighty sick. Ah'll drap in on mah way back fu' a word o' prayer wid John.

MAM SUE. Lonnie, yu'd bettah run erlon' as Brudder Moseby go an' tote dat wash tuh Mis' Ha't. An' drap in Mis' Hawkins' sto' an' git some soap an' starch; an' Ah reckons yu'd bettah bring me a bottle o' linimint— dis ole pain done come back in mah knee. (*To* MOSEBY.) Good eben, Brudder Moseby.

MOSEBY. Good eben, Mam Sue; Good eben, Millie, an' Gawd bles' yuh.

LONNIE (*as he is leaving*). Tell John I'll git back fo' he leaves.

(LONNIE *and* MOSEBY *leave.* MILLIE *closes the door behind them and then goes to the window and looks out anxiously.*)

MILLIE (*musingly*). Po' John! Po' John! (*Turning to* MAM SUE.) Mam Sue?

MAM SUE. Yas, Millie.

MILLIE (*hesitatingly*). Who's goin' to tell John 'bout dad?

MAM SUE (*realizing for the first time that the task must fall to someone*). Dunno. Ah reckons yu'd bettah.

MILLIE (*going to* MAM SUE *and kneeling softly at her side*). Mam Sue, don' let's tell him now! He's got only a li'l hour to spen' with us—an' it's the firs' time fu' so long! John loved daddy so! Let 'im be happy jes a li'l longer—we kin tell 'im the truth when he comes back fu' good. Please, Mam Sue!

MAM SUE (*softened by* MILLIE'S *pleading*). Honey chile, John gwine to be askin' for his daddy fust thing—dey ain't no way—

MILLIE (*gaining courage*). Oh, yes, 'tis! We kin tell 'im dad's gone to town—anything, jes so's he kin spen' these few lil'l minutes in peace! I'll fix the Bible jes like dad's been in an' been a-readin' in it! He won't know no bettah!

(MILLIE *takes the Bible from the mantel and opening it at random lays it on the table; she draws the old armchair close to the table as her father had been wont to do every evening when he read his Bible.*)

MAM SUE (*shaking her head doubtfully*). Ah ain't much on actin' dis lie, Millie.

(*The soft afterglow fades and the little cabin is filled with shadows.* MILLIE *goes again to the window and peers out.* MAM SUE *falls again to her crooning.*)

MAM SUE (*crooning*).
O, yes, yonder comes mah Lawd,
    He's comin' dis way
Wid his sword in his han'—
(*To* MILLIE.) Millie, bettah light de lamp; it's gittin' dark.—
    He's gwine ter hew dem sinners down
        Right lebbal to de groun'
    O, yes, yonder comes mah Lawd—
(*As* MILLIE *is lighting the lamp, whistling is heard in the distance.* MILLIE *listens intently, then rushes to the window. The whistling comes nearer; it rings out clear and familiar—"Though the boys are far away, they dream of home"!*)

MILLIE (*excitedly*). That's him! That's John, Mam Sue!

(MILLIE *rushes out of doors. The voices of* JOHN *and* MILLIE *are heard from without in greetings. Presently,* JOHN *and* MILLIE *enter the cabin.* JOHN *is tall and straight—a good soldier and a strong man. He wears the uniform of a private in the American Army. One hand is clasped in both of* MILLIE'S. *In the other, he carries an old fashioned valise. The War Cross is pinned on his breast. On his sleeve three chevrons tell mutely of wounds suffered in the cause of freedom. His brown face is aglow with life and the joy of homecoming.*)

JOHN (*eagerly*). Where's Dad? Where's Mam Sue?

MAM SUE (*hobbling painfully to meet him*). Heah's ole Mam Sue! (JOHN *takes her tenderly in his arms.*) Bles' yo' heart, chile, bles' yo' heart! Tuh think dat de good Lawd's done lemme live to see dis day!

JOHN. Dear old Mam Sue! Gee, but I'm glad to see you an' Millie again!

MAM SUE. Didn' Ah say dat yuh wuz comin' back hyeah?

JOHN (*smiling*). Same old Mam Sue with huh faith an' huh prayers! But where's dad? (*He glances toward the open Bible.*) He's been in from de field, ain't he?

MILLIE (*without lifting her eyes*). Yes, he's come in but he had to go out ag'in—to Sherley's feed sto'.

JOHN (*reaching for his cap that he has tossed upon the table*). That ain't far. I've jes a few minutes so I'd bettah run down there an' hunt him up. Won't he be surprised!

MILLIE (*confused*). No—no, John—I fu'got; he ain't gone to Sherley's, he's gont to town.

JOHN (*disappointed*). To town? I hope he'll git in befo' I'm leavin'. There's no tellin' how long they'll keep me at Camp Reed. Where's Lonnie?

MAM SUE. Lonnie's done gone to Mis' Ha't's wid de wash. He'll be back to-reckly

MILLIE (*admiring the medal on his breast*). An' this is the medal? Tell us all erbout it, John.

JOHN. Oh, Sis, it's an awful story—wait 'til I git back fu' good. Let's see whut I've got in dis bag fu' you. (*He places the worn valise on the table and opens it. He takes out a bright-colored dress pattern.*) That's fu' you, Millie, and quit wearin' them black clothes.

(MILLIE *takes the silk and hugs it eagerly to her breast, suddenly there sweeps into her mind the realization that she cannot wear it, and the silk falls to the floor.*)

MILLIE (*trying to be brave*). Oh, John, it's jes lovely! (*As she shows it to* MAM SUE.) Look, Mam Sue!

JOHN (*flourishing a bright shawl*). An' this is fu' Mam Sue. Mam Sue'll be so gay!

MAM SUE (*admiring the gift*). Who'd evah b'lieved dat yo' ole Mam Sue would live to be wearin' clo'es whut huh gran'chile done brung huh f'om Eu'ope!

JOHN. Never you mind, Mam Sue, one of these days I'm goin' to tek you an' Millie over there, so's you kin breathe free jes once befo' yuh die.

MAM SUE. It's got tuh be soon, 'cause dis ole body's mos' wo'e out; an' de good Lawd's gwine to be callin' me to pay mah debt 'fo' long.

JOHN (*showing some handkerchiefs, with gay borders*). These are fu' Lonnie. (*He next takes out a tiny box that might contain a bit of jewelry.*) An' this is fu' Dad. Sum'pin he's been wantin' fu' years. I ain't goin' to open it 'till he comes.

(MILLIE *walks into the shadows and furtively wipes a tear from her eyes.*

JOHN (*taking two army pistols from his bag and placing them on the table*). An' these las' are fu' *youahs truly.*

MILLIE (*looking at them, fearfully*). Oh, John, are them youahs?

JOHN. One of 'em's mine; the other's my Lieutenant's. I've been cleanin' it fu' him. Don' tech 'em—'cause mine's loaded.

MILLIE (*still looking at them in fearful wonder*). Did they learn yuh how to shoot 'em?

JOHN. Yep, an' I kin evah mo' pick 'em off!

MILLIE (*reproachfully*). Oh, John!

JOHN. Nevah you worry, li'l Sis, John's nevah goin' to use 'em 'less it's right fu' him to. (*He places the pistols on the mantel—on the very spot where the Bible has lain.*) My! but it's good to be home! I've been erway only two years but it seems like two cent'ries. All that life ovah there seems like some awful dream!

MAM SUE (*fervently*). Ah know it do! Many's de day yo' ole Mam Sue set in dis cheer an' prayed fu' yuh.

JOHN. Lots of times, too, in the trenches when I wuz dog-tired, an' sick, an' achin' wid the cold I uster say: well, if we're sufferin' all this for the oppressed, like they tell us, then Mam Sue, an' Dad, an' Millie come in on that—they'll git some good ou'n it if I don't! An' I'd shet my eyes an' fu'git the cold, an' the pain, an' them old guns spittin' death all 'round us; an' see you folks settin' here by this fire—Mam Sue, noddin, an' singin'; Dad a spellin' out his Bible—(*He glances toward the open book.*) Let's see whut he's been readin'—(JOHN *takes up the Bible and reads the first passage upon which his eye falls.*) "But I say unto you, love your enemies, bless them that curse you, an' do good to them that hate you"—(*He lets the Bible fall to the table.*) That ain't the dope they been feedin' us soljers on! 'Love your enemies!' It's been—git a good aim at 'em, an' let huh go!

MAM SUE (*surprised*). Honey, Ah hates to hyeah yuh talkin' lak dat! It sound lak yuh done fu'git yuh Gawd!

JOHN. No, Mam Sue, I ain't fu'got God, but I've quit thinkin' that prayers kin do ever'thing. I've seen a whole lot sence I've been erway from here. I've seen some men go into battle with a curse on their lips, and I've seen them same men come back with never a scratch; an' I've seen men whut read their Bibles befo' battle, an' prayed to live, left dead on the field. Yes, Mam Sue, I've seen a heap an' I've done a tall lot o' thinkin' sence I've been erway from here. An' I b'lieve it's jes like this—beyon' a certain point prayers ain't no good! The Lawd does jes so much for you, then it's up to you to do the res' fu' yourse'f. The Lawd's done His part when He's done give me strength an' courage; I got tuh do the res' fu' myse'f!

MAM SUE (*shaking her head*). Ah don' lak dat kin' o' talk—it don' 'bode no good!

(*The door opens and* LONNIE *enters with packages. He slips the bolt across the door.*)

JOHN (*rushing to* LONNIE *and seizing his hand*). Hello, Lonnie, ole man!

LONNIE. Hello, John. Gee, but Ah'm glad tuh see yuh!

JOHN. Boy, you should 'ave been with me! It would 'ave taken some of the skeeriness out o' yuh, an' done yuh a worl' o' good.

LONNIE (*ignoring* JOHN's *remark*). Here's the soap an' starch, Millie.

MAM SUE. Has yuh brung mah linimint?

LONNIE. Yassum, it's in de packige.

MILLIE (*unwrapping the package*). No, it ain't, Lonnie.

LONNIE. Mis' Hawkins give it tuh me. Ah mus' a lef' it on de counter. Ah'll git it w'en Ah goes to de train wid John.

MILLIE (*showing him the handkerchief*). See whut John done brought you! An' look on de mantel! (*Pointing to the pistols.*)

LONNIE (*drawing back in fear as he glances at the pistols*). You'd bettah hide them things! No cullud man bettah be seen wid dem things down heah!

JOHN. That's all right, Lonnie, nevah you fear. I'm goin' to keep 'em an' I ain't a-goin' to hide 'em either. See them (*pointing to the wound chevrons on his arm*), well, when I got them wounds, I let out all the rabbit-blood 'at wuz in me! (*Defiantly.*) Ef I kin be trusted with a gun in France, I kin be trusted with one in South Car'lina.

MAM SUE (*sensing trouble*). Millie, yu'd bettah fix some suppah fu' John.

JOHN (*looking at his watch*). I don' want a thing. I've got to be leavin' in a little while. I'm 'fraid I'm goin' to miss dad after all.

(*The knob of the door is turned as though someone is trying to enter. Then there is a loud knock on the door.*)

JOHN (*excitedly*). That's Dad! Don't tell him I'm here!

(JOHN *tips hurriedly into the adjoining room.* LONNIE *unbolts the door and* MRS. SELENA HAWKINS *enters.*)

MRS. HAWKINS. Lonnie fu'got de liniment so I thought I' bettah run ovah wid hit, 'cause when Mam Sue sen' fu' dis stuff she sho' needs hit. Brudder Moseby's been tellin' me dat John's done come home.

JOHN (*coming from his hiding place and trying to conceal his disappointment.*) Yes, I'm here. Good evenin', Mis' Hawkins. Glad to see you.

MRS. HAWKINS (*shaking hands with* JOHN). Well, lan' sakes alive! Ef it ain't John sho'nuf! An' ain't he lookin' gran'! Jes look at dat medal a-shining' on his coat! Put on yuh cap, boy, an' lemme see how yuh look!

JOHN. Sure! (JOHN *puts on his overseas cap and, smiling, stands at attention a few paces off, while* MAM SUE, LONNIE, *and* MILLIE *form an admiring circle around him.*)

MRS. HAWKINS. Now don' he sholy look gran'! I knows yo' sistah, an' gran'-mammy's proud o' yuh! (*A note of sadness creeps into her voice.*) Ef only yuh po' daddy had a-lived to see dis day!

(JOHN *looks at her in amazement.* MILLIE *and* MAM SUE *stand transfixed with terror over the sudden betrayal.*)

JOHN (*looking from one to the other and repeating her words as though he can scarcely realize their meaning*). 'Ef your po' daddy had lived—' (*To* MILLIE.) Whut does this mean?

(MILLIE *sinks sobbing into the chair at the table and buries her face in her hands.*)

MRS. HAWKINS. Lor', Millie, I thought you'd tole him!

(*Bewildered by the catastrophe that she has precipitated,* SELENA HAWKINS *slips out of the cabin.*)

JOHN (*shaking* MILLIE *almost roughly*). Come, Millie, have you been lyin' to me? Is Dad gone?

MILLIE (*through her sobs*). I jes hated to tell you—you wuz so far erway—

JOHN (*nervously*). Come, Millie, for God's sake don' keep me in this su'pense! I'm a brave soldier—I kin stan' it—did he suffer much? Wuz he sick long?

MILLIE. He wuzn't sick no time—them w'ite devuls come in heah an' dragged him—

JOHN (*desperately*). My God! You mean they lynched dad?

MILLIE (*sobbing piteously*). They burnt him down by the big gum tree!

JOHN (*desperately*). Whut fu,' Millie? What fu'?

MILLIE. He got in a row wid ole Mister Withrow 'bout the price of cotton—an' he called dad a liar an' struck him—an' dad he up an' struck him back—

JOHN (*brokenly*). Didn' they try him? Didn' they give him a chance? Whut'd the Sheriff do? An' the Gov-nur?

MILLIE (*through her sobs*). They didn't do nothin'.

JOHN. Oh, God! Oh, God! (*Then recovering from the first bitter anguish and speaking.*) So they've come into ouah home, have they! (*He strides over to* LONNIE *and seizes him by the collar.*) An' whut wuz you doin' when them hounds come in here after dad?

LONNIE (*hopelessly*). They wuz so many of 'em come an' git 'im—whut could Ah do?

JOHN. Do? You could 'ave fought 'em like a man!

MAM SUE (*pleadingly*). Don't be too hard on 'im, John, wese ain't got no gun 'round heah!

JOHN. Then he should 'ave burnt their damn kennels ovah their heads! Who was it leadin' em?

MILLIE. Old man Withrow and the Sherley boys, they started it all.

(*Gradually assuming the look of a man who has determined to do some terrible work that must be done,* JOHN *walks deliberately toward the mantel where the revolvers are lying.*)

JOHN (*bitterly*). I've been helpin' the w'ite man git his freedom, I reckon I'd bettah try now to get my own!

MAM SUE (*terrified*). Whut yuh gwine ter do?

JOHN (*with bitterness growing in his voice*). I'm sick o' these w'ite folks doin's—we're 'fine, trus'worthy feller citizuns' when they're handin' us out guns, an' Liberty Bonds, an' chuckin' us off to die; but we ain't a damn thing when it comes to handin' us the rights we done fought an' bled fu'! I'm sick o' this sort o' life—an' I'm goin' to put an' end to it!

MILLIE (*rushing to the mantel, and covering the revolvers with her hands*). Oh, no, no, John! Mam Sue, John's gwine to kill hisse'f!

MAM SUE (*piteously*). Oh, mah honey, don' yuh go do nothin' to bring sin on yo' soul! Pray to de good Lawd to tek all dis fiery feelin' out'n yo' heart! Wait 'tel Brudder Moseby come back—he's gwine to pray—

JOHN (*his speech growing more impassioned and bitter*). This ain't no time fu' preachers or prayers! You mean to tell me I mus' let them w'ite devuls send me miles erway to suffer an' be shot up fu' the freedom of people I ain't nevah seen, while they're burnin' an' killin' my folks here at home! To Hell with 'em!

(*He pushes* MILLIE *aside, and seizing the revolvers, thrusts the loaded one into his pocket and begins deliberately to load the other.*)

MILLIE (*throwing her arms about his neck*). Oh, John, they'll kill yuh!

JOHN (*defiantly*). Whut ef they do! I ain't skeered o' none of 'em! I've faced worse guns than any sneakin' hounds kin show me! To Hell with 'em! (*He thrusts the revolver that he has just loaded into* LONNIE's *hand.*) Take this, an' come on here, boy, an' we'll see what Withrow an' his gang have got to say!

(*Followed by* LONNIE, *who is bewildered and speechless,* JOHN *rushes out of the cabin and disappears in the gathering darkness.*)

CURTAIN

THREE FROM THE EARTH

by Djuna Barnes

CHARACTERS

JAMES }
HENRY } *Carson brothers*
JOHN }

KATE MORLEY, *an adventurist—a lady of leisure*

TIME: *Late afternoon.*

PLACE: *Kate Morley's boudoir. A long narrow room, with a great many lacquer screens in various shades of blue, a tastefully decorated room though rather extreme.*

At the rise of the curtain the three Carson brothers are discovered sitting together on a couch to the left. They look like peasants of the most obvious type. They are tall, rather heavy—and range in ages from nineteen to twenty-five. They have sandy, sun-bleached hair that insists upon sticking straight up—oily, sweaty skins—large hanging lips and small eyes on which a faint whitish down moves for lashes. They are clumsy and ill clothed. Russet shoes are on all six feet. They each wear a purple aster and each has on a tie of the super-stunning variety—they have evidently done their best to be as one might say "well dressed."

When they speak—aside from their grunts—their voices are rough, nasal and occasionally crack. They are stoop-shouldered and their hands are excessively ugly.

Yet in spite of all this, their eyes are intelligent, their smiles gentle, melancholy, compassionate. And though they have a look of formidable grossness and stupidity, there is, on second observation, a something beneath all this in no way in keeping with this first impression.

John—the youngest, and the smallest—looks around the room carefully.

JOHN. A nice room, eh? (*He tries to whisper but it comes forth buzzing and harsh.*)

JAMES. A woman's room.

HENRY. How?

JAMES. A narrow room, John.

JOHN. Well?

JAMES. Cats and narrow walls.

HENRY (*grunting*). Ugh.

JOHN. Hush—I hear her coming!

(The curtains part and KATE MORLEY enters. She is a woman of about forty. Handsome. Dark. She is beautifully dressed in a rather seductive fashion. She has a very interesting head; she has an air of one used to adulation and the pleasure of exerting her will. She has a trick of narrowing her eyes. As she comes forward there is a general commotion among the brothers but none manages to stand up).

KATE. Good day, gentlemen.

ALL THREE. Good day.

KATE. Nice of you to call on me (*She seats herself, crossing her legs.*) You are the three Carsons, John, James and Henry, aren't you. I haven't seen you for years, yet I think I should have known you.

ALL THREE. Ah, ha.

KATE. Yes I presume I should have known you. I have a good memory. Well, as I said, it's nice of you to come to see me. Social?

HENRY. You might call it that.

KATE. It's quite nice to get an unexpected visitor or so. I'm the kind of woman who knows just who is going to call on Monday, Tuesday, Thursday—

ALL THREE. Ah, ha.

KATE. How's the country?

JOHN. Just the same.

KATE. It always is.—Don't you go mad—watching it?

HENRY. Now and again.

KATE. And how's your father? (*Not pausing for an answer—almost to herself.*) I re-

DJUNA BARNES (1892–   )

Until the publication of her novel *Nightwood* in 1936, with its laudatory introduction by T. S. Eliot, author-playwright-journalist Djuna Barnes was almost entirely unknown to the general reading public. Long before then, however, she could be counted among that legendary group of expatriate American writers who, like Gertrude Stein, F. Scott Fitzgerald, and Ernest Hemingway, wandered between Paris and the Mediterranean. Stein described the life they led in *The Autobiography of Alice B. Toklas.*

Barnes's own description of her life in the Bronx—then a genteel suburb—reveals that, even before she left for Paris, her forays downtown to Greenwich Village conjured up visions of hell and damnation for her worried mother. Her growing reputation among the cultural elite as a writer for such esoteric publications as *The Dial, Smart Set,* and *The Little Review* earned her the attention of the Bohemian clique that controlled the Provincetown Players. Their 1919–20 season saw the production of three of Barnes's short plays—*An Irish Triangle,*

Kurzy of the Sea, and *Three from the Earth.* (This was a particularly memorable season for the Players; it also introduced *The Eldest* by Edna Ferber, O'Neill's *The Dreamy Kid,* and *Aria da Capo* by Edna St. Vincent Millay.)

Much of Barnes's early writings—*The Book of Repulsive Women* (1915) and *Ryder* (1928), to name just two—were privately and sometimes anonymously printed. Any public editions that appeared in this country were heavily expurgated. Her work was and is the province of only the most literate. Likewise, the performance of her plays was for a select audience accustomed to the avant garde and eager to support work that seemed "advanced," even though its full meaning was usually veiled by a peculiarly hermetic symbolism.

Barnes lives as a recluse in Greenwich Village. She is in frail health, saddened and embittered that a new generation has not banished the puritanism of old but has simply lost all sense of the subtlety of such human encounters as love and solitude.

---

member—*he* was always mad. He used to wear a green cloth suit, and he carried white rats all over his shoulders. (*Remembering the three.*) Ah, yes, your father—he was a barber, wasn't he?

HENRY. No, a chemist.

KATE (*laughing uneasily*). I have a bad memory after all. Well, anyway, in those days he had begun to be queer—everyone noticed it—even that funny man who had those three flaxen-haired daughters with the thin ankles who lives at the end of the street—And your mother—a prostitute I believe.

HENRY (*calmly*). At times.

KATE. A dancing girl without a clean word in her vocabulary, or a whole shirt to her name—

JAMES. But a woman with fancies.

KATE (*sarcastically*). And what ability?

HENRY. Oh, none, just a burning desire.

KATE. What's the use of going into that. How did you get here—what for?

ALL THREE. On bicycles.

KATE (*bursting into laughter*). How exactly ridiculous and appropriate—and what else?

JOHN. To see how the sun falls in a place like this.

KATE (*angrily, rising*). Well you see, from left to right, and right to left—

HENRY. True.

JOHN (*quietly*). And we wanted to see how you walked, and sat down, and crossed your legs—

HENRY. And to get father's letters.

KATE. Well you see how I walk, sit down, cross my legs. What letters?

JAMES. Letters to you.

KATE (*uneasily*). So you know about that —well, and what would you fellows do with them—read them to see how clever they are?

JAMES. No, we have the clever ones.

KATE. Mine?

JOHN and HENRY (*nodding*). Exactly.

KATE. Oh.

JOHN. You suffer?

KATE. From time to time—there's always a reaction.

HENRY. That's vulgar isn't it.

KATE. Not unusually.

JOHN. The letters?

KATE (*to herself*). Well, there is malice in me—what of it? We've all been a while with the dogs, we don't all learn to bark.

JOHN. Ah, ha.

KATE. See here, what will you do with your father's letters?

HENRY. Destroy them, perhaps.

KATE. And if I give them to you—will your father be as generous with mine?

HENRY. Father is undoubtedly a gentleman —even at this moment.

KATE. Well, we shall see about that—first tell me how you live.

JOHN. We go down on the earth and find things, tear them up, shaking the dirt off (*making the motions to illustrate*). Then there are the cows to be milked, the horses— a few—to be fed, shod and curried—do you wish me to continue?

KATE. Yes, yes, go on.

HENRY (*taking the tale up*). We get up at dawn, and our father turns over in bed and whispers: "If you meet anyone, say nothing; if you are asked a question look stupid—

KATE. I believe you.

JAMES. And he says: "Go about your work as if you had neither sight, speech nor hearing—"

KATE. Yes—

JOHN. And he adds: "If you should meet a woman in the road—"

KATE (*excited*). Then what?

HENRY. That's enough. Then of a Sunday we watch the people going to church, when we hear the "Amen" we lift a little and sit back—and then again—

KATE. Religion?

HENRY. Enough for our simple needs.

KATE. Poor sheep!

JAMES. Wise sheep!

KATE. What! Well perhaps, no one is any longer sure of anything. Then what?

JOHN. When we come home he says: "What have you seen and heard today?" He never asks "What have you said?"

KATE. He trusts you?

JOHN. Undoubtedly. Sometimes we say

"We saw a hawk flying" or "A badger passed," and sometimes we bring him the best treat of all—

KATE. Well?

JOHN. Something dead.

KATE. Dead?

HENRY. Anything that has destroyed the crops—a mole—a field-mouse.

KATE. And never anything that's harmless?

JOHN. Never.

KATE. Well see here, I'll give you those letters. Suddenly my heart says to me "Kate, give the oxen the rope, they won't run away." —Isn't it so? Very well, I put my hand on a certain package and all is over—I'm about to be married you know. (*She has risen and gone over to a little box standing on the desk. Out from this she takes a package of letters tied with a red ribbon. She turns and walks straight up to* JOHN). I'll give them to you. You are the youngest, the gentlest, and you have the nicest hands.

(*She sits down, breathing with difficulty.*)

JOHN (*putting them into his blouse*). Thank you, Kate Morley.

KATE. Now tell me about everything. How is that mother of yours? I remember her— she was on the stage—she danced as they say, and she sang. She had a pet monkey—fed it honey out of a jar kept full by her admirers: grooms, stage hands, what not—

HENRY. Yes, and she used to draw pictures of it in the style of Dürer—almost morbid— and later it caught a disease and died.

KATE. I don't doubt it—and she, she had an under-lip like a balloon—and your father kissed that mouth, was even tempted—

JAMES. My father often saw beyond the flesh.

KATE. Kissed such a creature!

HENRY. At such times she was beautiful.

KATE (*with a touch of humility*). Yes, I'm sorry—I remember. Once I passed her, and instead of saying something, something horrible—she might—she looked down.

JOHN. She was beautiful looking down.

KATE (*angry*). And I, I suppose I wasn't beautiful to look at—

HENRY. No I suppose not, that is, not for her.

KATE (*viciously*). Well let me tell you, you

haven't inherited her beauty. Look at your hands—thick, hard, ugly—and the life lines in them like the life lines in the hands of every laborer digging sewers—

JOHN. There's something in that, but they are just beginning.

KATE (*turning on them*). Look at you! You're ugly, and clumsy and uncouth. You grunt and roar, you wear abominable clothes —and you have no manners—and all because of your father, your mighty righteous and original father. You don't have to be like this. You needn't have little pigs' eyes with bleached lashes, and thick hanging lips and noses—but I suppose you've got adenoids, and you may suffer from the fact that your mother had a rupture, and in all probability you have the beginning of ulcers of the stomach, for God knows your father couldn't keep a meal down like a gentleman!

HENRY. He *was* delicate.

KATE. And why was he delicate? He called himself "The little Father," as one might say, "The great Emperor." Well, to have a father to whom you can go and say "All is not as it should be"—that would have been everything. But what could you say to him, and what had he to say to you? O we all have our pathetic moments of being at our best, but he wasn't satisfied with that, he wanted to be at it all the time. And the result, the life of a mole. "Listen and say nothing." Then he becomes the gentleman farmer because he discovers he cannot be the Beloved Fool. Suddenly he is the father of three creatures for all the world like Russian peasants—without an idea, a subtlety—it's wicked, that's all, wicked—and as for that, how do you know but that all three of you had a different mother. Why great God. I might be the mother of one of you!

JOHN (*significantly*). So I believe, madam.

KATE (*unheeding*). Do you think a man like your father had any right to bring such children as you in the world—three columns of flesh without one of the five senses! (*She suddenly buries her head in her hands*).

JOHN (*gently*). You loved our father.

HENRY. And you also had your pot of honey—

KATE. Thank God I had no ideals—I had a religion.

JOHN. Just what?

KATE. You wouldn't understand.

HENRY. Shoes to the needy?

KATE. No, I'm not that kind, vicious boy.

JOHN. Are you quite certain?

KATE. I'll admit all my candles are not burning for God. Well, then, blow them out, still I'll have a light burning somewhere, for all your great breaths, you oxen.

HENRY. You were never a tower builded of ivory—

KATE. You're too stupid to be bitter—your voices are too undeveloped—you say "love" and "hate" the same way.

JAMES. True, we have been shut away from intonations.

KATE. You wouldn't even wish to die.

JOHN. We shall learn.

KATE. Why bother.

JOHN (*abruptly rising*). You have posed for the madonna?

KATE. Every woman has.

JOHN. You have done it better than most.

KATE. What do you mean?

JOHN. I looked at it when I came in.

(*He picks up the photograph.*)

KATE. Let it be—I was playing in the "Crown of Thorns," an amateur theatrical.

JOHN. Yes, I presumed it was amateur—

JAMES. You were a devoted mother?

KATE. I have no virtues.

HENRY. And vices?

KATE. Weak in one, weak in the other.

JOHN. However the baby had nice hands—

KATE (*looking at him*). That is true.

JAMES. But then babies only use their hands to lift the breast, and occasionally to stroke the cheek—

KATE. Or to throw them up in despair— not a heavy career.

JOHN. And then?

KATE (*in an entirely new tone*). Won't you have tea? ——But no, pay no attention to me, that's another of my nasty malicious tricks. Curse life!

HENRY. Your life is drawing to a close.

JAMES. And from time to time you place your finger on a line of Nietzsche or Schopenhauer wondering "How did he say it all in two lines." Eh?

KATE. As you say (*she looks at them slowly, one by one*). You are strange things.

(*Coming back.*) But at least I've given up something—look at your mother, what did she give up for your father—a drunken husband—

JAMES. A drunken lover—that's different.

KATE. I can't help thinking of that great gross stomach of hers.

JAMES. Gross indeed, it won't trouble him anymore.

KATE. What's that?

JOHN. He cut his throat with a knife—

KATE. Oh my God! (*Pause.*) How did he look?

JOHN. You can't satisfy your aesthetic sense that way—he looked, well ugly, played out, yes, played out. Everything had been too much for him,—you—us—you could see that in the way he—

KATE (*in a whisper*). Well, that's strange—everything seems—I knew him you know (*She begins to laugh.*) And the dogs barked.

JAMES. So I believe.

KATE (*dazed*). And you, what are you three going to do?

HENRY. We are coming out of the country—we are going abroad—we can listen there.

KATE. Abroad,—listen—what are you saying?

HENRY. There are great men abroad.

JAMES. Anatol France, De Gourmont—

KATE. De Gourmont is dead.

JOHN. There will be others.

KATE (*still dully*). And how did you come to know such names—oh your father of course—

JOHN. We needed them.

KATE. Strange, I've been prepared for every hour but this—

JAMES. Yet I dare say you've never cried out.

KATE. You are mistaken. I've cried: "To the evil of mind all is evil—"

HENRY. Ah ha, and what happened?

KATE. Sometimes I found myself on my knees—

JAMES. And sometimes?

KATE. That's enough, haven't we about cleared all the shavings out of the carpenter shop?

HENRY. You at least will never kill yourself.

KATE. Not likely, I'll probably die in bed with my slippers on—you see I have a pretty foot.

HENRY. We understand, you are about to be married.

KATE. To a supreme court Judge—so I'm cleaning house.

JOHN (*standing with the photograph*). But it won't be quite cleared out until this goes (*He takes it out of the frame and turning it over reads*) "Little John, God bless him." (*He turns it back*) God bless him. Well just for that I'd like to keep it.

KATE. That's my affair.

JOHN. So I see. (*He puts the photo in his blouse with the letters.*)

KATE. Well, perhaps—well, you're not so stupid after all—Come, for the madonna give me back the letters, I'll burn them I swear, and you can put the madonna at the foot of the bed.

JOHN. I shan't put it at the foot of the bed—I don't look at the foot of the bed—

HENRY and JAMES (*rising*). And now we shall go.

KATE. (*her hands to her head*). But gentlemen, gentlemen—

HENRY. We won't need to bother you again. We are leaving the country and going elsewhere—and there was only one of us to whom you might have shown a little generosity—in other words we do not wish to be reminded, and now we can forget, and in time become quite hilarious—

KATE. But, gentlemen, gentlemen, not this way—

JOHN. Well? (*Quite suddenly he takes her in his arms, raises her face and kisses her on the mouth.*)

KATE. (*crying out*). Not that way! Not that way!

JAMES. That's the way you bore him!

(*The curtain drops behind them.*)

THE ELDEST

by **Edna Ferber**

CHARACTERS

ROSE
FLOSS
AL
PA
MA
HENRY SELZ
A NEIGHBOR

SCENE: *The dining room of a flat in a cheap neighborhood. It is evidently used as the common room. There are, besides the necessary dining-room furniture, one or two shabby armchairs and a small table. The room is in disorder. A small rug is rolled in one corner. The room, just cleaned, has not quite been set to rights. At the back, left, a door leading into outer hall. Another right, back, into bedrooms. At left a door into kitchen. At right, well down, door to MA's bedroom. This door stands open. The dining table is left center. On its bare top are two diningroom chairs back to back as though they had been put out of the way during the scrubbing of the floor. A small stepladder against the wall. At the foot of the ladder a scrubbing pail, with a brush beside it and a moist gray rag hanging over the top. A telephone on a small table, back. An old-fashioned sideboard, left, near dining table.*

ROSE *enters from kitchen wiping her flushed face with a corner of her damp apron. She is a woman of about forty, grown heavy about the hips and arms as houseworking women do. On her face is the vague mute look of one whose days are spent indoors at sordid tasks. Her features are good. She must have been pretty in her youth. She wears a calico work dress and apron. Her*

sleeves are rolled up, her hair wispy, but she does not look like a sloven. She is flushed and hurried. ROSE *comes quickly down to bare table, picks up the chairs that are on top of it and puts them in their places; unrolls the rug that lies in a corner and spreads it on the floor; goes to pail, stoops, wrings out the wet rag, meanwhile glancing anxiously about. All this is done hastily as one would hurry who is late with her work.*

A doorbell rings. ROSE *gives an annoyed exclamation and drops her rag.*

ROSE. Who's there?
NEIGHBOR. It's only me.
ROSE. Oh, come right in. (NEIGHBOR *enters from kitchen. She is a stout, florid woman in a flowered kimono.*)
NEIGHBOR. What smells so good?
ROSE (*wiping her hands on apron*). I guess it must be my rhubarb pie. I just took it out of the oven.
NEIGHBOR. My folks don't care for rhubarb in any form.
ROSE. It does make the worst pie in the world.
NEIGHBOR. Well, then, why in the world . . . !
ROSE (*almost sheepishly*). Oh, I don't know. I heard the vegetable man calling it down the street. And rhubarb, and spring, and housecleaning all seem to go together, somehow.
NEIGHBOR. (*glancing swiftly around*). My land! You started housecleaning already!
ROSE (*triumphantly*). This morning.
NEIGHBOR. Awful early, ain't it?
ROSE. When I woke up there was a fly buzzing around the room. And I noticed the Burkes across the court had taken down their lace curtains. That started me.

EDNA FERBER (1885–1968)

It was mere happenstance that Edna Ferber, one of America's most successful authors, came to write for a group of such limited means as the Provincetown Players. Before 1919 and (by all accounts) afterwards as well, Ferber, in addition to critical esteem, expected and got munificent financial rewards for her work. Still, the Players' 1919–20 season included *The Eldest* by Edna Ferber.

As Ferber herself described it, this all came about because she happened to spot an advertisement for the performance of a play by that title. Having just published a collection of short stories that included "The Eldest," she phoned the Provincetown's director, James Light, and learned that plagiarism had indeed occurred. Though angry, she did not wish to ruin the reputation of this promising company; so Ferber dashed off her own script. The revised version, published in 1925, is included in this anthology.

Perhaps the story is apocryphal, but Ferber's career as a writer was also unplanned. Born in Kalamazoo, Michigan, she soon moved to Appleton, Wisconsin. Financial hardships forced her to give up both of her ambitions, which were to attend college and to go on the stage; she took a job as a reporter for the Appleton *Daily Crescent* at three dollars per week. Although she had not considered journalism as a career, Ferber was not long in attracting the attention of editors in Milwaukee and later Chicago.

During her brief stint as a reporter, she became ill from overwork and returned to Appleton to recuperate. Weak, but longing for something to do (or so the story goes), Ferber purchased a secondhand typewriter and some yellow copypaper and began work on *Dawn O'Hara*. It was published in 1911, the first of 12 novels from the pen of Edna

Edna Ferber

Ferber. Her Emma McChesney stories began to appear four years later, and with them came fame and fortune.

Ferber received the Pulitzer Prize in 1924 for her third novel, *So Big*. The continued success of both her novels and their screen adaptations is legendary. It was only at the urging of George S. Kaufman that she turned to the Broadway stage. Over the next quarter of a century, they collaborated on six plays, two of which, *The Royal Family* (1927) and *Dinner at Eight* (1932), have become American classics.

NEIGHBOR. It's catching. I guess I'll start in tomorrow. It's certainly hot enough, for April. (*Turns to go.*) For goodness' sake, I'm forgetting what I came for! Can you let me have a cup of milk? Mine turned sour on me.

ROSE. Just help yourself out of the bottle in the icebox. All I need's enough for their tea and ma's glassful. (NEIGHBOR *exits*. ROSE *goes to sideboard, gets out tablecloth, begins to lay table for supper, with plates, knives, forks, etc. A sound, off, from kitchen, as though* NEIGHBOR *has slammed the ice box door.* NEIGHBOR *appears again at door, cup carefully held in hand.*)

NEIGHBOR. How's your ma today?

ROSE. Just the same.

NEIGHBOR. It's certainly awful. Keeps you tied right down, don't it?

ROSE. Yes.

NEIGHBOR. Well, I always say a person like that's better off out of their misery, really. It's been years, ain't it? How long?

ROSE. Fifteen years this month.

NEIGHBOR. You must have been just a young girl.

ROSE. Floss and Al were hardly more than babies. We didn't think, at first, it would go on the way it has. The doctors said a few months —then a year—then five years. . . .

NEIGHBOR. And everything on your shoulders. I s'pose you might of had a husband and a home of your own. I bet you wasn't bad looking.

ROSE. I looked a lot like Floss looks now, they say.

NEIGHBOR. No! (*Shakes her head commiseratingly.*) Well, I got to run along. (*From*

ROSE. That's all right. (ROSE *listens to make* tomorrow.

ROSE. That's all right. (ROSE *listens to make sure that she has gone. Takes from the capacious pocket of her apron a little sheaf of time-yellowed letters, worn with handling, and a faded bit of blue ribbon. She comes over to sideboard and stacks the letters neatly, fingering them one by one. On her lips is a wistful, reminiscent half smile.*)

MA (*from bedroom, in a high, thin voice*). Rose!

ROSE (*startled, spills letters on floor*). Yes, ma! [*Stoops, gathers letters in scrambling haste.*]

MA. It's cold in here.

ROSE. I'll get you a hot bag in a minute. (*Hurriedly ties letters together with the bit of ribbon, unlocks the top cabinet of the old-fashioned sideboard, thrusts the letters into it, locks the little door, pockets the key. Exits to kitchen, enters again almost immediately with rubber water bag. As she crosses to bedroom she is screwing the top on the bag and wiping its wet sides with her apron. Exits bedroom, off.*) Where'd you want it this time, ma? Your head or your feet?

MA. Here. . . . Ain't the folks home yet?

ROSE. They'll be here any minute now. I guess you've been dozing off a little.

MA (*whining*). I haven't closed my eyes.

(*The telephone rings.* ROSE *enters dining room, goes to telephone.*)

ROSE (*At telephone*). Hello! . . . Al isn't home yet. . . . Well, I'll tell him as soon as he comes in. . . . I told you that before. . . . Yes, Hill 2163. (*Hangs up receiver. Picks up pail and brush, carries them to kitchen. Re-enters with dish of butter and milk pitcher. Busies herself at table. An outer door slams.* PA *enters. He is a fussy, gray-haired, sprightly old man of the hack bookkeeper type. He looks warm and irritable.*)

PA. Whew! My God, but it was hot downtown! (*Throws hat and coat on nearby chair.*) What's all this muss?

ROSE. Housecleaning. (*Back and forth between sideboard, table, kitchen, with plates, bread, etc.*)

PA (*To* MA's *bedroom door; peers in. With a false cheeriness*). Well, well! And how's the old girl tonight, h'm? Feel like you could punish a little supper?

MA. I couldn't eat a thing. My head's killing me again. My head. . . . (*Her complaining voice goes on as* PA *stands a moment longer in the doorway. The outer door slams.* AL *enters. He is of the slim, furtive, weasel type. He walks lightly on the balls of his feet, like an Indian, but without the Indian's dignity. In figure a born fox-trotter. His coat is over his arm. He is wearing a flashy striped shirt.*)

AL. Can you beat this for April! My shirt's stuck to my back.

ROSE. Al, put that stepladder away for me, will you?

AL. (*To bedroom, back*). I will not. What d'you think I am! The janitor! (*Exits bedroom.* PA *to armchair, newspaper in hand. Reads.* ROSE *folds ladder, places it against wall.* AL *enters from bedroom.*)

ROSE. Oh, some girl's been calling you up. She said. . . .

AL. Well, why didn't you tell me! (*Goes to phone.*)

ROSE. I'm telling you now. Hill 2163. Pestering me all the time. I should think girls could wait till fellows call them. . . . (ROSE *to kitchen; picks up pail.*)

AL (*To operator*). Hill 2163. . . . No! Six three. . . . Yeh. (*To* ROSE.) Say, if they were all disappointed old maids like you, I guess they'd have to wait till. . . . Hello! (*A complete change of tone.*) That you, Kid? Say, listen. How about to-night, now? (*Drops his voice very low during remainder of conversation.* ROSE *exits, kitchen. Outer door slams.* FLOSS *enters. She is about twenty, very slim, very pretty, rather cheap, in flimsy dress, cut too low, light-colored shoes, short skirt. As she enters she is breathless and excited. She carries a paper hatbag in her hand.*)

FLOSS. Rose! Where's Rose? (ROSE *enters from kitchen, carrying a dish.*)

ROSE. What's the matter?

FLOSS. Did you press my pink georgette, like I asked you to?

ROSE. I didn't get time. I've been cleaning all day long.

FLOSS. But I've got to have it. I got to wear it tonight. Guess who was in the store today!

ROSE. Who? What's that? A hat?

FLOSS. Yes. But listen. . . .

ROSE. Let's see it.

FLOSS (*whips it out of bag*). There! But let me tell you. . . .

ROSE. How much?

FLOSS (*defiantly*). Nine-fifty—trimmed.

AL (*who, having finished telephoning, has been regarding his sisters, leaning idly against the wall, cigarette in mouth*). Trimmed is right!

FLOSS. Shut up, Al! Well, but I had to have it, Rose. I'm going to the theater tonight. And guess who with!

ROSE. Who?

FLOSS. Henry Selz! (ROSE *stares, then smiles uncertainly, puts the dish on the table with a hand that trembles a little.*)

ROSE. What's the joke?

FLOSS. Joke, nothing! Honest to God! I was standing back of the counter at about ten. The rush hadn't really begun. Glove trade always starts late. I was standing there, kidding Herb, the stock boy, when down the aisle comes a man in a big hat, like you see in the western pictures, hair a little gray at the temples, and everything, just like a movie actor. I said to Herb, "Is it real?" I hadn't got the words out of my mouth when the fellow sees me, stands stock-still in the middle of the aisle with his mouth open and his eyes sticking out. "Register surprise," I said to Herb, and looked around for the camera. At that minute he takes two jumps over to where I'm standing, grabs my hands and says, "Rose! Rose!" kind of

choky. "Not by about twenty years," I says. "I'm Floss, Rose's sister. Let go my hands!"

ROSE (*vibrantly*). You said, "I'm Floss, Rose's sister, let go my hands." And then—?

FLOSS. He looked kind of stunned, just for a minute. His face was a scream, honestly. Then he said, "But of course. Fifteen years. But I had always thought of her as just the same." And he kind of laughed, ashamed, like a kid. And the whitest teeth!

ROSE. Yes, they were—white. Well?

FLOSS. Well, I said, "Won't I do instead?" Like that. "You bet you'll do!" he said. And then he told me his name, and how he's living out in Spokane and his wife was dead, and he had made a lot of money—fruit, or real estate or something. He talked a lot about it at lunch, but I didn't pay any attention. As long as he's really got it, a lot I care how. . . .

ROSE. At lunch?

FLOSS. Everything from crab meat to coffee. I didn't believe it could be done in one hour. Believe me, he had those waiters jumping. It takes money. He asked all about you, and ma, and everything. And he kept looking at me and saying, "It's wonderful!" I said, "Isn't it!" but I meant the lunch. He wanted me to go driving this afternoon. Auto and everything. Kept calling me Rose and Rosebud. It made me kind of mad, and I told him how you look. He said, "I suppose so," and asked me to go to a show tonight. Listen, will you press my georgette? I got to have it.

ROSE. I'll iron it while you're eating. I'm not hungry. (*Turns. Goes to kitchen door.*) Did you say he was gray?

FLOSS. (*On her way to bedroom, beginning to unbutton her blouse*). Gray? Oh, you mean. . . . Why, just here and here. Interesting, but not a bit old. And he's got that money look that makes waiters and doormen jump. (*At door.*) I don't want any supper. Just a cup of tea. Haven't got time to dress decently, as it is.

AL (*Leaves wall and phone table, against which he has been lounging. Comes down*). Your story interests me strangely, little gell. But there's a couple other people would like to eat, even *if you wouldn't.* (FLOSS *exits with a withering glance at* AL.) Come on with that supper, Ro! Nobody staked me to a lunch to-day. (AL *and* PA *to table, seat themselves.*

Rose *dishes out the supper to them, though she eats nothing herself.*)

Rose. I'll dish up for you, and then I'll get ma's tray, and press out that dress. I'm late with everything tonight, seems.

Al (*eating*). Some doings ourself today, down at the store, believe me! The Old Man's son started in to learn the retail end of the business. Back of the cigar case with the rest of us, waiting on trade and looking like a Yale yell.

Pa (*looking over the top of his specs which he has put on while reading the paper*). Mannheim's son, you mean! The president of the company's son!

Al. Yep. And I guess he loves it, huh! The Old Man wants him to learn the cigar business from the ground up. I'll bet he never gets higher than the basement, that guy. Went out to lunch at one and never showed up till four. Wears English clothes and smokes a brand of cigarettes we don't even carry.

(Rose *has finished waiting on the men for the time. Goes to* Floss's *room. Out again at once with a pink georgette dress in her hand.*)

Pa (*rises, picks up newspaper, which he scans while eating*). I see the Fair's got a spring housecleaning sale. Advertise a new kind of extension curtain rod. And Rose, Scouro, three cakes for a quarter.

Rose (*off*). I'm not wasting money on truck like that when half the time I can't make the housekeeping money last through the week, as it is.

Pa. Your ma did it.

Rose. Fifteen years ago liver wasn't seventy cents a pound. (*Exits kitchen.*)

Floss (*calling from bedroom*). Rose, pour me out a cup of tea, will you? (Rose, *in kitchen, does not hear.*)

Al (*raises his voice*). Oh, Rose! Come on in here and pour out a cup of tea for the little lady.

Rose (*from kitchen*). Well, then, carry in ma's tray for me.

Floss (*enters from bedroom. She is in petticoat and flimsy kimono, evidently having stopped halfway in her toilette's progress. Her cheeks are very pink. Her hair is shiningly coiffed about her ears*). Tray! Well, I should say not. I haven't got time to eat. (*Sits at table. Pours herself a cup of tea, which she gulps hurriedly.*)

Al (*sneering*). Every move a Pickford! And so girlish withal.

Floss. Shut up, Al. (Rose *enters from kitchen with tray. Crosses to* Ma's *room.*) Guess who I waited on today, Rose!

Rose (*without interest. Into bedroom*). Who?

Floss. Gladys Moraine! I knew her the minute I saw her. She's prettier off than on, I think. She's playing here in "Our Wives." I waited on her, and the other girls in the department were wild. Bought a dozen pair of white kids and made me give 'em to her huge so she could shove her hand right into 'em, like a man does. Two sizes too big. All the swells wear 'em that way. And only one ring—an emerald the size of a dime.

Pa. What kind of clothes'd she wear?

Al (*in a dreamy falsetto*). Ah, yes! What *did* she wear?

Floss (*animatedly*). Just a suit, kind of plain, and yet you'd notice it. And sables! And a Gladys Moraine hat. Everything quiet and plain and dark; and yet she looked like a million dollars. (*Sighs.*) I felt like a roach while I was waiting on her, though she was awful sweet to me. . . . Hurry up with that dress, Rose.

Rose. In a minute. I've just got the collar to do.

Floss (*rises*). He'll be here any minute now. And this place looks like the devil.

Rose (*stops short*). Why—Floss! He isn't going to call for you, is he? Here?

Floss. Sure. With a taxi. Did you think I was going to meet him on the corner or something? (*Goes toward bedroom.*)

Rose. But listen! Floss!

Floss. Don't bother me. (*Exits bedroom.*)

Al (*rises from table, yawning*). Guess I'll do a little beautifying myself. (*Rubs an investigating hand over chin.* Rose *to kitchen, her whole figure drooping, shrunken somehow.* Al *to bedroom.* Pa *throws paper down, yawns elaborately, pushes back his chair. A sound as of some one pounding on a closed door, off.*)

Al (*off*). Hurry up and get through primping in there, will you! What d'you think this is—a Turkish bath!

Floss (*shrilly, off*). Shave in your own

room, can't you! (ROSE *enters from kitchen, the freshly pressed dress in her hand. She prinks out the pleatings and ruffles as she goes toward* FLOSS's *room.*)

PA. Well, I guess I'll just drop around to the movie.

ROSE. Don't you want to sit with ma a minute, first?

PA. When I get back. I don't want to come in the middle of the picture. They're showing the third installment of the "Adventures of Aline."

ROSE. Ma'll be asleep by that time. You know it.

PA. I been slaving all day. I guess I got the right to a little amusement! A man works his fingers to the bone for his family and then his own daughter nags him! (*Snatches up his hat and coat from chair, stamps out.* ROSE *looks after him, her shoulders sagging, her face drawn. The outer door slams noisily. From the bedroom comes the sound of* AL's *whistling and singing in an off-key tenor.*)

FLOSS (*enters hurriedly, making frantic passes at her finger nails with a dilapidated buffer. She is in petticoat and pink camisole*). Where's that dress?

ROSE. Here. (FLOSS *clutches it impatiently. The doorbell rings, three long, loud rings.*)

FLOSS (*panic-stricken*). It's him! (*Slips one arm into the dress.*) Rose, you'll have to go.

ROSE (*shrinking, cowering*). I can't! I can't! (*Her eyes dart to and fro like those of a hunted thing seeking to escape. She runs to* AL's *door.*) Al! Al, go to the door, will you?

AL (*In a smothered mumble*). Can't. Shaving. (*The bell sounds again, three loud, impatient rings.*)

FLOSS (*In a venomous whisper as though she could be heard downstairs*). Rose! I can't go with my waist open! For God's sake answer the door! (*Runs back to bedroom, fastening gown as she goes.*)

ROSE (*In a kind of moan*). I can't! I—can't! (*And goes. As she goes she passes a futile, work-worn hand over her hair, plucks off her apron, casts it in a corner, first wiping her flushed face with it. She presses an electric button that opens lower door. Opens hall door. Stands there, waiting. A brief pause.* HENRY SELZ *is heard approaching with a springy step.* HENRY SELZ *stands in the door. He is about forty-two or three, well dressed, prosperous looking, almost youthful. He stares at* ROSE *uncertainly.*)

ROSE (*tremulously*). How-do, Henry.

HENRY (*The look of uncertainty changing to pitying incredulity*). Why, how-do, Rose! I didn't know you—for a minute. Well, well! It's been a long time. Let's see. Ten—twelve—about thirteen, fourteen years, isn't it?

ROSE. Fifteen. This month. Won't you come in and sit down? Floss'll be ready in a minute. (*They sit, he a little ill at ease,* ROSE *nervously tucking back her wisps of hair, twisting her fingers.*) Things look a little upset around here. I've been housecleaning.

HENRY. That's all right. (*Dabs at his face with handkerchief.*) Certainly is warm for this time of year. Well, and how've you been? Did little sister tell you how flabbergasted I was when I saw her this morning? Say, it was the funniest thing! I got kind of balled up for a minute and thought it was you. I'm darned if it didn't take fifteen years off my age—just like that! She tell you?

ROSE. Yes. She told me.

HENRY. She's the image of the way you used to look.

ROSE. I've changed—quite a lot.

HENRY (*feebly*). Oh, I don't know, Rose. You're a pretty good looking girl yet.

ROSE. You've changed, too. But it's different with a man. You're better looking now than you were fifteen years ago.

HENRY. Things have kind of come my way. I was pretty late learning about golf, and caviar and tailors. But say, it doesn't take long. . . . I hear your ma's still sick. (ROSE *nods her head.*) That certainly is tough. And you never married, h'm?

ROSE. Never married.

HENRY. I guess you never held it up against me, did you, Rose? My marrying? When your ma took sick and we had to put it off, who'd have thought you'd be stuck here all these years?

ROSE. I never held it up against you, Henry. When you stopped writing I just knew. . . .

HENRY (*glances around the room*). You've been going on like this, taking care of the family?

ROSE. Yes.

(FLOSS *enters, a radiant, glowing, girlish vision. She is wearing the gown* ROSE *has pressed, and the pert new hat.*

HENRY SELZ *rises. His eyes are fixed admiringly on* FLOSS.)

HENRY. Ah! And how's the little girl tonight!

FLOSS (*gives him her hand*). Did I keep you waiting a terribly long time?

HENRY. No, not a bit. Rose and I were chinning over old times, weren't we, Rose? (*A kindly, clumsy thought strikes him.*) Say, look here, Rose. We're going to a show. Why don't you just run and put on your hat and come along, h'm? Come on!

ROSE. No, thanks, Henry. Not tonight. You and Floss run along.

HENRY. Well, remember me to your ma.

ROSE. I will, Henry. I'm sorry you can't see her. But she don't see anybody—poor ma.

HENRY (*Shakes her hand heartily.*) Good-by, Rose. Glad I saw you.

ROSE. Good-by.

FLOSS. I hope we won't be late. (*At door.*) I hate to come in after the curtain's up, don't you? (FLOSS *and* HENRY *go,* FLOSS *still chattering.*) I went to a show one night and the woman behind us was simply furious because. . . . (ROSE *peers after her, anxiously, as a mother would. The door closes.* ROSE *stands still, her arms hanging straight at her sides, staring after the door is shut. The outer door slams as before.* ROSE *turns, mechanically, and goes into her mother's room. She comes out immediately, carrying the littered supper tray.*)

MA (*in her high-pitched, thin voice*). Who was that?

ROSE (*over her shoulder*). That was—Henry Selz.

MA (*wanderingly*). Henry? Henry Selz? Henry—oh, yes. Did he go out with Floss?

ROSE. Yes. (*Goes slowly toward kitchen with tray.*)

MA (*in a whine*). It's cold in here.

ROSE. I'll get you a bag in a minute, ma. (*Exits kitchen.* AL *enters from bedroom, shrugging himself into his coat. He is shaved, brushed, powdered to a marvel. Glances around, furtively, goes toward kitchen, encounters* ROSE *entering with hot water bag.*)

AL. I'll take that to ma. (*Takes bag to* MA'S *bedroom.* ROSE *crosses to cluttered supper table, sits wearily. Pours a cup of cold tea.* AL *enters from* MA'S *bedroom, over to* ROSE, *after regarding her speculatively for a moment.*

Lays a hand on her shoulder.) Ro, lend me a couple of dollars, will you?

ROSE. I should say not!

AL. (*douses his cigarette in the dregs of a convenient teacup, leans over, presses his pale, powdered cheek to* ROSE's *sallow one. His arm is about her, his hand patting her shoulder*). Oh, come on, kid. Don't I always pay you back? Come on. Be a sweet ol' sis. (*Kisses her.* ROSE *shrugs away impatiently.*) I wouldn't ask you, only I've got a date to go to Luna Park and I couldn't get out of it. I tried, honest.

ROSE. Don't you think I ever get sick of slaving for a thankless bunch like you! Well, I do. Sick and tired of it, that's what! Coming around asking for money as if I was a bank.

AL. Oh, come on, Ro. Just this once.

ROSE (*grudgingly, wearily*). There's a dollar bill and some small change in the can on the second shelf in the china closet. (AL *is off like a terrier. From the kitchen pantry comes the clink of metal against metal. He is back in a flash, snatches his hat, is out without a backward glance at* ROSE. *The outer door slams loudly.* ROSE *sits stirring her cold tea, slowly, as one does who will not drink it. She is gazing dully down into the cup. She turns her head and looks at the closed door of the sideboard cabinet, where the packet of letters lies. She crosses to sideboard, unlocks door, takes out letters, comes slowly back to table, stands a moment, tears letters across, crushes them in her fingers, and throws the pieces among the greasy supper dishes. Suddenly her face puckers up almost comically, like a child's. She sinks into a chair at the table, her head comes down on her outstretched arms among the supper things, so that the dishes jump and tinkle.*)

MA (*off*). What's that! Rose!

ROSE (*raises her head, stifling her sobs*). Nothing, ma. (*Wipes her eyes with the palm and back of her hand, sniffling. Sits staring down at the table. Her eye is caught by a headline in the evening paper that* PA *has thrown down on the table. She picks it up almost unconsciously, scans it, her face, twisted with grief, gradually losing its look of pain. As the curtain descends she rises, gathers up a handful of dishes, and drags her accustomed way to the kitchen.*)

PLUMES

by Georgia Douglas Johnson

CHARACTERS

CHARITY BROWN, *the mother*
EMMERLINE BROWN, *the daughter*
TILDY, *the friend*
DOCTOR SCOTT, *physician*

Scene: A poor cottage in the South.
Time: Contemporary.

SCENE: THE KITCHEN *of a two-room cottage, A window overlooking the street. A door leading to the street, one leading to the back-yard and one to the inner room. A stove, a table with shelf over it, a washtub. A rocking-chair, a cane-bottom chair. Needle, thread, scissors, etc., on table.*

Scene opens with CHARITY BROWN *heating a poultice over the stove. A groaning is heard from the inner room.*

CHARITY. Yes, honey, mamma is fixing somethin' to do you good. Yes, my baby, jus' you wait—I'm a-coming.

    (*Knock is heard at door. It is gently pushed open and* TILDY *comes in cautiously.*)

TILDY (*whispering*). How is she?

CHARITY. Poorly, poorly. Didn't rest last night none hardly. Move that dress and set in th' rocker. I been trying to snatch a minute to finish it but don't seem like I can. She won't have nothing to wear if she—she—

TILDY. I understands. How near done is it?

CHARITY. Ain't so much more to do.

TILDY (*takes up dress from chair; looks at it*). I'll do some on it.

CHARITY. Thank you, sister Tildy. Whip that torshon on and turn down the hem in the skirt.

TILDY (*measuring dress against herself*). How deep?

CHARITY. Let me see, now (*Studies a minute with finger against lip*) I tell you—jus' baste it, 'cause you see—she wears 'em short, but—it might be—(*Stops.*)

TILDY (*bowing her head comprehendingly*). Huh-uh, I see exzackly. (*Sighs.*) You'd want it long—over her feet—then.

CHARITY. That's it, sister Tildy. (*Listening.*) She's some easy now! (*Stirring poultice.*) Jest can't get this poltis' hot enough somehow this morning.

TILDY. Put some red pepper in it. Got any?

CHARITY. Yes. There ought to be some in one of them boxes on the shelf there. (*Points.*)

TILDY (*goes to shelf, looks about and gets the pepper*). Here, put a-plenty of this in.

CHARITY. (*groans are heard from the next room*). Good Lord, them pains got her again. She suffers so, when she's 'wake.

TILDY. Poor little thing. How old is she now, sister Charity?

CHARITY. Turning fourteen this coming July.

TILDY (*shaking her head dubiously*). I sho' hope she'll be mended by then.

CHARITY. It don't look much like it, but I trusts so—(*looking worried.*) That doctor's mighty late this morning.

TILDY. I expect he'll be 'long in no time. Doctors is mighty onconcerned here lately.

CHARITY (*going toward inner room with poultice*). They surely is and I don't have too much confidence in none of 'em. (*You can hear her soothing the child.*)

TILDY (*listening*). Want me to help you put it on, sister Charity?

CHARITY (*from inner room*). No, I can fix it. (*Coming back from sick room shaking her head rather dejectedly.*)

TILDY. How is she, sister Charity?

GEORGIA DOUGLAS JOHNSON (1886–1966)

The literary renaissance in Ireland had been a particular inspiration to the noncommercial theatre in this country. The poetic realism of plays about the tradition-bound, superstitious, and uneducated Irish peasant had a special appeal for us, since it was thought to strike at the very roots of comedy and (more often) tragedy. In these "folk" plays the nobility of mankind was best revealed by the suffering and defeat that characterized the human condition.

The notion of a Harlem Renaissance had inspired black scholars such as Alain Locke to champion (as William Butler Yeats had done in Ireland) "folk" plays dealing with the poorest and the most economically and socially deprived natives of his own country. Locke's hope was that works about Negro life in America would prove to be "universal" even in sounding the most racial notes.

Georgia Douglas Johnson's *Plumes* (1927) is one of the few plays to be written in this country that proved itself a worthy heir to the "universals" of folk drama. By the time she had written *Plumes,* Johnson was already well known as the author of two volumes of poetry, *The Heart of a Woman and Other Poems* (1918) and *Bronze* (1922), and the play *Sunday Morning in the South* (1925), which was written in support of the antilynching campaign following World War I.

Plumes was presented by the Harlem Experimental Theatre, which had patterned itself after W. E. B. Du Bois' Krigwa (an acronym for Crisis Guild of Writers and Artists) Players. The stated purpose of both groups was to foster the development of the black folk play and to make these works available to the Negro community in New York City.

Johnson is credited with at least three other plays, among them *Blue Blood,* which appeared in a 1928 volume of contemporary

Georgia Douglas Johnson

one-acts. At heart, however, she remained a poet.

Born in the South, Johnson attended Oberlin College in Ohio. Upon graduation, she moved to Washington, D.C., where her home became a gathering place for artists and intellectuals such as Locke, May Miller, and Langston Hughes. In her final years Johnson found herself part of a new movement for the advancement of Negro rights and the appreciation of black culture in America.

CHARITY. Mighty feeble. Gone back to sleep now. My poor little baby. (*Bracing herself.*) I'm going to put on some coffee now.

TILDY. I'm sho' glad. I feel kinder low-spirited.

CHARITY. It's me that low-sperited. The doctor said last time he was here he might

have to operate—said, she mought have a chance then. But I tell you the truth, I've got no faith a-tall in 'em. They takes all your money for nothing.

TILDY. They sho' do and don't leave a cent for putting you away decent.

CHARITY. That's jest it. They takes all you

got and then you dies jest the same. It ain't like they was sure.

TILDY. No, they ain't sure. That's it exzactly. But they takes your money jest the same, and leaves you flat.

CHARITY. I been thinking 'bout Zeke these last few days—how he was put away—

TILDY. I wouldn't worry 'bout him now. He's out of his troubles.

CHARITY. I know. But it worries me when I think about how he was put away . . . that ugly pine coffin, jest one shabby old hack and nothing else to show—to show—what we thought about him.

TILDY. Hush, sister! Don't you worry over him. He's happy now, anyhow.

CHARITY. I can't help it! Then little Bessie. We all jest scrooged in one hack and took her little coffin in our lap all the way out to the graveyard. (*Breaks out crying.*)

TILDY. Do hush, sister Charity. You done the best you could. Poor folks got to make the best of it. The Lord understands—

CHARITY. I know that—but I made up my mind the time Bessie went that the next one of us what died would have a shore nuff funeral, everything grand,—with plumes!—I saved and saved and now—this yah doctor—

TILDY. All they think about is cuttin' and killing and taking your money. I got nothin' to put 'em doing.

CHARITY (*goes over to washtub and rubs on clothes*). Me neither. These clothes got to get out somehow, I needs every cent.

TILDY. How much that washing bring you?

CHARITY (*wipes hands on apron and goes to whole lot more. But what can you do?*

TILDY. You can't do nothing—Look there, sister Charity, ain't that coffee boiling?

CHARITY (*wipes hands on apron and goes to stove*). Yes it's boiling good fashioned. Come on, drink some.

TILDY. There ain't nothing I'd rather have than a good strong cup of coffee. (CHARITY *pours* TILDY's *cup.*) (*Sweetening and stirring hers.*) Pour you some. (CHARITY *pours her own cup.*) I'd been dead, too, long ago if it hadn't a been for my coffee.

CHARITY. I love it, but it don't love me— gives me the shortness of breath.

TILDY (*finishing her cup, taking up sugar with spoon*). Don't hurt me. I could drink a barrel.

CHARITY (*drinking more slowly—reach-ing for coffeepot*). Here, drink another cup.

TILDY. I shore will, that cup done me a lot of good.

CHARITY (*looking into her empty cup thoughtfully*). I wish Dinah Morris would drop in now. I'd ask her what these grounds mean.

TILDY. I can read 'em a little myself.

CHARITY. You can? Well, for the Lord's sake, look here and tell me what this cup says! (*Offers cup to* TILDY. TILDY *wards it off.*)

TILDY. You got to turn it 'round in your saucer three times first.

CHARITY. Yes, that's right, I forgot. (*Turns cup 'round, counting.*) One, two, three. (*Starts to pick it up.*)

TILDY. Huhudh (*meaning no*). Let it set a minute. It might be watery. (*After a minute, while she finishes her own cup.*) Now let me see. (*Takes cup and examines it very scruti-nizingly.*)

CHARITY. What you see?

TILDY (*hesitatingly*). I ain't seen a cup like this one for many a year. Not since—not since—

CHARITY. When?

TILDY. Not since jest before ma died. I looked in the cup then and saw things and—I stopped looking . . .

CHARITY. Tell me what you see, I want to know.

TILDY. I don't like to tell no bad news—

CHARITY. Go on. I can stan' anything after all I been thru'.

TILDY. Since you're bound to know I'll tell you. (CHARITY *draws nearer.*) I sees a big gethering!

CHARITY. Gethering, you say?

TILDY. Yes, a big gethering. People all crowded together. Then I see 'em going one by one and two by two. Long line stretching out and out and out!

CHARITY (*in a whisper*). What you think it is?

TILDY (*awed like*). Looks like (*hesitates*) a possession!

CHARITY (*shouting*). You sure!

TILDY. I know it is. (*Just then the toll of a church bell is heard and then the steady and slow tramp, tramp, of horses' hoofs. Both women look at each other.*)

TILDY (*in a hushed voice*). That must be Bell Gibson's funeral coming 'way from Mt. Zion. (*Gets up and goes to window.*) Yes, it sho' is.

CHARITY (*looking out of the window also*). Poor Bell suffered many a year; she's out of her pain now.

TILDY. Look, here comes the hearse now!

CHARITY. My Lord! ain't it grand! Look at them horses—look at their heads—plumes—how they shake 'em! Land o' mighty! It's a fine sight, sister Tildy.

TILDY. That must be Jer'miah in that first carriage, bending over like; he shorely is putting her away grand.

CHARITY. No mistake about it. That's Pickett's best funeral turnout he's got.

TILDY. I'll bet it cost a lot.

CHARITY. Fifty dollars, so Matilda Jenkins told me. She had it for Bud. The plumes is what cost.

TILDY. Look at the hacks— (*Counts.*) I believe to my soul there's eight.

CHARITY. Got somebody in all of 'em too—and flowers— She shore got a lot of 'em. (*Both women's eyes follow the tail end of the procession, horses' hoofs die away as they turn away from window. The two women look at each other significantly.*)

TILDY (*significantly*). Well!— (*They look at each other without speaking for a minute. CHARITY goes to the washtub.*) Want these cups washed up?

CHARITY. No don't mind 'em. I'd rather you get that dress done. I got to get these clothes out.

TILDY (*picking up dress*). Shore, there ain't so much more to do on it now. (*Knock is heard on the door. CHARITY answers knock and admits DR. SCOTT.*)

DR. SCOTT. Good morning. How's the patient today?

CHARITY. Not so good, doctor. When she ain't 'sleep she suffers so; but she sleeps mostly.

DR. SCOTT. Well, let's see, let's see. Just hand me a pan of warm water and I'll soon find out just what's what.

CHARITY. All right, doctor. I'll bring it to you right away. (*Bustles about fixing water—looking toward dress TILDY is working on.*) Poor little Emmerline's been wanting a white dress trimmed with torshon a long time—now she's got it and it looks like—well— (*hesitates*) t'warn't made to wear.

TILDY. Don't take on so, sister Charity— The Lord giveth and the Lord taketh.

CHARITY. I know—but it's hard—hard— (*Goes into inner room with water. You can hear her talking with the doctor after a minute and the doctor expostulating with her—in a minute she appears at the door, being led from the room by the doctor.*)

DR. SCOTT. No, my dear Mrs. Brown. It will be much better for you to remain outside.

CHARITY. But, doctor—

DR. SCOTT. NO. You stay outside and get your mind on something else. You can't possibly be of any service. Now be calm, will you?

CHARITY. I'll try, doctor.

TILDY. The doctor's right. You can't do no good in there.

CHARITY. I knows, but I thought I could hold the pan or somethin'. (*Lowering her voice.*) Says he got to see if her heart is all right or somethin'. I tell you—nowadays—

TILDY. I know.

CHARITY (*softly to TILDY*). Hope he won't come out here saying he got to operate. (*Goes to washtub.*)

TILDY. I hope so, too. Won't it cost a lot?

CHARITY. That's jest it. It would take all I got saved up.

TILDY. Of course, if he's goin' to get her up—but I don't believe in 'em. I don't believe in 'em.

CHARITY. He didn't promise tho'—even if he did, he said maybe it wouldn't do no good.

TILDY. I'd think a long time before I'd let him operate on my chile. Taking all yuh money, promising nothing and ten to one killing her to boot.

CHARITY. This is a hard world.

TILDY. Don't you trus' him. Coffee grounds don't lie!

CHARITY. I don't trust him. I jest want to do what's right by her. I ought to put these clothes on the line while you're settin' in here, but I jes hate to go outdoors while he's in there.

TILDY (*getting up*). I'll hang 'em out. You stay here. Where your clothespins at?

CHARITY. Hanging right there by the back door in the bag. They ought to dry before dark and then I can iron tonight.

TILDY (*picking up tub*). They ought to blow dry in no time. (*Goes toward back door.*)

CHARITY. Then I can shore rub 'em over tonight. Say, sister Tildy, hist 'em up with that long saplin' prop leaning in the fence corner.

TILDY (*going out*). All right.

CHARITY. (*Standing by the table beating nervously on it with her fingers—listens—and then starts to bustling about the kitchen*) (*Enter* DOCTOR *from inner room.*)

DR. SCOTT. Well, Mrs. Brown, I've decided I'll have to operate.

CHARITY. MY Lord! Doctor—don't say that!

DR. SCOTT. It's the only chance.

CHARITY. You mean she'll get well if you do?

DR. SCOTT. No, I can't say that— It's just a chance—a last chance. And I'll do just what I said, cut the price of the operation down to fifty dollars. I'm willing to do that for you. (CHARITY *throws up her hands in dismay.*)

CHARITY. Doctor, I was so in hopes you wouldn't operate—I—I— And yo' say you ain't a bit sure she'll get well—even then?

DR. SCOTT. No. I can't be sure. We'll just have to take the chance. But I'm sure you want to do everything—

CHARITY. Sure, doctor, I do want to—do—everything I can do to—to— Doctor, look at this cup. (*Picks up fortune cup and shows the doctor.*) My fortune's jes' been told this very morning—look at these grounds—they says—(*softly*) it ain't no use, no use a-tall.

DR. SCOTT. Why, my good woman, don't you believe in such senseless things! That cup of grounds can't show you anything. Wash them out and forget it.

CHARITY. I can't forget it. I feel like it ain't no use; I'd just be spendin' the money that I needs—for nothing—nothing.

DR. SCOTT. But you won't though— You'll have a clear conscience. You'd know that you did everything you could.

CHARITY. I know that, doctor. But there's things you don't know 'bout—there's other things I got to think about. If she goes—if she must go . . . I had plans—I been getting ready—now— Oh, doctor, I jest can't see how I can have this operation—you say you can't promise—nothing?

DR. SCOTT. I didn't think you'd hesitate about it—I imagined your love for your child—

CHARITY (*breaking in*). I do love my child. My God, I do love my child. You don't understand . . . but . . . but—can't I have a little time to think about it, doctor? It means so much—to her—and—me!

DR. SCOTT. I tell you. I'll go on over to the office. I'd have to get my— (*hesitates*) my things, anyhow. And as soon as you make up your mind, get one of the neighbors to run over and tell me. I'll come right back. But don't waste any time now, Mrs. Brown, every minute counts.

CHARITY. Thank you, doctor, thank you. I'll shore send you word as soon as I can. I'm so upset and worried I'm half crazy.

DR. SCOTT. I know you are . . . but don't take too long to make up your mind. . . . It ought to be done today. Remember—it may save her. (*Exits.*)

CHARITY. (*Goes to door of sick room—looks inside for a few minutes, then starts walking up and down the little kitchen, first holding a hand up to her head and then wringing them. Enter* TILDY *from yard with tub under her arm.*)

TILDY. Well, they're all out, sister Charity—(*Stops.*) Why, what's the matter?

CHARITY. The doctor wants to operate.

TILDY (*softly*). Where he—gone?

CHARITY. Yes—he's gone, but he's coming back—if I send for him.

TILDY. You going to? (*Puts down tub and picks up white dress and begins sewing.*)

CHARITY. I dunno—I got to think.

TILDY. I can't see what's the use myself. He can't save her with no operation— Coffee grounds don't lie.

CHARITY. It would take all the money I got for the operation and then what about puttin' her away? He can't save her—don't even promise ter. I know he can't—I feel it . . . I feel it . . .

TILDY. It's in the air. . . . (*Both women sit tense in the silence.* TILDY *has commenced sewing again. Just then a strange, strangling noise comes from the inner room.*)

TILDY. What's that?

CHARITY (*Running toward and into inner room*). Oh, my God! (*From inside.*) Sister Tildy—Come here—No,—Some water, quick. (TILDY *with dress in hand starts toward inner room. Stops at door, sighs and then goes hurriedly back for the water pitcher.* CHARITY *is heard moaning softly in the next room, then she appears at the doorway and leans against jamb of door.*) Rip the hem out, sister Tildy.

CURTAIN

WINTER'S NIGHT

by **Neith Boyce**

CHARACTERS

RACHEL WESTCOTT.
JACOB WESTCOTT.
SARAH, *a neighbor*

SCENE: *A room in the Westcott farmhouse. Through the two large windows at the back moonlight streams in. The curtains are drawn back, and without, ground and trees covered with snow can be seen.*

At one side of the room is a stove, with fire glowing dimly in it, and a teakettle singing on top. A large grandfather's chair stands beside stove. A sofa under one window, under the other a sewing machine with a basket piled with stuff. On the other side of room, cupboards with glass doors. Center, a round table with lamp. Tall clock in one corner, and near it a mirror. Over the mirror hangs a shotgun.

Sleigh bells heard off stage, stopping before the house. A man's voice.

VOICE. Whoa, boys! Steady now, steady!
(*Sound of key turning in lock. Door center back opens. Enter RACHEL. She turns and calls out.*)
RACHEL. Better blanket the team, Jacob. It'll be down to zero before morning.
JACOB (*off*). Yes, yes, I'll tend to it. Don't hold the door open.
(RACHEL *closes door, throws off heavy cloak, goes to lamp and lights it, looks at key. She has the door key, with note tied to it, in her hand. She is a woman of middle age, dressed in black, with a widow's bonnet and long crape veil hanging over her shoulders. She sits down in rocking chair beside table, reads the note, then looks absently about the room. In the light it is very attractive—the woodwork painted white, the curtains, couch cover and*

table covers of scarlet, several red and blue rugs on the floor, gay china showing in the cupboards, and some flowering plants on the windowsills. After a moment RACHEL *takes off her bonnet, holds it in her hand, shaking out the crape veil, looks at it fixedly, and lays it on table. She smooths her thick gray-black hair, rocks back and forth, then, clasping her hands, sits motionless, looking before her.*
Stamping of feet, off left. Enter JACOB, in heavy ulster and fur cap, carrying an armful of wood and a lighted lantern. He blows out lantern, hangs it by the door, goes to stove, and puts down the wood, then takes off his coat and cap. He is dressed in stiff black clothes. A lean man, gray, carefully shaved. He glances at RACHEL, who does not look at him; then makes up the fire, and stands warming his hands and staring at RACHEL.)
JACOB. You must want something to eat, don't you, Rachel?
RACHEL (*absently*). No. I don't want anything.
JACOB. It was a long drive, and cold. You'll have a cup of tea, anyway?
RACHEL. No—yes—I don't care. Sarah left a note, Jacob—she says she'll be over to stay the night.
JACOB. That so?
(*He goes to cupboard, takes out teapot, cup and saucer, sugar bowl, canister, makes tea, and brings it on small tray, puts it beside RACHEL on the table. She does not notice him, but sits folding and refolding her black-bordered handkerchief.*)
JACOB (*gently*). Drink your tea, Rachel. You must be mortal cold and tired.
RACHEL (*turning suddenly*). No— (*She stirs sugar in the tea and drinks it slowly.*) It's queer

79

NEITH BOYCE (1872–1951)

By the late 1890's Neith Boyce was living in Greenwich Village with two other young women, who, like herself, were budding novelists. They made their way, however, by writing for various New York City newspapers. As Hutchins Hapgood, whom Boyce was later to marry, described them, "Probably no girls ever enjoyed themselves more as journalists than these three; they had bid a kindly farewell to their homes and were tasting economic independence. These and many other young women of the day enjoyed the same spirit as the young men; they suggested the French Bohemia . . . and yet were the equals of their men friends."

In those halycon days before the turn of the century Boyce worked for Lincoln Steffens, then editor of *The Commercial Advertiser*. Her formal preparation for such a career was scant, however. Like many well-to-do young people of her day, Boyce had been educated at home in Franklin, Indiana, mainly by devouring her parents' library of classics. Later she attended "a sort of college, presided over by an old melancholy clerical gentleman." That, plus language and music lessons, was what prepared her for a career as a writer.

Boyce published her first book in 1896, "a miscellany of various and interesting tales, histories and etc.," whimsically entitled *The Chap-Book. The Forerunner* appeared in 1903, followed by *The Eternal Spring* and *The Folly of Others,* both in 1906, and *The Bond* in 1908. Her last two novels, *Harry* and *Proud Lady,* were published in 1923.

During her early years at *The Commercial Advertiser,* Boyce met and married Hutchins Hapgood, who was himself just starting out on a long career as an author and journalist. Over the years the couple would function as friends and advisers to such cultural celebrities as Mabel Dodge, Djuna Barnes, Alfred Stieglitz, Georgia O'Keeffe and, most notably, Gertrude Stein.

Early in their marriage the Hapgoods

Neith Boyce

took to spending summers in Provincetown, Massachusetts. Not surprisingly, all four of Boyce's works for the stage were first presented by the Provincetown Players. The first of them, *Constancy* (1914), deals with the tempestuous relationship between two of her summer neighbors, Mabel Dodge and John Reed. The Hapgoods collaborated on *Enemies* (1916), a dialogue between a man and a woman that reflected the then contemporary war between the sexes. She wrote the woman's lines, and he the man's. The couple also appeared in the play when it premiered in Provincetown. *Enemies'* other distinction is that of being one of the earliest plays to be produced for radio. *Two Sons* and *Winter's Night* also premiered in 1916, although the latter play was not to appear in print until 1928, by which time it had undergone numerous revisions. It is the 1928 version of *Winter's Night* that is included here.

—but I don't feel tired—nor anything. I didn't feel the cold so much, coming home. The wind was behind us. But going over— (*She shivers.*) It was a long journey—

JACOB (*moving chair and sitting down at the other side of the table*). Perhaps you'd better have stayed at the minister's tonight, after all. When they asked you, after the funeral, I thought—

RACHEL. Why? I didn't want to stay at the minister's.

JACOB. Well—I only thought it would seem so lonely to you, coming back here—

RACHEL. Lonely? It does seem strange to be here—without him—don't it, Jacob? It does seem strange—you and me alone here—without Daniel. I can hardly realize he's gone—

(JACOB *gets up hastily and goes right, opens a door, and takes down brown coat, changes his black coat for the brown. Takes pipe from pocket and fills it. Goes to cupboard for matches.*)

RACHEL. Death's a strange thing, Jacob. It changes everything, Daniel's going.

JACOB (*huskily*). Yes.

(RACHEL *sighs, turns to look at Jacob and starts.*)

RACHEL. Oh, you've taken off your black already!

JACOB. Well—it's too tight for me, you see, the black coat is— You don't mind, do you— Rachel?

RACHEL. No—I don't know as I do. Though I suppose you'll wear the black, when you go out, for awhile. That's no more than right, seeing Daniel was your brother—

JACOB (*hastily*). Oh, of course, of course—

RACHEL (*firmly*). I shall wear my crape a year for him, though heaven knows I've always hated black. But I always did my duty by my husband, and I shall now.

JACOB (*moving about restlessly*). Yes—of course—

RACHEL. And you did your duty by him, too, Jacob.

JACOB. I—hope so—

RACHEL (*taking up bonnet and smoothing strings*). Yes, you were a good brother to him, all these years he's been ill. And you've been a good brother to me. I don't know how I could have got on without you— (*She sighs.*)

JACOB *goes to window and looks out.*

Knocks over small flower pot, which falls and breaks.)

RACHEL (*getting up*). Mercy, what's that? It's one of my begonias! (JACOB *stoops to pick up flower pot. Drops his pipe.*) Mercy, what ails you, Jacob? Now you've broken your pipe, too! I never knew you to be so clumsy! (*Going toward him.*) Why, you're as pale as a sheet! I know what's the matter; you want your supper—

JACOB. No, Rachel, no—I don't want any supper—

RACHEL (*firmly*). Yes, you do. You need it, whether you want it or not. People have to eat, Jacob, as long as they're alive, whether there's death in the house or not— (*Sighs. She takes an apron out of a drawer in cupboard and ties it on. It is trimmed with lace and has a red bow in one corner.* JACOB *stands with his broken pipe in his hand, watching her. She moves briskly from cupboard to table.*) There— there's some bread and cheese and apple pie. Sit down, Jacob. I don't believe you've eaten a morsel all day.

JACOB (*sitting at table*). I don't want it, Rachel.

RACHEL. You feel it a great deal, Jacob— Daniel's going. I never thought you would feel it so much. But you've got deep feelings, though you're so quiet. You thought a lot of Daniel. I never heard a harsh word from you to him in all these years, though goodness knows he was unreasonable enough sometimes, poor man, with his pains. Well (*sighing*), it's a mercy he's at rest at last. These four years past were nothing but suffering for him— Aren't you going to eat anything, Jacob?

JACOB. I don't seem to want it, Rachel. It chokes me, somehow—

(*He pushes his chair back a little, looking up at her as she stands beside him. His eyes rest on the red bow on her apron; she notices it for the first time, and pulls off the ribbon.*)

RACHEL. Pshaw! I never thought—

JACOB (*putting out his hand*). Give it to me, Rachel.

RACHEL. The ribbon? Whatever do you want of it?

JACOB. I don't know—I like the color. I always did like red.

RACHEL (*giving him the bow*). Well, there,

then. It's my favorite color, too—bright red, scarlet—though I like purple, too, deep purple— Well, I mustn't think of such things now. (*Sighs.*) It's foolish, come to think of it—

> (*She moves about, taking things from table and putting them back in cupboard.*)

JACOB. No! It isn't foolish! It's wonderful, liking colors, the way you do, and fixing things up to look pretty. You made a wonderful difference in this old house, Rachel. Before you come into it, it was all gray and dull. You made it seem like a different place, all bright and cheerful, with flowers, too, even in winter — That reminds me. (*He gets up and goes to window.*) I came near forgetting your plants. They'd surely freeze there tonight; it's going to be mighty cold before morning. (*He moves the flower pots to table.*) I'm sorry I broke the begonia—

RACHEL. Oh, it doesn't matter. (*She looks out the window.*) It does look cold! I don't believe Sarah'll come over after all.

JACOB. Oh, I guess she'll come. She said she didn't think you'd ought to be alone tonight.

RACHEL. Well, it's kind of her—though I don't know as I need her. I don't feel much like talking. I'd rather be alone with my own thoughts— Draw the curtains, Jacob—it does look so mortal cold outside in the moonlight!

> (JACOB *draws the red curtains over the two windows.* RACHEL *moves rocker to stove and sits down.*)

RACHEL. I wish I had some work to do—I never could bear to sit idle. There's that dress of Mrs. Gray's—but I suppose it would seem terrible heartless of me to sit sewing tonight, and Daniel hardly in his grave—

JACOB. I don't think so, Rachel! It's got nothing to do with your feelings. Shall I bring you the dress?

RACHEL. I don't know—yes, just hand me the basket there—I guess everything's just where I left it when Daniel was took so bad a week ago—but Sarah mustn't see me sewing; it'd be all over the neighborhood—

> (JACOB *brings the basket from the sewing machine.*)

JACOB. Oh, we'll hear her, time enough, when she comes.

> (RACHEL *shakes out the dress, a purple cloth.*)

RACHEL. It's a nice color, but the stuff is cheap. I never would have cheap stuff.

> (*She begins to sew.* JACOB *wanders about the room. He takes down the shotgun from its hooks, draws up a chair near* RACHEL, *and looks the gun over carefully, loading it.*)

JACOB. I reckon I'll get that fox yet, one of these nights. I found his tracks again this morning and I think he got another of the white pullets.

RACHEL (*absently*). That so? (*Pause.*) I was thinking, Jacob—it's twenty-seven years since I came to this house. It don't seem possible.

JACOB. No.

> (*He finishes loading the gun and lays it across his knees.*)

RACHEL. It was June, though—when I married Daniel—twenty-eight years ago come next June. He was twenty-three and I was twenty. And you—let's see, you was four years older'n Daniel, wasn't you?

JACOB. Five years.

RACHEL. Well, you seemed more than that —always so queer, you were, and quiet. It's too bad, Jacob, you never married—you wouldn't be alone now.

> (JACOB *gets up and goes to put the gun back on its hooks.*)

JACOB. I'm not alone—so long as you're here.

RACHEL. No—but I don't suppose I'll be here forever. (JACOB *drops the gun.* RACHEL *jumps up, the basket falling from her lap.*) For goodness' sake, Jacob, what does ail you? Ain't that gun loaded?

JACOB (*huskily*). Yes—it's loaded.

> (*He picks up gun and stands looking at it.*)

RACHEL. Well, I declare! I could almost think you'd been drinking—you haven't been and broke your promise to me, have you—

JACOB. No. I haven't touched liquor for ten years, and you know it, Rachel.

RACHEL. Well, for goodness' sake, put up that gun. I think you'd better go to bed, Jacob. You must be tired out, the way you act.

> (*She picks up her basket and sits down again.*)

JACOB. No, I'm not tired. It isn't that. (*He hangs up gun.*) It was only—

RACHEL. Only what? (*He stands up with his back to her, his head bent.*) Only *what?* You've got one of your queer streaks again, Jacob. I declare there's times when I can't make you out, no more than the man in the moon—for all we've lived side by side for twenty-seven years!

JACOB. Side by side! Yes— It was what you said, Rachel, about my being alone. (*He turns suddenly and comes toward her.*) You said— "Perhaps I won't be here forever"—

RACHEL. Did I? Well—yes—I've been thinking—

JACOB. Thinking what, Rachel?

RACHEL. Thinking I've spent enough of my life here, Jacob. I never meant to stay here forever. (*She threads her needle and goes on, without looking at him.*) I've had my ambitions, Jacob, and for all I'm forty-seven I can't feel that my life's over yet. You know yourself, Jacob, there isn't enough here to keep me busy. If I'd had children now, it might've been different. But just looking after you two men, and with you taking all the care of the farm off me—no, it wasn't enough. 'Twas for that, you know, that I took up dressmaking. Not that I needed the money. But I like the work. And for years I've had a plan, only it was no use speaking of it—it would only have worried Daniel. I want to go into business—dressmaking—in some big town, Bridgeport, perhaps. I've got a little capital, even without my share of the farm. And I'm free now. (*She drops her sewing in her lap and looks eagerly round at* JACOB, *who stands rigid.*) I can have what I've always wanted—more life, something going on, and a business of my own—and, Jacob, you don't know how, all my life, I've loved colors and stuffs! What I want is to make clothes for people that are well off and can have nice things. Just to handle the velvets and silks and the rich colors would make me happy! I can't say why it is—it seems foolish —but a color I like—some of these deep reds or purples, why, it'll almost bring tears to my eyes, looking at it, I enjoy it so! Why, Jacob—

JACOB (*harshly*). And how about me? (RACHEL *stops and looks at him in astonishment.*) How about me, I say? You're just planning to go off and leave me, then, as if—as if—

RACHEL. Why, Jacob! I never thought of your taking it that way! Why, surely—

JACOB. You never thought a thing about me. (*He walks up and down the room, in excitement.*) You just planned to leave me here, to go and leave me—when all my life's been spent for you—

RACHEL. For me! Jacob!

JACOB. Yes—for you! Why else do you think I've stayed here? Wasn't there other things I might have done? Do you think I haven't had any ambitions, too? Haven't I got a man's heart in me? Why do you think I've lived lonely here beside you?— Don't you know, Rachel?

RACHEL (*getting up, dropping things from her lap*). Jacob!

JACOB. Don't you know I've loved you all my life?

RACHEL (*gasping*). Jacob! And your brother hardly cold in his grave!

JACOB. Oh, Rachel! I loved you before he did! I thought you knew—I thought you knew! (*He comes slowly toward her. She moves away. He stops near her.*) I loved you before he ever saw you. All my life—all my life. Do you mean to say you never knew?

RACHEL (*harshly*). You're crazy.

JACOB. Am I, Rachel? Perhaps— To hear you say, so cold, that it was too bad I never married, so I wouldn't be alone now— Alone! Haven't I always been alone? How could I think of another woman after you? Yes, I know this wasn't the time to speak to you— but I couldn't help it— When you said that about going away, my heart seemed to burst. Rachel—oh, Rachel!

RACHEL. Jacob, you are stark, stark crazy. You're an old man, and I'm an old woman. It's awful, that's what it is—it's awful! Even if I hadn't just buried your brother—

JACOB. Oh, Rachel, that doesn't count. He had his life. But I've never had mine! And no more have you had yours— Rachel, you never rightly loved Daniel.

RACHEL. And you say that to me! Me that was a faithful and dutiful wife to your brother all his years! I won't talk to you!

(*Trembling, she takes off her apron and folds it and moves toward the door.*)

JACOB. Rachel, for God's sake, don't be angry. Try to understand.

RACHEL. I don't want to understand anything you say. You've gone plumb out of your head, that's what it is.

JACOB (*barring her way to the door*). Rachel, you must listen to me now, after all these years I've kept silent. You wouldn't believe all I've had in my heart for you—you can't ever know how I would have loved you! And it's never changed, Rachel—it's just the same to me now—I can't feel I'm old—I can't feel you are. There's no age to feelings. Don't throw away my love for you now, Rachel—don't scorn it. Let me go with you, wherever you're going, if you won't stay here with me! Take me with you, Rachel! I can't live without you.

RACHEL. Move out of my way, Jacob.

JACOB. No! Why do you act like this? Do you think it's wrong of me to love you? There's no law against our marrying, if—

RACHEL. Marrying! You're stark crazy!

JACOB. Yes, marrying. Why not? It's lawful. And I thought it would come natural enough us living so long under the same roof and you being used to me—Of course I know you don't feel as I do to you. But yet you was always fond of me—

RACHEL. I was fond of you as a brother, but now—

JACOB. Now what, Rachel?

RACHEL. Now it's best for us to part, as quickly as may be.

JACOB. No! I can't part from you. If I could've gone, years ago, I would. But I couldn't. And I stayed. And you never thought anything against my staying. And you took the work of my hands and the love of my heart—yes, even if you say you didn't know it, you took it! And now you owe me something, Rachel!

RACHEL. You have your half of the farm, Jacob. And if you want more, you can have all of it—

(JACOB *seizes her by the arms.*)

JACOB. No, you don't speak like that to me! That's too heartless—you know better. Oh, I know you're heartless, right enough! I haven't lived near you and watched you, and not know that, for all you're kind and do your duty! There's no love in your duty! But you can't speak so to me. You owe me some kindness, anyhow—

RACHEL. Let me go! I'm afraid to be here with you. I always knew there was something crazy about you— First you know, you'll be in the asylum—

JACOB (*releasing her and staggering away*). Yes, that's a true word you say. You can drive me to it. If you leave me—

RACHEL. Jacob, listen to me. I don't want to part with you like this, after all our years together. You've done for me, and I've done for you too, and we've lived peaceful. Years ago you'd have drunk yourself to death, if it hadn't been for me, and you know it.

JACOB. Better if I had.

RACHEL. Better to lie in a drunkard's grave! I saved you from that—and you've lived decent. Maybe you've had some crazy ideas, but you had sense enough to keep them to yourself. And you have sense enough now, Jacob, to see things must change. You must see I can't stay here— You take the farm and run it, or we'll sell it, just as you like—

JACOB. So you mean to go?

RACHEL. Why, of course I mean to go! I'm in prison here, I have been for years!

JACOB (*huskily*). Rachel, take me with you. I'll go wherever you want. I'll work for you—

RACHEL (*shrinking away*). Jacob, I can't do that. I'll just have a room somewhere at first, till I get started—

JACOB. I could be somewhere near you—

RACHEL (*bursting out*). No! Can't you see after what you've said it can't be? I wouldn't have an easy minute. Anybody that could have such an idea—you and me marrying—

(*She laughs nervously.*)

JACOB (*starting*). Don't laugh, Rachel!

RACHEL (*placatingly*). Well, it did sound so foolish—but I guess you were just scared of being left alone—you didn't really mean it, and now we'll forget all about that—

JACOB (*dully*). We'll forget—all—

RACHEL (*increasingly nervous*). That's right, Jacob, and we'll part good friends. Two old people like us, we can't be thinking of such things—

(*She laughs a little, hysterically.*)

JACOB (*turning on her, seizing her*). Don't laugh.

RACHEL. Oh, my God, he's crazy! Help! help!

(*She breaks from him, rushes to door.*)

JACOB (*staggering, grasps back of chair,*

panting). Rachel—I wouldn't hurt you—don't be frightened—my dear, my dear—I'd never hurt you—I'll never say any more— We'll just forget—forget—

(*Stumbles, sinks into chair by table, buries his head on his arms.*)

(*Knock at door.*)

RACHEL. Oh, thank God! Sarah! (*Pulls door open and throws herself into Sarah's arms.*) Oh, I thought you'd never come—

SARAH (*pushing* RACHEL *gently from door and closing it*). Why, of course I wouldn't leave you alone this night, you want a woman with you. And Jacob—ah, poor man, he's feeling it too—

RACHEL (*hurriedly*). Yes, Jacob's feeling bad. Take off your things, Sarah, come and warm yourself, it's so cold. (*Shivers, takes* SARAH'S *cloak and hood and lays them aside, both women stand by stove.*) Oh, Sarah, I'm so thankful you came—

SARAH. I know, I've been through it too. Rachel. (*Sighs.*) It's so lonesome at first, it seems as if you can't stand it— (JACOB *rises slowly without looking at the women, moves stiffly, takes gun and goes out door back.* RACHEL *starts and looks after him.*) But we have to live on, Rachel. You must bear up best you can. Poor Jacob! he seems to feel it terrible. No wonder, fond of Daniel as he was. A lonely man like him, it's hard to see changes. It's lucky for him he could have a home here with you all these years. There's not many would've put up with his queer ways, for all he

was so faithful, working year in, year out. You couldn't've kept up the farm without him, Rachel, Daniel being laid up the way he was— But now it's to be hoped you'll have a good rest, and a little peace and quiet, and well you've earned it— (*Report of a gun outside. Both the women spring up.*) What's that?

RACHEL. It's Jacob—he went out—look, he's taken the shotgun—

SARAH. What on earth is he doing with the shotgun?

RACHEL. It must be the fox—he was talking tonight about getting the fox—we've lost a lot of chickens lately— (*She goes to the window and pulls aside the curtains.*) I can't see him, Sarah!

SARAH. What's the matter, Rachel? Why, you're all trembling! Whatever is the matter?

RACHEL. I'm going out—

SARAH. What are you thinking of? Why, you're shaking so you can hardly stand! Here —let me go—

(*Catches up her cloak.* RACHEL *comes forward, catches back of chair, and leans on it. Exit* SARAH, *left.* RACHEL *leans heavily on chair, gasping.*

A cry outside, repeated nearer. SARAH *rushes in, dropping her cloak.*)

SARAH (*shrieking*). Down by the barn his head all blown to pieces—Rachel! Rachel!

(*She falls, catching* RACHEL *round the knees.* RACHEL *pulls away from her, clapping her hands to her ears.*)

CURTAIN

CAN YOU HEAR THEIR VOICES?

by Hallie Flanagan and Margaret Ellen Clifford

based on a story by Whittaker Chambers

CHARACTERS

JIM WARDELL
ANN WARDELL
JOHN WARDELL
SAM WARDELL
MORT DAVIS
SHAY
DRDLA
ROSE DRDLA
DOSCHER
MRS. DOSCHER
BEN DOSCHER
FRANK FRANCIS
HILDA FRANCIS
MARTIN
MRS. MARTIN
MARY MARTIN
PURCELL
RED CROSS WORKER
REPRESENTATIVE BAGEHEOT
HARRIET BAGEHEOT
BILL
FIRST BOY
FIRST GIRL
SECOND BOY
SECOND GIRL
THIRD BOY
THIRD GIRL
FOURTH BOY
FOURTH GIRL
A SENATOR
DOWAGERS
A YOUNG ATTACHÉ
A PAINTED WOMAN
A SECOND SENATOR
A FOREIGN AMBASSADOR

(*When the audience is seated, the stage lights and auditorium lights dim out, and the screen is lowered to position in darkness.*)

SLIDE 1

CAN YOU HEAR THEIR VOICES?

SLIDE 2

A Play of our time, based on a story by Whittaker Chambers in the *New Masses* for March, 1931; also on material appearing in the *Congressional Record, Time, The Literary Digest, The New Republic, The Nation, The Christian Century,* and *The New York Times.* Every episode in the play is factual.

SLIDE 3

Colonel Arthur Woods, Chairman of the President's Emergency Committee for Unemployment, reports to the Appropriations Committee of the Senate:

Total number of totally unemployed persons in the United States .... 4–5 millions
Approximate number of persons affected by unemployment .... 25 millions

Of the $2,500,000 to be expended for "Public or private construction" to aid this situation, 40% is still in the plan or contract stage. Machinery is set in operation, but in the meantime people are starving.

SLIDE 4

No nation has successfully solved the problem of the relation between agriculture and industry.

For ten years American farmers have been growing more and more desperate. The drought of 1930 coincided with the greatest business depression in our history. It made all agricultural problems acute. It demanded immediate measures for relief.

HALLIE FLANAGAN (1890–1969)

Animated by the desire to introduce her students to the latest techniques of the European avant garde, Hallie Ferguson Flanagan Davis founded the Vassar College Experimental Theater in 1925. In the 1920's and early 1930's this meant German Expressionism. Plays such as Georg Kaiser's *From Morn to Midnight* (1916) and Ernst Toller's *Man and the Masses* (1920) were to influence such promising American dramatists as Eugene O'Neill and Elmer Rice. (O'Neill, in fact, taught himself German in order to read these authors and his intellectual idol, Friedrich Nietzsche, in the original.)

In the same way, Flanagan was alert to the activities of the League of Workers' Theatres, which was then introducing Soviet agitprop (short for agitation and propaganda) plays to American audiences. Two such works, *Miners Are Striking* and *We Demand,* had recently appeared in New York when Flanagan determined that Vassar should present its own version of this special genre. *Can You Hear Their Voices?* (1931), which she dramatized in collaboration with her teaching assistant, Margaret

Margaret Ellen Clifford

COURTESY SOPHIA SMITH COLLECTION

Hallie Flanagan

Ellen Clifford, was to become America's third agitprop play.

Flanagan left Vassar in 1935 to become Director of the Federal Theatre Project. By that time the Vassar Experimental Theater had gone beyond agitprop to produce the American premiere of T. S. Eliot's *Sweeney Agonistes* (1933). As the result of that production, Eliot made his next play, *Murder in the Cathedral* (1935), available to the Federal Theatre, and it became one of the project's first successes. Flanagan's productions of the famed Living Newspaper, together with the epic achievements of Orson Welles, gave luster to the Federal Theatre's four years of existence.

When in 1939 Congress voted to discontinue funding for the project, Flanagan resumed her academic career, this time at Smith College.

On her own, Flanagan wrote several other plays, among them *The Curtain* and $E = mc^2$, and histories of both the Federal Theatre Project and the Vassar Experimental Theater. She was, as well, the first woman ever to receive a Guggenheim Fellowship.

Hallie Flanagan's career in dealing with both radical and conservative elements in the politically charged climate of her time reveals her to be not only a master of modern theatrical techniques but a consummate politician as well.

MARGARET ELLEN CLIFFORD (1908–1971)

Can You Hear Their Voices? was a unique experience for Margaret Ellen Clifford, who was mainly interested in children's theatre. At the age of fourteen she organized a troupe of underprivileged boys and girls in her hometown of Portland, Maine.

Following her undergraduate years at Vassar, Clifford went on to the University of Chicago for an M.A. in Drama. She returned to Portland for several years as Director of the Community Children's Theater. At the time of her death, Clifford was on the faculty at Skidmore College.

She had several published plays to her credit, including *The Secret of the Worn-Out Shoes* and *Sleeping Beauty*, both for children.

SLIDE 5

Among the worst sufferers were the farmers of Arkansas, Mississippi, Tennessee, Kentucky, Virginia and the Carolinas. Through these regions the drought stunted the corn, dried the alfalfa, and burned up the kitchen gardens. On August 8 the Department of Agriculture made a preliminary report showing that 1,000,000 farm families were seriously affected. On August 1, 1930, the Department of Agriculture reported a decrease of 690,000,000 bushels in the corn crop up to August 1.

Streams, wells, and ponds went dry. Mules and cattle starved in the fields. Over a hundred banks failed. 250,000,000 people were destitute.

SCENE 1: *The lights reveal the exterior of Wardell's house. On the steps is* FRANK FRANCIS, *a young farmer, slightly built, with a sensitive face. Leaning against the porch post is* DAVIS, *an older farmer.* ANN WARDELL, *wife of* JIM WARDELL, *is standing in the doorway.*

FRANK. It's like a fire. Everything burns up. Nothin' for the cattle to eat.

DAVIS (*with a drawl*). It's all on account of the sun. Ever notice it up there, Frank? Warms the earth, makes the farmer's crops grow, ripens the apple on the bough! Just now it looks like a red-hot silver cartwheel. Better take a look at it—it's the only cartwheel you'll see this year.

FRANK. My cow died this morning.

ANN. That's the third right around here this week. But you tell Hilda she ain't to worry about milk—we got plenty.

FRANK. That's awful kind of you, Mrs. Wardell.

DAVIS. The water'll go like the corn and the alfalfa. If there's anything left, that'll go too.

FRANK. By the time the snow comes we'll starve.

DAVIS. You got your gun, ain't you?

FRANK. Oh, you mean huntin'?

DAVIS. Yeah, I mean huntin', all right.

(WARDELL, *a quiet man with a kindly, humorous face and a suggestion of latent power, appears in the doorway.*)

DAVIS. Hello, Jim. Just come over to hear the speech over the radio.

WARDELL. Hello, Mort. 'Lo, Frank. Where's the rest of the boys?

DAVIS. They'll be along, glad of an excuse. Don't know what we'd do without the radio.

WARDELL. Best investment the crowd of us ever made.

FRANK. With all the crops burned up there's nothin' to do but sit around and listen to the radio.

(*The two Wardell boys have come around the house at the mention of the radio.* JOHN *is fourteen, a strong, sturdy-looking boy.* SAM *is twelve, slight and rather frail-looking.*)

SAM. We got Tyrone on the radio the other night, Frank.

JOHN. See the rattlesnake I killed, Mr. Davis? It's around here.

WARDELL. Shows what the drought's done. Snakes never come down out of the hills.

ANN. I remember when Purcell started his mines up there, the men drove the snakes down, but when he closed the mines they went back again.

DAVIS. Funny they stayed down here when Purcell was in the hills. I sh'd think Purcell must be right at home with snakes.

(DAVIS *and* WARDELL *laugh.*)

FRANK. What's wrong with Purcell? Nothin' wrong with Purcell. He's the big man in this town all right. I mean beyond he's a little hard-fisted.

DAVIS. You've only been here a year, Frank. You're a newcomer yet.

(*A balalaika is heard offstage.*)

That'll be Drdla. He's taken to playin' his queer Russian fiddle. Makes Rose mad as anything.

SAM. I like it. Why does it make Rose mad?

DAVIS. Well, Sam, Drdla is an old-fashioned Russian and his daughter is a new Russian an' that seems to make quite a lot of difference nowadays.

(DRDLA, *a tall, fine-looking Russian, enters with his daughter,* ROSE, *a handsome girl of about eighteen. With them are* SHAY, *a young man, and* DOSCHER, *a rather plaintive-looking man of middle age.*)

SHAY. 'Lo Jim. 'Lo Mort. Mornin', Mrs. Wardell.

ROSE. Heard you boys killed a rattler. My, ain't he a big one!

DOSCHER. Dead rattler's news these days.

ROSE. 'Lo Mrs. Wardell. We have it pretty easy now, ain't we? Nothin' to do but sit around. Where's Hilda, Frank?

FRANK. Tried to get her to bring the baby and come on over to listen to the radio.

ROSE. She's awful pretty with the baby, Frank. Like to hear her singin' to it.

FRANK. She ain't singin' much these days.

(*He goes back to the bench,* ROSE *with him, and the men gather around the snake, talking about the drought.* DRDLA *approaches* ANN *with a courtesy foreign to the other men.*)

DRDLA. Good day. God bless you. The others talk. I play.

ANN (*smiling*). You know I like your music better'n their talk.

(DRDLA *sits down and plays his balalaika softly through the ensuing scene.*)

DOSCHER. How long this weather goin' to last, Davis?

DAVIS. The papers don't tell you. They say there's hope.

SHAY. They've been sayin' that a long time. Besides, it don't make any difference now if it does rain. The corn's done for.

DOSCHER. What do you think, Davis, will the government help us?

DAVIS. What do you think the government'll do for you? Do you think you're the only poor farmer in the country? They's 100,000 of us, remember.

SHAY. I need cheerin', John. How about tunin' in on something?

JOHN. Sure.

(*He goes into the house.*)

DOSCHER. The banks'll have to give us some kind of loans.

WARDELL. The banks are just as bad off as we are.

SHAY. If the cows keep on dyin' they'll have to do something about milk.

FRANK. What about winter comin'? What are we goin' to do if there ain't any food? How we goin' to feed the babies?

DAVIS. Anyway, Frank, your cow's dead; you've got one less mouth to feed.

(*The men laugh.*)

ROSE. Aw, that ain't funny!

FRANK. A dead cow ain't no joke.

(*The men laugh again.*)

WARDELL. Well, the government ain't going to do anything, if you want to know. At least not until it's too late.

(*At this minute the radio, after some pre-*

liminary static, gets under way with jazz.)

DAVIS. Well, music! Ain't this gay?

SHAY. Feel like dancin', Rose?

ROSE. No. I'm gonna sit this out.

DAVIS. Try W. G. P. U.

JOHN *(appearing at the door)*. There's gonna be a talk on farm relief.

WARDELL. Well, I don't know any better place to turn that talk on.

DAVIS. Yes, I feel just like a good, heartnin' talk on farm relief.

> *(Through the ensuing scene* DOSCHER *and* DRDLA *listen as if to divine wisdom;* SHAY, FRANK, *and* ANN *eagerly, wanting to believe;* ROSE *skeptically;* WARDELL *and* DAVIS *with frank disbelief.)*

RADIO. Ladies and gentlemen of the radio audience: this program comes to you through the courtesy of U.S. Purse and Co., Fancy Groceries. Ladies and gentlemen, have you ever experienced that hollow feeling that comes over you in the middle of the morning?

DAVIS. Well, I hadn't thought of puttin' it just that way.

RADIO. When that happens, go to the Frigidaire and select from your store of Purse's delicacies a crisp hors d'oeuvre or a bottle of U.S. Purse's sparkling fruit punch.

SHAY. Rose, just trot in to the Frigidaire and bring me a crisp er derv.

> *(Everybody laughs.)*

RADIO. This morning we have a great treat for our radio audience. The fifth of the series of farm-relief talks will be given to you by Mr. Wilton Wordsworth of the business school of Carver University.

DAVIS. This is a treat!

RADIO. Mr. Wordsworth.

> *(Another voice says)*

Thank you, Mr. Smythe.

RADIO. Ladies and gentlemen of my radio audience: on this bright, sunny morning it seems malapropos to discuss so sad a subject as the great drought which is affecting our southern farmers. Yet so closely woven is the fabric of American life that what affects one affects all.

> *(DAVIS spits.)*

But we cannot allow ourselves to be caught in these crucial days by a feeling of panic.

> *(SHAY rubs his stomach.)*

DAVIS. A feelin' of panic, Shay?

RADIO. We must remember the old adage that it is always darkest before dawn. We are now, it is true, on the ebb tide, but the rising tide is gathering even as we speak: has not our Chief Executive recently said that he will call into conference on drought relief the governors of twelve western states?

DAVIS. Well, well.

RADIO. As our great national leader has well said: "Our problems are the problems of growth, not the problems of decay. The fundamental assets of the nation, the education, intelligence, virility, and spiritual strength of our 120,000,000 people have been unimpaired."

WARDELL. Anyway, Davis, we're unimpaired.

RADIO. Although on the surface it seems a curious paradox, is it not true, as our leading economists are pointing out, that the drought is really a blessing in disguise?

DAVIS. Well, I'm blessed.

ROSE. Guess we don't know when we're well off.

RADIO. How is it a blessing, my friends? It has done away with over-production in the rural areas.

WARDELL. It has done away with everything in the rural areas.

RADIO. It has sent up the price of corn on the stock exchange.

DAVIS. Did you clean up much on your last deal on the stock exchange, Wardell?

RADIO. What, after all, my friends, is a brief period of depression, in the history of our vast cavalcade of progress? After each depression of the past—and such depressions are only normal, my friends, have we not risen to a new high tide of prosperity? Prosperity is on the way! Let our motto be BUY NOW—

ROSE. Turn that damn thing off!

> *(JOHN goes in and the radio stops.)*

DOSCHER. Anyway, he's got a real nice voice.

> *(Everybody laughs.)*

WARDELL. I used to wish I could get a good education for my boys but this speech consoles me some.

SHAY *(returning to the subject uppermost in the minds of all)*. Well, whatever Mr. Wilton Wordsworth says over the radio, I notice they're stoppin' credit at the stores in town.

WARDELL. Think they'd give it all through

the winter? To all of us? They've got to make a livin' too.

DOSCHER. You mean there ain't goin' to be nothin' to eat?

WARDELL. There's plenty to eat in the stores in town. All you've gotta have is the money to buy it.

DAVIS. You can eat like a hog—if you're a storekeeper. We only grow the food—they sell it.

WARDELL. But as I haven't got the money to buy and neither have you—

FRANK. We'll starve.

DAVIS. Or take it.

(*There is a moment's silence. They are slow to get this. A shocked look comes slowly over their faces.*)

SHAY (*in an alarmed voice*). You mean you'd steal it?

DAVIS. I mean that when I'm hungry I like to eat. And when my wife and kids are hungry, I'm likely to take food. If that's stealin', then you can say I like to steal.

(*There is a silence.*)

FRANK (*militantly*). Well, I'll be goin' along.

(*He starts off, then turns and looks fixedly at* DAVIS *and* WARDELL.)

And I think all of us better be goin' along and not listenin' to this kind of talk.

SHAY. Frank's right. Come along, Doscher.

DOSCHER. Sure he's right.

(*They start out.*)

DAVIS. You're young, Frank. I felt that way once.

DOSCHER. Who's car is that?

DAVIS. Well, it's no farmer's tin lizzie.

SHAY. It's Purcell. What's the boss doin' down here?

DRDLA. He don't like us to stand around and talk.

DAVIS. Probably get out an injunction against our lookin' at a dead rattlesnake.

SHAY. It's his war trainin' makes him like that. Once a colonel always a colonel.

(PURCELL, *a heavy, prosperous-looking man, comes over to the group, which opens slowly.* FRANK, SHAY, DOSCHER *and* DRDLA *nod in somewhat awed and embarrassed greeting.*)

PURCELL. Well, boys, what's this? A meetin'?

DAVIS. Wardell's John killed a rattler in front of the house. The folks came over to see what a dead snake looks like. You like to see?

(PURCELL *walks up to the snake and looks at it idly. On the way he sees* ROSE.)

PURCELL. Well, Rose, gettin' to be a mighty fine lookin' girl, ain't you?

(*He runs his hand down her arm.*)

ROSE (*dangerously*). You keep your hands off me, you hear?

PURCELL. Spunk, eh? (*He winks at the men.*) I like spunk in horses and women. Well boys—(*He strolls over to* JOHN *and draws him down-stage.*) Nice work, John. When you see a snake, kill him. Ain't that right, Frank?

FRANK (*pleased at attention from the great man*). That's right.

WARDELL (*meaningly.*) The drouth killed it —like everything else.

PURCELL. This drought has been a lucky break for you, Wardell. You were runnin' low on your line of trouble talk when the drought —or "drouth" as you call it—(*He winks companionably at the men*) came along.

ANN. We'll call it what we like. It's our babies are dyin'.

WARDELL (*facing* PURCELL *and speaking quietly*). Some of us call it drouth, and some of us call it drought, but we all mean the same thing—we mean that the crops are done for, water and forage are dried up, the cattle are dyin', the banks are on the rocks. We mean we'll be needin' food when our credit gives out at the stores in town.

SHAY. You ought to be able to do something about that, Purcell, bein' President of the bank, and all.

PURCELL (*turning from* WARDELL *and keeping his good temper with an effort*). I realize you fellows are up against it. All of us are, for the matter of that. (WARDELL *laughs and turns away.*) We all have to stick it out together. To do you justice none of you ain't done much whinin' except Wardell here. The trouble with Wardell is that he spends too much time nights readin' those books he has in the house, and lookin' up the words in the dictionary. So he gets sleepy and sore at the world, don't you, Jim?

(*The two boys glower and draw closer to their father. The rest of the group relaxes its tension and smiles, being let in on a secret by the big boss. All except* ROSE *and* DAVIS *draw toward*

PURCELL *and away from the little group on the porch.*)

PURCELL. "Socialism, Utopian and Scientific." (*He laughs.*) Well, every man's got a right to read what he wants in his own house, I guess—if he don't try to force others to think his crazy ways too. (*He starts off, then turns back to them.*) If you get hungry, boys, and he tries to feed you Socialism, Yewtopian and Scientific, and you don't feel full, and I guess you won't, I think the Red Cross will do more for you.

DOSCHER. But the Red Cross won't help you unless you're starvin'.

PURCELL. Well, you wouldn't want to take help unless you were starvin', would you? None of us would. Well, so long, boys. So long, Jim. (*He waves and goes off.*)

(*The men emerge from their speechlessness and say: "The Red Cross." "They did fine work in the Mississippi flood —The Red Cross!—maybe the Red Cross'll help us out!"*)

WARDELL. (*facing them suddenly*). So! You're goin' to ask for charity?

DOSCHER. Rather take charity than steal.

DRDLA. Always there has been rich and poor. The rich must help the poor. That's the way things are.

ROSE. The way things are don't make 'em right!

SHAY. Charity—hell! We gotta right to live, ain't we?

WARDELL. Think it's goin' to get you any further in your right to live to let the Red Cross hand you out a plate of beans?

SHAY (*coming up and facing WARDELL antagonistically*). Well, what would you do?

WARDELL. Probably just what you'd do— take the beans. But first I'd like to try to make the government see—

DAVIS. Make the government see—don't make me laugh!

WARDELL (*turning from DAVIS and facing the crowd*). Then I'd like to try to make you see, all of you, that it ain't charity we want. It's justice. Where's the justice in the Red Cross buyin' Purcell's grain and milk and dealin' it out to us as charity?

DAVIS. It belongs to us, anyway.

SHAY. Whaddaya mean, it belongs to us?

WARDELL. Didn't Purcell make all his money off of us? Hasn't he gone on year after year gettin' richer on the work we do for him? Hasn't he bought up mortgages on our farms and then foreclosed when we couldn't make payments?

DAVIS. We produce and he eats.

FRANK. It ain't no good talkin' against Purcell. He's a smart man—he made this town —and he's hit by the depression just the same as anybody else.

DAVIS. Oh, he is, is he? Well, he yaps a lot about it, but I notice it don't affect the car he drives, the clothes he wears, or the food he eats. Maybe he had to take a few of his securities out of the bank—that'd be just too bad!

FRANK. Well, it's no good you and Wardell gettin' off any of your Socialistic talk here— what you want us to do? Have a revolution, like in Russia?

WARDELL. No, Frank, that's just what Davis and I want to prevent.

DAVIS. Speak for yourself, Jim.

(*Everyone in the group starts and looks at DAVIS. The two Wardell boys, who have been listening eagerly to all the discussion, draw toward their father.*)

SHAY. You mean you want a revolution?

DAVIS. I ain't sure I wouldn't just as leave die by violent as by natural causes.

DRDLA. What did the revolution do for Russia? Once people laughed in the fields. Everyone was gay. Now, people are hungry there. No one laughs any more.

ROSE (*fiercely*). I don't notice any of us splittin' our sides laughin'!

ANN (*motions indignantly to the boys, who come to her.*) Well, there's one thing I'm sure of. I don't want Sam or John to grow up in this kind of mess. I don't want 'em to be where we are.

SHAY. They're smart boys, Mrs. Wardell. They might get to where Purcell is.

WARDELL. I don't want 'em to get where Purcell is.

ANN. They ain't goin' to get nowhere through this kind of talk! This is the United States of America we live in, and we got a President and a Congress and a government to look after our interests, and I want my boys should respect that government and know that that government ain't goin' to let us down!

(*She goes into the house, taking the two boys. There is a pause.*)

SHAY. You're wife's right. We're just shootin' off our faces. We're all right.

DOSCHER. Sure we're all right. We got plenty of beans.

ROSE. Beans!

DRDLA. We're better off than if we had a revolution.

FRANK. Yes, Mrs. Wardell's right. The government won't let anything happen.

DAVIS. This is only August, Frank. Wait till January and see how you feel. Ever notice strikes and revolutions usually break out in winter time?

(*Black Out.*)

SCENE 2: *The lights go up revealing* CONGRESSMAN BAGEHEOT'S *breakfast room. The* CONGRESSMAN *is an attractive gentleman past middle age. He has finished breakfast and is absorbing the morning* Times. HARRIET, *his daughter, home from college for a week-end, enters. She is a clean-cut, good looking young woman who, in the manner of her generation, covers most of her convictions and ideas with a mask of flippancy.*

HARRIET. Good morning, darling. How are you this morning? Up late last night filibustering? Where's mother?

CONGRESSMAN. She's having her tray. What do you want, my dear?

HARRIET. I want two tremendous fried eggs immediately. I'm going to conquer a young man at golf this morning. What I'm having, however, is orange juice. Must do what we can for the figure.

(*She picks up the newspaper and scans the headlines.*)

H'm. Jimmie Walker again. One wing of the Fisher Body plant turned into a flop-house for the destitute.

(*She looks off into the distance.*)

That's not bad. "Bodies by Fisher." How respectable the New York Times is. Couldn't you start taking a few tabloids, Father—at least while I'm home for the week-end? Vice investigation continues—more drought suffering. Why don't they do something about the drought, Father?

CONGRESSMAN (*tolerantly*). What should you suggest doing, my dear? The bishops have prayed for rain, I believe.

HARRIET. I mean seriously, Father. The Red Cross is a fine, upstanding institution. Why don't you give it a break? If you'll excuse my saying so, the members of the respected body which you adorn are doing as fine a job as I've ever seen done in my life, of parking on their tails and doing absolutely nothing.

CONGRESSMAN. I'll excuse your saying so, my dear, because you don't know what you're talking about. Congress is a body of wise, elder men who have the country's good primarily at heart. It's true we're in the grip of a severe crisis, but just for that reason we have to proceed with caution. We can't rush headlong into things.

HARRIET. Well, personally, if I saw a guy starving I'd rush headlong for a loaf of bread.

CONGRESSMAN. Don't bother your pretty head about it, dear. It takes an economist to understand a crisis as wide in its national import as the drought.

HARRIET. They've got more sense in Russia. When the farmers go on the rocks there, they've got something solidly back of them— they don't have to sit around for the Red Cross to dish them out charity.

CONGRESSMAN. My dear child, what do you know about Russia? Who's been talking to you?

HARRIET. Come out of the fog, old dear. I'm one of the country's educated women. I go to college. I take a course in government and one in charities and corrections.

CONGRESSMAN. College professors—impractical dreamers! Can't even secure an adequate living wage. What do you think they know about world affairs?

HARRIET. I thought it showed a lovely spirit in a young woman to try to get the low-down on what the great ones of her father's profession were doing.

CONGRESSMAN. But my dear child, I didn't send you to college to acquire biased, radical ideas about Russia and collective farming.

HARRIET (*with a delightful smile but an edge of steel in her voice*). What did you send me for, darling?

CONGRESSMAN. Why, why—that is—of course—I wanted you to have the best education that money could buy. I wanted you to be as beautiful and cultured as your mother is—so that you could do the same credit to your—social position and family, and my name—or your husband's name—that your mother has always done.

HARRIET. You mean you wanted me to learn to be a lady?

CONGRESSMAN. Exactly.

HARRIET. They don't have those any more, dear. If that's what you wanted you should have sent me to one of those emporiums of culture for young ladies. There are a few of them, I believe, left over from the last century, tucked away in the hills.

CONGRESSMAN. Harriet!

HARRIET. I'll never be an ornament to society, father. You might as well give up the idea now. By the way, speaking of ornaments to society, mother said I was to chat with you about this burst of glory we're having on Christmas Eve, to introduce me to society.

CONGRESSMAN (*expanding with pride*). Yes! Well! Your mother and I have talked a good deal about it, and I told her I wanted to talk to you about it a little.

HARRIET. Sounds like a carnival, from what mother said. It's very white of you, father.

CONGRESSMAN. Well, my dear, we wanted our little girl to have the best of everything. Of course it's going to be rather expensive—those things get more and more expensive as people give more and more of them.

HARRIET. How much?

CONGRESSMAN. Well, I haven't figured exactly—I should say—upwards of two hundred and fifty thousand dollars.

HARRIET. Good God, where does it all go? I'm only a simple college girl.

CONGRESSMAN. We have been extremely fortunate in securing the Arden Park Hotel for that night and the services of Mr. Joseph Durban.

HARRIET. Durban? What's this going to be—a musical show? Doesn't the Arden Park satisfy you?

CONGRESSMAN. As a hotel, yes. On this occasion, no. Mr. Durban is going to do it over for your party, a temporary redesigning of the whole lower floor in silver and black. Then your mother will dress in black shot with silver, and you in silver shot with black.

HARRIET. Shot with black—God!

CONGRESSMAN. Mr. Durban sent the designs yesterday. I thought them a little extreme, but your mother liked them, and as she pointed out, I don't understand these things as she does.

HARRIET. Strikes me I'm nothing but the corpse.

CONGRESSMAN. You don't seem particularly pleased, Harriet. It isn't the attitude I should have expected from a young woman who is having everything done for her.

HARRIET. Well, frankly, I'm not turning handsprings. What do I get out of it? This Durban guy for a preposterous sum of money turns the lower floor of the Arden Park Hotel into a night club; you and mother glad-hand around with the legislative body and wives; there are pools of champagne in the corners and bathtubs full of hard liquor in the hall; attachés neck debutantes in the foyer; thousands of Harvard and Yale freshmen get drunk and I have to hold up one after another when they dance with me; a few horrid old fat men snuffle amorously down by neck; I get pulled and hauled and slapped on the back, and tossed from hand to hand like a bag of meal; somebody spills gin on my new dress and everybody steps on my feet, and what with too much liquor and caterer's lobster eaten at two in the morning, I'm sick the next day. Personally, the whole thing almost completely feeds me up.

CONGRESSMAN. But my dear, I thought you liked parties. You like to dance, don't you?

HARRIET. Sure, I love to dance. But you don't call that free-for-all, dancing, do you? I like cocktails, too, but I know when to stop, which is more than you can say for most of your friends. I like to go places with some of my friends, and I like to dance and I like to drink, and I like a little love-making—nicely done. But this organizing everything on an automobile factory basis—big business in the debutante world—I don't think it's so hot. Sorry to seem unappreciative, but I thought I'd better let you see how I felt before you went ahead and blew yourself on this Roman orgy.

CONGRESSMAN. I'm frank to say, Harriet, I'm very much surprised. I had hoped we were giving you something you would appreciate—would always remember. I understood from your mother that a girl's coming-out party was something she looked forward to all her girl-hood, and treasured the memory of all her life —like her wedding day. Why your mother has a scrap book with all the clippings relating to her coming-out party in it. She had more flowers than any debutante in town ever had.

HARRIET. Mother came out in 1900, father. An introduction to society meant an introduction to society, then. But I've smoked and drunk and necked with these same boys for five years—or others just like them. Where's the kick?

CONGRESSMAN. But, my dear, society demands of people in our position a certain formality, a certain duty in the graces of living . . .

HARRIET. The three graces—drinking, cursing, and necking . . .

CONGRESSMAN (rising, outraged). I'm very sorry, Harriet. If I had realized how you felt about it I should never have gone ahead with it. I'm frank to admit that your attitude still seems quite incomprehensible to me. I feel worried about the education you are getting. It's expensive enough, heaven knows. I should be disturbed if I thought that all you were getting out of it was to become maladjusted to the life you were born to. But to get back to the question of the party—considering your peculiarly unsympathetic attitude I should throw the whole thing over, but we can't—on account of your mother. She's importing a musical comedy troupe from New York by airplane. She's set her heart on it. Why, she gets almost as much pleasure out of it as if it were her coming-out party. We couldn't disappoint her like that.

HARRIET. Allowing for differences in phraseology, that's exactly what she said about you.

CONGRESSMAN. What? Oh, well, yes—doubtless she doesn't admit it to herself.

HARRIET (facing him, putting her hands on his shoulders, and looking squarely at him). Look here, father, if I have to set this in bigger type I will—doesn't it seem a little incongruous to be giving parties with the country in the state it is? With people standing in bread lines and dying of hunger? I don't suppose 250 thousand would be anything but a drop in the bucket, but it ought to feed a mouth here and there. Sounds like Louis XVI at Versailles to me.

CONGRESSMAN. On the contrary, my child, this is just another case of your inability to understand these great economic problems. While this depression affects us all, I feel that it would be selfish to retrench—the thing to do is to keep money in circulation—

(Black Out.)

In the darkness the screen is lowered to position and the following slides projected:

SLIDE 6

In the meantime, between August and November, the President's State Committees on Drought Relief were investigating. On October 20th they recommended to both Congressional Committees on Agriculture a $60,000,000 appropriation for farm loans. The Senate passed the bill, but the House Committee cut it to $30,000,000.

SLIDE 7

From early December until Christmas, Congress wrangled with the Administration as to the amount of money needed and its disposition. Should the money be loaned for tools, seed, fertilizer,—or should it include food for farmers?

SLIDE 8

The Senate insisted that since the money was a loan to farmers it should be used when necessary to keep them alive. The President, backed by a majority in the House, maintained that the money should not be used for food because this would constitute a dole. The farmers said, "Millions for mules but not a cent for humans."

(In darkness the screen is raised.)

SCENE 3: *The interior of FRANK'S kitchen. Evening late in autumn. HILDA, FRANK'S wife, a slight girl of about twenty, is pacing up and down with the baby in her arms. FRANK comes in and sits down. He puts his head in his hands. HILDA stands motionless with the baby in her arms. She looks at the baby, then at FRANK, turns and puts the baby down in the bunk, crosses to FRANK and stands by him awkwardly.*

HILDA (*touching his shoulder*). Don't.

(*He turns and puts his arms about her, and buries his head against her. They lean against each other and cry without making much sound. Then she wipes the back of her hand across her eyes and goes back to the bunk.* FRANK *gets control of himself. After a while she speaks.*)

Did you stop at Wardell's for the milk?

FRANK. Wardell'll be over with it after a while.

HILDA. You don't like Wardell, do you Frank?

FRANK. Wardell's a trouble maker, Hilda.

HILDA. He's kept the baby alive, 'till now.

FRANK. I'm afraid of Wardell. I'm afraid of all these queer ideas he's got. It was easy enough to answer all the things he said in the summer. Things weren't so bad then—we could sit around and listen to the radio. Now we ain't got that no more, there's nobody to tell us everything's alright and the government is going to help us out. It's hard to think straight when you're hungry.

(*There is a knock and* WARDELL *comes in.*)

HILDA. Did you bring the milk, Mr. Wardell?

(WARDELL *slowly shakes his head "no."* HILDA *makes a frightened movement toward* FRANK. WARDELL *goes up to* FRANK.)

WARDELL. Don't you think the time is comin', Frank, when poor farmers—people like you and me, and the Martins, and Doscher, and Drdla, will have to go and take the food and milk out of the store windows? There's plenty of it there.

FRANK. That's communism you're talkin' about.

WARDELL. Right now communism means free groceries to all poor farmers. No rent for two years, free seed, free milk for babies.

FRANK. You Reds want everything free.

(WARDELL *looks at them pityingly, then speaks with gravity.*)

WARDELL. You will, too, before the baby's dead.

HILDA. Frank!

WARDELL. I know what I'm tellin' him, Hilda. We're both tenant farmers. Both came from the same class, so there's no reproach in you takin' something from me when you need it. And there's no reproach meant in my tellin' you that your kid would be dead but for your gettin' the milk from my cow. You couldn't buy it—not from me—I wouldn't sell it to you—we need it too bad ourselves—and you couldn't buy it from Purcell because he would sell it to you, and you haven't the money to buy it. Well, my cow's dead. Now what do you think about having milk free?

FRANK (*dully*). Dead?

HILDA (*in a panic*). What are we going to do?

WARDELL. Some people come into communism through their minds and others through their bellies, but I guess most of 'em come in because they can't stand to see the folks they care about go hungry.

(*At this moment the door opens and* MRS. WARDELL *comes in, followed by* SAM *and* JOHN. *She is excited and breathing rapidly. She looks defiant. Three women are with her:* ROSE, MRS. DOSCHER, *a frightened, little woman, middle-aged, and* MRS. MARTIN, *a tall, raw-boned woman with a gaunt face.* MARY MARTIN, *seven years old, and two smaller Martin children huddle near the door.*)

ANN. We got you some milk after all, Hilda.

HILDA. Milk! God bless you, Mrs. Wardell.

MRS. MARTIN. Let's have a look at the baby.

MARY MARTIN. Yes, can we see the baby?

(*The women go over and look at the baby and exchange glances.*)

ANN. A funny God that brings babies into the world and takes away their mothers' milk and kills the cows that feed them.

WARDELL (*to* ANN). You bought milk at Purcell's.

ANN. Yes!

WARDELL (*quietly*). You got to stop. We ain't got the money. You got to think of your own boys.

SAM. We don't care, Pa.

JOHN. No, we ain't hungry.

ANN. You can't let a baby die.

(WARDELL *goes out without looking around.* FRANK *gets up slowly and goes after him.* SAM *and* JOHN *follow the men. The women and the little girls are left with* HILDA *and the baby.*)

MRS. MARTIN. Does the baby cry much?

HILDA. No.

(*There is a pause.*)

MRS. DOSCHER. Well, they say there's folks up the creek that's worse off than us.

ROSE (*with a hard laugh*). That make you feel any better, Mrs. Doscher? Well, it don't me. It don't seem to cheer me none, to think there's folks yonder in the woods eatin' roots.

MRS. DOSCHER. The thing I mind most is not havin' anything to do. Usually I'm cannin' way into November.

ROSE. I'll bet Purcell's cellar's full of fruit and vegetables. He had enough to get water from outside. If we was all, Purcell and all, workin' together on one big farm, like in Russia, we could a kept our gardens goin'. We could a kept our cows alive.

ANN. This ain't Russia. I been listenin' to this communist talk ever since I married Jim and it ain't never got us nowhere. The ideas of it are all right in some foreign country, but we got a government back of us.

MRS. DOSCHER. Men get a lot of comfort out of talkin' and it don't do them no harm.

ANN. It don't do us no good.

ROSE (*in a hard voice*). So you're goin' to let Hilda's baby die?

(*There is a startled silence.* MRS. DOSCHER *goes over and touches* HILDA *protectingly.*)

MRS. MARTIN. What can we do?

ROSE. We can take the men's guns and we can go to Purcell's, and take the milk.

(*There is a silence. The women draw back startled.*)

ANN (*after a pause*). I ain't goin'. I'd go without milk myself to give it to Hilda and I'd spend the last cent I got to buy it for her, but I ain't goin' to do nothing against the government!

(ANN *goes out.*)

MRS. MARTIN (*looking at her children*). I'll come with you, Rose.

(*She takes the children and goes out.*)

MRS. DOSCHER. Well, I won't go. What do you think I am, a thief?

ROSE. Lend me your husband's gun then, will you? Our farms are too near together. I can't stand hearin' your kids whine themselves to death.

(MRS. DOSCHER *starts to cry and goes out.* ROSE *goes out.* HILDA, *left alone, stands motionless. Then she goes over, takes the gun from behind the door and goes out.*)

(*Fade Out.*)

SCENE 4: *An alcove off the ballroom of the Arden Park Hotel in Washington, Christmas Eve. A flight of steps leads down from the ballroom. Silver and black. Artificiality. Jazz and high laughter. Girls' voices. The actors playing in this scene, as in the breakfast scene, should remember that they represent the upper classes. They should interpret the vulgarity of the lines with staccato brilliance. Four couples dance the climax of "Tiger Rag," ending in a whirl. They go off clapping. Boys and girls walk on lighting cigarettes.*

FIRST GIRL. It seems it was one of those parties where everybody jumps into the swimming pool with evening clothes on at five o'clock in the morning. Pool was strung with lanterns. Harriet said it was like animals led to the slaughter, and besides, she had on a new dress, and she was damned if she'd ruin it, what with the depression and all.

FIRST BOY. She's a high grade moron, but she's damn funny.

FIRST GIRL. What more do you want? She gives the town something to talk about, anyway, and that's a godsend—

(*The music starts "You're Driving Me Crazy." They dance off. Another couple comes on dancing. The boy sings with the music.*)

SECOND BOY. "My love for you makes everything hazy—"

(*They stop and indulge in a violent embrace. They emerge.*)

SECOND GIRL (*very blasé*). My God, my feet are tired!

(*She kicks off her shoes. They walk wearily over to the steps, sit down and embrace again. Enter another couple dancing.*)

THIRD BOY. Can't you Garbo-Gilbert somewhere else, children?

THIRD GIRL. Love may make things hazy for you, but we're all too clear-headed.

(*The two on the steps uncoil languidly.*)

SECOND BOY. May I suggest that the champagne is right around the corner. Possibly that would help you?

THIRD BOY (*fastidiously*). Speak to your girl friend, Lemuel. She takes things too seriously. My dear young lady, do you have to take off your shoes when you neck?

(*The* THIRD BOY *and* GIRL *go off. The* SECOND BOY *and* GIRL—*the embracing ones—straighten up, and the* BOY *lights the* GIRL *a cigarette. She strolls over in time to the music and steps into her slippers.*)

SECOND BOY (*listening to the music*). They're playing "Sweet and Hot"—that music calls me, Genevieve.

SECOND GIRL (*composedly*). Sir, you've been drinking. The name is Katharine.

SECOND BOY (*holding her off and looking at her*). Oh, well, you never can tell, can you? (*They start to dance.*) I've always had a bad memory for names. Katharine. It's written in fire on my heart.

SECOND GIRL. Written in lipstick on your shirt-front's more to the point.

(*They dance off. Enter two* DOWAGERS *with a* SENATOR, *the latter slightly tippled.*)

FIRST DOWAGER. I was saying to Mrs. Harkness, Senator—you'd never know she was Clarissa Bageheot's daughter.

SENATOR. S'a very pretty girl.

FIRST DOWAGER. Yes, but so reckless. A sort of brazen look. Same hair as Clarissa's, same eyes,—but the expression—I don't know what it is.

MRS. HARKNESS. I know what it is. It's too much drinking, if you ask me.

SENATOR. S'a very pretty girl, but she'll never be the girl her mother was.

FIRST DOWAGER. I should think the old Senator, Clarissa's father, must be turning in his grave. I wanted to slap her painted little face, and tell her she comes of some of the best blood in the country.

MRS. HARKNESS. And she behaves like a common street woman.

SENATOR. Take it from a man that knows horses, Mrs. Randall,—you can overbreed any stock.

(*They go off. Another dance starts and other people stroll on. A* SENATOR *and an* AMBASSADOR *enter.*)

SENATOR. Can you look at this scene, my friend, and doubt the prosperity of these United States?

AMBASSADOR. Yes, it is easy to shorten a dress, but not quite so easy to make it long. (*He points to the dancers.*) They must be prosperous to wipe the dust from the floor.

SENATOR. Where in this scene can you find the germs of revolution?

AMBASSADOR. You are right. It is as safe from revolution here as in my own country—in Spain.

(*They go off.*

Enter a PAINTED WOMAN *with a strident voice, speaking to a young* ATTACHÉ.*)

PAINTED WOMAN. Had the most awful day—Young Tom Farrel wanted me to have tea with him.

YOUNG ATTACHÉ. Farrel has all the luck.

PAINTED WOMAN. I told him I had a full day's work to get this aged frame ready for public inspection. I was three hours at the hairdresser's alone—talk about keeping body and soul together—I never have time to get as far as the soul!

YOUNG ATTACHÉ. It's not your soul I'm interested in, darling,—let's dance.

PAINTED WOMAN. Oh, you wicked boy!

(*They dance off to the music of "Mood Indigo" which continues through the following scene.* HARRIET *enters, dancing with a boy named* BILL.*)

HARRIET. God!

(*She sinks down on the steps.*)

BILL. I say, Harriet, why doesn't this barrage of elderly white elephants go home? They ought to be in bed. They've been blocking the traffic too long. I've had my elbow in three women's hair.

HARRIET. I've had my hand in four men's mouths.

BILL. Cigarette?

HARRIET. I think a drink would set me up more.

(*He goes out for a drink.* HARRIET *closes her eyes and proceeds to take a short nap.* BILL *comes back with a silver pitcher of champagne. She comes to and takes it.*)

HARRIET. A pitcher, b' God! (*She drinks.*)

I feel better. I feel that I am rapidly becoming drunk, and that I shall rapidly become drunker.

(BILL *has sunk, exhausted, onto the steps and is gloomily regarding his legs stuck out straight in front of him.*)

BILL. At this time of the night you have to be drunk or you go to sleep. I usually go to sleep anyway. Being drunk makes it easier.

HARRIET (*sentimentally*). We could have gone to a movie tonight, Bill.

BILL. And if we wanted to stay up all night we could have done it privately in a speak-easy or romantically on a hill-side.

HARRIET. And if anyone thinks I get any pleasure out of screaming into the leering faces of my mother's girlhood friends, they're crazy. I could have bitten the lorgnettes off the hatchet-face of that old Mrs. Harkness and chewed them up and swallowed them and never even felt it.

BILL. That's because your stomach's lined with good, hard liquor, dear.

HARRIET. Every Bageheot is either a gourmand or a drunkard, and I have to keep thin so I can wear this kind of dress. I wouldn't be surprised if I just dropped this dress somewhere. I have to keep checking up on myself to make sure it's still with me.

BILL (*still regarding his legs gloomily*). I don't think I'd notice if it fell off, myself.

HARRIET (*Her tone changing as she listens to the waves of shrill laughter from the ballroom*). Sometimes I get so fed up on this stuff I could scream.

(*Flippant and hard again.*)

William, I'm afraid I'm going to have one of those scenes where the poor little rich girl bares her heart to the thoughtless young man who does not understand. I'm going to tell you I wish I were a fish-wife—that you should marry me and we could go to Abyssinia and raise cockle-shells and start all over again—

BILL. Well, it's an interesting version of the old tale. I might ask the orchestra to put on "The Little Things in Life."

(*He starts to rise.*)

HARRIET. Don't bother. Or I might be a revolutionary—I look well in red—I might be pretty fascinating with a red flag around my brows and my arms thrust through an Internationale—what is an Internationale, Bill?

BILL. I don't know. Going Bolshevik, huh?

HARRIET (*bitterly*). Yeah. Parlor Bolshevik. (*As the music and drunken laughter reach a climax.*) Well, if we want the country to go Communist, carrying on stampedes like this one—

(*She waves her cigarette towards the ballroom.*)

—is the quickest and surest way to do it. If I were a dirt farmer, or a dirt farmer's woman, I know which side I'd be on.

(*The orchestra starts to play "Hello Beautiful." The* CONGRESSMAN *enters.*)

Well, let's get back to the carnage. Aha, here's the pillar of the State himself. Your health, Pillar!

CONGRESSMAN. Harriet, must you drink like a road-laborer? Really, my dear, at your own party. People are talking—

HARRIET. My, that must be a change.

CONGRESSMAN. It's one thing to take a quiet, ladylike cocktail, but champagne in pitchers—it's perverted!

HARRIET. Come, Father, when did you ever take a quiet, ladylike cocktail? The only reason you never drank champagne in pitchers is because you never thought of it. No, sir, you forget that this is something I've looked forward to all my girlhood, and am going to remember for the rest of my life! And boy, so is everyone else!

(*Another dance is over. People begin to come back.* COUPLES ONE, TWO *and* THREE *come in, also the* PAINTED WOMAN *and the* YOUNG ATTACHÉ. *A boy calls off-stage, "Paging* CONGRESSMAN BAGEHEOT." *"Telephone—Long Distance—*CONGRESSMAN BAGEHEOT." *The* CONGRESSMAN *goes out. There is a burst of laughter in the group around* HARRIET *who is on the steps. Somebody cries: "Speech! Speech!" She looks bewildered for a moment and then says:*)

Drink, please!

(*They shout approval and hand her the silver pitcher. She holds it in one hand during the following.*)

Listen! I've got something to tell you. Come here, everybody!

(*She is quite drunk now. They all gather around shouting, "Speech! Speech!"*)

FIRST YOUNG MAN. It's an announcement.

BILL. Who's the lucky man, Harriet?

HARRIET. No, there's nothing tender about this. I want to tell you something important. I want to tell you about the drought.

(*One of the men snatches the pitcher and drinks.*)

EVERYONE. Hurrah! The drought! Is there a drought?

HARRIET (*under the stress of terrific excitement*). There's a drought—In the United States—In the South. It's a terrible thing—It's killing the crops—It's making people hungry—It's making people thirsty—And you know what it is to be thirsty, my children!

(*Chorus of groans and cries of, "Give the girl a drink! Let's all have a drink!" HARRIET leaps to the top step and her voice crashes through their drunken laughter.*)

Well! We're the educated classes! We're the strength of the nation! What're we going to do about it? What're we going to do about the drought?

(*There is a moment of complete silence, then renewed hysteria. Everybody shouts, "Down with the drought!" The orchestra begins "Just a Gigolo." The lights dim to a flood of scarlet. Everyone except HARRIET begins to dance. She stands motionless, looking down at them. The jazz is muted and the dancers posture in strange, grotesque positions. Above the jazz a telephone conversation is heard.*

The CONGRESSMAN's voice comes from the general region of the ball scene, and the GOVERNOR's from the other side of the stage.)

CONGRESSMAN. Hello! Hello! Yes, this is October 1–9–1–7—yes, this is Congressman Bageheot.

GOVERNOR. This is the Governor speaking—Governor Lee.

CONGRESSMAN. Oh, yes, Governor.

GOVERNOR. I'm sorry to disturb you, Bageheot, but the fact is we're having some difficulty here. Central! Central! What's the matter with this connection? Why can't you give me a clear wire? Bageheot!

CONGRESSMAN. Yes.

GOVERNOR. That's better. I say we've had some trouble with the farmers. Because of the drought, you know—and the bank failures.

CONGRESSMAN. Oh, yes, the drought.

GOVERNOR. There's a good deal of talk about communism. A man named Wardell is something of a trouble maker.

CONGRESSMAN (*exploding*). A cheap demagogue! Trading on the sufferings of these poor farmers. They always come to the front at times like this.

GOVERNOR. He's just one of a good many in different districts. Even a very little relief—

CONGRESSMAN. What's that? Isn't your local Red Cross functioning?

GOVERNOR. It seems to be tied with orders from higher up.

CONGRESSMAN (*coldly*). Well, you know, Governor, I'm opposed to the dole. A few of our Senators seem willing to sacrifice principle to expediency, but I am not one of them. I am opposed to the dole. You know the situation in the House—you know where the President stands. The Red Cross exists to take care of just such situations.

GOVERNOR. Well, I don't want to be responsible—

CONGRESSMAN (*with irritation*). You really think it's serious, then? Well, I'll see what can be done. I'll appoint an investigating committee tomorrow. I'll send a notice to the press. Now if that's everything I'll ring off now. (*Self-consciously*). It's rather a gala night for us here.

GOVERNOR. Oh, yes,—your daughter—Mrs. Lee and I were so sorry—Please present my compliments—

CONGRESSMAN. Thank you, Governor, thank you. How is it down there—cold as it is here?

GOVERNOR (*His voice receding and dying*). Yes, very cold. We're having snow—

(*His voice dies away at the same moment that the dancing figures fade out.*)

(*Fade Out.*)

SCENE 5: FRANK's *kitchen, Christmas Eve. The scene opens in darkness. There is a woman's scream, instantly suppressed. Dim figures are revealed in the darkness; HILDA standing, and FRANK lying on the bench. Their movements cast gigantic shadows on the wall.*

FRANK (*startled*). What is it, Hil?

HILDA (*tonelessly*). Baby's dead.

FRANK (*in terror*). No. (*He leaps up. He listens for its breathing.*) I'll get someone—I'll get the doctor.

HILDA. What's the use of the doctor? He won't come now.

FRANK. He will!

HILDA. You can't get him in time.

FRANK. I'll go. I'll run.

HILDA. How can you run two miles through all this snow? You haven't even got shoes.

FRANK. I must go.

HILDA (*with finality*). Don't go. I know she's dead. (*She faces him fiercely.*) What do we mean bringin' a baby into the world when we can't even take care of it? What did we get married for? Folks like us haven't got no right to get married and have kids.

(FRANK *sits down at the table and sobs.* HILDA *looks at him and laughs hysterically.* FRANK, *goaded almost to madness, springs to his feet.*)

FRANK. Wardell killed her. She's never been right since he stopped the milk on her. The dirty, lousy Red! He did it! He killed her!

HILDA. Don't be a fool. He gave us the milk as long as his cow lived. And his wife bought milk for her as long as the money held out. She got us milk as long as there was any to get. Now there ain't none. I been to the Red Cross all day long. They say maybe tomorrow. Tomorrow!

FRANK. Then Purcell killed her—that's it. He moved all his cows where he could get more money for the milk. He killed her! Somebody killed her—God curse 'em!

HILDA. Don't be a fool. I killed her myself. Do you think I wanted to see her tortured to death by inches? I killed her—with the blanket.

(FRANK *shudders away from her.*)
(*Black Out.*)

SCENE 6: *Dawn of Christmas Day outside the local Red Cross Bureau.* FRANK *is standing, motionless, gun in hand. He is hard and desperate looking. All traces of boyishness are gone.* WARDELL *comes in right, followed by* DAVIS, SHAY, DRDLA, DOSCHER, ROSE, MRS. DOSCHER, MRS. WARDELL, *the two boys, and about ten others. They crowd about the entrance and there is confused talk.* ROSE, *in the center of the group, going from one to another, is easily seen to be leading the women.*

WARDELL (*speaking off-stage where there is a confused sound of voices*). No need your all comin'—a few of us can handle this! Then we'll all be needed to go to the stores.

(*He turns to the group.*)

I'm glad to see they're so few of us here.

ROSE. The rest are afraid, the cowards—

WARDELL. It means that only the most reliable and the most needy are here. It means that we can move together easier and have more confidence in each other.

DAVIS. We need a little confidence in something.

WARDELL. Frank, you've decided to come in with us?

FRANK (*in a hard tone*). I'm in with you.

WARDELL. Good.

ANN. How's the baby, Frank?

FRANK. The baby's—better.

WARDELL. I'm glad you women have brought your babies with you. It's another sign that you're not afraid, and it means that we'll not lose sight of why we're here and what we've decided to do, and why we're movin' from here on the town.

(*There is a murmur, partly of opposition.*)

DRDLA (*shaking his head*). There'll be trouble.

ROSE (*scornfully*). Go home if you're afraid.

WARDELL (*his voice gaining firmness*). Because we're movin' on the town next. We're starvin' and we're goin' to the town to get food.

(*At this moment* ANN *forces her way fiercely through the crowd, drawing the boys with her. She faces* ROSE *and* WARDELL.)

ANN. But first we're goin' to give the Red Cross another chance to help us out!

WARDELL. Best you should keep out of this, Ann. We're here to take the food.

ANN. I say we're givin' the Red Cross one more chance—

ROSE. And you know how they're takin' that chance, Ann Wardell! You know Purcell promised us Red Cross help way back in August and here it is Christmas Day. Christmas Day! You know we been hangin' round here for three weeks signin' blanks to get a mean little drizzle of beans and bread.

DOSCHER. Well, we ain't as bad off as they are in factory towns at that. Look at Detroit.

MRS. DOSCHER. The Red Cross doin' the best they can.

(ROSE *laughs.*)

WARDELL. You're right, Ann, it ain't the fault of the Red Cross; they got to take orders from higher up. But no matter whose fault it is, we've stopped askin'. From now on, we're takin'.

ANN. I say we're givin' the Red Cross one more chance.

ROSE (*laughs*). One more chance! That's a good one! All the kids in this town got rickets and all the sick and old folks has died, and you talk about one more chance. Well, I'll tell you how they'll take their chance. First they'll ask us to prove that we're not impostors. That's what they're callin' some of us now. They'll tell us to prove that we're starvin'.

(*She laughs.*)

Well, can you prove it?

(*The murmur throughout the crowd grows to an ominous roar.*)

Then when we've proved we're starvin', I'll tell you what they'll give us.

ANN. How do you know what they'll give us?

ROSE. How do I know? Because I ain't got no way of tellin' what's going to happen except by lookin' at what has! What have they give us in the past? One loaf of bread, not one apiece, but one to a family—one bag of flour —same! Maybe some bacon.

MRS. MARTIN. How much milk?

ROSE. Enough for two days.

MRS. MARTIN. What good does two days do? We had a day's before and we made it last three. Now if they give us two days' and we make it last five, what'll we do when it's gone?

ROSE. It's the same with all relief.

WARDELL. It's the same with all charity.

FRANK (*menacingly*). We don't want charity.

ROSE. There's food enough in here and in the stores in town to last till Spring. The thing to do is to force them to give it to us. How many of you got guns?

(*Murmurs from the crowd, some excited, some in opposition.*)

DAVIS. We got guns and we know how to use 'em.

DRDLA. Rose—Rose . . .

WARDELL. Wait a minute, Rose. Wait a minute, Mort. You've got to be careful not to use your guns unless somebody starts shootin' at you first.

ROSE (*enraged*). There you go, Jim Wardell —tellin' 'em to be careful when what we ought to do is put some guts in 'em.

ANN. We don't want shootin'!

DAVIS. This ain't no time to be careful.

WARDELL. I'll tell you why we got to be careful. If we start fightin' they can call in the police and we'll be outnumbered ten to one, and those of us that ain't killed that way—they can shoot us, you see, because they'd be "in defense of their duty"—will land in the pen— and our children will be hungry just the same —but there'll be nobody to get 'em food.

ROSE (*still angry*). You're yellow, Jim Wardell! If I could put a bullet through Purcell I'd go to jail happy!

(*Some of the men shout approval.*)

WARDELL (*his voice lashing the whole crowd into attention*). Don't you see, Rose, it ain't Purcell that's wrong. It's the plan we live under: it's the whole system. Listen! Maybe I think, like you, that there'll come a time when there'll be shootin'. But today ain't the time. Maybe there'll come a time when we can stand our feet like free men instead of crawlin' on our bellies askin' for help. But that time ain't come yet. Some of us believe in a time comin' when everybody will have to work, and there'll be enough work for everybody. Some of us believe that the land and the crops and the cattle and the factories belong to the men that work 'em. But we ain't strong enough yet to take 'em. And that's why some of us think it's more important to work for that time than to shoot up a few rich guys now.

(*At this moment there is a murmur in the crowd offstage. PURCELL comes through the crowd with a woman, a Red Cross worker, who has a kind, troubled face. The crowd makes way for her respectfully, but regards PUR-CELL with suspicion.*)

PURCELL. Another meetin', I see. Wardell,

you've taken strong to public speaking, ain't you?

(WARDELL *looks at him, does not reply, does not retreat.*)

RED CROSS WORKER. You're here early, Mrs. Doscher. Good morning, Mrs. Wardell.

(*The women murmur, "Good morning." There is a dead silence as* PURCELL *and the woman go up and unlock the door.*)

PURCELL (*turning and facing the crowd*). I'm glad to see you're behaving in an orderly way. Everything will be attended to if you just keep quiet and decent.

(*They go in and shut the door.*)

ROSE. Quiet and decent! Starve and be quiet and decent about it or you'll go to jail and rot!

PURCELL *opens the doors and appears with a paper in his hand.*) I've got the names of those who signed blanks yesterday and didn't get food because it gave out before we got to 'em. (*Reading.*) Rose Drdla—wouldn't forget you, Rose—

ROSE. Bah!

(*The men murmur ominously as* PURCELL *continues to read.*)

Frank Francis, Jim Wardell, Higgins, Carrillo, Gombos, Wells, Sitka—that's all for today.

CROWD. What's that? How about us. We'll signs blanks!

WARDELL. What you mean, Purcell? We're ready to sign blanks.

PURCELL (*nervously*). Now I got to ask you to co-operate with us in this. You see—

ROSE. Don't you tell us the food's give out. We know it ain't!

PURCELL. No, the food ain't give out. But the blanks have.

(*A moment's silence.*)

WARDELL. Just what do you mean, Purcell?

PURCELL. You know we got orders not to give out food to anyone who doesn't sign a blank for it. Well, all the blanks have run out and I can't give out no more food until a new lot of blanks come from Washington.

(*A stunned silence.*)

ROSE. Well, what do you say to that, Ann Wardell?

SHAY. When'll the blanks get here?

PURCELL. Well, we can't tell. Maybe by tomorrow.

ROSE. And you think we're going to sit around and sing hymns till then, do you? We came here for food.

DAVIS. Yes, and we're takin' what we came for.

WARDELL. What you givin' us?

(*The men surge up around* PURCELL.)

PURCELL. I don't know that we're goin' to give you anything. At least till you put those guns down. I'm chairman of the Red Cross and I'm not takin' orders here. I'm givin' 'em.

(*The men laugh and their laughter is not pleasant to hear.*)

You'll get food when the blanks come and not a second sooner. This place is closed. Get out!

(*He goes in and bangs the door.*)

ROSE. Closed! The hell it is! (*She turns to the mob.*) Did you say your kids was dyin'? Come on!

(*Gun in hand she throws herself against the door.* WARDELL *and* DAVIS *are with her. Most of the men and women surge after her shouting.* ANN *tries to hold the two boys back but they follow their father.* DRDLA *remains wringing his hands. The door gives and the crowd rushes in and there is a struggle. The Red Cross worker emerges. She looks ill and frightened, and* PURCELL, *his coat half torn off, is white with rage.* FRANK *comes after him, a fanatic look in his face.*)

PURCELL. It's all the work of that lousy Red!

FRANK. It ain't food I come here for.

(*He turns and summons the crowd who spill out of the store in response to the madness in his voice.*)

You see that man? He ain't a man—he's a murderer. He's a rattlesnake—that's what he is, a rattlesnake, he and the rest of the ones on top!

(*He fires at* PURCELL *and misses him. The men surround him and take his gun.*)

PURCELL. Well, I'm damned! Tried to kill me, the little shrimp. I'll have you all jailed if it's the last thing I do!

(*He goes out. The men, silent and motionless, watch him.*)

(*Fade Out.*)

SCENE 7: *Christmas Night, outside* WARDELL'S *house. It is very dark.* DAVIS *comes in and goes up to the house.*

DAVIS (*in a low voice*). Jim.
WARDELL (*inside*). That you, Mort?
DAVIS. Come out, will you?
   (WARDELL *comes out.*)
WARDELL. Anything new?
DAVIS. State troopers on the way. We'll be under arrest by mornin'.
WARDELL. I know. Ann and I been talkin'. We're sendin' the boys away.
DAVIS. Is Ann willin'?
WARDELL. There ain't anything else she can do. They can hitch hike out over the north road.
DAVIS. They're pretty small for that.
WARDELL. Think I don't know that? What is there for them to do here? Fightin' for food, goin' to jail.
   (*The door opens and* ANN *comes out followed by the two boys. Their faces look white and frightened in the dim light. They have small bundles on sticks over their shoulders.*)
ANN (*in a hard, dead voice*). They're ready, Jim.
SAM (*suddenly*). Oh, Ma, I don't wanta go.
ANN (*still hard*). You'll be all right. Anybody see two boys alone like that'll take you in and maybe even feed you.
WARDELL. You can hitch hike it as far as Tyrone and then you go straight to communist headquarters and tell 'em Jim Wardell sent you. They'll take care of you. And John, you remember all you're to say to 'em?
JOHN (*as if reciting from memory*). I'm to say that things have gone too far and that you're organizing, that you may be sent to jail, and that the comrades here need help.
WARDELL. That's right.
ANN (*suddenly, desperately*). You boys'll stick together, won't you? You'll try to get jobs and stick together?
SAM. Yes, Ma, we'll stick together—
JOHN. We'll come back in the spring, Ma.
ANN. Yes, in the spring.
   (*They start off. Suddenly* WARDELL *goes after them.*)
WARDELL. Try to remember all you've seen here, boys. Try to remember it and understand it. Remember that every man, every man, mind you, ought to have a right to work and eat. Every man ought to have the right to think things out for himself. Listen to everything, look at everything, and decide for yourselves. Then see if you can't help make a better kind of world for kids to live in.
JOHN. Yes, Pa.
SAM. We'll come back in the spring.
   (*The boys go off.* WARDELL *and* ANN *stand looking at them.*)
WARDELL (*as if the cry is forced out of him*). Try to remember.
BOYS' VOICES (*faintly*). We'll remember.
ANN. Can you—hear their voices?
   (*Fade Out.*)

   (*In the darkness the screen is lowered.*)

SLIDE 9

These boys are symbols of thousands of our people who are turning somewhere for leaders. Will it be to the educated minority?

AUF WIEDERSEHEN

by Sada Cowan

CHARACTERS

FRAU FRIEDA NEUBERG, *an attractive Jewish woman, of 38 to 40. She is refined, well educated, and lovable, with none of the objectionable characteristics sometimes portrayed. She is dark and handsome, with a slender, wiry figure.*

ELSA, *a blonde Christian girl of about 15, well educated and refined.*

HARTWIG, *Elsa's brother, a trifle older, about 19.*

LEVINSKI, *an old Orthodox Jew, of lower class. He is bearded, and none too tidy. He could be from 40 to 55.*

JOHANN, *a boy of the same age as Hartwig. He is of military bearing.*

A SOLDIER, *typical militarist.*

SCENE: Living quarters of Frau Neuberg's trousseau shop, Germany.
TIME: The present. Afternoon.

The room is a sitting room, simply and stiffly furnished with horsehair furniture, tidies on the chairs, and various bits of German pottery and Dresden china in what-nots. There is a large window at the back, draped with crisp white curtains, a door left leading to the outside, and a door right leading into the bedrooms. On various tables and chairs are bags and large wicker hampers in the process of being packed.

At the rise of the curtain, ELSA, *a girl of about fifteen, blonde, fresh-looking and pretty, is busily packing. She is humming gaily as she folds different pieces of wearing apparel and puts them in the bags.*

FRIEDA, *a Jewish woman of thirty-eight*

or forty, enters. She is simple and direct in her manner, and has a face of great character.

FRIEDA. The Baroness ordered a dozen more linen sheets to be embroidered with crown and monogram.

(FRIEDA *sits and picks up a dress which is almost completed, and starts sewing.*)

ELSA (*folding clothes*). Oh, how lovely! I wish Baronesses would get married every day.

FRIEDA (*smiling*). So do some of the Baronesses. Come here, dear. (ELSA *does so.*) Let me see if this wristband is tight enough.

(*She measures* ELSA'S *wrist with the dress on which she is sewing.*)

ELSA. You've such a lot to do, Aunt Frieda; you ought not to be sewing for me.

FRIEDA (*releases her, and she goes back to her packing*). Aren't you packing for me?

ELSA (*holding up frock*). Do you think you'll use this on the steamer or . . .

FRIEDA (*quietly*). No, I won't need it.

ELSA. Then it can go down in the . . . what do you call it . . . the hold. I'll put it in here.

(*She packs it into a case.*)

FRIEDA. That's right.

ELSA (*packing, very gaily*). It doesn't seem to me you are taking enough warm things. New York is very cold in winter, they say.

FRIEDA. I can get everything I need after I get there.

ELSA. Why don't you smile when you say that? If I were going, I'd be dancing with joy all over the place.

FRIEDA (*not convincingly*). Oh, I'm delighted to be going.

ELSA (*dreamily*). New York, with Aunt Emma and Uncle Charlie . . . Oh!

FRIEDA (*as before*). It's going to be just lovely.

SADA COWAN (1883–1943)

Long before Great Britain and its allies declared war on the Axis powers in 1939, many Americans could see that Hitler's dictatorship had cast a dark pall across the face of Europe. Anti-Semitism had become the official government policy in Germany by 1934. Liberals and radicals alike in this country held that any group persecuted by the Third Reich—be it Communist, Socialist, Catholic, or Jewish—was worthy of their support.

A spate of anti-Nazi plays appeared before 1939. Six of these plays were anthologized by Stephen Moore, who described them as an attempt "to calmly and dispassionately present the fear, terror and ruthlessness as exercised by the Nazis on the great mass of German people today." Like Sada Cowan's *Auf Wiedersehen* (1937), these plays were neither calm nor dispassionate. Their authors utilized the strategies of classic horror tales in an attempt to rouse their fellow countrymen to take up the cause of a people without hope.

Cowan's earlier plays, although not about political atrocities, still exhibited a pre-occupation with the grotesque and supernatural. *In the Morgue* (1920) was as chilling as its title, and her very first play, *Sintram of Skagerrak* (1917), introduces the themes of violence and unnatural death in a Germanic setting.

This affinity for and revulsion at things German seems to have entered Cowan's private consciousness long before the advent of the Nazis. At the age of fifteen she left her home in Boston to study music in Frankfort. It was an unsettling experience, and she soon left. Although written many years later, *Sintram of Skagerrak* is said to have been inspired by a piano recital she attended in Frankfort.

Whether a similar inspiration was responsible for *The State Forbids, The Investigation,* or any of her other titles is unknown. In time, however, she discovered that motion pictures were the natural outlet for her peculiar talents, and aside from an occasional return to the stage, the bulk of Cowan's professional life was spent as a Hollywood screenwriter.

ELSA (*going to* FRIEDA). Aunt Frieda, tell me something.

FRIEDA. Yes, child?

ELSA. You're going to America because you really want to, aren't you? Not because you have to on account of . . .

FRIEDA. O dear, no! The Nazi have nothing to do with my going. I've really wanted to for a long time and this is such a splendid opportunity.

ELSA (*dropping on her knees beside* FRIEDA). I'm not sure, Aunt Frieda, and I want to be sure. I couldn't bear to think of you way over there, lonely, longing for us . . .

FRIEDA (*smiling*). Don't you want me to miss you and Hartwig?

ELSA. Of course. But not too much.

FRIEDA. I see, just a little. Like when I see a pretty bit of material that might make you a dress, or a necktie for Hartwig.

(*For a moment she can hardly bear the thought of leaving.*)

ELSA. And you won't stay long, will you?

FRIEDA (*with meaning*). Not longer than I have to. But don't you worry. Frau Hahn will take the best of care of you both.

ELSA. It isn't that. (*Impetuously she throws her arms around the woman.*) I love you. You've been just like a mother to Hartwig and me.

FRIEDA (*staring ahead, caressing the girl*). A hen that raised two goslings, two little Christian chicks with a Jewish mother.

ELSA. But we're just the same. Jews and Gentiles are all alike.

FRIEDA. They used to be, when your mother and I kept this shop while our men went to war . . . when they didn't come back. She and I were like sisters.

ELSA. Of course, I don't remember mother, but I'm sure she couldn't have been any better to us than you have been.

FRIEDA (*affectionately*). Liebchen!

ELSA. I'm so glad she gave us to you to raise.

FRIEDA. I'm glad, too. (*Then suddenly very*

serious.) But it would have been better if it had been one of your own people.

ELSA. Why do you say a thing like that? Race doesn't make any difference. Nobody thought a thing about it until all this fuss started.

FRIEDA (*abruptly*). Get up off your knees, child. You'll get your stockings dusty. (ELSA *rises and brushes off her white stockings.* FRIEDA *is much troubled by the conversation, but tries to throw it off.*) I wonder what's keeping Hartwig so long.

ELSA. He probably had to wait. There has been a big crowd down there every day getting their passports viséed.

FRIEDA. Yes, so many of my people are going. (*She catches herself and forces a gay note into her voice.*) It will be nice to have friends on board.

ELSA (*encouragingly*). And you can play pinochle with Frau Hammer.

FRIEDA. Yes. And Friday nights Herr Hammer can make Shabbos. It won't be like being away from home at all. (*She sews rapidly to keep from breaking down.*) Elsa, I want you to promise me that while I'm in America you'll work hard and get ahead with your studies so that . . . (*Her voice catches.*) by the time I come back you'll . . .

ELSA. I'll do everything I can to make you proud of me. I promise. So will Hartwig.

FRIEDA. I'm proud of him now. Why, just the other day Herr Folger told me he had never had so clever an apprentice. (*Thinks.*) I hope Hartwig stays with him for years and years. He might develop into a great goldsmith, a real artist like Leonardo da Vinci used to be or . . . (*Abruptly she rises and walks to the window.*) If Hartwig doesn't come soon he'll be late for the picnic. What time are the boys coming for him?

ELSA. At two.

FRIEDA. I shouldn't have sent him to the Rathaus. I should have gone myself.

(*She watches for him out the window. As she stands there, the sound of hammering is heard outside.*)

ELSA (*leaving her packing*). I'll run next door and see if your shoes are ready.

FRIEDA. Thanks, dear. And bring some apples for Hartwig to take with him.

ELSA (*starts, then stops near the window*). What's the hammering?

FRIEDA. Nothing, dear.

ELSA (*looking out*). Oh! The Nazi are putting a sign on Levinski's shop.

FRIEDA (*looking out*). Yes, a boycott! Herr Gott! Will they never stop!

ELSA. I suppose we'll be the next.

FRIEDA. Oh, no. They know I'm going away, and they wouldn't do that to Frau Hahn. You see, it's really a very good thing she is taking over the shop. Yes, everything is working out for the best. (*Then abruptly.*) Run along, child. Get the apples for Hartwig.

ELSA. Yes, Aunt Frieda. (ELSA *goes. As she reaches the outer room, the sound is heard of a door opening and closing. Her voice is heard off stage.*) Thought *you'd* gone to America! You've been an age!

HARTWIG (*off stage*). Terrible crowd there.

(HARTWIG *enters. He is a boy of eighteen, tall, strong, blond, good-looking. At present he is very much downcast.*)

FRIEDA (*as* HARTWIG *enters*). Well! I'm glad you're back. I was worried for fear the boys would come and you'd be late for the picnic. Better hurry and wash up a little. (HARTWIG *is crossing the room very slowly, the picture of desolation, his head low, his hands thrust deep into his pockets.*) Did you have any trouble with my visé? (*She watches him, and senses that something is wrong.*) What's wrong, Hartwig?

(*She crosses to him.*)

HARTWIG. Nothing.

FRIEDA. But there is. (*She tries to force a smile.*) You can't fool me. I've known you too long. Anything go wrong at the shop? (*No answer.*) Something did. You haven't done anything to displease Herr Folger, have you.

HARTWIG (*turning to her, still disconsolate*). Yes, and no. (*Drops into a chair.*) That is, nothing I can help. (*Pause.*) I'd rather not talk about it, if you don't mind.

FRIEDA. But I do mind. Remember, I'm going away tomorrow and I can't go with anything on my mind, troubling me. You'd better tell me, dear.

HARTWIG. Well, if you must know, I've lost my job.

FRIEDA (*aghast*). You've . . . ? No, it isn't possible. Why, only the other day Herr Folger told me . . .

HARTWIG. I know. It has nothing to do with

him. He can't help it, and it's no fault of mine. It's a new edict, that's all.

FRIEDA. I see! More persecution! (*Pause.*) But you're not a Jew! (*He glances up swiftly, not wishing to hurt her but hoping she will understand. She does.*) It's because you are living in the same house with one. Is that it? Tell me, Hartwig. You *must* tell me.

HARTWIG. Oh, don't ask me, Aunt Frieda.

FRIEDA. That's it. Of course that's it. But darling, why didn't you tell them that your Aunt Frieda wouldn't be in your way much longer? Why didn't you tell them that I'm sailing the day after tomorrow, and that I'm leaving for good?

HARTWIG (*loath to say what he must*). You're not leaving, Aunt Frieda.

FRIEDA. I'm not leav . . .

(*She pauses, dumbfounded. He shakes his head.*)

HARTWIG. They are not issuing any more visés to Jews. (*He tries to smile.*) I'm sorry if you're disappointed. But I'm glad, really I am. It means you will stay right here with us.

FRIEDA. It's impossible. You can't mean what you're saying. I'm not to go . . . they won't let me . . .

HARTWIG (*putting an arm around her affectionately*). You're staying right here with us. Now, tell the truth, aren't you glad, honestly?

FRIEDA (*letting herself go, almost gaily*). Yes. Yes I didn't want to go away. I just thought it was best. But now they won't let me. (*Suddenly her mood changes. She moves away from the boy.*) But no. It's impossible for me to stay with you two children. Can't you see what it would do? Through me, you've even lost your job. But I can send you to live with someone else, then you'll be all right. Herr Folger would give you back your job then.

HARTWIG. He can't, unless I join the Nazi.

FRIEDA. Oh!

HARTWIG. Of course I can't do that. But I'm all mixed up. I don't know what to do. All the boys belong. Johann has been made a captain. He keeps at me to join.

FRIEDA. I see.

HARTWIG. Honest, Aunt Frieda, I don't know. I love Germany just as much as they do. I want to see her on her feet again, fine, strong, proud as we used to be.

FRIEDA. But darling, it's not the Jews who are hurting Germany.

HARTWIG. Of course it's not Jews like you, Aunt Frieda, but most of them aren't like you. They are like Levinski, and Grunebaum, and . . . you haven't been listening, as I have, to the speeches at the meetings . . .

FRIEDA. So you've been going to the meetings?

HARTWIG. Yes.

FRIEDA. I see. And you'd join if it weren't for me, wouldn't you? (*As he does not answer, she asks with more insistence.*) Wouldn't you?

HARTWIG. Well, maybe. I've got to think of my future, and of Elsa's. Somehow I've got to get work; and you know as well as I do there is only one way I can get it. (*Comes closer to her.*) Don't feel bad about it. I don't want to hurt you, but . . .

FRIEDA. I'm not hurt. I understand. You'll join the Nazi. Of course, you'll have to join.

HARTWIG. No, I won't. I'll stick to you, Aunt Frieda, honest. I was just thinking about it.

(*The clock strikes two.*)

FRIEDA (*pretending to toss the whole thing off*). The boys will be here any minute. You'll find a box of lunch all done up, on top of the ice box.

HARTWIG. Great! (*Rises.*) Did you put in some of your apfelkuchen?

FRIEDA. Yes, a whole one.

(*HARTWIG starts for the door. Outside, a street commotion is heard. HARTWIG turns back and steps to the window.*)

HARTWIG. There's a crowd gathering outside of Levinski's. Wonder what's going on!

FRIEDA. Possibly he is objecting to the boycott sign they put on his place.

HARTWIG. Pretty dangerous to object to anything the Nazi do.

FRIEDA (*half to herself*). Yes.

(*ELSA enters with a pair of shoes wrapped in a newspaper.*)

ELSA. There's an awful crowd outside. I could hardly get through. (*Hands package to FRIEDA.*) Here are your shoes, Aunt Frieda.

FRIEDA. Thanks, dear. And the apples for Hartwig? Did you forget them?

ELSA (*confused, on the verge of tears*). No, I didn't forget.

(*The noise from the street grows louder. HARTWIG enters with his lunch neatly done up in a newspaper.*)

HARTWIG. What's going on out there?

ELSA. A row over at Levinski's. A fight, I think. His son sort of went out of his head when they nailed the sign on the shop, and he resisted the soldiers. They are taking him away.

FRIEDA. Oh, God! Those poor people! My people!

ELSA. Don't worry, Aunt Frieda. You'll be away from all this soon. Day after tomorrow . . .

HARTWIG. Aunt Frieda isn't going.

FRIEDA (*quickly*). No. I, I've changed my mind.

ELSA. You're going to stay with us? Oh, I'm so glad. I would have missed you terribly.

HARTWIG (*at the window*). I'll take a run over there and see what's going on. Tell the boys where I am. They can pick me up there.

(*He takes his lunch and starts out.*)

ELSA (*haltingly*). Oh, Hartwig, I was going to tell you, the boys have gone.

HARTWIG. What do you mean? It's only just two.

ELSA. They have gone.

HARTWIG. Without calling for me?

ELSA. Yes. They passed me as I came in.

HARTWIG. That's funny. Well, I'll go and meet them.

ELSA. They don't want you.

HARTWIG. What do you mean? They don't want me?

ELSA (*haltingly*). They said to tell you . . . they were sorry . . . but it was getting too dangerous to be seen with . . .

FRIEDA (*quietly*). With people who associate with Jews.

ELSA (*bursting out crying*). Yes, that's it.

(*She flings herself in* FRIEDA'S *arms, sobbing.*)

FRIEDA (*holding her close and cradling her, while Hartwig throws down his package of lunch*). Don't cry, Elsa, don't. You break Aunt Frieda's heart. I'm just beginning to realize all that I've done to you, that I *will* do to you. Hartwig has lost his job, and his friends; that's why Johann and the other boys haven't been here lately, all because of me. But Frieda mustn't stand in your way. Don't cry, darling. We'll find some way out. I'll tell you; you can both go live with Frau Hahn. She'll take you. Then everything will be all right.

ELSA (*clinging to her*). And leave you here alone?

HARTWIG (*heatedly*). We couldn't do that. If you were here without us, then it *would* be hard on you. They'd boycott the shop; you couldn't make a living; you'd starve, and we couldn't stand that. We'd come back to help you, and then the Nazi . . .

FRIEDA. Oh, darling, stop. Stop! Don't talk about it. I must think it all over. There must be some way out.

(*The noise from the street increases.* HARTWIG *rushes to the window to watch.*)

HARTWIG. Look! They're breaking in the front of Levinski's store. They're ruining the place.

(*There is the sound of shattered glass, and noise of the crowd.*)

FRIEDA. Trouble, more trouble! God help my people!

(HARTWIG *starts from the window to the door.*)

ELSA. Don't go. Stay here with us. I'm frightened.

HARTWIG (*turning back*). Nothing will happen as long as we mind our own business.

ELSA. But I'm afraid . . .

(*The door bursts open unceremoniously.* LEVINSKI, *dirty and disheveled, stands there, a gun in his hand. He is an old man with a grey beard. Now he is almost hysterical with excitement and fear. He comes in quickly, closing the door behind him and turning the key in the lock.*)

FRIEDA. Herr Levinski!

LEVINSKI. Quick, hide me some place! They are after me! I shot at a soldier. He laid his hands on my wife! (*He looks about him dazed, mumbling.*) They took my boy away . . .

HARTWIG. You shouldn't come in here. You'll get us into trouble.

LEVINSKI. No one saw me. I slipped through the crowd. They are looking for me down the street.

ELSA. You mustn't stay here!

LEVINSKI (*to* FRIEDA). My friend, help one of your people!

FRIEDA. But what can I . . .

(*Knocking is heard on the door.*)

LEVINSKI. That's the soldiers. They've found me.

FRIEDA. You children mustn't be in this. Go quickly, out over the roof. You can get to

Frau Hahn's. Stay there . . . until I come for you. Run. Hurry.

(ELSA *takes* HARTWIG *by the hand and tries to drag him away, but he will not go.*)

HARTWIG (*to* FRIEDA). I'm not going to leave you in this trouble.

FRIEDA (*frantically*). You must. You must get Elsa out of here.

(*Knocking is repeated.*)

FRIEDA. I'll be all right. It will be easier without you. Go, please.

HARTWIG (*taking* ELSA *by the hand*). All right. I'll take Elsa to Frau Hahn's, and come right back to you.

FRIEDA. Yes, that's right. Do.

(ELSA *and* HARTWIG *go.*)

LEVINSKI (*pleading hysterically*). You won't give me up? They'll shoot me like a dog . . . and my Lena, and my children . . .

FRIEDA. No. No. I'll help you.

(*Knocking is repeated.*)

JOHANN (*outside door*). Open in the name of the law.

LEVINSKI. What shall I do?

FRIEDA. Here, you mustn't be found with a gun. Give it to me.

(*She takes the gun, looks about her hurriedly, and then hides it under some clothing in one of the bags on the table.*)

JOHANN (*outside*). Open!

FRIEDA. And now, try the roof. You may get away. (*She goes to the door, and* LEVINSKI *leaves. Then she pretends to be fumbling with the key in the lock.*) I am trying to open the door, but the key has stuck.

JOHANN (*outside*). Open, or we break down the door.

FRIEDA (*throwing open the door*). There!

(JOHANN, *a Captain, and a soldier, both dressed in Nazi uniform, enter.*)

FRIEDA (*trying to be light*). You frightened me so I couldn't get the key to work. (*Then, recognizing* JOHANN.) Oh, Johann, it's you!

JOHANN (*also surprised*). Frau Neuberg! I, I came in in such a hurry I didn't realize this was your house.

FRIEDA. Yes.

JOHANN (*changing his tone*). Well, I'm a Captain now. Where is he?

FRIEDA. Who?

JOHANN. That Jew.

FRIEDA (*wishing to gain time*). If you mean my Hartwig, you know as well as I that he is not a Jew.

JOHANN. I mean that old man who shot at one of our soldiers. He's here and we know it.

FRIEDA (*looking about her*). No one is here.

JOHANN (*also looking about*). We'll soon see. Search the rest of the place.

(*The soldier goes out.*)

FRIEDA. How strange it seems to see you in that uniform, unkind, unfriendly towards me.

JOHANN. I'm sorry, but I have my duty to perform.

FRIEDA. Of course. It is strange. When I think of the times you and Hartwig used to play together, sleep in the same bed, wake me up at daybreak to get your breakfast so you could go fishing, beg for cookies out of my old Meissen jar . . . I can't believe that you are here, standing stiff and unfriendly before me, ready to act against me and my people.

JOHANN (*uncomfortably*). Conditions have changed.

FRIEDA. But you haven't changed, and I haven't changed. We're still the same people. Must we be enemies?

JOHANN. That remains to be seen.

SOLDIER (*returning*). Excuse me, Herr Captain, but we got him. He was hiding in the next room. When I entered he tried to escape, and one of the soldiers shot him. He is dead.

FRIEDA (*stifling a cry*). Oh!

JOHANN. That's all, then. You may go.

(*The soldier goes.*)

FRIEDA (*her face in her hands*). Oh! That poor old man . . . and for no reason, dead!

JOHANN. And you, Frau Neuberg, I'm sorry to inform you, are under arrest.

FRIEDA. What!

JOHANN. For sheltering a fugitive from justice.

FRIEDA. I didn't know he was there. I told him to go out over the roof.

JOHANN. It's one and the same thing. You were aiding him in his escape.

FRIEDA. And why shouldn't I? He'd done nothing wrong. He was only defending his family. Wouldn't you have helped him if you had been in my place?

JOHANN (*stiffly*). That I cannot say. I am not a Jew.

FRIEDA. And what difference does that make? Oh, why are you all so hard on us? What have we done to deserve the treatment we are getting. I love Germany just as you do. I'm just as much a part of the Fatherland. I've lived here all my life, and my father before me, and my grandfather before him. We've all loved Germany. We've all sacrificed for her. In the war I gave my beloved man, just as the Gentile women gave theirs. We all gave, just as Christians gave. We fought and bled and suffered exactly as they. After the war we pinched and scraped and paid our taxes, Christian and Jew alike, gladly, for the good of the Fatherland. And now, that there is no war and you don't need fodder for your cannon, you turn on us and say we are not Germans, we are different! But look out. The years are long. And much may happen. Germany may yet cringe on her knees, and beg the Jews for their money and for the life blood of their sons!

JOHANN (stern and angry). Quiet! All you say will only make it worse for you. Get your things. Come with me.

FRIEDA. You're not going to take me away?

JOHANN. I must.

FRIEDA. Oh, but you can't. What will they do with me?

JOHANN. That I cannot say.

FRIEDA. I will be tried for treason?

JOHANN. Yes.

FRIEDA. Then I know what that means: conviction. Oh, but it mustn't be. Don't you see what that would mean for the children, for Elsa and Hartwig, to have been living with a Jew who is convicted of treason? It will mean disgrace for them. They will be outcasts.

JOHANN. Yes.

FRIEDA. Then you can't take me away. For their sake, let me stay here.

JOHANN. I'm afraid I . . .

FRIEDA. Oh, please! You've known me a long time; you know I won't do any harm, I won't cause any trouble. And you've known Elsa and Hartwig all their lives. You've been Hartwig's best friend, until recently. Think of all the good times you've had together, all that you've meant to each other. And think of Hartwig: what this will mean to him; he won't have a chance. But if you do nothing about all this, Hartwig will join the Nazi, he'll . . .

JOHANN. He has refused.

FRIEDA. But he wants to join, and he will. I'll see that he joins.

JOHANN. But he couldn't be a Nazi, with you . . . here in the house.

FRIEDA. Oh, no, no; that's right, of course.

JOHANN (sincerely). I'm sorry, Frau Neuberg, truly I am. But if you're thinking of Hartwig, don't you see it would be much worse for you to stay on here than to go with me?

FRIEDA (realizing all that he means). Yes, yes, I suppose it would be. But there must be something I can do, some way out. There must be. (She is standing near the table on which is the bag where she hid the gun. She drops her hand on the open bag for support and feels the gun there. She reacts to it and suddenly sees the solution to her problem.) Yes, yes. There's always some way out.

JOHANN. But how?

FRIEDA. Listen to me. I've thought of something. Suppose I were to go away, far away . . .

JOHANN. They're not issuing any more visés.

FRIEDA. I won't need a visé. But I'll go, I promise you, where neither you nor Elsa nor Hartwig will ever see me or hear of me again.

JOHANN. Where will you go?

FRIEDA. Don't ask me that. But I give you my word. If you'll leave me now, before the children come back, I'll go . . . and not return.

JOHANN. But . . .

FRIEDA. Say that you will, I beg of you. Give Hartwig and Elsa their chance.

JOHANN. But Frau Neuberg, where can you go?

FRIEDA (looking at him with meaning). Johann, one can go where one does not return.

JOHANN (understanding). Oh!

FRIEDA. Please, let me. What harm can it do? You will have accomplished your purpose. You will have one more Nazi in your ranks, and one less Jew.

JOHANN. I see. Very well, Frau Neuberg, since you ask it. I will go back to headquarters, and report nothing.

FRIEDA. God bless you! And I give you my word, as a Jew, when you come back in the morning I'll not be here. (She holds out her hand, which he takes.) And now, go. I . . . I have some things to do first.

JOHANN (still holding her hand). I will. But first I want to say I think Elsa and Hartwig have been blessed . . . to have you. Auf wiedersehen, Frau Neuberg.

FRIEDA. Auf wiedersehen. (JOHANN goes.) Auf wiedersehen.

(*Tears come to her eyes, but she brushes them away. She takes the gun out of the bag, looks at it, lays it on the table, looks around the room, picks up* HART-WIG'S *luncheon, looks at it, lays it on a table, goes to* ELSA'S *dress, takes the last stitch in it, presses it to her breast and puts it on a hanger. Then she goes back to the table, picks up the gun, looks at it, looks around the room once more, saying again,* "Auf wiedersehen." *Then, with the gun in her hand, she goes quickly off stage. A second later a shot is heard, and the curtain falls.*)

JOURNEY FOR AN UNKNOWN SOLDIER

by **Doris Frankel**

CHARACTERS

    ARCHIE
    DICK
    TARO
    GERMAN COUPLE
    A COP
    TICKET-AGENT
    YOUNG COUPLE
    NEGRO YOUTH

TIME: In the weeks after Pearl Harbor.

PLACE: A bus station somewhere outside of Los Angeles.

AT RISE: *A bare stage, or some portion of it. A ticket-booth may or may not be visible. There might be a blackboard with chalked announcements of bus departures; or possibly a large calendar. There is surely and prominently an American flag tacked on the wall.*

Two men are standing waiting, one behind the other. If there were more of them it would be a line. They ignore one another after the custom of public waiting rooms. The first is DICK, *Caucasian, American, Irish, or what-have-you. His hands are thrust in his pockets, and he is contemplating the ceiling. The second man is* TARO, *a Japanese youth. He lounges against a suitcase, his face completely obscured by a newspaper.*

A third man, ARCHIE, *enters and pushes in front of* DICK. *He is also a white American, remarkable only for the fact that he wears evening clothes, and evidently has not slept all night.*

ARCHIE (*belligerently to the ticket-booth*). Recruiting station?

    (*There is no answer.*)

DICK. Bus station.

ARCHIE. I want to enlist.

DICK. Take a bus. Fort Sinclair.

ARCHIE. Give me a ticket.

DICK. The ticket-agent left. House on fire or something. Said he'd be back.

ARCHIE. How much a ticket?

DICK. I don't know.

ARCHIE. Give me two!

DICK. Two?

ARCHIE (*beaming*). I'm going to kill twice as many Japs!

DICK (*with a bitter laugh*). Sure.

    (ARCHIE *leans over and taps the other man genially on the shoulder.*)

ARCHIE. He don't like me. Me, either. (*The other man lowers his newspaper, and we discover that he is Japanese.*) Oops! beg your pardon. (DICK *stares at* TARO.) Friend of yours?

DICK (*contemptuously*). What do you think?

ARCHIE (*taps* TARO *again*) Hey, you remind me of a story—

DICK. Don't start something—

ARCHIE. About a black duck. There were a lot of white ones—

TARO. The Ugly Duckling.

ARCHIE. Yeah! Mama didn't love him. But he turned out all right—a white swan or something—

TARO. No resemblance.

ARCHIE. Yeah, you remind me—

TARO. I'll never be white.

DICK (*tugs* ARCHIE *away*). They won't take you in the army drunk.

ARCHIE. I haven't had a drink since—what time is it?

DICK. Four o'clock.

ARCHIE. Four o'clock.

DICK. The washroom's over there. Dunk your head.

ARCHIE. Thanks. (*He moves off in the direction indicated.*) You're a pal!

DICK (*smiles*). Sure, Archie, I'm a pal.

DORIS FRANKEL (1909–   )

Despite optioning her first play, *Outcry*, to Broadway at the age of twenty, Doris Frankel has spent most of her professional life away from the stage. In the 1930's she was writing for radio—from the folksy "Ma Perkins" to the public-spirited "Cavalcade of America" to the dramas of "Counterspy," "The Thin Man," and "Theatre of Today." Following World War II she wrote screenplays for Warner Brothers and Universal Pictures. Her television work includes "Circle Theater," "Suspense," "Actors Studio," and "Playhouse 90," as well as most of the soap operas.

Four of her plays have appeared in New York. They are *Hail the Conqueror* (1935), *Don't Throw Glass Houses* (1939), *Love Me Long* (1949), and *The Woman and the Warriors* (1972). She is also the author of a volume of poetry, *The Sun Beats Down,* published in 1930.

Frankel describes her life very succinctly, indeed. "I was born in the year that Robert E. Perry reached the North Pole—and have been going to extremes ever since." She was one of the youngest graduates of Radcliffe College, and from there enrolled in George Pierce Baker's celebrated Drama 47 Workshop at Yale. In addition to writing, she has worked as a radio commentator and photographer's model.

Journey for an Unknown Soldier was written during a professional hiatus in 1943, when Frankel took her two sons and rejoined her husband at the Heart Mountain Relocation Center for Japanese-American evacuees, where he was Chief of Community Services. These relocation centers were, in fact, concentration camps to which wartime hysteria had relegated a segment of the population without regard to its constitutional rights. There was again, however, as in World War I, the feeling that America's ultimate victory would conquer injustice at home as well as abroad. *Journey for an Unknown Soldier* embraces that view.

Doris Frankel (fifth from right) at the first rehearsal of Love Me Long. *Actresses Shirley Booth and Anne Jackson are at her right.*

ARCHIE (*delighted*). He knows my name!
(*He exits.* DICK *covertly watches the* JAP- ANESE BOY, *who finally raises his eyes. Their glances hold.*)

DICK (*tense*). I don't want to make trouble —(*He breaks off.*) Well? (TARO *doesn't an- swer.*) What are you doing here?

TARO. Waiting for a street-car. (*Smiles con- temptuously.*) Or is it a bus?

DICK. These buses go out to camp.

TARO. Me, too.

(DICK *inspects him deliberately from head to foot.*)

DICK. Yeah? What for—military informa- tion?

TARO. That's right. About whether I weigh enough to get in the army.

DICK. Maybe Hirohito isn't so particular!

TARO. Maybe. But I am.

[DICK *clenches fingers and* TARO'S *jaw stiffens. They are interrupted by the en- trance of an elderly German refugee couple. The* OLD WOMAN *looks around, uncertainly.*)

WOMAN. Bitte—we get the bus here—for the soldiers' camp? Isn't it?

DICK. Yes.

WOMAN (*relieved*). Ach! Is all right, Papa.

DICK (*smiles*). Joining up, Grandpa?

WOMAN. Nein, we're getting a medal.

DICK. Medal?

WOMAN. He was twenty-two years old. (*To the* OLD MAN.) Is a bench over there—you should sit. (*The* MAN *walks heavily off.*) Papa don't feel good— (*Her eyes follow him.*) So sit already—sit! (*She watches till he does, then turns back to* DICK.) Only the day before, it comes a letter from him—how it never rains in Pearl Harbor. Such good weather! (*She shakes her head sadly, then calls.*) Ja, Ja—I'm coming— (*She walks offstage to sit on the bench with her husband.*)

DICK (*to* TARO). Shall I translate that into Japanese? (TARO *doesn't answer.* DICK *glares at him.*) What's the matter with your chin?

TARO. Nothing.

DICK. It's bleeding.

TARO (*shortly*). Cut myself with a razor.

DICK. Looks more like a rock.

TARO. Yes. Some kids threw a rock.

DICK. What for?

TARO. Ask them!

(ARCHIE *returns from the washroom.*)

ARCHIE. How do I look?

DICK. Better.

ARCHIE. I feel great!—See that flag— (*He points to the wall.*) You get one on your coffin if anything happens. I've got a soft spot for a military funeral. They all walk, see, but they carry you—

DICK. Shut up.

ARCHIE. It was *my* funeral—

DICK. Shut up!

(*Pause.*)

ARCHIE. What did you say my name was?

DICK. Archie.

ARCHIE (*admiringly*). How do you know?

DICK. I went to school with you.

ARCHIE. But I never went to school.

DICK. In Santa Monica. Remember Miss Griscome?

ARCHIE. Nope.

DICK. She taught us Latin.

ARCHIE. Who?

DICK. Miss Griscome. I'm Richard Clark.

ARCHIE. Nope.

DICK. I sat right behind you—third row near the windows—

ARCHIE (*happy recognition*). Dirty Dick! Why didn't you say so? You used to copy my exams, we got swell marks— How are you?

DICK (*with a frown over the nickname*). All right.

ARCHIE. How's the other fellow—what was his name? The one you always hung around with—Oh, hell—

DICK. Ryan.

ARCHIE. Ryan—yeah. Nice guy, I liked him. He loaned me his turtle once.

DICK. It was my turtle.

ARCHIE. No kidding? How's Ryan getting on? (DICK *doesn't answer.*) I suppose you hear from him?

DICK. No.

ARCHIE. Don't you see him any more?

DICK. No.

ARCHIE (*lightly*). Well, well, here today and gone—the best of friends—etcetera.

DICK (*vehemently*). That's not what hap- pened!

ARCHIE (*surprised*). Okay.

(*Pause.*)

DICK. We were salesmen together. Life in- surance policies.

ARCHIE (*politely*). Yeah?

DICK. The first month we sold two. I sold one to him. He sold one to me.

ARCHIE. What did you do then—retire on the profits?

DICK. We worked out a system. We'd go up to an office—they'd kick Ryan out—while the door was still open, I'd slip in—

ARCHIE. Suppose they kicked you out?

DICK. By that time Ryan was back.

ARCHIE. Blitzkrieg.

DICK. We did fine! Ryan bought a house for his mother and sister—you remember Gertie?

ARCHIE. Nope.

DICK (*surprised*). You don't? She was awfully pretty. She wanted to be an actress—you know—in pictures—

ARCHIE (*he knows*). Ah huh.

DICK. It didn't pan out. Ryan used to tell her never mind, someday he'd buy her Cecil B. De Mille. He would have, too—

(*His voice trails to a stop.*)

ARCHIE. What stopped him?

DICK. Overwork. He lost eleven pounds. The boss gave him a bonus—a sunburn on the house.

ARCHIE. Any relation to a gin sling?

DICK. A sunburn on the house is a winter vacation—all expenses paid.

ARCHIE (*whistles*). Not bad!

DICK (*flatly*). Ryan went to Hawaii.

ARCHIE. Oh.

(*Pause.*)

DICK. Well—lucky I sold him that policy —damn lucky—

ARCHIE. And now you're joining the army?

DICK. Yeah.

ARCHIE. About Ryan's sister—do you ever see her?

DICK. Every time I pass the Ansonia Café. She's in the window—making flapjacks. (*Pause—with a cynical laugh.*) And what brings you here? An initiation?

ARCHIE. I have reasons. When I was six years old my mother took me to Washington to see Abraham Lincoln and the cherry blossoms.

DICK. How interesting. Well, Lincoln was all right.

ARCHIE. The cherry blossoms were nice, too. I can't get them out of my mind.

DICK. Get back to the reasons.

ARCHIE. I like to fly. Had a little cub plane. Called her Tom.

DICK. Called *her* Tom?

ARCHIE. You could drop her on her tail, and she always landed on her feet. We used to do tricks—Tom has nine lives— (*Sighs.*) I had to sell her for scrap—red paint and all. (*Brightens.*) But anyhow, we sure gave the airplane spotters one hell of a night!

(*The* OLD LADY *comes over nervously.*)

DICK (*to* ARCHIE, *sneering*). So you want to make the world safe for cherry blossoms?

WOMAN (*to* TARO). Papa wants to know are you Chinese? Ja?

TARO. No.

WOMAN. Ach!

TARO. I'm not Filipino, either.

WOMAN (*sadly*). No?

TARO. I'm Japanese. American-Japanese.

WOMAN. Ach! (*The old man stamps on; she anxiously tries to intercept him.*) Papa! Please—*he* didn't do it— (*The* OLD MAN *goes up to the group, stops by the Japanese boy—and spits.*) Papa! It says on the sign you shouldn't spit on the floor!

MAN. On the floor I wasn't spitting! Nein.

(*He goes out the street entrance. She follows him.* TARO *makes an angry move to go after them.*)

ARCHIE (*placating*). Hell, they're old— they don't know—

TARO (*calling after them, though they can't hear*). I'm an American! I was born here! Where were you born? Germany? Austria? Things aren't so good over there, either! I was born here—my country—

DICK. Why don't you Japs keep off the streets for a while?

TARO (*turning, like a baited animal*). Maybe we need air.

DICK. Why? Something got you hot and bothered?

TARO. Yes! Something!—

DICK. If you say Pearl Harbor, so help me I'll kill you!

ARCHIE. Dick!

DICK. I had a friend there!

TARO. I had friends—many friends—

DICK. I'll bet. *In Jap planes!*

TARO. Don't say that!

DICK. It's true—whether I say it or not—it's true!

TARO. It's a goddamned lie!

DICK. Don't you curse me!

TARO. It's a lie! I care more than you—I care for this country— (*He is almost sobbing.*)

DICK (*sneers*). Can you sing the Star Spangled Banner?

TARO. No! I can't sing!—Leave me alone! (*He covers his eyes.*) All of you—my father —you—everyone—leave me alone! (*Pause— he straightens up, calm again.*) I won't go back. I'm going to enlist. No matter what you do.

DICK. I'm going to do plenty!

ARCHIE (*quietly*). Leave him alone.

DICK. What are you? A Jap-lover?

ARCHIE. What are you? A storm-trooper?

DICK. I don't like that crack—

ARCHIE. I don't like fascism.

DICK. Want to start something?

ARCHIE. No. I'm a pacifist.

DICK (*jeers*). A pacifist—joining the army!

ARCHIE (*earnestly*). To make peace—for the world. I can't stand blood. I have to kill them—get it over—

DICK. Don't look now if you can't stand blood. (*To* TARO.) Take off your glasses.

(*He does at once.*)

ARCHIE. You fool! What does Ryan get out of this?

TARO. Be careful—I know Judo.

DICK. Then use it—fast.

(*He slaps him across the face.* TARO *throws him.*)

ARCHIE. Don't fight—you fools!

(*He leaps in—the three of them roll on the floor, hitting and punching. A* COP *comes running in.*)

COP. What goes on here? Break it up! (*He tries to separate them.*) You waitin' for a bus —or an ambulance?—Go on, break it up! (*They rise, brushing themselves off.*) Wait a minute—this Jap's a Jap!

ARCHIE. It's all right, we're pals.

COP (*indicating* TARO). What about him?

ARCHIE. He's my brother.

COP. Brother!

ARCHIE. Sure. He looks like my uncle's sister on my mother's side, whereas I've got more my paternal grandfather's nose. But there's a family resemblance.

COP. Are you guys nuts?

ARCHIE. I'm Peanuts—that's Walnuts— (*Nods at* TARO.) And over there is Almonds. But we go together lovely on a sundae.

COP (*with heavy humor*). Well, this ain't Sunday. And you better sober up—all of you. (*He starts off.*)

ARCHIE. Thanks, Kelly.

COP. My name ain't Kelly.

ARCHIE. Well, thank Kelly when you see him, will you?

COP (*turning back*). If you want to know what I think of you—

ARCHIE (*hastily*). We'll think of you, too —when we're bombing Tokio.

COP (*sarcastic*). With what—wise cracks?

ARCHIE. If we can't find any bombs, we'll drop each other. Him first— (*Winks at* TARO.) Then him— (*Nods at* DICK.)

(*The* COP *exits.*)

ARCHIE. Come on, you dopes, kiss and make up.

DICK. Sure. The kiss of death.

ARCHIE. What's the matter with you? Maybe he doesn't like your face, either.

DICK. It's more than his face.

TARO. Sure—it's my color!

DICK (*mimicking* ARCHIE). Maybe I don't like fascism.

TARO. Neither do I.

DICK. Aaah—

ARCHIE. How do you know? How do you know whether he does or not? You haven't looked at him—except to see the yellow ribbon in his hair.

DICK. What do you want me to do? Wait around till he sticks a knife in my back?

TARO (*to* DICK). Where were you born?

DICK. Missouri. So what?

TARO. I was born in California—five miles from here.

DICK. You think that makes you an American?

TARO. Yes!

DICK. Didn't you ever look in a mirror?

(*Pause.*)

ARCHIE. Listen, moron—

DICK. Listen to what? More sweetness and light? I bet you're kind to babies, and pet animals in the street. Because you're soft. Well, I'm not. It's our duty to be tough. Kill or be killed! We won't win this war with mush. We'll win it with iron and hate!

ARCHIE. Then hate principles—not races.

DICK. I'll hate Japs. We're fighting 'em, for God's sake—

ARCHIE. We're fighting a system, a government—

DICK. Japs are Japs!

ARCHIE. Then why is this one breaking his neck to get into the United States Army?

DICK. Search me—but I sure hope he breaks it!

ARCHIE. Okay. . . . Just go ahead like you're doing. You hate him—he'll hate the Bohunks and the Micks—the Micks will hate the Polacks, the Jews and the Wops—and the Wops will hate the Blacks.—You're sure fixing it so our great grandsons can all have fine military funerals!

(*Pause.*)

DICK (*tight-lipped*). You've said your piece.

ARCHIE. Yeah. (*Turns to* TARO.) There's a bad smell in here. Let's go over to the windows.

(*They cross away from* DICK, *who stares after them bitterly.*)

DICK (*calls*). It's a free country, isn't it? Don't we have free speech?

ARCHIE. He don't. (*To* TARO.) What's your name?

TARO. Taro.

ARCHIE. Mine's Archie.

(TARO *nods.* DICK *has moved over to them.*)

DICK. What do you mean "Taro"? Is that a name? You mean Tom?

ARCHIE. Tom's an airplane. He means Taro.

DICK. I like Tom.

ARCHIE. Taro, meet Dirty Dick.

DICK. Don't be funny.

ARCHIE. Why don't you go tear up a magazine? (*Turns his back on him.*) Got folks, Taro?

TARO. My father.

ARCHIE. Does he want his boy to be a soldier?

TARO. Not much. He would like me to raise flowers.

ARCHIE. Yeah—that's parents. But they're good eggs.

TARO (*diffidently*). I don't know my father very well.

DICK (*bursting out*). You see! No family feeling!

TARO (*smiles*). Too much.

DICK. What's your father do?

TARO. Why, he's Secretary—

DICK (*interrupting*). Secretary! that's a hot one! Does he take shorthand in Japanese?

TARO (*continuing quietly*). Secretary of the Florists' League. He doesn't have much time for his greenhouses. That's why he wanted me to—

DICK. His—come again—greenhouses?

TARO. Yes.

DICK (*shakes his head*). My error! I thought all Japs ran Chinese restaurants. (*Laughs at his own joke.*) Or is it Greeks I'm thinking of?

ARCHIE (*dryly*). Couldn't be. The Greeks have stopped eating.

DICK. So Pop's in the money. You know, any yellow, pink, or greenhorn can get on a boat and make a fortune in America.

TARO. Yes, my people came on a boat. Did yours walk?

ARCHIE (*chuckles*). His came on the Mayflower. That's the English line.

DICK. Very funny.

ARCHIE. Thank you.

DICK. Your clothes are funny, too. I suppose you always wear evening clothes in the day time.

ARCHIE. No.

DICK. It wouldn't surprise me.

ARCHIE. I've been to a wedding. My girl just got married.

DICK (*startled*). Today?

ARCHIE. Yeah.—No, yesterday.—No, Sunday, dammit. R.A.F. flier.

DICK. Your girl?—You mean—another guy—?

ARCHIE. Yeah.

DICK. Why didn't you stop 'em?

ARCHIE. He got six Messerschmitts. He might as well have her. (*They laugh.* ARCHIE *pulls a handkerchief out of his pocket. A flood of rice comes with it.*) Oops, Taro—here's your dish!

(*They laugh again, and relax slightly.*)

DICK (*making general conversation*). I hear the Germans are going to use gas if it gets tough in Russia.

TARO (*accepting the truce*). Same old gas. We've got lots newer stuff here.

DICK. Have you heard about this synthetic rubber they're making?

ARCHIE. Sawdust and glue, isn't it?

(*They laugh.*)

DICK. They'll have new tires on all cars by spring.

(*There is a distant noise of a motor and brakes outside as a bus pulls up to the curb.* TARO *goes toward the entrance.*)

TARO. Looks like our bus pulling in.

DICK. That's good.

(TARO *comes back.*)

ARCHIE (*with a sudden shiver*). Somebody got a cigarette?

(DICK *hands him a pack.* ARCHIE *takes one.*)

DICK (*offering pack to* TARO). Tom?

TARO (*takes a cigarette*). Thanks.

(DICK *also takes one.* TARO *strikes a match and lights all three cigarettes—then they stare at the match.*)

DICK. Three on a match—

ARCHIE (*laughs*). Yeah. One of us is a dead duck.

(*They look at each other.*)

TARO. Not me.

DICK (*bravado*). They don't kill my kind with bullets!

ARCHIE. Not unless they're shot out of a gun, they don't!

(*The* TICKET AGENT *enters from outside.*)

DICK. What's fifty years more or less, once you're dead?

ARCHIE (*snaps his fingers—then grins*). It's while you're alive!

AGENT. Tickets on sale in a minute. (*He crosses over to the booth.*)

DICK. Our missing pal.

(*A young couple enter and cross to the* AGENT.)

YOUNG MAN. Grove Park?

AGENT. Next bus. Wait over there.

YOUNG MAN. Come on, darling.

(*They exit to the bench.* ARCHIE *steps up to the ticket window as the* AGENT *enters the booth.*)

DICK. Let me—

ARCHIE (*waving him away*). I'll get 'em.

TARO (*taking out his wallet*). Here—

ARCHIE. Forget it.

AGENT. Fort Sinclair?

ARCHIE. Three.

AGENT. Three? (*Referring to* TARO.) He's going, too?

ARCHIE. That's right.

AGENT (*gruffly*). H'm. Cost you each eighty cents.

ARCHIE. That's a long journey for eighty cents.

(*He puts down the money. A* COLORED BOY *in a soldier's uniform enters, and gets in line behind* ARCHIE.]

AGENT. Coming back?

ARCHIE [*turns to* TARO *and* DICK]. He wants to know if we're coming back. [*They all laugh.*] Mister, we've got no guarantee.

[*He takes the tickets. The* COLORED BOY *steps up to the booth.*]

AGENT. Ticket for you, Rastus?

COLORED BOY. Yes.

AGENT. Eighty cents—same as the white boys. (*He winks broadly at* ARCHIE.) Uncle Sam must be getting color-blind, hey, Rastus? (*The* COLORED BOY *pays for his ticket.*) Well —that's America! Everybody's got a chance.

COLORED BOY. Yes. Even you. (*He takes his ticket and goes out.*)

AGENT (*calling after him*). Hey! (*Shakes his head.*) You can't get friendly with niggers!

(ARCHIE *steps up to the booth.*)

ARCHIE. You know something? I'm going to change my will.

AGENT (*startled*). What's that?

ARCHIE. I don't think I'm going to leave this country to fellows like you. (*He goes back to* DICK *and* TARO.) Come on, boys— (*Tossing an arm about* TARO.) Our carriage awaits!

(*The three exit together as*

THE CURTAIN FALLS

ON THE WAY HOME

by Esther M. Hawley

CHARACTERS

ANN MAITLAND, *a war wife, very warm-hearted but not given to emotional display.*
JULIE BYRNES, *her sister-in-law, young, pretty, feminine and gentle.*
PAUL BYRNES, *Ann's brother, usually good-natured, nervous veteran.*

TIME: The present.
PLACE: The Byrnes' apartment, late afternoon.

> *Door up left to hall and outside right to house. Window, left center. Chair above window. Table. Three chairs to simulate davenport right. End table below davenport.*
> *The stage is empty when the curtain rises.* ANN, *in outdoor clothes, comes in, speaking as she enters.*

ANN. Where's that conquering hero home from the wars? (*Enters from left through door. Voice trails off as she sees empty room. In conversational tone.*) Hey, where is everybody? (*Back to door, calls.*) Julie! Paul! Where are you?

JULIE (*off*). Be right with you. (ANN *takes off her coat and leaves it on table.* JULIE, *upset, enters, straightening her hair. Goes to* ANN *and kisses her.*) Hello, darling. It's good to have you back.

ANN. What a trip!

JULIE. It must have been. Tell me, how's Hank? What did the doctor say?

ANN. He's fine. He's got his new prosthetic leg and he sat around by the hour mooning over it instead of me. I'm only his wife—but the leg! That's his real love. But where's that brother of mine? I want to see him.

JULIE. Paul—Paul's gone out for a while.

ANN. Well, I like that!

JULIE. He'll be back soon—I guess. I know he's dying to see you.

ANN. It looks like it. (*Affectionately. Crosses to* JULIE.) How is he? How does he look?

JULIE (*crosses to window, looking out*). He's very well, but he looks older.

ANN (*slight pause*). He would, I suppose.

JULIE (*in a strained voice*). But he does look well.

ANN. Julie, what's the trouble?

JULIE. Nothing's the trouble. (*Turns to face* ANN.) Why on earth should there be anything the matter? Whatever made you ask such a silly . . . Oh, Ann! (*Runs up to* ANN *and begins to cry.*) I'm so miserable!

ANN (*soothes her*). There, darling. It's all right. Come and sit down. (*Leads her to left end of davenport and seats her.*) There . . . (*Sits on right end of davenport.*)

JULIE. I'm so frightened, Ann. Paul's been acting so strange. Everything's going all wrong. I was so happy he was coming back to me after all those months and months. Everything we'd planned was going to come true. Now he's here, and it's all so—awful! I don't know what to do.

ANN. Poor baby!

JULIE. He acts like he's sorry he came home, sometimes. I don't think he loves me any more.

ANN. Nonsense!

JULIE. You don't know what he's like. One minute he's on top of the world, and the next, everything I say, everything I do, makes him cross. I spent hours yesterday cooking the kind of dinner he liked, and then just when it was almost ready he went out and didn't come back till nearly midnight. And when I tried to tell him what it was like trying to get anything nice to eat, he swore at me and told me to shut up. (*Pause.*) Oh, Ann, what am I going to do?

ANN. Nothing.

JULIE (*startled*). Nothing! But I've got to do something!

PAUL (*off, breaking in on* JULIE's *speech*).

ESTHER M. HAWLEY (1906–1968)

During World War II and the years that immediately followed it, the stage became part of a national effort to bolster morale and to ensure the successful readjustment of our troops to the prospects of postwar life. Some Broadway plays, such as Arthur Laurents' *Home of the Brave* and Arthur Miller's *All My Sons* (1947), spoke, if pseudo-seriously, of extreme situations. But it was even less dramatic problems than those posed by Laurents and Miller that became standard fare.

Hundreds of thousands of wartime veterans were returning home either physically or psychically wounded. Esther Hawley's *On the Way Home* (1945) is a mildly didactic drama on how civilians might cope with this situation. In retrospect, the award-winning film *The Best Years of Our Lives* (1946) is but a longer version of this same theme, and one that offers much the same wisdom.

Hawley had spent the war years develop-ing a type of one-act play that the New York *Times* credited with "bringing humanity into what would otherwise be simple propaganda." They became part of the catalog of plays used by the American Theatre Wing's production unit, The Victory Players, and performed throughout the rest of the country by local amateur groups. Among the best of them was Hawley's *You Give What You Got* (1944), an appeal for blood donors. After the war she wrote *Recreation Is Fun* (1948), which takes up the special recreation problems that were being encountered in military and VA hospitals.

A native of Chicago, Hawley was graduated from the University of Wisconsin. She started out as a copywriter, then became associated with the Irish Players during their New York engagement in 1931. Most of her later career in the theatre was as part of government service.

Julie! (JULIE *jumps up and starts toward door.* ANN *sits up expectantly.*)

JULIE (*with relief*). He's back.

PAUL (*comes in door from left, picks up* JULIE *and swings her around*). Hi, baby! Miss me?

JULIE. Oh, darling, where on earth did you go? I worried so.

PAUL. (*sees* ANN, *who rises. Sets* JULIE *down and goes to* ANN). So finally you found time to look me up!

ANN. My hero! (*Gives him a big hug. Steps back, holding him by his arms, and looks him over.*) I must say war hasn't improved your looks. (*Kisses him with emotion.*) Welcome home, dear. (*Breaks away quickly and sits on davenport.*)

JULIE (*going to* PAUL, *takes his arm*). Are you tired, dear? Can I get you something to eat?

PAUL. I'm O.K. (*Ignores* JULIE *and sits beside* ANN.) What's the word about Hank? (JULIE *stands alone.*)

ANN. He's fine. He's got his eye on a blond nurse who's going to teach him to jitterbug as soon as he can keep his balance a little better.

JULIE. You're not serious?

ANN. Sure. I'm learning, too.

JULIE. But Hank's a cripple!

PAUL (*sharply*). Don't say things like that, Julie! Hank's no cripple just because he lost a leg.

ANN (*gently*). Men like Hank don't think of themselves as cripples, dear, any more than a man does with, well—one kidney or one lung. they're amputees.

JULIE. But he is . . .

PAUL. No, he isn't. A cripple's helpless. Guys like Hank will be able to do as many things as they ever did. (*Enthusiastically.*) Why, one guy I know has a wonderful hook on his right arm—he has a fancy cosmetic hand for dress-up—but with that hook he can do anything I can do with both my hands—lift, carry, write letters, tie his shoes . . . I'll bet he'll even be able to tie a dress tie.

JULIE. Oh, Paul, I'm so grateful you didn't come home disabled.

PAUL. I told you not to say things like that.

ANN (*slapping his hand*). Manners, Paul. You're not in the Army now.

PAUL (*to* JULIE). Sorry, kid. (*To* ANN.) I'm so used to yelling at that dope Kowalski I forget it's Julie, even though she looks different and feels different—and smells different. (*To* JULIE.) Don't stand so far away. Come to Papa. (JULIE *stands beside him. He puts his arm around her and pats her back.*) Isn't she wonderful, Ann? And you're wonderful. (JULIE *goes up behind davenport, puts hands on* PAUL's *shoulders.*) Hank's wonderful. Everything's wonderful—and I'm home again!

ANN. Yippee!

PAUL. Let's celebrate! (*Jumps up and starts for door.*) The Scotch still in the same place? (*Takes out cigarettes.*)

JULIE. Scotch! We haven't had any Scotch for years! You just can't get it. (PAUL *lights cigarette.*) It's simply awful—and the prices! I keep telling you, Paul, you just won't believe it. Why, one day I went . . .

PAUL. O.K. Skip it. (*Sits down, smoking.*)

ANN. The saga of the sad civilian. Come around to my place later. I'm a hoarder.

PAUL. Swell. Trust you.

JULIE. Heaven knows, I tried . . .

PAUL. Sure, I know. What say, we all go out for dinner and do the town?

JULIE. Oh, Paul, I've got dinner all planned.

PAUL. It'll keep. How about it, Ann?

ANN. Sorry, Paul. I'm night shift at the Children's Hospital. Seven to one.

PAUL. That's new, isn't it?

ANN. Four months.

PAUL. What could you do? Not give any medicine, I hope.

ANN. I could do it in a pinch. I seem to remember being pretty handy with the castor oil.

PAUL (*to* JULIE). She's a born tyrant.

JULIE. I know how you suffered. (*Smiles.*) Gee, you two must have had fun together!

PAUL (*reminiscently*). Yeah!

JULIE. Paul! You didn't show Ann your medal. Go get it for her. It's so beautiful, Ann. (*Steps toward end of davenport.*)

PAUL. Skip it.

JULIE. The citation just says something about bravery above the call of duty. It's beautiful, but it isn't very explicit. And Paul's so modest he won't explain. Tell us about it, darling.

PAUL. Skip it, I said. (*Rises and crushes out cigarette on floor. Turns toward window.*)

JULIE (*steps toward him*). But we want to know all about it. We're proud of you.

PAUL (*tensely*). I helped take a gun emplacement. That's all.

JULIE. But how did you do it? What happenend? It wasn't as simple as just taking it.

PAUL (*swings back to face her. Starts quietly*). No, it wasn't as simple as just taking it. It was tough as hell and it cost three of the best guys I ever knew —and will you, for God's sake, shut up about it!

JULIE. Paul! (*Begins to cry. Turns up to table.*)

PAUL. And stop sniveling. If you didn't ask such questions, you wouldn't get such answers.

ANN (*rises*). Paul, may I have a cigarette?

PAUL (*crosses to her*). Oh, sure. (*Offers and lights cigarette.*)

ANN. I hope you brought a few cartons home.

PAUL. A couple.

ANN. Remember how I used to snitch the last piece of apple pie for you when you were sent to bed without your supper?

PAUL. I've paid for that pie so many times already.

ANN. I never mentioned it before in all my life. (*Sits at right end of davenport.*)

PAUL. Only when you wanted a new compact for the junior prom and an extra buck for a show when you'd spent your allowance and . . . (*Sits at right end of davenport.*)

ANN. Well, of course, if you're going to bring up things like that, I could . . .

PAUL. O.K. I'll give you a carton. But why the heck can't Hank send you some from Walter Reed?

ANN. The P.X. only lets them have two packs a day there, and smoking's the only vice he can enjoy in the ward.

PAUL. When are you going down again?

ANN. Not till the end of the month.

PAUL. So long?

ANN. I can't get away from work too often.

PAUL. Maybe I'll go down with you. (JULIE *turns to look at him.*)

ANN. That will be wonderful. Hank would love it.

PAUL. It's a date. (JULIE *steps down toward him.*)

JULIE. Won't you be working by that time?

PAUL. I don't know.

JULIE. But Mr. Hamilton is expecting you on the fifteenth. Told me so last week.

PAUL. Well, I haven't made up my mind.

JULIE. About what? (*Steps toward him.*) What do you mean?

PAUL. I'm not sure I'm going back with him.

JULIE. But—what else would you do? That's your job.

PAUL. I'm not so sure it is. Hamilton's a good guy, but there's no life in the job—nothing happening. Same old thing day after day. Every six months you get a two-buck raise, and by the time you're sixty-five you can retire if you've kept up your endowment policies.

ANN. I thought you liked it there.

PAUL. I did—before. It was all right then. But a guy has to be doing something constructive—see that he's getting somewhere. I don't mean just promotions. Oh . . . (*Rises and walks up to door.*)

ANN. Seeing something concrete come out of his work?

PAUL. Sort of. (*Steps down.*)

JULIE. But what will you do?

PAUL. I'm not sure. I thought I might try at McAllister's.

JULIE. The factory!

PAUL. I learned a lot about machines and things in the Army. I was pretty good at them. I could try my hand out there, and maybe take some government engineering courses at night.

ANN. Golly, Paul, that could be exciting. (PAUL *comes down to back of davenport.*)

JULIE. But that factory! And what about Mr. Hamilton? He's expecting you back.

PAUL. At twenty-seven fifty a week! I'm not a kid now, Julie.

JULIE. But there are such nice people at Hamilton's.

PAUL (*paces back of davenport*). A lot of stuffed shirts that can't understand anything except stock market reports and golf scores.

JULIE. What'll we live on?

PAUL. A darn sight more than twenty-seven fifty once I find my right job (*Crosses to center.*)

JULIE (*rises*). I'll never see you if you go to school nights. Oh, Paul, I had such lovely plans for the two of us. There's a darling little house right next to the Crawfords' (PAUL *turns away to right.*)—you know who Elmer Craw-

ford is!—and with your mustering out pay and what I've saved from my salary, we could make the down payment, and you'd be at Hamilton's, and everything would be just like it used to be.

PAUL. Nothing's going to be like it used to be. (*Crosses to* JULIE.) Can't you get it through that pretty head of yours that we've been fighting a war to get rid of a lot of things "that used to be"? Some of them we want to keep, sure, but they've got to be different. And we think about them in a different way. (*Pause.*) I don't want to fight another war and I don't want my kids to fight one, but they'll have to, sure as God made little apples, if I sit back on my fanny and shut myself up in a fog of phony dreams about everything being just like it always was. (*Crosses back of davenport.*)

JULIE. I'm not dumb. I know things aren't like they used to be. I didn't spend all those months working behind a counter and standing on corners for buses and standing in lines at the Super Market without knowing things were a whole lot different. But that's all over now, and I don't see why we can't go back . . .

PAUL. Go back! Gosh almighty—we just begin to climb out of all that mess—oh, you women are just like cats: curl up by your own fire with your own dreams and to hell with what goes on outside. (*Steps down to window. Pause.*) Well, I'm not going to do it, and I'm not going to let you sweet-talk me into doing it, either. I don't know what the answer is yet, but I'm sure as hell going to try to find out. And when I do, I'm going on from there.

JULIE (*alarmed*). Don't get so excited, darling (*Takes his arms.*), all about nothing.

PAUL. Nothing! (*Breaks loose.*) Won't you ever grow up? The most important thing—nothing! "Don't get so excited, Paul!"

JULIE. You're tired now.

PAUL. I'm not tired. For Pete's sake, stop saying I am! Stop fussing!

JULIE (*steps to him*). I'm not fussing, but you say—such . . .

PAUL. I say what? Make up your mind. Oh, what's the use of trying to talk to you? (*Rushes through door and off right.*)

JULIE (*following toward door*). Paul!

ANN. Let him go, Julie.

JULIE (*faintly*). Paul—please— (*Crosses slowly and sits in chair.*)

ANN. You poor kid!

JULIE. What did I do? I can't understand him. Oh, Ann, I'd do anything to make him happy.

ANN. I know.

JULIE. But he doesn't want me any more.

ANN. That's not true. It's because he does love you that he lets go. People always take out their irritation on the ones they love best.

JULIE. But it isn't fair.

ANN. No, but it's human nature.

JULIE (*rises*). Paul never used to be like that. (*Crosses to sofa.*) I mean, he'd be cross once in a while, but now—one moment he's all keyed up, and the next, he's biting my head off (*Sits.*)

ANN. It's so hard for us to understand, but it's sort of like being between two worlds. (*Sits left end of sofa.*) Paul's not a soldier any more, but he's not the old easy-going Paul, either. Not yet.

JULIE. But, Ann, the war's all behind him now.

ANN. Not far enough behind. We can say the words he's been living—filth and horror and suffering and fear—but what do they mean to us? What's it like to live with fear? Not knowing what—or when. Oh, Julie, you can't forget that in a week.

JULIE. But he's at home now, safe.

ANN. Yes, thank God, he's safe. (*Thinking her words.*) But he's not really home. Part of him is still in that distorted world he's been living in. We have to remember that. His values are all upset—even the little things. Like being clean. A bath a day isn't so important when you haven't had one for three months at a time. Men living together lose their knack of polite conversation. After they've been living on K rations, and eating in and out of mess kits, their table manners get rusty. They've forgotten how to pay full attention, because half their minds are listening to things beyond. They've been living by extremes so long—tension, then nerve-racking inactivity, then tension again.

JULIE. I'm trying to understand. I've got to. My mind does—but *I* don't really, and I've got to.

ANN. I know it's hard. We've changed, too, living without our men, having to depend on ourselves, making our decisions alone; but we haven't changed emotionally, the way Paul has.

JULIE. All I know is that I want Paul. I don't care about anything else.

ANN. That's all any of us wants—and the men want it desperately. But we've been driven so far apart. It takes time to find the way home.

JULIE. But how . . .

ANN. *We* have to find the way. For a while we can't matter. We can't indulge in hurt feelings and self-pity.

JULIE. I don't care about myself.

ANN. Not really. But pride pops up—and nerves. It takes so much watching.

JULIE. But what if I can't do it?

ANN. For a little while—till he really gets to be the old Paul—you have to be the one to give in. Do what *he* wants—no matter if it seems silly—no matter how tired you get. If he wants to run wild, let him. If he wants to sit around without talking, don't bother him. (*Intensely.*) He's got to be on his own to find his own way back.

JULIE. Did Hank teach you all this?

ANN. In a way. I talked a lot to the doctors at Walter Reed. With Hank hurt, I *had* to make him sure of himself and of me, absolutely sure nothing that had happened to him changed—us. So that when he comes home, no matter what stupid people say to him, no matter how they stare at him, they won't be able to hurt him. You and Paul will have to help me then—to keep him certain we know he's not a—cripple.

JULIE (*eagerly*). We will—we will (*Hesitates.*) if Paul comes back. Oh, Ann, where do you think he's gone?

ANN. He'll be all right. These—outbursts are all on top. They don't go deep. Just hang on (PAUL *comes to door with a bag of groceries.*) and keep on loving him extra hard.

PAUL (*in doorway*). That's the kind of talk I like from my women.

JULIE (*runs to him*). Darling!

ANN (*with relief*). Paul!

PAUL. Hey! You'll bust the beer bottles.

ANN. What did you do? Buy out the store?

PAUL. Sure. Liverwurst, limburger, rye bread.

JULIE. Oh, Paul, I was so worried.

PAUL (*good-naturedly*). How's that for a devoted little woman? Afraid I'll get run over crossing the street?

JULIE. No, but when you went out . . .

PAUL. What are you talking about?

JULIE. Why, darling, you were so cross.

PAUL. Was I?

JULIE. Why, you said . . .

ANN (*warning*). Julie! Paul's a big boy now.

JULIE (*with understanding*). Yes! We're both grown up now. Here, give me that. (*Takes bag.*) We're going to have a party. (*Exits through door and right.*)

PAUL (*in doorway*). Isn't she something? Golly, it's wonderful to be home with my two girls. Come on, let's eat (*Exits through door right. ANN sits thinking of them and of Hank. PAUL calls from off.*) Ann!

ANN (*straightens*). Coming! (*Rises and walks quickly to door and out right.*)

CURTAIN

THE MOTHER OF US ALL

by Gertrude Stein

ACT I

(Prologue sung by VIRGIL T.*)*

Pity the poor persecutor.
    Why,
If money is money isn't money money,
    Why,
Pity the poor persecutor,
    Why,
Is money money or isn't money money.
    Why.
Pity the poor persecutor.
Pity the poor persecutor because the poor persecutor always gets to be poor
    Why,
Because the persecutor gets persecuted
Because is money money or isn't money money,
    That's why,
When the poor persecutor is persecuted he has to cry,
    Why,
Because the persecutor always ends by being persecuted,
    That is the reason why.
    *(*VIRGIL T. *after he has sung his prelude begins to sit.)*
VIRGIL T. Begins to sit. Begins to sit. He begins to sit. That's why. Begins to sit. He begins to sit. And that is the reason why.

ACT I — SCENE I

DANIEL WEBSTER.
He digged a pit, he digged it deep he digged it for his brother.
Into the pit he did fall in the pit he digged for tother.

ALL THE CHARACTERS.
Daniel was my father's name,
My father's name was Daniel.
JO THE LOITERER.
Not Daniel.
CHRIS THE CITIZEN.
Not Daniel in the lion's den.
ALL THE CHARACTERS.
My father's name was Daniel.
G. S.
My father's name was Daniel, Daniel and a bear, a bearded Daniel,
not Daniel in the lion's den not Daniel, yes Daniel my father had
a beard my father's name was Daniel,
DANIEL WEBSTER.
He digged a pit he digged it deep he digged it for his brother,
Into the pit he did fall in the pit he digged for tother.
INDIANA ELLIOT. Choose a name.
SUSAN B. ANTHONY. Susan B. Anthony is my name to choose a name is feeble, Susan B. Anthony is my name, a name can only be a name my name can only be my name, I have a name, Susan B. Anthony is my name, to choose a name is feeble.
INDIANA ELLIOT. Yes that's easy, Susan B. Anthony is that kind of a name but my name Indiana Elliot. What's in a name.
SUSAN B. ANTHONY. Everything.
G. S. My father's name was Daniel he had a black beard he was not tall not at all tall, he had a black beard his name was Daniel.
ALL THE CHARACTERS. My father had a name his name was Daniel.
JO THE LOITERER. Not Daniel
CHRIS THE CITIZEN. Not Daniel not Daniel in the lion's den not Daniel.
SUSAN B. ANTHONY. I had a father, Daniel was not his name.
INDIANA ELLIOT. I had no father no father.

126

GERTRUDE STEIN (1874–1946)

As soon after her birth (in Allegheny, Pennsylvania) as she was able to travel, her parents took Gertrude and their four other children on an extended European tour. Upon their return some five years later, the Steins resided for a short time in Baltimore, Maryland, before settling in East Oakland, California.

Gertrude and her older brother, Leo, shared an especially close relationship. Eventually they would both leave America to take up residence in Paris. At their now legendary address, 27, rue de Fleurus, Gertrude and Leo collected the paintings of Matisse, Cézanne, and Picasso and established a salon where artists and writers came together. Their early years in Paris and Gertrude's long struggle to achieve recognition for her unique style of writing are described in her lively narrative *The Autobiography of Alice B. Toklas* (1933). This book also proved to be her first popular success.

Among her early works were a number of portraits in words, probably the most significant of which was "A Portrait of Mabel Dodge at the Villa Curonia" (1912). Dodge was well known in literary circles both here and abroad, and such was her delight that she responded in kind with an article on Stein's work entitled "Speculations, or Post-Impressionism in Prose" for the March, 1913, issue of *Arts and Decoration* magazine. This article was reprinted the following year in the catalog for the exhibit that introduced Cubism to New York, and thereafter Stein's name was linked with those of Picasso, Picabia, Delauney, Braque, and Gris. In the beginning all of them met with ridicule and scorn from the general public, but over the years they have emerged as seminal figures in what has come to be called "modern" art.

Another early work, *Three Lives* (1906), was later to attract the attention of writers such as Ernest Hemingway and Sherwood Anderson, both of whom helped to give Stein a reputation among the literary avant garde long before the rest of the world looked seriously at her work.

Stein's method of writing is not easy to describe. She used simple words in unique combinations for the purpose of arriving at their most objective meaning. It was a method comparable to that of the Cubist painters, who pictured simple objects in ways that seemed distorted.

The Mother of Us All was written in 1946 as the libretto for an opera by Virgil Thomson. Stein knew at the time that she was dying. Her choice of Susan B. Anthony as the play's heroine was made, in part, because both women had faced death knowing that their life's work was incomplete.

Gertrude Stein began to think seriously of writing as a career after graduating from Radcliffe College and dropping out of the Johns Hopkins Medical School. This followed an unhappy triangular love affair with two other women. Much of Stein's unhappiness stemmed from the misunderstandings created by the nuances of meaning in the words spoken between the three women. In the novella *Q.E.D.* (1903) she described the affair in a way that became her earliest attempt to find a better, more accurate use of words than language traditionally conveyed.

DANIEL WEBSTER. He digged a pit he digged it deep he digged it for his brother, into the pit he did fall in the pit he digged for tother.

ACT I — SCENE II

JO THE LOITERER. I want to tell

CHRIS THE CITIZEN. Very well

JO THE LOITERER. I want to tell oh hell.

CHRIS THE CITIZEN. Oh very well.

JO THE LOITERER. I want to tell oh hell I want to tell about my wife.

CHRIS THE CITIZEN. And have you got one.

JO THE LOITERER. No not one.

CHRIS THE CITIZEN. Two then

JO THE LOITERER. No not two.

CHRIS. How many then

JO THE LOITERER. I haven't got one. I want to tell oh hell about my wife I haven't got one.

CHRIS THE CITIZEN. Well.

JO THE LOITERER. My wife, she had a garden.

CHRIS THE CITIZEN. Yes

Jo the Loiterer. And I bought one.

Chris the Citizen. A wife.

No said Jo I was poor and I bought a garden. And then said Chris. She said, said Jo, she said my wife said one tree in my garden was her tree in her garden. And said Chris, Was it. Jo, We quarreled about it. And then said Chris. And then said Jo, we took a train and we went where we went. And then said Chris. She gave me a little package said Jo. And was it a tree said Chris. No it was money said Jo. And was she your wife said Chris, yes said Jo when she was funny, How funny said Chris. Very funny said Jo. Very funny said Jo. To be funny you have to take everything in the kitchen and put it on the floor, you have to take all your money and all your jewels and put them near the door you have to go to bed then and leave the door ajar. That is the way you do when you are funny.

Chris the Citizen. Was she funny.

Jo the Loiterer. Yes she was funny.

(Chris and Jo *put their arms around each other.*)

Angel More. Not any more I am not a martyr any more, not any more.

Be a martyr said Chris.

Angel More. Not any more. I am not a martyr any more. Surrounded by sweet smelling flowers I fell asleep three times.

Darn and wash and patch, darn and wash and patch, darn and wash and patch darn and wash and patch.

Jo the Loiterer. Anybody can be accused of loitering.

Chris Blake a Citizen. Any loiterer can be accused of loitering.

Henrietta M. Daniel Webster needs an artichoke.

Angel More. Susan B. is cold in wet weather.

Henry B. She swore an oath she'd quickly come to any one to any one.

Anthony Comstock. Caution and curiosity, oil and obligation, wheels and appurtenances, in the way of means.

Virgil T. What means.

John Adams. I wish to say I also wish to stay, I also wish to go away, I also wish I endeavor to also wish.

Angel More. I wept on a wish.

John Adams. Whenever I hear any one say of course, do I deny it, yes I do deny it whenever I hear any one say of course I deny it, I do deny it.

Thaddeus S. Be mean.

Daniel Webster. Be there.

Henrietta M. Be where

Constance Fletcher. I do and I do not declare that roses and wreaths, wreaths and roses around and around, blind as a bat, curled as a hat and a plume, be mine when I die, farewell to a thought, he left all alone, be firm in despair dear dear never share, dear dear, dear dear, I Constance Fletcher dear dear, I am a dear, I am dear dear I am a dear, here there everywhere. I bow myself out.

Indiana Elliot. Anybody else would be sorry.

Susan B. Anthony. Hush, I hush, you hush, they hush, we hush. Hush.

Gloster Heming and Isabel Wentworth. We, hush, dear as we are, we are very dear to us and to you we hush, we hush you say hush, dear hush. Hush dear.

Anna Hope. I open any door, that is the way that any day is today, any day is today I open any door every door a door.

Lillian Russell. Thank you.

Anthony Comstock. Quilts are not crazy, they are kind.

Jenny Reefer. My goodness gracious me.

Ulysses S. Grant. He knew that his name was not Eisenhower. Yes he knew it. He did know it.

Herman Atlan. He asked me to come he did ask me.

Donald Gallup. I chose a long time, a very long time, four hours are a very long time, I chose, I took a very long time, I took a very long time. Yes I took a very long time to choose, yes I did.

T. T. and A. A. They missed the boat yes they did they missed the boat.

Jo a Loiterer. I came again but not when I was expected, but yes when I was expected because they did expect me.

Chris the Citizen. I came to dinner.

(*They all sit down.*)

CURTAIN

ACT I — Scene III

(Susan B. Anthony *and* Daniel Webster *seated in two straight-backed chairs not too near each other.* JO THE LOITERER *comes in.*)

JO THE LOITERER. I don't know where a mouse is I don't know what a mouse is. What is a mouse.

ANGEL MORE. I am a mouse

JO THE LOITERER. Well

ANGEL MORE. Yes Well

JO THE LOITERER. All right well. Well what is a mouse

ANGEL MORE. I am a mouse

JO THE LOITERER. Well if you are what is a mouse

ANGEL MORE. You know what a mouse is, I am a mouse.

JO THE LOITERER. Yes well, And she.

(SUSAN B. *dressed like a Quakeress turns around.*)

SUSAN B. I hear a sound.

JO THE LOITERER. Yes well

DANIEL WEBSTER. I do not hear a sound. When I am told.

SUSAN B. ANTHONY. Silence.

(*Everybody is silent.*)

SUSAN B. ANTHONY. Youth is young, I am not old.

DANIEL WEBSTER. When the mariner has been tossed for many days, in thick weather, and on an unknown sea, he naturally avails himself of the first pause in the storm.

SUSAN B. ANTHONY. For instance. They should always fight. They should be martyrs. Some should be martyrs. Will they. They will.

DANIEL WEBSTER. We have thus heard sir what a resolution is.

SUSAN B. ANTHONY. I am resolved.

DANIEL WEBSTER. When this debate sir was to be resumed on Thursday it so happened that it would have been convenient for me to be elsewhere.

SUSAN B. I am here, ready to be here. Ready to be where. Ready to be here. It is my habit.

DANIEL WEBSTER. The honorable member complained that I had slept on his speech.

SUSAN B. The right to sleep is given to no woman.

DANIEL WEBSTER. I did sleep on the gentleman's speech; and slept soundly.

SUSAN B. I too have slept soundly when I have slept, yes when I have slept I too have slept soundly.

DANIEL WEBSTER. Matches and over matches.

SUSAN B. I understand you undertake to overthrow my undertaking.

DANIEL WEBSTER. I can tell the honorable member once for all that he is greatly mistaken, and that he is dealing with one of whose temper and character he has yet much to learn.

SUSAN B. I have declared that patience is never more than patient. I too have declared, that I who am not patient am patient.

DANIEL WEBSTER. What interest asks he has South Carolina in a canal in Ohio.

SUSAN B. What interest have they in me, what interest have I in them, who holds the head of whom, who can bite their lips to avoid a swoon.

DANIEL WEBSTER. The harvest of neutrality had been great, but we had gathered it all.

SUSAN B. Near hours are made not by shade not by heat not by joy, I always know that not now rather not now, yes and I do not stamp but I know that now yes now is now. I have never asked any one to forgive me.

DANIEL WEBSTER. On yet another point I was still more unaccountably misunderstood.

SUSAN B. Do we do what we have to do or do we have to do what we do. I answer.

DANIEL WEBSTER. Mr. President I shall enter on no encomium upon Massachusetts she need none. There she is behold her and judge for yourselves.

SUSAN B. I enter into a tabernacle I was born a believer in peace, I say fight for the right, be a martyr and live, be a coward and die, and why, because they, yes they, sooner or later go away. They leave us here. They come again. Don't forget, they come again.

DANIEL WEBSTER. So sir I understand the gentleman and am happy to find I did not misunderstand him.

SUSAN B. I should believe, what they ask, but they know, they know.

DANIEL WEBSTER. It has been to us all a copious fountain of national, social and personal happiness.

SUSAN B. Shall I protest, not while I live and breathe, I shall protest, shall I protest, shall I protest while I live and breathe.

DANIEL WEBSTER. When my eyes shall be turned to behold for the last time the sun in heaven.

SUSAN B. Yes.

JO THE LOITERER. I like a mouse

ANGEL MORE. I hate mice.

JO THE LOITERER. I am not talking about mice, I am talking about a mouse. I like a mouse.

ANGEL MORE. I hate a mouse.

JO THE LOITERER. Now do you.

CURTAIN

INTERLUDE

(SUSAN B. *A Short Story.*)

Yes I was said Susan.

You mean you are, said Anne.

No said Susan no.

When this you see remember me said Susan B.

I do said Anne.

After a while there was education. Who is educated said Anne.

Susan began to follow, she began to follow herself. I am not tired said Susan. No not said Anne. No I am not said Susan. This was the beginning. They began to travel not to travel you know but to go from one place to another place. In each place Susan B. said here I am I am here. Well said Anne. Do not let it trouble you said Susan politely. By the time she was there she was polite. She often thought about politeness. She said politeness was so agreeable. Is it said Anne. Yes said Susan yes I think so that is to say politeness is agreeable that is to say it could be agreeable if everybody were polite but when it is only me, ah me, said Susan B.

Anne was reproachful why do you not speak louder she said to Susan B. I speak as loudly as I can said Susan B. I even speak louder I even speak louder than I can. Do you really said Anne. Yes I really do said Susan B. it was dark and as it was dark it was necessary to speak louder or very softly, very softly. Dear me said Susan B., if it was not so early I would be sleepy. I myself said Anne never like to look at a newspaper. You are entirely right said Susan B. only I disagree with you. You do said Anne. You know very well I do said Susan B.

Men said Susan B. are so conservative, so selfish, so boresome and said Susan B. they are so ugly, and said Susan B. they are gullible, anybody can convince them, listen said Susan B. they listen to me. Well said Anne anybody would. I know said Susan B. I know anybody would I know that.

Once upon a time any day was full of occupation. You were never tired said Anne. No I was never tired said Susan B. And now, said Anne. Now I am never tired said Susan B. Let us said Anne let us think about everything. No said Susan B. no, no no, I know, I know said Susan B. no, said Susan B. No. But said Anne. But me no buts said Susan B. I know, now you like every one, every one and you each one and you they all do, they all listen to me, utterly unnecessary to deny, why deny, they themselves will they deny that they listen to me but let them deny it, all the same they do they do listen to me all the men do, see them said Susan B., do see them, see them, why not, said Susan B., they are men, and men, well of course they know that they cannot either see or hear unless I tell them so, poor things said Susan B. I do not pity them. Poor things. Yes said Anne they are poor things. Yes said Susan B. they are poor things. They are poor things said Susan B. men are poor things. Yes they are said Anne. Yes they are said Susan B. and nobody pities them. No said Anne no, nobody pities them. Very likely said Susan B. More than likely, said Anne. Yes said Susan B. yes.

It was not easy to go away but Susan B. did go away. She kept on going away and every time she went away she went away again. Oh my said Susan B. why do I go away, I go away because if I did not go away I would stay. Yes of course said Anne yes of course, if you did not go away you would stay. Yes of course said Susan B. Now said Susan B., let us not forget that in each place men are the same just the same, they are conservative, they are selfish and they listen to me. Yes they do said Anne. Yes they do said Susan B.

Susan B. was right, she said she was right and she was right. Susan B. was right. She was right because she was right. It is easy to be right, everybody else is wrong so it is easy to be right, and Susan B. was right, of course she was right, it is easy to be right, everybody else is wrong it is easy to be right. And said Susan B., in a way yes in a way yes really in a way, in a way really it is useful to be right. It does what it does, it does do what it does, if you are right, it does do what it does. It is very remarkable said Anne. Not very remarkable said Susan B. not very remarkable, no not very remarkable. It is not very remarkable really not very remarkable said Anne. No said Susan B. no not very remarkable.

And said Susan B. that is what I mean by not very remarkable.

Susan B. said she would not leave home. No said Susan B. I will not leave home. Why not said Anne. Why not said Susan B. all right I will I always have I always will. Yes you always will said Anne. Yes I always will said Susan B. In a little while anything began again and Susan B. said she did not mind. Really and truly said Susan B. really and truly I do not mind. No said Anne you do not mind, no said Susan B. no really and truly truly and really I do not mind. It was very necessary never to be cautious said Susan B. Yes said Anne it is very necessary.

In a little while they found everything very mixed. It is not really mixed said Susan B. How can anything be really mixed when men are conservative, dull, monotonous, deceived, stupid, unchanging and bullies, how said Susan B. how when men are men can they be mixed. Yes said Anne, yes men are men, how can they when men are men how can they be mixed yes how can they. Well said Susan B. let us go on they always listen to me. Yes said Anne yes they always listen to you. Yes said Susan B. yes they always listen to me.

ACT II

ANDREW J. It is cold weather.

HENRIETTA M. In winter.

ANDREW J. Wherever I am

(THADDEUS S. *comes in singing a song*.)

THADDEUS S. I believe in public school education, I do not believe in free masons I believe in public school education, I do not believe that every one can do whatever he likes because (a pause) I have not always done what I liked, but, I would, if I could, and so I will, I will do what I will, I will have my will, and they, when the they, where are they, beside a poll, Gallup the poll. It is remarkable that there could be any nice person by the name of Gallup, but there is, yes there is, that is my decision.

ANDREW J. Bother your decision, I tell you it is cold weather.

HENRIETTA M. In winter.

ANDREW J. Wherever I am.

CONSTANCE FLETCHER. Antagonises is a pleasant name, antagonises is a pleasant word, antagonises has occurred, bless you all and one.

JOHN ADAMS. Dear Miss Constance Fletcher, it is a great pleasure that I kneel at your feet, but I am Adams, I kneel at the feet of none, not any one, dear Miss Constance Fletcher dear dear Miss Constance Fletcher I kneel at your feet, you would have ruined my father if I had had one but I have had one and you had ruined him, dear Miss Constance Fletcher if I had not been an Adams I would have kneeled at your feet.

CONSTANCE FLETCHER. And kissed my hand.

J. ADAMS (*shuddering*). And kissed your hand.

CONSTANCE FLETCHER. What a pity, no not what a pity it is better so, but what a pity what a pity it is what a pity.

J. ADAMS. Do not pity me kind beautiful lovely Miss Constance Fletcher do not pity me, no do not pity me, I am an Adams and not pitiable.

CONSTANCE FLETCHER. Dear dear me if he had not been an Adams he would have kneeled at my feet and he would have kissed my hand. Do you mean that you would have kissed my hand or my hands, dear Mr. Adams.

J. ADAMS. I mean that I would have first kneeled at your feet and then I would have kissed one of your hands and then I would still kneeling have kissed both of your hands, if I had not been an Adams.

CONSTANCE FLETCHER. Dear me Mr. Adams dear me.

ALL THE CHARACTERS. If he had not been an Adams he would have kneeled at her feet and he would have kissed one of her hands, and then still kneeling he would have kissed both of her hands still kneeling if he had not been an Adams.

ANDREW J. It is cold weather.

HENRIETTA M. In winter.

ANDREW J. Wherever I am.

THADDEUS S. When I look at him I fly, I mean when he looks at me he can cry.

LILLIAN RUSSELL. It is very naughty for men to quarrel so.

HERMAN ATLAN. They do quarrel so.

LILLIAN RUSSELL. It is very naughty of them very naughty.

(JENNY REEFER *begins to waltz with* HERMAN ATLAN.)

A SLOW CHORUS. Naughty men, they quarrel so

Quarrel about what.
About how late the moon
can rise.
About how soon the earth
can turn.
About how naked are the
stars.
About how black are
blacker men.
About how pink are pinks
in spring.
About what corn is best
to pop.
About how many feet the
ocean has dropped.
Naughty men naughty
men, they are always
always quarreling.

JENNY REEFER. Ulysses S. Grant was not the most earnest nor the most noble of men, but he was not always quarreling.

DONALD GALLUP. No he was not.

JO THE LOITERER. Has everybody forgotten Isabel Wentworth. I just want to say has everybody forgotten Isabel Wentworth.

CHRIS THE CITIZEN. Why shouldn't everybody forget Isabel Wentworth.

JO THE LOITERER. Well that is just what I want to know I just want to know if everybody has forgotten Isabel Wentworth. That is all I want to know I just want to know if everybody has forgotten Isabel Wentworth.

ACT II — SCENE II

SUSAN B. Shall I regret having been born, will I regret having been born, shall and will, will and shall, I regret having been born.

ANNE. Is Henrietta M. a sister of Angel More.

SUSAN B. No, I used to feel that sisters should be sisters, and that sisters prefer sisters, and I.

ANNE. Is Angel More the sister of Henrietta M. It is important that I know important.

SUSAN B. Yes important.

ANNE. An Indiana Elliot are there any other Elliots beside Indiana Elliot. It is important that I should know, very important.

SUSAN B. Should one work up excitement, or should one turn it low so that it will explode louder, should one work up excitement should one.

ANNE. Are there any other Elliots beside Indiana Elliot, had she sisters or even cousins, it is very important that I should know, very important.

SUSAN B. A life is never given for a life, when a life is given a life is gone, if no life is gone there is no room for more life, life and strife, I give my life, that is to say, I live my life every day.

ANNE. And Isabel Wentworth, is she older or younger than she was it is very important very important that I should know just how old she is. I must have a list I must of how old every one is, it is very important.

SUSAN B. I am ready.

ANNE. We have forgotten we have forgotten Jenny Reefer, I don't know even who she is, it is very important that I know who Jenny Reefer is very important.

SUSAN B. And perhaps it is important to know who Lillian Russell is, perhaps it is important.

ANNE. It is not important to know who Lillian Russell is.

SUSAN B. Then you do know.

ANNE. It is not important for me to know who Lillian Russell is.

SUSAN B. I must choose I do choose, men and women women and men I do choose. I must choose colored or white white or colored I must choose, I must choose, weak or strong, strong or weak I must choose.

(*All the men coming forward together.*)

SUSAN B. I must choose

JO THE LOITERER. Fight fight fight, between the nigger and the white.

CHRIS THE CITIZEN. And the women.

ANDREW J. I wish to say that little men are bigger than big men, that they know how to drink and to get drunk. They say I was a little man next to that big man, nobody can say what they do say nobody can.

CHORUS OF ALL THE MEN. No nobody can, we feel that way too, no nobody can.

ANDREW JOHNSON. Begin to be drunk when you can so be a bigger man than a big man, you can.

CHORUS OF MEN. You can.

ANDREW J. I often think, I am a bigger man than a bigger man. I often think I am.

(ANDREW J. *moves around and as he moves around he sees himself in a mirror.*)

Nobody can say little as I am I am not bigger than anybody bigger bigger bigger (and then in a low whisper) bigger than him bigger than him.

JO THE LOITERER. Fight fight between the big and the big never between the little and the big.

CHRIS THE CITIZEN. They don't fight.

VIRGIL T. *makes them all gather around him.*)

VIRGIL T. Hear me he says hear me in every way I have satisfaction, I sit I stand I walk around and I am grand, and you all know it.

CHORUS OF MEN. Yes we all know it. That's that.

And Said VIRGIL T. I will call you up one by one and then you will know which one is which, I know, then you will be known. Very well, Henry B.

HENRY B. (*comes forward*). I almost thought that I was Tommy I almost did I almost thought I was Tommy W. but if I were Tommy W. I would never come again, not if I could do better no not if I could do better.

VIRGIL T. Useless. John Adams. (JOHN ADAMS *advances.*) Tell me are you the real John Adams you know I sometimes doubt it not really doubt it you know but doubt it.

JOHN ADAMS. If you were silent I would speak.

JO THE LOITERER. Fight fight fight between day and night.

CHRIS THE CITIZEN. Which is day and which is night.

JO THE LOITERER. Hush, which.

JOHN ADAMS. I ask you Virgil T. do you love women, I do. I love women but I am never subdued by them never.

VIRGIL T. He is no good. Andrew J. and Thaddeus S. better come together.

JO THE LOITERER. He wants to fight fight fight between.

CHRIS. Between what.

JO THE LOITERER. Between the dead.

ANDREW J. I tell you I am bigger bigger is not biggest is not bigger. I am bigger and just to the last minute, I stick, it's better to stick than to die, it's better to itch than to cry, I have tried them all.

VIRGIL T. You bet you have.

THADDEUS S. I can be carried in dying but I will never quit trying.

JO THE LOITERER. Oh go to bed when all is said oh go to bed, everybody, let's hear the women.

CHRIS THE CITIZEN. Fight fight between the nigger and the white and the women.

(ANDREW J. and THADDEUS S. *begin to quarrel violently.*)

Tell me said Virgil T. tell me I am from Missouri.

(*Everybody suddenly stricken dumb.*)

DANIEL *advances holding* HENRIETTA M. *by the hand.*)

DANIEL. Ladies and gentlemen let me present you let me present to you Henrietta M. it is rare in this troubled world to find a woman without a last name rare delicious and troubling, ladies and gentlemen let me present Henrietta M.

CURTAIN

ACT II — SCENE III

SUSAN B. I do not know whether I am asleep or awake, awake or asleep, asleep or awake. Do I know.

JO THE LOITERER. I know, you are awake Susan B.

(*A snowy landscape. A negro man and a negro woman.*)

SUSAN B. Negro man would you vote if you only can and not she.

NEGRO MAN. You bet.

SUSAN B. I fought for you that you could vote would you vote if they would not let me.

NEGRO MAN. Holy gee.

SUSAN B. (*moving down in the snow*). If I believe that I am right and I am right if they believe that they are right and they are not in the right, might, might, might there be what might be.

NEGRO MAN AND WOMAN (*following her*). All right Susan B. all right.

SUSAN B. How then can we entertain a hope that they will act differently, we may pretend to go in good faith but there will be no faith in us.

DONALD GALLUP. Let me help you Susan B.

SUSAN B. And if you do and I annoy you what will you do.

DONALD GALLUP. But I will help you Susan B.

SUSAN B. I tell you if you do and I annoy you what will you do.

DONALD GALLUP. I wonder if I can help you Susan B.

SUSAN B. I wonder.

(ANDREW G., THADDEUS *and* DANIEL WEBSTER *come in together*.)

We are the chorus of the V.I.P. Very important persons to every one who can hear and see, we are the chorus of the V.I.P.

SUSAN B. Yes, so they are. I am important but not that way, not that way.

THE THREE V.I.P.'s. We you see we V.I.P. very important to any one who can hear or you can see, just we three, of course lots of others but just we three, just we three we are the chorus of V.I.P. Very important persons to any one who can hear or can see.

SUSAN B. My constantly recurring thought and prayer now are that no word or act of mine may lessen the might of this country in the scale of truth and right.

THE CHORUS OF V.I.P.

DANIEL WEBSTER. When they all listen to me.

THADDEUS S. When they all listen to me.

ANDREW J. When they all listen to him, by him I mean me.

DANIEL WEBSTER. By him I mean me.

THADDEUS S. It is not necessary to have any meaning I am he, he is me I am a V.I.P.

THE THREE. We are the V.I.P. the very important persons, we have special rights, they ask us first and they wait for us last and wherever we are well there we are everybody knows we are there, we are the V.I.P. Very important persons for everybody to see.

JO THE LOITERER. I wished that I knew the difference between rich and poor, I used to think I was poor, now I think I am rich and I am rich, quite rich not very rich quite rich, I wish I knew the difference between rich and poor.

CHRIS THE CITIZEN. Ask her, ask Susan B. I always ask, I find they like it and I like it, and if I like it, and if they like it, I am not rich and I am not poor, just like that Jo just like that.

JO THE LOITERER. Susan B. listen to me, what is the difference between rich and poor poor and rich no use to ask the V.I.P., they never answer me but you Susan B. you answer, answer me.

SUSAN B. Rich, to be rich, is to be so rich that when they are rich they have it to be that they do not listen and when they do they do not hear, and to be poor to be poor, is to be so poor they listen and listen and what they hear well what do they hear, they hear that they listen, they listen to hear, that is what it is to be poor, but I, I Susan B., there is no wealth nor poverty, there is no wealth, what is wealth, there is no poverty, what is poverty, has a pen ink, has it.

JO THE LOITERER. I had a pen that was to have ink for a year and it only lasted six weeks.

SUSAN B. Yes I know Jo. I know.

CURTAIN

ACT II—SCENE IV

(*A Meeting*.)

SUSAN B. (*on the platform*). Ladies there is no neutral position for us to assume. If we say we love the cause and then sit down at our ease, surely does our action speak the lie.

And now will Daniel Webster take the platform as never before.

DANIEL WEBSTER. Coming and coming alone, no man is alone when he comes, when he comes when he is coming he is not alone and now ladies and gentlemen I have done, remember that remember me remember each one.

SUSAN B. And now Virgil T. Virgil T. will bow and speak and when it is necessary they will know that he is he.

VIRGIL T. I make what I make, I make a noise, there is a poise in making a noise.

(*An interruption at the door*.)

JO THE LOITERER. I have behind me a crowd, are we allowed.

SUSAN B. A crowd is never allowed but each one of you can come in.

CHRIS THE CITIZEN. But if we are allowed then we are a crowd.

SUSAN B. No, this is the cause, and a cause is a pause. Pause before you come in.

JO THE LOITERER. Yes ma'am.

(*All the characters crowd in.* CONSTANCE FLETCHER *and* INDIANA ELLIOT *leading*).

DANIEL WEBSTER. I resist it today and always. Who ever falters or whoever flies I continue the contest.

(CONSTANCE FLETCHER *and* INDIANA ELLIOT *bowing low say*): Dear man, he can make us glad that we have had so great so dear a man here with us now and now we bow before him here, this dear this dear great man.

SUSAN B. Hush, this is slush. Hush.

JOHN ADAMS. I cannot be still when still and until I see Constance Fletcher dear Constance Fletcher noble Constance Fletcher and I spill I spill over like a thrill and a trill, dear Constance Fletcher there is no cause in her presence, how can there be a cause. Women what are women. There is Constance Fletcher, men what are men, there is Constance Fletcher, Adams, yes, Adams, I am John Adams, there is Constance Fletcher, when this you see listen to me, Constance, no I cannot call her Constance I can only call her Constance Fletcher.

INDIANA ELLIOT. And how about me.

JO THE LOITERER. Whist shut up I have just had an awful letter from home, shut up.

INDIANA ELLIOT. What did they say.

JO THE LOITERER. They said I must come home and not marry you.

INDIANA. Who ever said we were going to marry.

JO THE LOITERER. Believe me I never did.

INDIANA. Disgrace to the cause of women, out. (*And she shoves him out.*)

JO THE LOITERER. Help Susan B. help me.

SUSAN B. I know that we suffer, and as we suffer we grow strong, I know that we wait and as we wait we are bold, I know that we are beaten and as we are beaten we win, I know that men know that this is not so but it is so, I know, yes I know.

JO THE LOITERER. There didn't I tell you she knew best, you just give me a kiss and let me alone.

DANIEL WEBSTER. I who was once old am now young, I who was once weak am now strong, I who have left every one behind am now overtaken.

SUSAN B. I undertake to overthrow your undertaking.

JO THE LOITERER. You bet.

CHRIS THE CITIZEN. I always repeat everything I hear.

JO THE LOITERER. You sure do.

(*While all this is going on, all the characters are crowding up on the platform.*)

(*They Say*):

Now we are all here there is nobody down there to hear, now if it is we're always like that there would be no reason why anybody should cry, because very likely if at all it would be so nice to be the head, we are the head we have all the bread.

JO THE LOITERER. And the butter too.

CHRIS THE CITIZEN. And Kalamazoo.

SUSAN B. (*advancing*). I speak to those below who are not there who are not there who are not there. I speak to those below to those below who are not there to those below who are not there.

CURTAIN

ACT II — SCENE V

SUSAN B. Will they remember that it is true that neither they that neither you, will they marry will they carry, aloud, the right to know that even if they love them so, they are alone to live and die, they are alone to sink and swim they are alone to have what they own, to have no idea but that they are here, to struggle and thirst to do everything first, because until it is done there is no other one.

(JO THE LOITERER *leads in* INDIANA ELLIOT *in wedding attire, followed by* JOHN ADAMS *and* CONSTANCE FLETCHER *and followed by* DANIEL WEBSTER *and* ANGEL MORE. *All the other characters follow after.* ANNE *and* JENNY REEFER *come and stand by* SUSAN B. ULYSSES S. GRANT *sits down in a chair right behind the procession.*)

ANNE. Marriage.

JENNY REEFER. Marry marriage.

SUSAN B. I know I know and I have told you so, but if no one marries how can there be women to tell men, women to tell men.

ANNE. What

JENNY REEFER. Women should not tell men.

SUSAN B. Men can not count, they do not know that two and two make four if women do not tell them so. There is a devil creeps into men when their hands are strengthened. Men want to be half slave half free. Women want to be all slave or all free, therefore men govern and women know, and yet.

ANNE. Yet.

JENNY REEFER. There is no yet in paradise.

SUSAN B. Let them marry.

(*The marrying commences.*)

JO THE LOITERER. I tell her if she marries me do I marry her.

INDIANA ELLIOT. Listen to what he says so you can answer, have you the ring.

JO THE LOITERER. You did not like the ring and mine is too large.

INDIANA ELLIOT. Hush.

Jo the Loiterer. I wish my name was Adams.

Indiana Elliot. Hush.

John Adams. I never marry I have been twice divorced but I have never married, fair Constance Fletcher fair Constance Fletcher do you not admire me that I never can married be. I who have been twice divorced. Dear Constance Fletcher dear dear Constance Fletcher do you not admire me.

Constance Fletcher. So beautiful. It is so beautiful to meet you here, so beautiful, so beautiful to meet you here dear, dear John Adams, so beautiful to meet you here.

Daniel Webster. When I have joined and not having joined have separated and not having separated have led, and not having led have thundered, when I having thundered have provoked and having provoked have dominated, may I dear Angel More not kneel at your feet because I cannot kneel my knees are not kneeling knees but dear Angel More be my Angel More for evermore.

Angel More. I join the choir that is visible, because the choir that is visible is as visible.

Daniel Webster. As what Angel More.

Angel More. As visible as visible, do you not hear me, as visible.

Daniel Webster. You do not and I do not.

Angel More. What.

Daniel Webster. Separate marriage from marriage.

Angel More. And why not.

Daniel Webster. And.

(*Just at this moment* Ulysses S. Grant *makes his chair pound on the floor.*)

Ulysses S. Grant. As long as I sit I am sitting, silence again as you were, you were all silent, as long as I sit I am sitting.

All Together. We are silent, as we were.

Susan B. We are all here to celebrate the civil and religious marriage of Jo the Loiterer and Indiana Elliot.

Jo the Loiterer. Who is civil and who is religious.

Anne. Who is, listen to Susan B. She knows.

(*The Brother of* Indiana Elliot *rushes in.*)

Nobody knows who I am but I forbid the marriage, do we know whether Jo the Loiterer is a bigamist or a grandfather or an uncle or a refugee. Do we know, no we do not know and I forbid the marriage, I forbid it, I am Indiana

Elliot's brother and I forbid it, I am known as Herman Atlan and I forbid it, I am known as Anthony Comstock and I forbid it. I am Indiana Elliot's brother and I forbid it.

Jo the Loiterer. Well well well, I knew that ring of mine was too large, It could not fall off on account of my joints but I knew it was too large.

Indiana Elliot. I renounce my brother.

Jo the Loiterer. That's right my dear that's all right.

Susan B. What is marriage, is marriage protection or religion, is marriage renunciation or abundance, is marriage a stepping-stone or an end. What is marriage.

Anne. I will never marry.

Jenny Reefer. If I marry I will divorce but I will not marry because if I did marry, I would be married.

(Ulysses S. Grant *pounds his chair.*)

Ulysses S. Grant. Didn't I say I do not like noise, I do not like cannon balls, I do not like storms, I do not like talking, I do not like noise. I like everything and everybody to be silent and what I like I have. Everybody be silent.

Jo the Loiterer. I know I was silent, everybody can tell just by listening to me just how silent I am, dear General, dear General Ulysses, dear General Ulysses Simpson dear General Ulysses Simpson Grant, dear dear sir, am I not a perfect example of what you like, am I not silent.

(Ulysses S. Grant's *chair pounds and he is silent.*)

Susan B. I am not married and the reason why is that I have had to do what I have had to do, I have had to be what I have had to be, I could never be one of two I could never be two in one as married couples do and can, I am but one all one, one and all one, and so I have never been married to any one.

Anne. But I I have been, I have been married to what you have been to that one.

Susan B. No no, no, you may be married to the past one, the one that is not the present one, no one can be married to the present one, the one, the one, the present one.

Jenny Reefer. I understand you undertake to overthrow their undertaking.

Susan B. I love the sound of these, one over two, two under one, three under four, four over more.

ANNE. Dear Susan B. Anthony thank you.

JOHN ADAMS. All this time I have been lost in my thoughts in my thoughts of thee beautiful thee, Constance Fletcher, do you see, I have been lost in my thoughts of thee.

CONSTANCE FLETCHER. I am blind and therefore I dream.

DANIEL WEBSTER. Dear Angel More, dear Angel More, there have been men who have stammered and stuttered but not, not I.

ANGEL MORE. Speak louder.

DANIEL WEBSTER. Not I.

THE CHORUS. Why the hell don't you all get married, why don't you, we want to go home, why don't you.

JO THE LOITERER. Why don't you.

INDIANA ELLIOT. Why don't you.

INDIANA ELLIOT'S BROTHER. Why don't you because I am here.

The crowd removed him forcibly

SUSAN B. ANTHONY (*suddenly*). They are married all married and their children women as well as men will have the vote, they will they will, they will have the vote.

CURTAIN

ACT II—SCENE VI

(SUSAN B. *doing her house-work in her house.*)

Enter ANNE. Susan B. they want you.

SUSAN B. Do they

ANNE. Yes. You must go.

SUSAN B. No.

JENNY REEFER. (*Comes in*) Oh yes they want to know if you are here.

SUSAN B. Yes still alive. Painters paint and writers write and soldiers drink and fight and I am still alive.

ANNE. They want you.

SUSAN B. And when they have me.

JENNY REEFER. Then they will want you again.

SUSAN B. Yes I know, they love me so, they tell me so and they tell me so, but I, I do not tell them so because I know, they will not do what they could do and I I will be left alone to die but they will not have done what I need to have done to make it right that I live lived my life and fight.

JO THE LOITERER (*at the window*). Indiana Elliot wants to come in, she will not take my name she says it is not all the same, she says

that she is Indiana Elliot and that I am Jo, and that she will not take my name and that she will always tell me so. Oh yes she is right of course she is right it is not all the same Indiana Elliot is her name, she is only married to me, but there is no difference that I can see, but all the same there she is and she will not change her name, yes it is all the same.

SUSAN B. Let her in.

INDIANA ELLIOT. Oh Susan B. they want you they have to have you, can I tell them you are coming I have not changed my name can I tell them you are coming and that you will do everything.

SUSAN B. No but there is no use in telling them so, they won't vote my laws, there is always a clause, there is always a pause, they won't vote my laws.

(ANDREW JOHNSON *puts his head in at the door.*)

ANDREW JOHNSON. Will the good lady come right along.

THADDEUS STEVENS (*behind him*). We are waiting, will the good lady not keep us waiting, will the good lady not keep us waiting.

SUSAN B. You you know so well that you will not vote my laws.

STEVENS. Dear lady remember humanity comes first.

SUSAN B. You mean men come first, women, you will not vote my laws, how can you dare when you do not care, how can you dare, there is no humanity in humans, there is only law, and you will not because you know so well that there is no humanity there are only laws, you know it so well that you will not you will not vote my laws.

(SUSAN B. *goes back to her housework. All the characters crowd in.*)

CHORUS. Do come Susan B. Anthony do come nobody no nobody can make them come the way you make them come, do come do come Susan B. Anthony, it is your duty, Susan B. Anthony, you know you know your duty, you come, do come, come.

SUSAN B. ANTHONY. I suppose I will be coming, is it because you flatter me, is it because if I do not come you will forget me and never vote my laws, you will never vote my laws even if I do come but if I do not come you will never vote my laws, come or not come it always comes to the same thing it comes to their not voting my laws, not voting my laws, tell me all you men tell me you know you will never vote my laws.

ALL THE MEN. Dear kind lady we count on you, and as we count on you so can you count on us.

SUSAN B. ANTHONY. Yes but I work for you I do, I say never again, never again, never never, and yet I know I do say no but I do not mean no, I know I always hope that if I go that if I go and go and go, perhaps then you men will vote my laws but I know how well I know, a little this way a little that way you steal away, you steal a piece away you steal yourselves away, you do not intend to stay and vote my laws, and still when you call I go, I go, I go, I say no, no, no, and I go, but no, this time no, this time you have to do more than promise, you must write it down that you will vote my laws, but no, you will pay no attention to what is written, well then swear by my hearth, as you hope to have a home and hearth, swear after I work for you swear that you will vote my laws, but no, no oaths, no thoughts, no decisions, no intentions, no gratitude, no convictions, no nothing will make you pass my laws. Tell me can any of you be honest now, and say you will not pass my laws.

JO THE LOITERER. I can I can be honest I can say I will not pass your laws, because you see I have no vote, no loiterer has a vote so it is easy Susan B. Anthony easy for one man among all these men to be honest and to say I will not pass your laws. Anyway Susan B. Anthony what are your laws. Would it really be all right to pass them, if you say so it is all right with me. I have no vote myself but I'll make them as long as I don't have to change my name don't have to don't have to change my name.

T. STEVENS. Thanks dear Susan B. Anthony, thanks we all know that whatever happens we all can depend upon you to do your best for any cause which is a cause, and any cause is a cause and because any cause is a cause therefore you will always do your best for any cause, and now you will be doing your best for this cause our cause the cause.

SUSAN B. Because. Very well is it snowing.

CHORUS. Not just now.

SUSAN B. ANTHONY. Is it cold.

CHORUS. A little.

SUSAN B. ANTHONY. I am not well

CHORUS. But you look so well and once started it will be all right.

SUSAN B. ANTHONY. All right

CURTAIN

ACT II — SCENE VII

(SUSAN B. ANTHONY *busy with her housework.*)

ANNE (*comes in*). Oh it was wonderful, wonderful, they listen to nobody the way they listen to you.

SUSAN B. Yes it is wonderful as the result of my work for the first time the word male has been written into the constitution of the United States concerning suffrage. Yes it is wonderful.

ANNE. But

SUSAN B. Yes but, what is man, what are they. I do not say that they haven't kind hearts, if I fall down in a faint, they will rush to pick me up, if my house is on fire, they will rush in to put the fire out and help me, yes they have kind hearts but they are afraid, afraid, they are afraid, they are afraid. They fear women, they fear each other, they fear their neighbor, they fear other countries and then they hearten themselves in their fear by crowding together and following each other, and when they crowd together and follow each other they are brutes, like animals who stampede, and so they have written in the name male into the United States constitution, because they are afraid of black men because they are afraid of women, because they are afraid afraid. Men are afraid.

ANNE (*timidly*). And women.

SUSAN B. Ah women often have not any sense of danger, after all a hen screams pitifully when she sees an eagle but she is only afraid for her children, men are afraid for themselves, that is the real difference between men and women.

ANNE. But Susan B. why do you not say these things out loud.

SUSAN B. Why not, because if I did they would not listen they not alone would not listen they would revenge themselves. Men have kind hearts when they are not afraid but they are afraid afraid afraid. I say they are afraid, but if I were to tell them so their kindness would turn to hate. Yes the Quakers are right, they are not afraid because they do not fight, they do not fight.

ANNE. But Susan B. you fight and you are not afraid.

SUSAN B. I fight and I am not afraid, I fight but I am not afraid.

ANNE. And you will win.

SUSAN B. Win what, win what.

ANNE. Win the vote for women.

SUSAN B. Yes some day some day the women will vote and by that time.

ANNE. By that time oh wonderful time.

SUSAN B. By that time it will do them no good because having the vote they will become like men, they will be afraid, having the vote will make them afraid, oh I know it, but I will fight for the right, for the right to vote for them even though they become like men, become afraid like men, become like men.

(ANNE *bursts into tears.* JENNY REEFER *rushes in.*)

JENNY REEFER. I have just converted Lillian Russell to the cause of woman's suffrage, I have converted her, she will give all herself and all she earns oh wonderful day I know you will say, here she comes isn't she beautiful.

(LILLIAN RUSSELL *comes in followed by all the women in the chorus. Women crowding around,* CONSTANCE FLETCHER *in the background.*)

LILLIAN RUSSELL. Dear friends, it is so beautiful to meet you all, so beautiful, so beautiful to meet you all.

(JOHN ADAMS *comes in and sees* CONSTANCE FLETCHER.)

JOHN ADAMS. Dear friend beautiful friend, there is no beauty where you are not.

CONSTANCE FLETCHER. Yes dear friend but look look at real beauty look at Lillian Russell look at real beauty.

JOHN ADAMS. Real beauty real beauty is all there is of beauty and why should my eye wander where no eye can look without having looked before. Dear friend I kneel to you because dear friend each time I see you I have never looked before, dear friend you are an open door.

(DANIEL WEBSTER *strides in, the women separate.*)

DANIEL WEBSTER. What what is it, what is it, what is the false and the true and I say to you you Susan B. Anthony, you know the false from the true and yet you will not wait you will not wait, I say you will you will wait. When my eyes, and I have eyes when my eyes, beyond that I seek not to penetrate the veil, why should you want what you have chosen, when mine eyes, why do you want that the curtain may rise, why when mine eyes, why should the vision be opened to what lies behind, why, Susan B. Anthony fight the fight that is the fight, that any fight may be a fight for the right. I hear that you say that the word male should not be written into the constitution of the United States of America, but I say, I say, that so long that the gorgeous ensign of the republic, still full high advanced, its arms and trophies streaming in their original luster not a stripe erased or polluted not a single star obscured.

JO THE LOITERER. She has decided to change her name.

INDIANA ELLIOT. Not because it is his name but it is such a pretty name, Indiana Loiterer is such a pretty name I think all the same he will have to change his name, he must be Jo Elliot, yes he must, it is what he has to do, he has to be Jo Elliot and I am going to be Indiana Loiterer, dear friends, all friends is it not a lovely name, Indiana Loiterer all the same.

JO THE LOITERER. All right I never fight, nobody will know it's men, but what can I do, if I am not she and I am not me, what can I do, if a name is not true, what can I do but do as she tells me.

ALL THE CHORUS. She is quite right, Indiana Loiterer is so harmonious, so harmonious, Indiana Loiterer is so harmonious.

(*All the men come in.*)
What did she say.

JO. I was talking not she but nobody no nobody ever wants to listen to me.

ALL THE CHORUS (*men and women.*) Susan B. Anthony was very successful we are all very grateful to Susan B. Anthony because she was so successful, she worked for the votes for women and she worked for the vote for colored men and she was so successful, they wrote the word male into the constitution of the United States of America, dear Susan B. Anthony. Dear Susan B., whenever she wants to be and she always wants to be she is always so successful so very successful.

SUSAN B. So successful.

CURTAIN

ACT II — SCENE VIII

(*The Congressional Hall, the replica of the statue of* SUSAN B. ANTHONY *and her comrades in the suffrage fight.*)

ANNE (*alone in front of the statuary*). The Vote. Women have the vote. They have it each and every one, it is glorious glorious glorious.

SUSAN B. ANTHONY (*behind the statue*). Yes women have the vote, all my long life of strength and strife, all my long life, women have it, they can vote, every man and every woman have the vote, the word male is not there any more, that is to say, that is to say.

(*Silence.* VIRGIL T. *comes in very nicely, he looks around and sees* ANNE.)

VIRGIL T. Very well indeed, very well indeed, you are looking very well indeed, have you a chair anywhere, very well indeed, as we sit, we sit, some day very soon some day they will vote sitting and that will be a very successful day any day, every day.

(HENRY B. *comes in. He looks all around at the statue and then he sighs.*)

HENRY B. Does it really mean that women are as white and cold as marble does it really mean that.

(ANGEL MORE *comes in and bows gracefully to the sculptured group.*)

ANGEL MORE. I can always think of dear Daniel Webster daily.

(JOHN ADAMS *comes in and looks around, and then carefully examines the statue.*)

JOHN ADAMS. I think that they might have added dear delicate Constance Fletcher I do think they might have added her wonderful profile, I do think they might have, I do, I really do. (ANDREW JOHNSON *shuffles in.*)

ANDREW JOHNSON. I have no hope in black or white in white or black in black or black or white or white, no hope.

(THADDEUS STEVENS *comes in, he does not address anybody, he stands before the statue and frowns.*)

THADDEUS S. Rob the cradle, rob it, rob the robber, rob him, rob whatever there is to be taken, rob, rob the cradle, rob it.

DANIEL WEBSTER (*he sees nothing else*). Angel More, more more Angel More, did you hear me, can you hear shall you hear me, when they come and they do come, when they go and they do go, Angel More can you will you shall you may you might you would you hear me, when they have lost and won, when they have won and lost, when words are bitter and snow is white, Angel More come to me and we wil leave together.

ANGEL MORE. Dear sir, not leave, stay.

HENRIETTA M. I have never been mentioned again. (*She curtseys.*)

CONSTANCE FLETCHER. Here I am, I am almost blind but here I am, dear dear here I am, I cannot see what is so white, here I am.

JOHN ADAMS (*kissing her hand*). Here you are, blind as a bat and beautiful as a bird, here you are, white and cold as marble, beautiful as marble, yes that is marble but you you are the living marble dear Constance Fletcher, you are.

CONSTANCE FLETCHER. Thank you yes I am here, blind as a bat, I am here.

INDIANA ELLIOT. I am sorry to interrupt so sorry to interrupt but I have a great deal to say about marriage, either one or the other married must be economical, either one or the other, if either one or the other of a married couple are economical then a marriage is successful, if not not, I have a great deal to say about marriage, and dear Susan B. Anthony was never married, how wonderful it is to be never married how wonderful. I have a great deal to say about marriage.

SUSAN B. ANTHONY (*voice from behind the statue*). It is a puzzle, I am not puzzled but it is a puzzle, if there are no children there are no men and women, and if there are men and women, it is rather horrible, and if it is rather horrible, then there are children, I am not puzzled but it is very puzzling, women and men vote and children, I am not puzzled but it is very puzzling.

GLOSTER HEMING. I have only been a man who has a very fine name, and it must be said I made it up yes I did, so many do why not I, so many do, so many do, and why not two, when anybody might, and you can vote and you can dote with any name. Thank you.

ISABEL WENTWORTH. They looked for me and they found me, I like to talk about it. It is very nearly necessary not to be noisy not to be noisy and hope, hope and hope, no use in enjoying men and women no use, I wonder why we are all happy, yes.

ANNIE HOPE. There is another Anne and she believes, I am hopey hope and I do not believe I have been in California and Kalamazoo, and I do not believe I burst into tears and I do not believe.

(*They all crowd closer together and* LILLIAN RUSSELL *who comes in stands quite alone.*)

LILLIAN RUSSELL. I can act so drunk that I never drink, I can drink so drunk that I never act, I have a curl I was a girl and I am old and fat but very handsome for all that.

(ANTHONY COMSTOCK *comes in and glares at her.*)

ANTHONY COMSTOCK. I have heard that they have thought that they would wish that one like you could vote a vote and help to let the ones who want do what they like, I have heard that even you, and I am through, I cannot hope that there is dope, oh yes a horrid word. I have never heard, short.

JENNY REEFER. I have hope and faith, not charity no not charity, I have hope and faith, no not, not charity, no not charity.

ULYSSES S. GRANT. Women are women, soldiers are soldiers, men are not men, lies are not lies, do, and then a dog barks, listen to him and then a dog barks, a dog barks a dog barks any dog barks, listen to him any dog barks. (*He sits down.*)

HERMAN ATLAN. I am not loved any more, I was loved oh yes I was loved but I am not loved any more. I am not, was I not, I knew I would refuse what a woman would choose and so I am not loved any more, not loved any more.

DONALD GALLUP. Last but not least, first and not best, I am tall as a man, I am firm as a clam, and I never change, from day to day.

(JO THE LOITERER *and* CHRIS A CITIZEN.)

JO THE LOITERER. Let us dance and sing, Chrissy Chris, wet and not in debt, I am a married man and I know how I show I am a married man. She votes, she changes her name and she votes.

(*They all crowd together in front of the statue, there is a moment of silence and then a chorus.*)

CHORUS. To vote the vote, the vote we vote, can vote do vote will vote could vote, the vote the vote.

JO THE LOITERER. I am the only one who cannot vote, no loiterer can vote.

INDIANA ELLIOT. I am a loiterer Indiana Loiterer and I can vote.

JO THE LOITERER. You only have the name, you have not got the game.

CHORUS. The vote the vote we will have the vote.

LILLIAN RUSSELL. It is so beautiful to meet you all here so beautiful.

ULYSSES S. GRANT. Vote the vote, the army does not vote, the general generals, there is no vote, bah vote.

THE CHORUS. The vote we vote we note the vote.

(*They all bow and smile to the statue. Suddenly* SUSAN B.'s *voice is heard.*)

SUSAN B.'s *voice*. We cannot retrace our steps, going forward may be the same as going backwards. We cannot retrace our steps, retrace our steps. All my long life, all my life, we do not retrace our steps, all my long life, but.

(*A silence a long silence.*)

But—we do not retrace our steps, all my long life, and here, here we are here, in marble and gold, did I say gold, yes I said gold, in marble and gold and where—

(*A silence.*)

Where is where, In my long life of effort and strife, dear life, life is strife, in my long life, it will not come and go, I tell you so, it will stay it will pay but

(*A long silence.*)

But do I want what we have got, has it not gone, what made it live, has it not gone because now it is had, in my long life in my long life

(*Silence.*)

Life is strife, I was a martyr all my life not to what I won but to what was done.

(*Silence.*)

Do you know because I tell you so, or do you know, do you know.

(*Silence.*)

My long life, my long life.

CURTAIN

DOPE

by Maryat Lee

THE PEOPLE

Louie
Hum
Marc
Friends (dancers)
Porse
Dream Man
Women
Crezell
Drunk

Time: *Present.*

Place: *On or near the street in a crowded neighborhood. The stage is bare except for a garbage can, a crate, tin cans, rubbish. Since the stage is a sidewalk, people are moving along as they talk, except where indicated.*

At Rise: Louie *enters, his eyes half shut. He is slightly bent over; he nods, sighs, scratches his chest, and sits down peacefully on the garbage can at Left, then lights a cigarette and drags slowly. MUSIC starts before his entrance and goes down softly.*

Marc (*runs on; he is younger than* Louie; *gives the stage a glance, then turns and yells Offstage, Right*). Hey, Hum! We can do it here. There's plenty of room. Go get a broom. (*He turns shyly to* Louie.) Hi, Louie.—Hi, we're going to dance, man. (Louie *doesn't move.* Marc *dances to hide his embarassment.*)

Hum (*enters Right*). Yeah—this is crazy. Just wait till I get my little head. Hi, Louie! Hey, get a doll, man. (*To* Marc.) Did you tell Rosie and Mamie?—And get Ruby.

Marc. And Davie! (*He bolts off, Right.*)

Hum. Hey, get Nilsa, too. And don't forget the broom. (*He fixes the place, moves a crate, finds an old broom with the handle broken off, dances to the MUSIC and begins to brush tin cans into a pile next to the garbage can.*) Louie! Hey! Move, man, remember how you used to dance? (*Tries to dance like* Louie.) Hey, come on. You tore it up. (Louie *pays no attention.*) Hey. Hey, Louie —LOUIE! Hey, man, listen, I'm talking. Look—don't you want to dance?

Louie. Dance?

Hum. Yeah!

Louie. I— (*Then shakes his head slowly.*) I don't feel like dancing.

Hum. Why not? What's the matter with you?

Louie. I don't need to dance, man.

Hum. Don't need to dance? (*Hops in the air.*)

Louie. I'm dancing. (*He taps his head.*)

Hum (*whispers*). You high again?

Louie. Ah—what you talking about?

(*MUSIC: up and strong.* Marc *and the* Dancers *begin to enter, Right. The MUSIC, discordant and ominous, has a strong beat and is full for about two minutes.* Everyone *dances—several couples—not all at the same time. They talk or greet* Louie *while each couple in turn takes Center Stage.* Louie *takes one or two half-hearted steps at their encouragement, then stops and looks out and away up at the sky. A hiccupping is heard in the beat of the MUSIC. The* Dancers *lose themselves in a wild dance with clapping and shouts. As the MUSIC begins to fade, they leave one by one, and* Hum *and* Marc *dance closer to* Louie. *MUSIC fades out.*)

Hum (*talks silently with* Marc. *They glance at* Louie *a couple of times and then:*) Go ahead—ask him.

Marc. *You* ask him.

Hum (*pushes* Marc *toward* Louie, *then* Marc *gets around and pushes* Hum, *then:*) Hey, Louie—is that pot that lifts you up?

MARYAT LEE (1923–   )

Fully a decade before such notable avant-garde groups as the Living Theatre and the Open Theatre began to combine improvisation and audience participation with relevant themes, *Dope* (1951) was presented on the streets of Harlem. Maryat Lee cast her play with local residents, who were then encouraged to tell their story in, more or less, their own words. One could not as yet think of an author's work as a scenario along whose lines actors freely improvised; that idea remained to be fully articulated by more self-conscious innovators. Still, every description of Lee's production leaves us with the shock of déjà vu, as we discover that what was thought to have been first—the much-publicized avant garde—in fact came after.

Dope reminded some onlookers of the Living Newspaper performers of the 1930's whose audiences, themselves participants in the real-life drama of the Great Depression, responded to the problems being presented on stage as if they were actually happening. The specific problem confronting the audiences of East Harlem was drug addiction, and, even if not by the design of the play, their very environment made them active participants in Lee's modern morality.

It was only natural, therefore, that *Dope* made use of a jazz ensemble (in much the same way that Jack Gelber does in *The Connection*) and a representative of Narcotics Anonymous, who climbed on the stage to complete the performance. "I was an addict, too," he would tell others that he spotted in the crowd, "for some twenty-four years. I'm okay now. If you want me . . ." And he gave them his telephone number. Looking on from his own fire escape, East Harlem's reputed dope prince attended the opening night.

This was Maryat Lee's first play, and it came about as the result of a year's undirected research into life on a single block in Harlem. Lee was born in Covington,

PHOTO BY FRANCES BELIN

Maryat Lee

Kentucky, where she also grew up. *Dope* represents quite a different education from the one she received at Wellesley College, the Union Theological Seminary, and Columbia University, where her course of study was the history of religion.

Lee has taught street theater at the New School for Social Research. In 1968 she founded the Soul and Latin Theater, producing and writing street plays in various places throughout New York City. She is also the author of *After the Fashion Show* (1968), *Day to Day* (1969), and other plays. In 1974 Maryat Lee left New York to live in Hinton, West Virginia, where she is currently writing a book about her experiences with street and indigenous theatre, as well as preparing a volume of correspondence with Flannery O'Connor.

LOUIE. Pot? (*Smiles.*) Come on, man, where you been at? I got a bigger kick than that, man.

MARC. See? What I told you. Horse!

LOUIE (*lovingly*). Junk, yeah. It whirls you. It—(*Breaks off.*) Hey—get in the wind, will you, man.

HUM. Wait, Louie. How much you pay for that stuff? How much is it right now, I mean?

LOUIE (*turns away, but then after a struggle—softly*). You got any dough? (*They produce two dollars. It isn't enough.*) Look—I think I can work it so I can turn you on free the first time. Then next time you can give me the dough and we can get down together.

Hum. That sounds boss, man.

Marc. I heard you can pick up the first shots free.

Louie. No, man. Not now.

Marc. Oh.

Louie. But if you get it through me—from my guy . . .

Hum. Yeah?

Louie. He's got good stuff—I do jobs for him. And he ain't as slick as some.

Marc. Yeah but how much that kick cost you?

Louie (shrugs). A pound. It depends.

Hum (whistles). For one of them pills?

Louie. Not pill, man. Bag! Bag!

Marc. Wow! That's a lot of dough, man. How often you have to take it?

Louie (sizes him up). Oh you'd take one a week.

Hum. How many do you take, Louie?

Louie (pause). Ah—you're just a couple of punks worrying about a few bucks.

Marc. Is it true you can't stop?

Louie (walking away—they follow). You believe everything you hear?

Marc. Well, I heard it. Everybody says it, and I just thought—

Louie. Man, if I wanted, I could stop just like that. Sure.

Marc. Have you tried?

Louie (pauses). Why should I? (Shrugs.)

Hum. I heard it takes ten years off your life.

Louie. So? Who wants to live a hundred years around here in this—this—cage! (The word turns him on.)

Hum. That stuff must do a lot for you.

Louie. Man, it does. A cage! Ssh, don't interrupt. I'm seeing it. This whole jungle, all of it, man, inside a cage. Everything wild—mashed flat and stuffed into this cage. And look at them—all these faces, thousands of faces in there flattened out and dead, man—and one or two soft, alive faces—their bodies stuffed in there, too—their heads hanging out, trying to sneak through—or breathe. Yeah—Porse and them are in there, too. They're all in there. We're *all* inside! (Pause.) See—once you take it, man, you can see what is a cage and what ain't—and you can get free, free of all this ace-king-and-queen crap, free like a bird way up there that flies up, up, up and busts itself right through space. . . .

That's what it is. No troubles, nobody telling you where you're at, no kids running around loose, no women yelling. (Sighs.) Yeah. No women yelling.

Marc. Oh, man. . . . Well, what do they do?

Louie. What do you mean what do they do?

Hum. If they don't yell.

Louie. Oh, they come around and they're nice to you. They stroke you, like— (Imitates stroking Hum. The Boys laugh and pound each other.) They look at you and they LISTEN. Yeah, they look at you while you— Oh—you can talk—like you got a gold tongue in your mouth. You just never heard yourself talk till then—the words ooze —and you can just get anybody wrapped around your toe. Just tell them—! (Marc and Hum laugh.) Tell them climb in a rat-hole and they just about do it.

Hum. Say, man, that sounds all right.

(Marc yells and jumps.)

Louie. I could tell you lots of things. You know Celee?

(Hum suddenly grabs Marc and whispers.)

Marc. Yeah—once wouldn't hurt.

Louie. Yeh, Celee sings right out so pretty when I come home high, feeling good. (Stops.) She used to. She ain't done it for a while. Ah, but when she sings, my head buzzes, man. (Scratches.)

Marc. Uh—Louie?

Louie. Yeah, man, I hear you. I could do with some myself. (He's looking out over the audience seeing a familiar, necessary person.) Hey! Hey! (Shouts at Porse, who is making his way through the crowd.) Porse! Hi, Porse! (To Marc and Hum.) Listen, you guys. Don't stand there looking like that. Cool it. (Goes to meet Porse.) Say, Porse —how you doing? Hey man, you looking clean today.

Porse (tired). Hi, Louie. Uh—stick around. I want you to pick up something a little later.

Louie. Okay. Uh—look, Porse—?

Porse. Later. Later.

Louie. Listen, I got a couple of new guys, man. (Motions to the Boys across Stage.) Friends of mine.

Porse. You ain't paid up.

Louie. Porse! I've got two new cats. (Points to them.) Hum and Marc.

Porse. How well you know them?

LOUIE. They're my men.

PORSE (*glances at them*). A little young.

LOUIE. What's it to you?

PORSE. Say—hey—you— (*To the* BOYS.) Come here. (*They cross.*) How old are you?

HUM *and* MARC (*look at each other, together*). About eighteen.

PORSE. *About* eighteen? Man, give me the exact.

MARC (*swallows*). Eighteen.

HUM. Eighteen!

PORSE (*he finds them funny*). Eighteen. Well, well.

LOUIE. I know them, Porse. They're okay.

PORSE. I seen them around. But you got to be careful.

HUM. We know where it's at, man. (MARC *agrees.*)

PORSE. Yeah? Where is that? I wish I knew. Now look—I'm going to run it to you like it is.

LOUIE. Porse!

PORSE. My advice is—you'll get in trouble and get me in bad trouble. Now—I don't want no minors messing me up.

LOUIE. Porse!

PORSE (*self-satisfied; to* LOUIE). What about that? See—I try. I try to do good.—Of course, on the other hand—someday when they find out about all them highup officials — When they find *why* the man upstairs is pushing the penalties, they'll make the whole thing legit and then wooee! Where will poor old corrup-tainted Porse peddle his goodies? —You'll see *me* in a clinic? So he done the best he could, you know? On my slab. So make it fast, Porse. Right? You understand me? See—I done give you warning. Well— (*He moves off with* LOUIE.) I'll meet you at the place, five or ten minutes. (LOUIE *holds him back.*) Yeah—I'll have some for them, too.

LOUIE. Come on—sometimes you're late. Sometimes you don't come at all. Make it right now.

PORSE. I told you I'll meet you at the place. I don't have nothing on me. Things are rough. You guys don't realize. (*He keeps his eye roving.*)

LOUIE (*quickly*). Okay. Okay. Five—ten minutes. Thanks, Porse. Thanks! See you. Five—ten minutes!

(PORSE *exits, Left.* LOUIE *starts back to the* BOYS, *then suddenly plays it cool and waits for them. They wait but finally walk over to him.*)

HUM. Well?

(LOUIE *nods.*)

MARC. Will he let us?

LOUIE. You're in. Now remember, you're my customers, see? We'll get it and then go to where I keep my works and get fixed together. (CELEE *enters, Right.*) Man, there ain't nothing like it.

MARC (*points behind* LOUIE). Sssh— there's your sister.

(CELEE *sees* LOUIE *and puts her head down, trying to go by without being noticed.*)

LOUIE. Celee—! Celee? What you doing out? You know—not till you're sixteen. Now go on home.

CELEE. I *am* sixteen.

LOUIE (*disarmed, then guilty*). Oh. . . . (*Pause. Sudden anger.*) Where you going?

CELEE (*looks at him*). I *am* sixteen and you forgot.

LOUIE. Where you going! By yourself!

CELEE. You forgot my birthday. You didn't come home.

LOUIE. Where are you going?!

CELEE (*shouts*). Do I know where you go?

LOUIE (*shouts*). You don't need to.

CELEE (*softly*). You didn't have to bring a present.

LOUIE (*shouts*). Beat it. Go home. (*He turns to the* BOYS.) Hey, itch my back, man. (CELEE *continues Left and exits, Left.*) Hey what's the matter with her? She walking funny?

MARC (*To* HUM). Like that hophead, Jenny? (*He and* HUM *laugh.*)

LOUIE (*grabbing him*). You talk that way about my sister and I'll— (*Nearly knocks him over.*)

MARC. Hey, I'm kidding you, man.

(MUSIC *begins low.*)

LOUIE (*Goes Left and watches her disappear*). Celee! Hey, CELEE! (*He turns back, not noticing the* BOYS.) What I do now? (MARC *and* HUM *whisper, look at* LOUIE *and exit, Right.* MUSIC *comes up slowly.* LOUIE *doesn't know whether to follow* CELEE *or the* BOYS—*whether to see about her or get his customers before they are gone. The conflict makes him feel his need for more drugs. He wipes his eyes and nose.*) I have a terrible feeling. (MUSIC *comes up full. He looks in all pockets for a coin. Pulls one out and tosses it)* Oh no! *(He throws one more look in* CELEE'S *direction and runs off, Right. Offstage he yells.)* Hey wait, you guys. I'm coming!

> *(MUSIC stays up. A* DRUNK *enters and stumbles across the Stage from Right to Left.* PORSE *and* CELEE *enter from Left.)*

CELEE. Porse—what I'm trying to say is— and all you need to do is—give me a chance. That's all. That's all I'm asking.

PORSE *(enjoying himself).* But why—why pick on me, baby? I got my hands full, you know. So to speak. Why me?

CELEE *(knowing his number).* Well—every girl on this block.

PORSE *(pleased).* Yeah?

CELEE. Sure they do. Talking about you all the time.

PORSE. Why, baby? Why is that?

CELEE *(change).* Look—you want to know the truth?

PORSE. Well—I don't know, sweetheart— that depends. Sometimes—like right now—I don't.

CELEE. Well, see?—you know my brother, Lou?

PORSE *(stops her).* Your brother? Ooh now, baby, I never know women that got brothers, that's a fact.

CELEE. Oh. Well never mind that—you know Jenny?

PORSE. Everybody know Jenny.

CELEE *(impatient).* Well, don't you see?

PORSE. See what, Sugar? Go ahead. Spell it out, baby, you ex-cite me.

CELEE. Well—look how good she's got it —fancy clothes . . .

PORSE. Oh yes.

CELEE. Crazy car, and everything. How she get all of them things?

PORSE *(mock surprise).* You're asking me?

CELEE. That's what I mean.

PORSE *(gives her a second look, then after a pleased pause).* Wooee, girl. You know a lot.

CELEE. Sure I do. She works for you. And so does— *(Stops herself. With emphasis.)* And everybody know Jenny. *(Pause.)* Don't you see?

PORSE. And—what about your brother?— Who's your brother?

CELEE *(quietly).* Never mind. No one knows my brother *(pause).* Not even you. He can't hurt nobody.

PORSE. But—if you work for me—what about *that?*

CELEE *(flares up).* Never mind that, mister. That part ain't your business and never will be. *(Kindly.)* See?

PORSE *(intrigued).* Um. Now wait a minute. *(He studies her. Taps his foot. Looks at his watch. Looks up and down the street. Then smiles, turns away and gets a couple of bills from his wallet.)* Here—go get yourself some clothes. *(CELEE hesitates.)* Go on— take it. What's the matter with it? *(She still hesitates.)* Look, baby—besides looks, you've got fight. That's what I like. I don't know why. I don't like *to* fight—but I like—fight. Understand?

CELEE *(suddenly takes the money).* Well? —what do I do?

PORSE *(laughs).* Nothing—if you don't want to. Think about it.—But come on. I'll show you some places—the candy store over there, and the—well, come on—I'll show you a place right now—see if you feel like trying it. —Oh baby—I'm feeling young again. *(As they exit.)* I'm going to open a new world to you.

> *(MUSIC up.* DRUNK *re-enters from Left and takes a longer time getting off. He tries to fight an imaginary passerby, wants company, or makes dumbshow conversation with someone in the audience. Takes a swig from his bottle, looks into garbage can, etc., then exits.)*

LOUIE *(runs in from Right. He looks around wildly. To audience).* Hey, have you seen Porse? He was just here. Have you seen Porse? *(To someone in audience.)* Yeah, Porse! You know him. Have you seen him? —the guy with the brown coat?—or those other two guys?

> *(CELEE, in a dazed state, and* PORSE, *enter from Right.* CELEE *stops when she sees* LOUIE.)

CELEE. Hi, Lou— Look—

LOUIE *(hearing her voice before he sees her, cries joyfully).* Celee! *(Then, turning, sees* PORSE *too.)* You. YOU!

PORSE. Hey, Louie—I want you to run across town for me.

LOUIE. I—I didn't find you at the place.

PORSE. That's right. I had a little business come up.

LOUIE. Where did you meet him, Celee? Where?

CELEE. He's your friend.

PORSE (*to her*). He—your brother?

LOUIE. Where did you meet my sister?

CELEE. Wait.

PORSE. She your sister?!

LOUIE (*shouts*). Yes, she's my sister! (*Softly.*) Your eyes look heavy, Celee.

PORSE. She's tired.

CELEE. I'm tired.

LOUIE. Celee, your hair's messed up, Celee.

PORSE. It's the wind.

CELEE. The wind.

LOUIE. Ain't no wind!

PORSE. Take it easy, boy.

CELEE. Lou—

LOUIE. Celee, why don't you look at me?

PORSE. She's thinking about other things.

CELEE. Other things. Listen—

LOUIE (*interrupts*). *Look* at me, Celee! (*She does.*) Show me your arm.

CELEE (*drawing back*). No.

LOUIE. Show me your ARM! (*He grabs her arm and pushes up the sleeve and sees the needle mark.*) Celee! Celee!

PORSE. *You* like it, Louie.

LOUIE. You took it, Celee. You *took* it.

CELEE. *You* took it, Louie.

LOUIE (*slaps* CELEE). Oh, Celee! (*Slaps her again, calling her name.*) Celee!

CELEE. Porse!

PORSE (*pushes them apart, and* LOUIE *struggles to get at her*). Beat it, girl. (CELEE *runs off.*)

LOUIE (*turns on* PORSE). Porse! Porse! Oooooh—You did it. You started her! You—

(*Local language useful here. They fight.*

LOUIE *throws* PORSE *down, then* PORSE *trips and throws* LOUIE *down with a swipe at* LOUIE's *neck.*)

PORSE (*brushing himself off*). Wait a minute, man. What you trying to do? Gone off your bat?

LOUIE (*beginning to pick himself up slowly*). Porse? How—how long? How long has she—?

PORSE. You want to know something?

LOUIE (*interrupting*). How long! How many times? (LOUIE *has begun to moan and strike himself—his chest, his head.*)

PORSE (*taking all this in*). Oh—nuts. (*Pause.*) Hey, look—listen to me, man, you better watch out. Don't worry about Celee—

she's gone home. And don't get hung up— you're just a little sick, that's all. Look, I'm a right guy. She's your sister—

LOUIE (*softly*). No.

PORSE. No? You say no? That's good. (*He laughs, but then is very thoughtful.*) You sure you want to say that? You rather look after Celee than have some stuff?

LOUIE (*softly*). I am going to kill you, man. (*He begins to exit, Left.*)

PORSE. What if there was some stuff right in back of you? (LOUIE *stops in his tracks as though frozen.*) You—you running off to be a—hero? (LOUIE *doesn't move. His eyes are wild.* PORSE *mimics* LOUIE.) "Please, Porse, lay off, will you. Please, PLEASE, Porse, give me some stuff." Right, Louie?

LOUIE (*his shoulders sag; he breaks*). Oh.

PORSE. But you want to be the main man, don't you?

LOUIE (*screams*). Lay off it!

PORSE (*knows his game; takes out his watch, looks at it*). Well, I can't be messing around here all day. I got to go. Take it light, man. (*Starts to exit.*)

LOUIE (*tries to hold him*). Porse—Porse—

PORSE. Take your hands off, man. You're taking up my time.

LOUIE. Porse—

PORSE. Why don't you make up your mind?

LOUIE. Look, Porse!

PORSE. Can't be worrying around with punks like you. You sound like you're going to talk. You owe me some coin.

LOUIE. Porse, please—one last time.

PORSE. You are trouble.

LOUIE. No more after this. No more.

PORSE. Will you stay out of my hair?

LOUIE. Yeah, I will, I will.

PORSE. Where's your money?

LOUIE. Here's a buck. (*Tears it out of his pocket. Gives it to* PORSE, *who looks at it and drops it with scorn.*)

PORSE. That don't cover it.

LOUIE. I'll get it, I swear I'll get it.

PORSE. Sssh—shut up, man.

(*MUSIC begins.*)

LOUIE. Give me some stuff. GIVE ME SOME STU—

PORSE. Shut up, man. Cool it!

LOUIE. Now!

PORSE. Okay. (*He looks around casually, pulls* LOUIE *aside, slips him a tiny envelope, then exits. MUSIC up.* LOUIE *walks quickly around the stage. He is frantically hurried, yet careful. From a hiding place, he pulls out an old cigarette pack in which his works are stored. He squats down, picks up the dollar, keeps watch. He opens the small cellophane bag, empties the powder into a soft drink bottle cap, adds a little water and lights a match under it. He attaches a needle to the eyedropper and soaks the fluid up through a bit of cotton. He takes off his belt and tightens it around his arm and waits with great impatience for his vein to bulge. He sticks in the needle, has difficulty getting it into the vein. He mutters.)* Hit it. Hit it hard. Go home, goddam you, go home. *(As it finally goes in, his head goes back suddenly as a rush of relief floods him.)* Oh Mm, Mama, Mama. *(The LIGHTS change from ordinary daylight to blue.* IMPORTANT NOTE: *All of the following action is in slow motion—as if in water—until the next light change.* LOUIE *pulls out the needle. He slowly takes it apart and stores it in the cigarette packet and hides it again. Then with a great sigh he begins to move across stage, his jaw hanging open. He sits, nodding, on a garbage can.* CELEE *enters and floats past him, dropping her handkerchief at his feet. He slowly picks it up and returns it to her. A* DREAM MAN *enters and heads for* CELEE. *She struggles as he tries to kiss her.* LOUIE *pulls him around and they fight, and* LOUIE *slowly knocks him down. As in slow motion film fights, the* MAN'S *face crumples.* LOUIE *gets rid of him and bids* CELEE *farewell as she exits. Then* PORSE *appears—also part of* LOUIE'S *imagination.* LOUIE *has begun to wander back and forth looking for* CELEE *and calling out her name, slowly. Finally as he sits,* PORSE *ties the end of a rope to the front of* LOUIE'S *belt. Then slowly he pulls it out, umbilical like, to its full length—the width of the stage. As* LOUIE *seeks* CELEE, *he slowly winds himself up in the rope until he is face to face with* PORSE. PORSE *laughs, tucks in the rope and hauls* LOUIE *Downstage before the audience. Shouting like a barker, in slow motion.)* Jun-kie! Blow—your—horn. *(*LOUIE *imitates a horn.* PORSE *talks over* LOUIE'S *sounds.)* The—law—will—get—you.

LOUIE *(like a siren).* OoooooooooOOOOooooooooOOOOooooo.

PORSE *(talking over* LOUIE*).* The—cats—will—kill—the—dogs. *(*LOUIE *meows and barks.* PORSE *is enjoying himself.)* Kiss—my

—foot. *(*LOUIE *kneels down and slowly does so.* PORSE.*)* Now—the—other—one. *(*LOUIE *looks up at* PORSE *before doing it.* PORSE *lifts* LOUIE *by the back of the neck and speaks to the crowd.)* Ladies—and gentlemen.—Step—right—up. See—for yourselves—. I pre-sent—to you—, yes—here—he is—none other—than—the world's—one hundred—per-cent—suckuh.

LOUIE. *(Screaming out slowly as if in a nightmare.)* Mama! *(MUSIC up.* PORSE *unwinds* LOUIE *like a top and exits.* LOUIE *sinks slowly to the sidewalk. MUSIC down. LIGHTS change back to daylight. Ordinary movement is resumed. A* WOMAN *with a sack of groceries comes down the street with a little girl,* CREZELL.*)*

WOMAN *(sees* LOUIE *and shakes her head).* Things is just getting worse and worse. Crezell! *(The little* GIRL *goes to look at* LOUIE.*)* Crezell, come along. You hear me? *(To herself or audience.)* Can't let children out of your sight one minute. Crezell! Get away from there, you hear me?

CREZELL. Mama, I just want to see if he's sick.

WOMAN. He sick all right. Now just mind your own business.

CREZELL *(kneeling).* But, Mama, he's sick.

WOMAN. What he done to himself, just might as well be dead, poor Jesus. Come on, Crezell. Crezell! CREZELL. *(Gives her a smack and pulls her off.)*

CREZELL. Waah. He hurt himself. *(Boxed.)* Ow! You never let me do nothing. *(Yanked.)* Wah. *(They exit.)*

LOUIE *(wakes, stretches painfully and groans. Suddenly feels in his pockets—they are empty except for the dollar).* He give me bad stuff—garbage! *(Suddenly closes his eyes.)* If you thought hard enough maybe you could just think yourself into it. *(Tries to remember.)* Say—what was it happened to me. Let's see—that's funny. *(He feels around himself as if he still felt the rope.)* A rope—I had a rope around me. Wound round me. I wonder where Porse is. Porse? Porse—had that rope around me. That's funny, very funny. He was laughing with that grin—gives you the creeps sometimes. Porse had that rope and then I got wound up. Going back and forth I got *wound* up, *bound* up—and there I was—at the end of this goddam—rope, dancing like some APE. And then! then he called me— He told me— Oh God—he told me to kiss his—his oh no, his dirty rotting— Oh no, no, NO! And I—so help me, I did! God strike me deaf and dumb, I did! Ughgh. Not—not just one. BOTH! (*He pounds on the garbage can.*) No. No. NO. I won't. NEVER. I won't do it. Never again. NEVER! You hear? You hear me?—NEVER! (*Suddenly he is quiet—as if listening to the echoes of his shouts.*) But—how—how will I remember—when it comes on me again? How? But I'll have to. Oh Jesus—it's already coming—it's coming, it's sneaking, creeping up me, it's coming—Oh God, it's coming. I need somebody. I need— Or am I trapped? Am I trapped?

WOMAN (*entering with laundry bag*). Louie, Louie, what's the matter with you, honey?

LOUIE. Maybe I'm trapped.

WOMAN. What you mean, trapped?

LOUIE. I want to cut loose—

WOMAN (*catching on*). Oho. Well, you should of thought of that a long time ago.

LOUIE. I want to kick it. (*Kicks the can.*) I want to kick—him!

WOMAN. Why you want to pull out?

LOUIE. Where can I go?

WOMAN. I suppose you got nothing going for you.

LOUIE. Well, what's it look like!

WOMAN. Sweetheart, you waited a long time to find this out. It's happened, honey. You can't pull way from junk. You been too long. You should've know better in the first place.

LOUIE. Don't preach at me, for Chrisake. Tell me yes or no, do you know where I can get some help?

WOMAN. You should've thought of that a long time ago.

LOUIE (*can't stand it any longer*). Go away, woman.

WOMAN. You might just as well save yourself the trouble.

LOUIE (*maddened, he shouts her Offstage*). GO AWAY! (*Tries now to think clearly.*) Now—! If—if I am trapped—if I *am* trapped —yeah—let me feel walls, four walls and a ceiling around me, and bars. And if I'm at the end of a ROPE!—then let me feel AIR beneath these feet. (*Stamps his boot hard.*) But—but if— Oh Jesus!

(MARC *and* HUM *enter.*)

MARC. Hey, Louie, we got something to

talk over with you, Louie. What's the matter, man? (LOUIE *groans.*) I guess he's sick.

HUM. Hey, Louie—about that free shot, you remember—

LOUIE (*softly*). There ain't no free shot.

HUM. But you told us he gave you the first shot fr—.

LOUIE. There ain't no free shot, man.

MARC. Yeah? But—?

LOUIE (*painfully trying to continue his thought*). But—but if I ain't trapped—NOT trapped—if the walls ain't yet closed around me, and my feet still feel this load—then— (*He reaches for something hard to grasp.*) Then—?

MARC (*whispers*). Louie?

LOUIE. WHAT!—Go away, man, you're bugging me.

MARC. What's wrong?

LOUIE (*turns on him*). Yeah. Now make it, man. Leave me alone! (HUM *and* MARC *leave slowly.* LOUIE *starts to follow, then stops.*) No—no—crum. Why does it matter anyhow? People do it everyday and die doing it. You can't stop—everybody says it, what the hell. (*He wipes his nose.*) I could sure do with a shot right now. Wouldn't have to worry any more about it. Yeah. (*Yawns, but right in the middle, stops.*) Oh Celee, Celee, he made me kiss his— I got to get some help. I could go to a hospital. But maybe they'd make me talk. (*Cries out.*) Why, why should I turn around now and go the other way after so long? Why? (*He holds his head.*) Ooooooouh. (MUSIC *begins thinly, builds louder and deeper, becomes very intense.* LOUIE *clutches his head, stomach, falls, rolls, gets up.*) God! Oh God! Help me, man, help me!

PORSE (*enters*). Hi, Louie.

LOUIE (*turns with joy at the sound of this voice, then pulls back*). Go away.

PORSE. What's up, man?

LOUIE. I'm telling you. Go away. (PORSE *takes a step closer.*) Don't come closer. I'm telling you, man. I'm through, THROUGH! (PORSE *looks at him not unkindly.* LOUIE *waits for some sign that* PORSE *believes or understands him. Whispers.*) Get outa here.

PORSE (*more joking than cruel*). Fine. That's all right. If you want to kick the stuff, I'll leave you alone. Don't worry about that. (*He starts to leave, then thinks, and slowly turns back.*) Someone going to help you?

LOUIE (*gasps. He begins to weaken*). Oh, God.

PORSE. What are you going to do?

LOUIE. Get OUT OF HERE.

PORSE. What are you going to do?

LOUIE. I'm—I'm— (*With dismay realizes he doesn't know. After a pause he turns on* PORSE.) You goddam lizard. You ask me what I'm going to do! *Me* who thought I had a square foot of this world to stand on, who thought I was rich and all these women were waiting around for me. But all the time, all the time boosting, begging, bumming, going lower and lower, smaller and smaller—each time losing a piece of me—my fingers, my hand, my arm, eyes, legs, liver, guts—piece by piece. And Porse, there isn't much left of me. See? (*Wildly shoves him.*) Go. Goddam you. GO.

PORSE. Take it easy, man, take it easy. You know I'm a right guy. If you want to kick it —go ahead. God bless. I got plenty else to do. (*Begins to exit.*) Bye, baby, say hello to old man Straight for me.—So long.

LOUIE (PORSE *gets to the edge of the Stage, almost off.* LOUIE *looks away; can't let him go; whirls around, shouting*). PORSE!

PORSE (*turns slowly, grins*). Yeah?—Yeah, man?

LOUIE (*remembers*). No.

PORSE. Look, man. Let me tell it to you.

LOUIE. No.

PORSE. You gotta make up your mind.

LOUIE. No! Get out. I'm kicking.

PORSE. Yeah? Who's going to help?

LOUIE (*pause. Softly*). Help? (*Gasping at a straw.*) Yeah—Celee.

PORSE. Celee?

LOUIE (*low*). Porse—where is Celee?

PORSE. Celee? Celee's busy somewhere, I expect.

LOUIE. Busy WHERE?

PORSE. Now look, let me tell you something. *I'm* willing to help you out. What's the good of making a big scene?

LOUIE. Celee'll help. I'll take her and—

PORSE. Yeah.

LOUIE (*threatening*). Where is she, man? Tell me or I might surprise you.

PORSE. Don't give me that kind of talk. I ain't afraid. (*Pats his pocket.*) Now look— you know how it is. You can't do anything about it. People get cures, but they go back.

LOUIE. God. God. (*Rubbing his eyes and nose.*)

PORSE. Man, don't fight it. Come on, let me help you. Here, I'll—

LOUIE (*crouches*). WAIT. You bring out anything, man, I'll call a cop.

PORSE. Ah, I was waiting for you to say something like that. Now that's a different matter, man. I don't think it will help you to do that.

LOUIE (*starts to go, rubbing his nose*). You'll see.

PORSE. Wait a second. You know what that would mean? Listen. The cops come to me. I'd say, "Well, officer, let me see—" We'd talk a little and I'd say, "Oh yes, let's see, the first time I seen some, uh, narcotics was—on Louie's little sister." And "Officer," I'd say, "she said she got it from Louie."

LOUIE (*shouts*). They won't believe you.

PORSE. Louie, listen. I'm not a junkie and you are. They'll take my word, not yours. So —relax, man. Forget it. You can't do it.

LOUIE. I am doing it.

PORSE. How long, man? Five minutes.

LOUIE. I'm taking my sister and we're getting OUT.

PORSE. Man, you're a junkie and your sister is a junkie. Forget it.

LOUIE (*screams and leaps on* PORSE, *getting a tight hold around his neck*). NO. NO. NO, she ain't. Leave her alone, you hear, or I'm gone kill you. And leave me alone. I won't take it. Won't take it. Won't take it. (*They struggle,* LOUIE *about to kill him.* PORSE, *not able to bear the jerks of the strangle hold, pulls out his knife and tries to hit* LOUIE, *and then finally cuts him.* LOUIE *cries out, but still hangs on.* PORSE *lifts the knife high and cuts him to kill.* LOUIE *cries out and lets go.* PORSE *holds his neck with one hand and runs Offstage.* LOUIE *reels and grabs his stomach and then looks up as the realization dawns.*) I didn't take it. Goddam! (*Long triumphant shout.*) Porse! POR—SE! Hear me! I didn't take it. DIDN'T TAKE IT. Hear that? (*Smiles.*) Wow. That's funny. Celee! (*Long shout.*) CE—LEE! Listen! I won. I WON. I— (*Interrupted by a spasm of pain in his stomach.*) Oh, no. No, no, no! (*He topples over and dies.*)

(*MUSIC comes up strong, as:*)

CURTAIN

A TRAP IS A SMALL PLACE

by Marjean Perry

CHARACTERS

STELLA
MRS. ASHER
JESSICA
ANDREW MIDDLETON

TIME: November. The present.
PLACE: A small apartment in New York City.

The scene is a New York City living room and dinette apartment. In the background, somewhat to the left, is the doorway to the kitchen, through which can be seen a cupboard made to hold dishes in the upper section. In the left wall of the kitchen is a large window with thin curtains and a sill full of plants.

To the left of the kitchen door is a desk and telephone. Against the wall is a small dining table and two chairs, beneath a window with heavy drapes and venetian blinds rolled half-way up to allow space for another row of potted plants. In the corner is a folding screen. To the front is the bathroom door.

To the right of the kitchen door is a row of bookcases. Beside them is an easy chair with a hassock. Farther down stage is a daybed that can open out into a double bed. A small table and lamp are near it. Against the wall is a chest of drawers with a mirror above. At the sides of the chest of drawers are two doors, one the entrance door, the other a closet door.

By the easy chair, there is a bird cage with two canaries in it. On the dining table, there is a small goldfish bowl with a few greens and one fish. By the entrance door is an umbrella stand. On the rear wall are three pictures. One is rather large, an abstract painting in bright colors. The other

two are pastoral scenes, of the type found on calendars.

Vases, ashtrays and figurines are scattered about, too many for the sake of order or simplicity.

It is about two o'clock on a rainy day in November.

When the curtain rises, the stage is empty. In a moment, STELLA comes in from the kitchen with a tablecloth, which she arranges on the dining table. STELLA is a young woman of about thirty, with a dark and pale kind of beauty, liquid and soft. She is an immaculate person and is dressed in a stiff little house dress with an apron over it.

There is the sound of subdued hammering from the next apartment. Someone taps irregularly and then seems to stop.

STELLA makes several trips to the kitchen and back in the process of setting the table for two, with wine glasses, plates, silver and, finally, a bottle of wine, cake and a vase overflowing with red roses. She performs everything with fussy care, dusting off the plates with a towel, shifting and reshifting each object until she has accomplished what she considers to be a composition. She rearranges the roses for a moment and then bends over the goldfish bowl.

STELLA. Hello in there! Is it a nice glass cage? (She picks up a box of fish food and sprinkles some on the water.) I love you, Puddles; but you don't love me. (Watches for a moment.) Oh, plup-plup. Greedy! (She shifts a plate and then pulls the screen out so that it is in front of the table. There is a knock at the door. She goes to open it, giving a quick flourish with her towel at some imaginary dust as she passes the bookcases. A young housewife, MRS. ASHER, enters. She is wearing clothes obviously meant for house cleaning, with a big apron and a kerchief

MARJEAN PERRY (1927–   )

While seeming to be just another well-made play about the eternal triangle, *A Trap Is a Small Place* (1953) explores a more interesting if normally taboo subject —that of one woman's love for another. Thus, unlike so many other one-act plays of the 1950's, its most notable production was neither for television nor Off-Broadway, but at the Kleines Theater in Vienna. At the end of the decade Edward Albee also would be forced to go abroad—to Berlin—for the premiere of *The Zoo Story,* because it too offended American tastes.

A Trap Is a Small Place was sandwiched in between plays by Goethe and Johann Nestroy, and the consensus of the Vienna critics was that "only the middle part can claim perfection." The Perry play was subsequently acquired by Margaret Mayorga for *The Best Short Plays* series and reprinted in her *Twentieth Anniversary Edition.*

Marjean Perry was born in a small town along the Maryland shore. Her family moved to Towson, Maryland, where she attended both elementary and high school. Her college years were divided between the University of North Carolina and Indiana University, but at both she pursued the same course of study—art and creative writing.

Perry began her career as a poet, not a playwright. She settled in New York City, where, among other things, she managed the Unicorn Theatre during the early 1960's.

---

around her head. The way she is continually moving about reminds one of a honey bee in a clover patch. She is constantly picking things up, looking at them and putting them down again as she goes on talking. She speaks with emphatic enthusiasm. STELLA *takes off her apron.*) Oh, Mrs. Asher.

MRS. ASHER. Hi, Stella! (*Walking to the middle of the room.*) My! How nice everything looks.

STELLA (*amused*). Come in, won't you?

MRS. ASHER. Oh, but I *am* in! (*Walking over and just looking behind the screen.*) I can't stay but a minute. Such pretty roses! They look like an occasion!

STELLA. It is.

MRS. ASHER. I hope I was supposed to look. I'm an awful pry. Where's Jessica?

STELLA. Still at the office.

MRS. ASHER. Again? Something ought to be done. That girl works too hard.

STELLA. Perhaps you can convince her for me that Saturdays should be her own.

MRS. ASHER. Me? Now, tell me, Stella. I bet one of your beaux sent those flowers.

STELLA. No. They're a surprise for Jess. We met each other just ten years ago.

MRS. ASHER. Oh, how sweet! You know, Mr. Asher and I just celebrated our tenth anniversary. He brought me red roses. Red roses for love. I just cried my eyes out. But then the baby set up such a howl I had to laugh at myself. (*Laughs.*) I bet you've asked that nice young salesman to come.

STELLA (*coldly*). No. You mean Andrew Middleton, I suppose. No, I didn't.

MRS. ASHER. Such a nice young man. Jessica brought him by to see me once. Baby adored him. (*Laughs.*) That's the acid test, you know. He'll make a wonderful papa.

STELLA. He'll have to become one first.

MRS. ASHER (*Looking at the abstract painting*). Stella, honey, do me a favor and tell me what this *is.*

STELLA. A painting.

MRS. ASHER. You have such a sense of humor. But what *is* it? I've never had the courage to ask Jessica for fear she'd be insulted.

STELLA. I believe Jess calls it a composition in spaces and lines.

MRS. ASHER. Oh.

STELLA. That was done a long time ago. She doesn't paint any more.

MRS. ASHER. Well, I don't know. It reminds *me* of all that stuff done by that poor crazy old maid that used to live in the building. They took her (*Significantly.*) away finally. All she could say was: "Please— Please."

STELLA. She might have thought of *something* else.

MRS. ASHER. Are you teasing me? I never know when you are and when you aren't.

STELLA. You mean—I confuse you?

MRS. ASHER. Yes, you do! (*Looking at a vase.*) How pretty! Just my taste . . . It's really very sad.

STELLA. Your taste?

MRS. ASHER. Oh, Stella! I meant, how some people end up—like the old maid. There she was, painting and painting. Such crazy things! And her sister crying and crying. (*Shuddering.*) It gave me the creeps!

STELLA. A poor old lady? I'm afraid you're not very brave, Mrs. Asher.

MRS. ASHER. Well, maybe I'm not. But the doctor said the oddest thing.

STELLA. Doctor?

MRS. ASHER. About old maids.

STELLA. What did the doctor say?

MRS. ASHER. Trapped each other. He said: "Trapped each other." (*Laughs suddenly.*) So, you tell Jessica for me she's better marry that salesman. He's a nice fellow.

STELLA (*sarcastically*). An upstanding American citizen.

MRS. ASHER (*earnestly*). Yes, he is. He certainly is. (*Taking a breath.*) Well, now, Stella, honey, I've got to rush. I left the baby alone and she's right at that climbing stage. Now, my ulterior motive in coming was to see if Jessica might have a couple of hours free this afternoon to mind the baby. (*Laughs.*) I know better than to ask you.

STELLA. I could ask her.

MRS. ASHER. You're to say "No," if it's not convenient.

STELLA. Then, it isn't. (*Indicating the screen.*) You see—I've made plans.

MRS. ASHER. Oh. Well, that's perfectly all right. I'll think of some scheme.

(JESS *enters, wearing boots and a raincoat and carrying an umbrella. She is quite tall, with a slight stoop to her shoulders. She is pretty enough if she takes care of herself; generally, she doesn't bother. She is about twenty-eight or twenty-nine.*)

JESS. Oh, hello, Mrs. Asher. (*Drops the umbrella into the umbrella stand.*) I was afraid you wouldn't be here, Stella. I forgot my keys again.

MRS. ASHER. Hello, Jessica. I'm just going. (*Laughing.*) If I say that again without acting upon it, Stella's going to take me for a liar.

JESS (*warmly*). Oh, stay awhile. We could gossip.

MRS. ASHER. I'd just love to. But baby's probably at the top of the Empire State Building by this time. I left her alone.

JESS. She's a beautiful child.

MRS. ASHER. My husband says she's getting too fat but I . . .

STELLA (*holding the door and imitating* MRS. ASHER'S *tone of voice*). Bye-bye.

MRS. ASHER (*finishing her sentence lamely*). . . . . think she's just right. Bye-bye.

(MRS. ASHER *leaves.* STELLA *closes the door after her.*)

STELLA. Now for a little peace.

(*When the door closes,* JESS *listlessly begins to take off her raincoat, throwing it on the daybed. She sits down in the easy chair and removes her boots, then her shoes from her boots, leaving them on the floor.* STELLA *watches her, trying to repress a desire to scold.*)

JESS. What did she want?

STELLA. What does she always want? I wish I could hate that woman. Unfortunately, she doesn't seem to know she's a hypocrite.

JESS. Was that necessary?

STELLA. Necessary?

JESS. Pushing her out that way.

STELLA. She would have stayed forever if I hadn't.

JESS. Yes. She might have stayed.

STELLA. You're tired?

JESS. Yes, I'm tired.

STELLA (*sitting down on the hassock and reaching for* JESS'S *foot*). Let me help you.

JESS (*looking up for a moment*). Why?

STELLA (*laughing uncertainly*). Because you're tired.

JESS. Never mind.

STELLA (*after a pause, gets up*). Shall I play some music?

JESS. If you want.

STELLA. I guess I won't then. (*A pause.*) Did you get the mail on your way up?

JESS. There wasn't any.

STELLA (*after a pause*). Is something the matter, Jess?

JESS. No. Nothing at all.

STELLA. You're just tired.

JESS. Yes. I'm tired.

(*She leans back in the chair and lights a cigarette.*)

STELLA. Could I get you something? An aspirin, maybe?

JESS. I don't have a headache.

(*She drops the match absent-mindedly on the floor.*)

STELLA (*sharply*). Jess! (*Picking up the match.*) Do you know what an ashtray is for?

JESS (*automatically*). I'm sorry, Stella.

STELLA (*with appeal in her voice*). I—I didn't mean to snap at you.

JESS (*surprised*). That's all right. I guess I deserve it sometimes.

STELLA (*playfully*). You do. But I don't really mind.

(*Quietly, she picks up the boots and raincoat and puts them in the closet, then sets* JESS's *shoes by the easy chair.*)

JESS (*watching her*). I'm sorry, Stella. I let you do everything, don't I?

STELLA (*laughing*). Just about.

JESS. It's only that I'm always tired. . . . The place looks very nice.

STELLA (*gaily*). It's about time you took notice of that fact. It's in your honor.

JESS (*surprised that she was to notice*). You're always cleaning it. . . . In my honor? Why in my honor?

STELLA. In our honor, then.

JESS (*trying to think*). What's happened to us?

STELLA. You're worse than men are reputed to be. Don't you realize that just today makes ten years since we first met each other?

JESS. Ten years. Has it really been ten years? (*Slowly.*) That means we can start measuring it in—decades. (*Quickly.*) Oh, no, that sounds terrible.

STELLA. Not so terrible. (*Arms akimbo.*) I don't believe you even remember meeting me.

JESS. I just remember knowing you, not getting to know you.

(*As she speaks,* STELLA *goes to the bookcase and gets a box of bird food, then goes to the bird cage and fills the seed dish. She stands, poking her fingers through the wires of the cage at the birds.*)

STELLA. That's not in the least flattering. It puts me exactly at zero. Really, don't you remember at all?

JESS (*leaning back in her chair and stubbing out the cigarette*). Give me a clue.

STELLA. Paise College, Institute for Women. I am sitting in my room, studying. I still think I want to be a lawyer. A young lady, in boots and raincoat, marches boldly in. "I've lost my keys," she says, sitting down. "May I sit down?" "Do," I say. "Have you some coffee?" she says. "Regulations," I say. "Ah, yes," she says. "Rule No. 257. No student may keep a hotplate in her room. Rule No. 258. Gargling is not permitted. Have you some paper?" "Here," I say (JESS *chuckles.* STELLA *is pleased with the response.*) Aha! I've struck a spark.

JESS. Fan it a little.

STELLA. Term paper: The Effects of Going Without Sleep on the Human Nervous System.

JESS (*gives a shout of laughter*). Professor Alamander's psychology course. Five days and five nights without sleep. He thought I was a little fool.

STELLA. Do you remember meeting me now?

JESS (*thinking*). No.

STELLA (*turns away from the bird cage*). Oh. Well, it doesn't matter.

JESS (*after a pause*). When does Mrs. Asher want me to come?

STELLA. I told her you couldn't come.

(*She goes to the kitchen.*)

JESS (*pushing the hassock with her feet*). Oh? Why?

(STELLA *doesn't answer. There is a pause. Then she appears in the kitchen door with a little watering pot in her hands, waters the plants on the kitchen sill, comes out to the bird cage and fills the drinking dish.* JESS *watches her for a moment.*) Why did you say I couldn't come?

STELLA. Because—I knew you'd be tired.

(*She crosses the room and goes behind the screen to water the plants there.*)

JESS. I am. But I always am. (*She pushes the hassock away and drops her foot.*) I always feel such a—lassitude. Continual lassitude. (*She likes the word.*) Lassitude.

(STELLA *emerges suddenly from behind the screen and drops down beside* JESS's *chair with one hand on the arm.*)

STELLA. I told her you couldn't come because *I* wanted to see you. I wanted a few of your hours just for myself. Lately, somehow, you're always busy. You always talk as if you do nothing, have nothing to do. And yet, you're never here. You spend hours with Mrs. Asher, or I don't know where. (*She gets up and drifts across the room.*) You seem to know everyone in the building—to have spent hours with them. Or Andy comes and you two take a walk, or take a drive. And then you take another walk. And then you go home to see your mother. And that's the week ends and the evenings and the occasional holiday.

JESS (*thoughtfully*). It has seemed to me that I'm continually here instead of, as you say. . . . It's a small place. I've been in one small place or another. I don't know, I seem to have hurt you. Though I never intended to. And as for Andy, I've not seen much of him. He used to come almost every day.

STELLA (*comes and sits on the hassock*). I understand your disappointment. The treachery of men is—terrible. I've been disappointed enough to know that.

JESS [*half smiling*]. I wasn't thinking of "the treachery of men."

STELLA. I know. Your generous mind doesn't allow such thoughts.

JESS. It hasn't much to do with generosity, I'm afraid, but with "catch him if you can."

STELLA. Sweet Jess. How like you—to joke of something, to you, so deadly serious. Your feelings all numb and raw—yet, you joke.

JESS. Stella, you know you make me uncomfortable when you begin extolling my virtues.

STELLA. It's only that (*Quickly.*) I've been picking at you, lately, Jess. So you go away. (*Tentatively.*) Now, I'm asking you to come home.

JESS (*embarrassed*). Really . . .

STELLA. We can be true friends to one another, if we choose.

JESS. You've been a true friend, Stella. I haven't forgotten that. You've put up with a great deal of nonsense.

STELLA. Not nonsense at all! (*Jumping up*). Now, tell me, do you have any plans for the afternoon?

JESS. None. Except to—pamper my lassitude.

STELLA. Then you're to sit right there and see what I've gotten together.

JESS (*starting to get up*). You've planned something?

STELLA (*restraining her*). Yes, but sit there. And close your eyes for a minute.

JESS. All right.

STELLA (*almost running*). Just for a minute. (*She folds the screen back into the corner, then pours the wine. She gives an anxious final look at the table.*) Now! Look!

JESS (*staring for a moment*). Why, how pretty, Stella! (*She gets up, slips into her shoes and walks slowly to the table.*) Roses. There must be dozens! And wine. And what is this? My favorite cake. (*She smells the roses.*) So that's why you had the screen out in the middle of the room!

STELLA (*delighted*). You never notice anything.

JESS. Only one thing missing. (STELLA *looks at the table, puzzled.*) There should be a little sunlight to make the wine glow.

STELLA (*happy*). Oh. (*Picking up a glass of wine.*) To you, Jess! To our friendship.

JESS (*going to the other end of the table and picking up her glass*). To our friendship. To the big, old, damnable world. (*They touch glasses, take a sip, sit down. Both reach for the cake cutter, draw back, reach for the cutter again simultaneously. They laugh.* JESS *puts one hand in her lap and leans her chin on the other.* STELLA *begins cutting the cake.*) How ever many dozen roses *is* that?

STELLA (*holding out a slice of cake*). Only three. Your plate, Jess. Quick.

JESS (*handing her the plate*). Three dozen!

STELLA (*cutting another piece of cake*). Go ahead and start.

JESS. Catch Andy ever remembering when he first met me. (*Taking a bite.*) Mmm.

STELLA. I baked it myself. All this morning. I was so afraid you'd come home before I finished.

JESS. Fat chance! Mr. Gruin merely looks surprised when I suggest that working overtime without pay is illegal. It is illegal, isn't it?

STELLA. I should hope so.

JESS. Anyway, I refused once, and he went around looking hurt for the next entire week.

STELLA. Why do you stay with him, then?

JESS. I'm used to him. Besides, who else would put up with him?

STELLA (*tentatively*). I don't believe you have any ambition.

JESS. Why do you say that?

STELLA (*laying down her fork*). When you came to New York you ran your finger down the Help Wanted column and came across an item marked "Girl Friday" at the remarkable salary of thirty-five dollars a week. You stepped into the job and haven't stepped since. After almost ten years, you've achieved three raises to attain the new, remarkable salary of fifty dollars a week. Add it up yourself.

JESS (*evasively*). Eat your cake.

STELLA. I also started at a low salary . . .

JESS (*interrupting*). But you now have six people working under you, an interesting, responsible position and a salary of ninety-five dollars a week. I know.

STELLA. But you have ability, Jess—above the level of a Mr. Gruin.

JESS. I know. I wrote a couple of little stories once. And painted that picture over there, which you don't understand, but about which some wistful professor once said: "You have talent." You seem to forget, Stella, that I've heard this argument before.

STELLA. But this is different, Jess. There's a definite opening. Just listen how nice! If you choose, you can be my advertising assistant. We could be in the same department. We could work together.

JESS. No.

STELLA. You always say "No."

JESS. I mean: "No, you're wrong." I do have an ambition.

STELLA (*sighing*). What's that?

JESS. Mr. Andrew Middleton. He's been my ambition for the last three years.

STELLA. Excuse me, but where's that gotten you?

JESS. Well—it's gotten me an engagement ring—and an annual proposal of marriage. Or is it perennial, the flower that comes back every year?

STELLA. Perennial.

JESS (*wistfully*). I almost thought it wouldn't bother this year. (*With mock cheer.*) But no. It bloomed last week. A little pale. It seemed to be saying: "What? Same old sun? Same old world?"

STELLA. Andy—proposed to you last week?

JESS. I didn't see any point in mentioning it. It was hardly news.

STELLA. Oh. (*After a pause.*) Jess, I want to talk to you very seriously.

JESS. I thought this was a party.

STELLA. All right. But how long can you go on this way?

JESS. Which way?

STELLA. This way! Maybe. Sometime. Perhaps. It's about time you realized that Andy is never going to marry you.

JESS (*stiffening*). Do you really think that? Never?

STELLA. He never will. I've thought that for a long time.

JESS. I see.

STELLA (*reaching across the table and putting her hand on* JESS's). Oh, Jessica. Life is very difficult. (JESS *withdraws her hand*.) I'm only thinking of you, my dear. Don't draw away and stop up your ears and think, "No," before I even say anything.

JESS (*folding her arms and slumping back in her chair*). Say it, then.

(*They both seem to have forgotten why they are sitting at the table.*)

STELLA (*carefully*). Well, first, I wish you would consider the job.

JESS. Go on. Second?

STELLA. Stop saying "No."

(*Slaps* JESS's *hand playfully.*)

JESS. All right. I'll pretend you're saying something new.

STELLA. I wish you would be—sympathetic, Jess—just a little.

(*At this moment, someone in another apartment starts playing the piano, alternating between jazz and quick, lively polkas, with an occasional slow sentimental piece thrown in. The music acts as a foil to the mood of the two women. It continues throughout the rest of the scene, with some brief pauses. The tones are considerably subdued.*)

JESS. I've plenty of sympathy—for other people; but not much sympathy for suggestions intended to improve my character.

STELLA (*Getting up and walking part way across the room*). Why not?

JESS. Because no suggestion ever made to me has—sat right. (*Vaguely.*) If you know what I mean.

STELLA. I can't say that I do.

JESS. I mean: when Andy asks me to marry him, *that* sits right. It seems like a perfectly wonderful suggestion. All the other suggestions seem to be evading the issue. When Andy asks me to marry him . . .

STELLA (*interrupting*). *He* is evading the issue—because that's his way of keeping you on a string a mile long. He dangles you there with his perennial proposals. He likes dangling you.

JESS (*hurt*). It's not true.

STELLA. If you'd only admit what you actually know to be true . . .

JESS. I don't. I don't know it at all. You seem to know it, but I don't. You—you aren't looking into his eyes when he's proposing.

STELLA (*calmly*). Why hasn't he married you then? Or why hasn't he set a date?

JESS. Because—because—of money.

STELLA. If, at the age of thirty-six, he's not making enough money to support a wife, then when do you suppose he will?

JESS. He makes enough money for that. He's a good salesman. It's other considerations— that prevent an immediate marriage. In a year or so, perhaps less, those other considerations —won't have to be considered.

STELLA. Then it isn't money?

JESS. Yes. Yes, it's money. He wants to see his mother settled comfortably in a house of her own before he takes on other responsibilities. He's expecting a promotion soon, almost any day now. And he's almost done paying for the house and—his mother's a very sweet person.

STELLA. I see.

JESS. After all, his mother had to work very hard after her husband died—after Andy's father died—to support them both. And, of course, she did it for love. But then Andy feels a duty toward her and wants her comfortable. Though, of course, he wants to do it. . . . And we can live in the house, too, when we're married. But you can't have everything you want, all at once.

STELLA. I see.

JESS (*trying to sound convincing*). And that's how it is.

(*She picks at the tablecloth.*)

STELLA (*after a pause*). Jess.

JESS. What, Stella?

STELLA (*gently*). If you believed all that before, you don't now, do you?

JESS (*despairingly*). I don't know. I haven't a way with words. It sounded so different before, when Andy explained it. And I wish he were here now to explain it, so you'd believe in—all that.

STELLA. No, Jess, so *you* would believe.

JESS (*making a vague gesture with her hand*). Oh, I don't know.

STELLA. Jess. Jessica. Let's take a step, Jess, you and I. We needn't stay here, crushed into a space too small for us. (*Bitterly.*) That tinny piano! Soot drifting in! That man that hammers till he hammers through your nerves! You can hear him singing in his bath from our bathroom. Thousands of people crowding in around us, as if we forever wanted to remember their sweaty presence. (*Softly.*) We can go outside the city, with grass and trees and sunlight. We can get a bigger place and furnish it ourselves—with a little elegance. No more makeshifts. No more wrack and strain. Something like peace. We can have a home. We can have something that will be a real home.

JESS (*slowly*). A real home has a man and his wife and a child in it.

STELLA. A real home has love and affection in it. We must take what is available to us.

JESS. Am I the only thing left for you? Are you the only thing left for me?

STELLA. As true friends, it's not so little.

JESS. This is how it is, then? I'm to give up . . .

STELLA. It's not giving up, but filling your life with things worth while. It's an end to drifting and a world without meaning.

JESS. Do you really think so, Stella?

STELLA. I know it. Lean on me for a while. Just at first, while you're getting used to a new arrangement of your life.

JESS (*utterly tired*). I feel like leaning on somebody. I feel—is it silly?—rather tired.

STELLA. No. No. (*Going over to* JESS.) Lean on me. You'll see—we'll find such an adorable apartment. I know all the best places to look. We can spend the afternoon looking —our anniversary afternoon. (JESS *pulls away from her with a look of protest.*) Never mind if it's raining. I think it's stopping. I think the sun will come out.

JESS. Go now?

STELLA. Yes. And why not? Shall we wait for that tomorrow that never comes? Depend on me, Jess!

JESS (*frightened*). The cake. The wine. We haven't even finished them.

STELLA. Even my cake can wait for something as important as this.

JESS (*shrinking*). I can't go now.

STELLA (*briskly*). Nonsense; of course you can. I'll get your coat and you'll put it on. I'll open the door and you'll walk out. It's as simple as that.

JESS. If it's simple to do this, then it should be simple to do other things. Why must I do this, when it's so hard, and other things would be—so easy?

STELLA (*bringing* JESS's *coat*). This is possible. Here, put it on!

JESS (*allowing* STELLA *to put the coat on*). I like the city crowding in around me.

> (*In the next apartment, the same person as before begins hammering. This person goes on hammering intermittently throughout the rest of the scene.*)

STELLA (*getting her own coat*). Like that, I suppose?

JESS (*hopefully*). That's Mr. Ferris. He's very clever. Let's just stop by and see what he's making.

STELLA (*maneuvering* JESS *toward the door*). When we come back.

> (STELLA *picks two umbrellas out of the umbrella stand with her free hand, not letting go of* JESS *for a moment. She opens the door and closes it after them, as they go out. The telephone rings. The door flies open as* JESS *bounds back in to answer it.*)

JESS (*into the phone*). Hello? . . . What? . . . No. No. (*She puts the phone down slowly.*) Wrong number.

STELLA (*from the doorway*). Come along, then.

JESS (*her face brightening*). Why don't I just call Andy? He has a car and can drive us around.

STELLA (*coming back into the room*). We must take this step alone, Jess.

JESS (*picking up the phone*). That's silly. It won't take a minute for me to call. And I'm sure he'd love to.

STELLA (*coming quickly, and holding* JESS's *hand*). You mustn't.

JESS. Mustn't? (*Decisively.*) "Must. Must not. Must." Take away your hand, Stella! I will.

> (*She starts to dial.*)

STELLA (*violently*). No!

> (*She jerks* JESS's *hand awkwardly, so that the telephone falls off the desk.*)

JESS (*jumping up*). You're so close to me. Why do you always keep so close?

STELLA (*impulsively moving forward*). I want you . . . (*But withdrawing.*) . . . to come with me now, Jess. That's all. Let's not be childish and fight over nothing.

JESS. Then, shall I call Andy?

STELLA (*turning away, at the end of her patience*). Yes, call him! Don't pay any attention to me or what I want! (JESS *sits down again at the desk.*) How could I have been so silly as to think we could do anything alone— just the two of us? (*A pause.*) No, we must have a conducted tour. (*A pause.*) Why don't we give Andy's mother a ring, too? We could have her mature opinion. (*A pause.*) And there must be dozens of people right in this building that could give invaluable advice.

> (JESS *gets up and goes to the table. She stands with her back to* STELLA.) Don't worry. I'm halfway across the room. I can't touch you from here. (JESS *picks up a glass of wine, but stops and puts it down again.*) Ah, be careful! That's my wine. Don't drink Stella's wine! Or eat Stella's cake. Or smell Stella's roses. (JESS *wheels suddenly and walks rapidly to the open hall door.*) But do run away! Do run to the next-door neighbor! Tell them how you're being treated!

JESS (*turns, slamming the door shut*). I can't stand this, Stella. You've said too much. I've tried to say nothing but . . . I've said nothing but, "Yes, yes, Stella," all afternoon. All year. All the years I've known you. "Yes, yes, Stella."

> (*They are standing face to face.*)

STELLA. I've never forced you to anything.

JESS (*wonderingly*). How beautifully logical it all is.

STELLA. Now, for the first time, I'm asking you to do something for *me*. For the sake of friendship, if nothing else.

JESS (*amazed*). For the sake of friendship, I'm to give up my life—only the whole rest of my life!

STELLA (*sarcastically*). I ask for one afternoon, but she rises in irate rebellion. Oh, it's superb! What cause is this you've taken up? After the banner of art, the banner of writing, the banner of the scrapbooks, the stamps, the photographs, the postcards, we come to the banner of marriage. The banner of Andrew Middleton. The banner of children. The banner of rebellion. Don't you know what it adds up to? The banner of the balloon!

JESS (*slides past* STELLA). You like everything in cages, don't you, Stella? Oh, what a way you have with words! I stand in admiration. Everything in cages and bedecked beautifully in words, everything so graceful and so pretty, everything fine, everything in cups and vases. The ivy twines. And the birds sing. You have an instinct for it. You're like one of those —plants. A vegetable—with a trap! But I won't be meshed and tangled. I want to run away. I want to make mistakes. I want *not* to walk serenely to the fatal sweetness.

STELLA. Listen to me!

JESS (*in crescendo*). Listen to you? Listen to you? I've listened to you. I've listened to you till my ears are throbbing!

STELLA (*running to* JESS *and taking her by the arms*). Jess. Jess. Jessica. (*Recoils as* JESS *stiffens.*) This is my dream.

JESS. Dream it, then; and let me dream mine.

(*There is a pause during which neither moves. They stare at each other like two cats standing head to head. The silence is broken by the sharp sound of three quick rings of the doorbell. They both start.* JESS *exclaims with tremendous joy.*) Andy!

STELLA (*frightened*). If I'm sorry . . . ? If I'm sorry, Jess . . . ?

JESS. It's Andy. I know it. It's his ring.

(STELLA *turns blindly. She wheels slowly, but stops, putting her hand to her mouth. She takes a step, then hunches over, clasping herself with her arms.* JESS *stands for a frozen moment, rigid with joy. Then she runs forward to the hall door, slipping out of her coat as she does so. She doesn't notice* STELLA.)

STELLA (*choking*). Jess.

JESS (*without looking, but frightened by the tone*). What?

STELLA (*choking*). So sudden.

JESS (*still not looking*). What is it?

STELLA. Help me!

JESS (*turning, genuinely frightened*). What is it?

STELLA. Such a pain. . . . Don't leave, Jess! Don't answer!

(*There are three more sharp rings of the bell.* JESS *turns and, pushing the buzzer, runs out into the hall.* STELLA *straightens slowly. Her face registers bewilderment and hurt, but no physical pain.*)

She limply removes her coat, walks to the daybed and sits down, looking straight in front of her.)

ANDY'S VOICE (*from the hall*). Hey! Hey, what's this?

(STELLA *stiffens at the sound of his voice.*)

JESS'S VOICE. Andy. Andy. Andy.

ANDY'S VOICE. Well—well, honey!

JESS'S VOICE. Take me out, Andy! Take me for a drive!

ANDY'S VOICE. I don't know what to . . . Honey!

JESS'S VOICE. Take me for a drive!

ANDY'S VOICE. Let a fella sit down a minute.

(*They come in.* JESS *has both arms around* ANDY *and is hanging on for dear life.* ANDY *has one arm around* JESS, *patting her shoulder, and looking at her with a pleased but half-embarrassed grin on his face. He is wearing a grey suit, vest and flashy tie. He is about the same height as* JESS, *and is a man in the process of becoming overweight.*)

ANDY. You're certainly—different today.

JESS (*putting her head on his shoulder*). I guess I am.

ANDY (*considering her*). I like it. I wish I understood it.

JESS (*raising her head and looking at him*). Do you like *me*?

ANDY. It's the same thing, isn't it?

JESS (*smiling*). I guess it is.

ANDY (*suddenly*). You haven't been talking to mom, have you?

JESS (*puzzled*). No.

ANDY (*seeing* STELLA). Oh, hi, Stell!

(STELLA *doesn't answer. She has been watching them, with a half-irritated, half-supercilious expression on her face.*)

JESS. Take me out, Andy. Let's go somewhere.

ANDY. Mom's waiting outside.

JESS. Oh, I'd love to see her.

ANDY. She didn't feel quite up to the stairs today.

STELLA (*softly, but derisively*). Pooh!

JESS (*sympathetically*). Of course. Let's run down, then. I want to say, "Hello."

ANDY. You really haven't been talking to her?

JESS. No. Why? You asked me that before.

ANDY. I thought maybe you had—the way you leaped at me.

JESS. I'm just glad to see you. So glad!

ANDY (*blurting out the words*). Jess, I've something important to tell you. (STELLA *gives a low, deriding laugh.* ANDY *looks at* STELLA *uncomfortably.*) Say, uh, did I come at the wrong time?

JESS (*vehemently*). No!

STELLA. I'm sick.

JESS (*quickly*). Tell me. Tell me your news.

ANDY (*looks at* STELLA *a moment, but shrugs his shoulders in bewilderment*). Maybe you'd better sit down.

JESS (*sitting slowly*). It's—your promotion?

ANDY (*grinning*). Yeah.

JESS. I knew it.

ANDY. You *have* been talking to mom.

JESS. No. No, I haven't.

ANDY. Well, I am now an executive. (*Eagerly.*) How does it sound?

JESS. Oh, Andy.

ANDY. An executive—after sixteen years. There were times when I didn't think I'd make it. But you know that, don't you, Jess? You always told me I would. That I'd have to believe I could. From office boy to an executive! Now, now I go out to lunch with the boss. Yesterday morning when he told me he said: "We can have lunch together and discuss some of the details then."

JESS. How wonderful it is!

ANDY. Do you know, I wouldn't tell anybody else, but I remember almost every word he said.. (*Laughing a little as he thinks about it.*) He doesn't waste words, you know. I'd hardly gotten in the door when he said: (*Without quite realizing it, he speaks more briskly and in a deeper tone in imitation of the boss.*) "Middleton, I want you to head the new branch. Get it rolling. It's a lot of work and a lot of responsibility. But I know you can handle it. I'll be out myself in another month to see how you're doing."

JESS. What does it all mean?

ANDY. Why, I'm to start the new branch office in . . . (*His voice drops off.*) . . . California.

(STELLA *turns her head and looks intently at* ANDY.)

JESS (*Taken aback*). What . . .

ANDY (*Sitting down beside her*). I didn't mean to say it so quick.

JESS. California?

ANDY. I know, honey. I'd like it better if I didn't have to go so far, but it's an opportunity I can't afford to miss.

JESS. When are you going?

ANDY (*after a pause*). Day after tomorrow. Monday.

JESS (*dryly*). I see. That's quite soon, isn't it?

ANDY. I wish it weren't so soon, but it can't be helped. The boss intended to send someone else, but the man pulled out at the last minute. (STELLA *gets up lazily and wanders into the kitchen.*) The boss, himself, wasn't sure what to do. He said, "You'll do."

JESS (*flaring up*). Like that? He said it like that?

ANDY. He never says anything good about anybody. But he's sending me, isn't he?

JESS (*angrily*). No, he never does say anything good—or do anything good.

ANDY. Jess, this doesn't sound like you.

JESS. All he does is mess up people's lives. He can't give something free and clear; he has to include a nice sharp little knife.

ANDY. Jess . . .

JESS. He knows you're buying a house. He knows you're trying to settle down.

ANDY. He has a business to run. He isn't being deliberately . . . Jess, I don't understand you.

JESS. Don't you know him at all? He knows and you know this is the one and only chance, the first and last offer. If you said "No" to this, he'd never give you another chance. Don't you care? Don't you care about that part of it?

(STELLA *returns from the kitchen. She goes to the dining table and fusses around with the plants on the window sill. She sits down and picks up the cake crumbs, which she lazily carries to her mouth. From time to time, she glances at* ANDY *and* JESS.)

ANDY. Honey, I don't like everything about it, but what can I do?

JESS. Oh, I don't know.

ANDY. It means being unsettled for a while, and I'll miss seeing you, but it *is* more money; it is a better position.

JESS. Will you miss me?

ANDY. Sure, I'll miss you. Don't you know I'll miss you?

JESS. You're not just saying that? You mean it—with—with your whole heart, don't you?

ANDY. Yes.

JESS. Say it so I can hear it.

ANDY. I'll miss you. I don't know how to say it any louder.

JESS. You could take me with you.

ANDY. What?

JESS. Let me come with you.

ANDY. Now, honey . . .

JESS. I won't be any trouble and—I can't stay here!

ANDY. Look, Jessie, mom's coming with me.

JESS. Ooh. I—could—look—after—her. (*Abruptly.*) Let's go out, Andy; I can't seem to breathe.

ANDY (*patting her on the back*). Come, now, come . . .

JESS. Andy, I can be ready in nothing flat. Take me to California. Marry me. Marry me now!

ANDY. I told you, honey, mom . . .

JESS. It's now or never, Andy. If you've ever meant anything you've ever said, you'll marry me now. You'll take me with you.

ANDY. This is mom's trip, Jess; I promised her it was her trip.

JESS. If you explain . . .

ANDY. She has her heart set on it; she's looking forward to it so. You know how it would affect her.

JESS. Yes, I know.

ANDY. Look, I'll write to you. I'm a good letter writer, regular as a clock. I was away from home once and mom always used to tell everybody how good I was about writing regularly. (JESS *doesn't say anything.*) It'll be something quite new, you know; we've never written each other before.

JESS. That—will be—nice.

ANDY. Sure it will! And I'll see you tomorrow before I leave—tomorrow evening. I won't have much more time than that. But we'll go wherever you want, do whatever you want. How about it? (JESS *nods.*) I'll come at eight o'clock. It'll be your night. Something to be remembered.

JESS (*choking*). Ye-es.

ANDY. And we'll write each other.

JESS (*suddenly*). Andy. (*Throwing her arms around him.*) Andy!

ANDY (*awkwardly*). Now, look, honey. (*Pats her on the shoulder.*) It's not so bad. It's not forever, Jessie?

JESS (*sitting up*). I'm sorry.

ANDY. You shouldn't take it so hard.

JESS (*smiling a little*). I'm sensible now. . . . You must have things to do. And your mother's waiting downstairs.

ANDY. Well, yes, I do. But I'm worried about you.

JESS. I'm all right now. I don't seem to feel anything, all of a sudden.

ANDY. I'll see you tomorrow then? At eight? (JESS *nods. He kisses her on the cheek.*) Tomorrow. (*He starts for the door. As he is about to go out, he looks at* STELLA.) So long, Stell!

STELLA (*waving her hand in a vague gesture*). Good-bye—Andrew. (ANDY *goes out, shutting the door.* JESS *remains sitting, dazed.* STELLA *watches her, still picking up crumbs with one finger and putting them in her mouth.* JESS *gets up, without looking at* STELLA, *and walks, first upstage, stops, then toward the kitchen, stops, then starts toward the hall door, but stops. Then she runs into the bathroom, shutting the door behind her.* STELLA *remains sitting for a moment, listening. Then she languidly gets up, goes to a mirror and stands, touching up her hair. Bored with this activity, she goes to the closet, pushes several articles of clothing back and forth along the rod, finally removing a wine-colored dressing gown, which she puts on. She takes several half-waltzing steps, ending up by the easy chair; she kneels on the chair while inserting a cigarette into a holder; she lights the cigarette. She then goes to the dining table and refills the wine glasses.* JESS *comes out of the bathroom.* STELLA *looks back over her shoulder.*) We haven't finished our party. (JESS *looks at her dumbly.*) See? I've filled your glass. (*She picks up a wine glass and holds it out to* JESS.) And the sun's out now. (*She holds it in a ray of sunshine.*) Isn't it pretty?

(*Without speaking,* JESS *comes up and takes the glass.*)

CURTAIN

EX-MISS COPPER QUEEN
ON A SET OF PILLS

by Megan Terry

The scene opens on a street somewhere on the Lower East Side of New York City. It's about 5:30 A.M. Garbage cans are near the curb ready for the Sanitation Department. There's a slight chill in the air. An old Puerto Rican woman hauls the last can of ash up from the cellar of one of the houses, sets it in its place along the row of other cans, then disappears under the steps of her house. As the light grows stronger we make out the figure of COPPER QUEEN, *who is sleeping on the top step of a brownstone stoop. She fights through drugs and drink to wake up.*

COPPER QUEEN (*tries to pull herself to a sitting position, but falls back. She rolls over on her belly and tries to focus her bleary eyes. She thinks she sees a man*). Hey there, Mister . . . this is your dance. Sidewalk's as good a place as any. Say, Mister, you've got my number. You know . . . I'm giving it to you . . . If you take it I'll let ya buy this little gal a great big drink . . . Cig's gone out. Buy me a . . . buy me a . . . (*Her mind clears a bit more and she sees the sidewalk. She wants to get to it, but it's too far. This makes her angry, but first she tries to talk the sidewalk into coming closer.*) Why hello there . . . pleased to see ya. I spot you down there, you sidewalk . . . nine million miles away. Sure beats the hell out of me to know why this city builds its sidewalks so far down from the houses. By God . . . Only a big city sidewalk would build itself so darn far away from a gal's boot. Swallowed me a blue heaven, man . . . Pretty Man . . . dance? (*She painfully pulls herself to a sitting position, and reaches for her bottle*

of wine. She thinks it's farther from her hand than it actually is, so she reaches beyond it, and works back toward it. She repeats this several times, almost knocking it over.) No you don't. I got ya, thought you'd get away again, I betcha? Can't get away. I take care a the important things. Getting too bright out. You S.O.B. can't make off with my wine. (*It takes two hands and great concentration to get the wine bottle to her mouth. It's without a top.*) Momma needs sugar . . . dry . . . cut to the rawhide squaw-chewed dust! All right. Git to work. Git to work. Gotta cut outta this here place soon's I can see my way. This ain't no Yellowstone Park, that's for damn sure . . . (*laughs and sips some more wine*) All them dresses waitin' to be shown . . . I damn well still git myself to work . . . In my blue heaven. (*takes a blue pill*) Yeah, but the heaven's in me now, yes it is!

(COPPER QUEEN *is about twenty-six. She wears tight black pants, run-over heels, low-cut blouse, and some tattered scarves. She's half in and half out of a mangy fur coat. Behind the drugs, drinks, and ten years of little sleep lies a beautiful girl. While the* COPPER QUEEN *sips her wine, two old women enter. One pushes a baby carriage; both search the garbage cans with expert hands and appraising eyes. B.A., the larger of the two women, definitely the manager, wears many watches on each arm. She has three wigs on her head, each a different color and age. She wears one rubber glove and one canvas one. There's a record book chained to her belt and several pens and pencils on cords. The carriage she pushes sports an alarm clock. Several whisk brooms hang on the side of the car-*

MEGAN TERRY (1932–   )

In 1973 Megan Terry proclaimed that "America is witnessing the greatest flowering of playwriting talent since the Elizabethans and the Greeks." If this is so, Terry can take personal credit for having had a hand in the nurturing of much of this talent. In that same year she joined forces with Rosalyn Drexler, Maria Irene Fornes, and some 20 other Off-Off-Broadway authors to form the New York Theatre Strategy, whose purpose is the encouragement of experimental playwrights. Today Terry is also the creative mentor of the Omaha Magic Theatre, a group of young writers and actors who travel to colleges and theatre festivals to perform. Following a recent stint as an adjudicator for the American Theatre Association's new-play competition, Terry expressed her wonder and delight at the variety and caliber of the work she had seen.

Her own plays run the gamut from heavy drama to musical comedy. She has received innumerable awards for her work, among them the 1970 Obie for *Approaching Simone,* and her more than 40 plays have been translated into every major language.

A native of Seattle, Megan Terry studied all aspects of the theatre at the University of Washington, the University of Alberta, and the Banff School of Fine Arts. Not only as a playwright, but also as a founding member of the Open Theatre, she is one of the people who helped to shape the critically acclaimed avant garde of the 1960's. The Open Theatre was consciously innovative in both its methods of performance

PHOTO BY MEGAN TERRY

Megan Terry

and its approach to political activism. *Viet Rock,* which Terry developed for this company in 1966, was an unprecedented anti-war document, as well as the first in a long series of rock musicals.

The noted journal *Theatre Quarterly* said of Megan Terry that she "has constantly moved ahead of the currents, whether with the brilliant Open Theatre or on her own, creating plays across the country."

---

riage. The carriage is ancient, but polished and shining. B.A.'s clothes are strange, but they're clean and ironed. CRISSIE *is uncertain of her age, but she does know that she comes from San Francisco. She'd never be seen on any street without her hat and gloves. Like* B.A.'s, *her clothes are clean and pressed, and she wears one rubber glove, but the other glove is white lace. She moves with delicacy and grace.*)

B.A. Crissie! Crissie Rutherford Denny!

What in the name of a snake's insides is this junk you've deposited in my clean carriage?

CRISSIE. Are you calling me, dear? Did you want me, B.A.?

B. A. What do you think you're trying to do to me!

CRISSIE. I beg your pardon, dear?

B.A. Don't beg my pardon. Give me an answer.

CRISSIE. What was the question?

B.A. What is this junk?

CRISSIE. Let me see the item, B.A.

B. A. Have you lost all your senses? Are you going through this trash properly?

CRISSIE. I'm always proper, B.A.

B.A. I nearly, I very nearly wrote it down in my record book. Come here! Closer! I want to see your face, hands. Aha! How much eye-opener this morning?

CRISSIE. Hardly a smitch. We were very low.

B.A. I think you had more than a smitch. I think you finished the jug. Let me smell your breath.

CRISSIE. Please, B.A. That's offensive and hurtful.

B.A. Hurtful! Look who's being hurtful to *me*. What is this? What is this filthy thing you've carelessly tossed in my carriage?

CRISSIE. Excuse me, B.A. But you promised it would be *our* carriage.

B.A. What's this cardboard thing? You know I detest cardboard. What is this waxed and runny lice-filled carton?

CRISSIE. Let me see? (*Reaches for it*).

B.A. Don't touch it, you dope. It's covered with germs. (*Takes some tongs that hang on the side of the carriage and gingerly fishes the milk carton out of the carriage and throws it into the garbage can.*) I'll never get you trained. Why do I keep trying? I'll never get you to understand the true value of anything.

CRISSIE. Oh, B.A., I know we could use it.

B.A. Oh yes? How?

CRISSIE. Why I read in last week's lovely issue of *Woman's Day* we found behind the A & P that you just melt lots of different colored candles into one of these empty milk cartons, and then you sprinkle sequins on top, any color you like, and then behold; you have a lovely, lovely Christmas candle that will burn the twelve days of Christmas.

B.A. At your funeral! Do you realize you could bring typhoid into our home by picking up filth like this? Why you might as well drink water from a toilet.

CRISSIE. I'm sorry, sorry, sorry, B.A. I thought it would be so pretty at mealtimes.

B.A. We prospect for salable items. Will you get that through your head? I don't bring garbage into our home, and neither do you. We can *buy* a Christmas candle, if you have your heart set on one. But I won't have you endangering your health *or* mine, by such careless . . .

CRISSIE (*starting to cry*). Oh, B.A., please don't raise your voice like that, I can't . . .

B.A. For God's teeth and jawbone, will you stop! This instant! Don't try to shirk your responsibility to our business with a lot of teary . . . I'll go back to Alaska . . . I'll go back to Alaska and leave you to prospect this whole city . . . this whole city . . . all by your little dopey self . . . all by your . . .

CRISSIE. Don't go back to that dangerous country, B.A. . . . See? I'm not crying. Earthquakes and polars and . . . I couldn't stand it. See . . . I'm not crying.

B.A. What's all that water swimming in your eyes?

CRISSIE. Oh, B.A., I try so hard. I've worked so hard to please you. I've learned so much . . . you've truly taught me a great deal . . . I was such a tenderfoot when we met . . . you've . . . I'm so grateful . . .

B.A. I wish you'd show it more, then.

CRISSIE (*plunging into a can*). I'll show you. I'll find treasures all the rest of the morning.

B.A. You couldn't tell a salable item if it bit you in the behind. (*Takes her record book up to write in it; looks at her watches, adjusts one.*) Let's see, we took seven minutes, eighteen seconds for Avenue C, from Fourteenth Street to Eleventh. That's good. That's very good. We're ahead of ourselves by twelve minutes. Best morning's record since the mock air raid of April 13, 1943. (*Records the time.*)

CRISSIE. I told you. I told you I would, B.A. See here, look, B.A. See, it's a little red jacket. (COPPER QUEEN *puts down her wine at the word "little."*) A dear little child's, little red jacket.

COPPER QUEEN. Child? Dear . . . little? . . .

CRISSIE. Yes, B.A. A dear little jacket. I can wash it in the boiler room and press it. You'll get us a grand price on Orchard Street.

B.A. (*plucking the jacket from* CRISSIE *and going over it with expert care*). Here . . . mmmmmm . . . I don't know . . . maybe . . . Ah . . . Sure as hell couldn't wear it down into a mine! Mmmm . . . perhaps . . . not more than two bits, though. Is this the best you can do?

CRISSIE. Oh a dear little child's jacket as red as this should fetch much more than a quarter, I'd say.

COPPER QUEEN. Was it a boy's or a girl's?

CRISSIE. I said it was a child's, B.A. It's a fine jacket. A little boy I knew in San Francisco had a jacket like that. Do you suppose he lost it?

B.A. Nonsense. He couldn't have lost it this far . . . of course, he might have been visiting the city and lost it . . . Did he come to New York often?

CRISSIE. Not often, I think. I think he would not come too often. He was only five.

B.A. Then it's bound and determined that your friend didn't lose the jacket. So we'll wash it and sell it on Orchard Street. Put it in the carriage.

COPPER QUEEN. He lost it . . . a boy . . . a little boy lost . . . his . . . little jacket . . .

CRISSIE. See how nicely I fold you, little jacket . . . See . . . see there, B.A.?

B.A. Idiot! Don't put it on that side, that's where the blue pants go. Put it on the other side with red top wear.

CRISSIE. I'm so sorry, B.A. I was too excited. Of course I know that red top wear goes here, and blue bottom wear goes there.

B.A. There, that's better. Balances the color inside the carriage better. I can't have a messy carriage. It'll look like cheap linoleum. Order. We must have order or the carriage will collapse.

CRISSIE. Yes, B.A. See, it's in order now. It's balanced . . . perfect . . . balance . . .

B.A. (considers a moment, then rearranges the jacket ever so slightly). There, that's better. I have an eye for order you know. There. It won't collapse . . . I've balanced the carriage. (Pushes the carriage to the next can)

CRISSIE. It's in order now, B.A.

COPPER QUEEN (watching the carriage, fascinated). A baby . . . a baby . . . in a buggy . . . (Reaches out and makes an effort to stand, but can't.) Say . . . lady . . . ladies! . . . you there . . . Say . . . ? May I ask you . . . with sugar on it . . . may I ask . . .

CRISSIE. B.A., look at that poor young woman. I think she wants to meet us. I'd love to . . . I believe she's calling to us . . .

B.A. Pay no attention; we're on a work schedule. The carriage isn't half filled yet.

CRISSIE. I distinctly heard that poor young woman ask . . .

B.A. Just some whore sobering up.

CRISSIE. Oh, the poor little whore.

B.A. Did you go through all these cans? How about that one? That one on the end?

CRISSIE. I'm just about to, B.A. I was on my way.

B.A. Get your gloves in there. One twenty-five-cent jacket doesn't get you off the hook for that milk carton.

CRISSIE. Please don't use that carton against me.

B.A. Don't let it happen again.

COPPER QUEEN. Say lady . . .

CRISSIE. We have to speak to her, B.A. She's made the first gesture. It's only common courtesy.

B.A. To work!

CRISSIE. I was brought up to attend the less fortunate, B.A. There're some things you could learn, too, you know. It's our duty to aid that poor girl.

B.A. That's no girl. That's a sick whore. We're respectable business women.

COPPER QUEEN. Say there, ladies, may I just ask . . . to . . . a "red bird" baby . . .

CRISSIE. B.A., I must see if I can help . . .

B.A. You stay here, she's more diseased than that filthy milk carton you tried to slip in the carriage.

CRISSIE. Oh, please, B.A.

COPPER QUEEN. May I just have a tiny peek at the . . . (Leans over the steps and loses her balance.) Who tipped these stairs!

CRISSIE (worried, she runs to COPPER QUEEN). Are you all right, my dear? Here, let me help. There you go. (Steadies her.)

COPPER QUEEN. Much obliged. Just on my way to work . . . saw your buggy . . .

CRISSIE. Allow me to introduce myself. I'm Crissie Rutherford Denny, and my partner is Miss Mayhew. I don't believe I caught your name.

COPPER QUEEN. I didn't give it. Your partner?

CRISSIE. We're business partners. However, Miss Mayhew is senior partner.

COPPER QUEEN. What line you in?

CRISSIE. We . . . we . . . 'er, we find things.

B.A. We're prospectors! We deal in salable items.

CRISSIE. You have no idea how many treasures you can find in the city. Just for the picking.

COPPER QUEEN. Picking! What the hell berries grow on this street?

B.A. We're business women.

COPPER QUEEN. Some business, picking through crud!

CRISSIE (*matter-of-fact*). Oh, crud brings a good price, if you know where to sell it!

COPPER QUEEN. How can you drag a poor little baby around while you pick through garbage cans?

B.A. It's a darn sight more ordered job than whoring.

COPPER QUEEN (*pulling her ray gun*). Zap! Zap! I've dissolved millions for less than that! (*Laughs.*)

B.A. You can't even stand up. Crissie, get away from that mess.

COPPER QUEEN. I'm on my way to work. I work. You're not so smart. I work. Zap! Blackjack! (*Takes a pill.*)

B.A. In doorways, at night!

COPPER QUEEN. I got a good job. I'm appreciated. People look at me. What do you get from picking rags?

CRISSIE. We've earned the dearest place. We live in the most secure unit of our building. I've completely redone the inside. It was lots of scrubbing and white tornado, but it was worth it, wasn't it, B.A.?

B.A. You couldn't never even tell it was ever a coal bin.

CRISSIE. Never, never in a million years. And it's so San Francisco cool in summer. We have so much storage for our treasures.

B.A. And room for expansion!

COPPER QUEEN. Do you keep the baby in a coal bin? Well blackjack! Why not!

CRISSIE. I'd love you to call on me, my dear. I have the loveliest room all draped in brocade; it completely covers the stone. Keeps dampness out.

B.A. I've plugged all the rat holes.

COPPER QUEEN. Brocade. Yes, that's it. I wore brocade.

B.A. Yeah, the latest uniform at the House of Detention. Burlap brocade!

COPPER QUEEN. I did. I had a whole gown of brocade. White brocade.

CRISSIE. White! White for your wedding, dear?

COPPER QUEEN. The contest! Hearts! (*Pops another pill into her mouth.*)

B.A. Last time you wore a gown was the day you were born.

CRISSIE. You won a contest? I'm honored to meet you. I've never won a contest, but then I've never entered one.

COPPER QUEEN. Copper Queen. Miss Copper Queen of all the dirt you could see on the whole state of Montana. Baby blue heaven . . . let's see your baby? . . .

CRISSIE. How do you do again. Miss Queen, I'm so very pleased to make your acquaintance. I'm Crissie Rutherford Denny and this is Miss Beatrice Anderson Mayhew.

COPPER QUEEN. And I'm very pleased to meet you, too, little ladies.

B.A. Where'd you say that contest was?

COPPER QUEEN. Don't talk so fast. Hey baby, boy . . . Football! (*Calls at carriage and leans toward it as she takes another pill.*)

B.A. She don't know where she is. All right, Miss Crissie Rutherford Denny, you have just ten seconds to live up to your partnership agreement.

CRISSIE. But, B.A. . . .

B.A. March with me now, Crissie . . . or I'll cancel your orders. (*Goes through the cans, brushing and dusting and wiping things before placing any good item in the carriage; when she does find something good, she writes it down.*) We're going to finish up here, and get lickety-split to Avenue D. We're making good time, and I aim to keep it that way. What's this? A nearly new pair of Hart, Schaffner & Marx! That's promising. (*Pulls pair of shoes out.*) Crissie!

CRISSIE (*to* COPPER QUEEN). It's not what it used to be, my dear. We do very well, but we have to work fast to earn enough.

B.A. Another throwaway beer bottle! Plastic and cardboard—the scourge of our times. Once we earned our food on beer bottles alone! The bread, right out of our mouths!

CRISSIE. You know what I saw in a Third Avenue antique shop on Tuesday? A Prince Albert can! And do you know what they were asking for it? You'll never guess, my dear.

B.A. Don't tell me, I'll get sick.

CRISSIE (*sotto voce to* COPPER QUEEN). Two dollars and fifty cents. Two dollars and fifty cents for an old tin tobacco can that we used to pass by.

COPPER QUEEN (*pounding her temples, beginning to tremble*). Hello, do you have Prince Albert in the can? Well, let him out!

CRISSIE. I understand, my dear. I have days like this, too. Sometimes they last for months.

B.A. Our partnership is dissolved. Good-bye, Crissie!

CRISSIE. Oh, no.

B.A. This is it, Miss Denny. I'm leaving. You have one tenth of a second to move your bones, or I'll tell the vacuum cleaner where you are.

CRISSIE. Very good, but you can't trick me that way. I'm coming. I want to come with you, B.A. But I do so enjoy visiting. I haven't had a day off in years.

B.A. The vacuum cleaner.

CRISSIE. Go ahead and tell the vacuum cleaner, B.A. It can't do anything because it ruined its suction when it tried to swallow my little jade frog.

B.A. I fixed it, Crissie, and I'll turn it on full power if you don't come immediately.

COPPER QUEEN. I want to see your baby . . .

CRISSIE (*jumping up, tries to shake hands with* COPPER QUEEN). Good-bye, my dear. I must go back to work. It's been so nice to make your acquaintance. If you're ever in San Francisco, I'll take you to lunch at Fisherman's Wharf, and then to the opera. Do you like *Der Rosenkavalier?*

COPPER QUEEN. You're such a nice lady . . . (*Pulls her pillbox out of her coat but can't get it open—pleads sweetly.*) Could you please open this little tiny box for me?

B.A. Oh, Crissie . . . oh, Crissie, how you'll cry when you're sucked into the dirt chamber. How black your gloves will get! Where's the . . .

CRISSIE. Why, of course, my dear, if you'll pardon my fingers. (*Removes her gloves gracefully and opens the box.*) What a pretty box. Look, B.A.

B.A. Mmmhmmm . . . At least eighteen dollars. Come on or I'll plug in the cleaner.

CRISSIE (*opening the box*). What pretty pills. You can't fool me, B.A. There are no electrical outlets on Avenue A.

COPPER QUEEN (*grabs for pills*). I can't wait any more. I need a set. Stone me honey! Give me blackjack hearts in my blue heaven.

CRISSIE. Pretty pills, B.A. Look at these colors. I know you'd approve of the arrangement. You'd love these colors, B.A. Love them! There's red heart-shaped babies, and black and white clown tinys and long ball-shaped littles and greenies with small colored balls and yellow-jacket bee-like sweeties and blue blue blue . . . the color of . . . Oops. (*The box spills.*)

COPPER QUEEN. My blue heaven . . . (*Reaches and pills get spilled.*) Get them. Give me. I got to have . . . I can't make it . . .

B.A. (*shrugs*). She's on goofballs, too, eh?

COPPER QUEEN. Hand them to me. I've got to stay stoned. I can't stand my own company . . . the baby . . . please lady . . . hand me . . .

CRISSIE (*fetching pills*). Here, my dear Miss Queen. How clumsy of me . . . I fear in your haste you knocked . . .

COPPER QUEEN. Three, give me . . . any three as long as they're different colors.

B.A. Good-bye, Crissie. I'm taking down all that nice brocade when I get home, and you'll have to look at the damp, runny, black, stone walls.

CRISSIE (*hands pills to* COPPER QUEEN). Here's what I found, my dear . . . See, I'm coming now, B.A. Good-bye . . . (*Makes an effort to shake* COPPER QUEEN'S *hand but she is busily struggling to get the pills in her mouth and wash them down with wine.*)

COPPER QUEEN (*then grabs for* CRISSIE). You've been so good to me. Let me buy you a drink?

B.A. A lush, too!

COPPER QUEEN. Let me buy you little ladies a great big drink! (CRISSIE, *embarrassed, looks to* B.A.) See, got nearly a whole bottle of . . . of Chablis. I hate the stuff, but it comes in handy if I run out of . . . of . . .

CRISSIE. I'm coming with you now, B.A.

B.A. Is it really wine?

CRISSIE. I believe so. I think I recognize the shape of the bottle.

B.A. What kind?

CRISSIE. I thought we only had a tenth of a second.

B.A. What brand of Chablis?

CRISSIE. Gall— Gall— Gallo . . . I know that . . . They come from the same state as I do. The Gallo brothers. They make lovely wines.

B.A. It must be filthy.

CRISSIE. B.A., it's nearly a full bottle.

B.A. Fifth?

CRISSIE. I think it's a full quart.

B.A. Full?

CRISSIE. Nearly . . .

COPPER QUEEN. If you'll let me hold the baby . . . just one hold . . . just one . . . I'll give you more than a drink . . . I'll give you the whole bottle.

CRISSIE. Did you hear, B.A.? She wants to give us the bottle.

B.A. Give?

CRISSIE. If we let her see the baby.

B.A. Baby! What baby?

CRISSIE (*bewildered*). That's right, B.A. We don't have a baby in the carriage.

B.A. But she doesn't know that.

CRISSIE (*a bit mournfully*). We'll have to give back the wine.

B.A. No, we won't. We'll drink the wine. Then we'll let her look.

CRISSIE. But I couldn't deceive *her,* B.A. She trusts me.

B.A. (*ominously*). Stand still a minute, Crissie.

CRISSIE. No. No. No. Who is it?

B.A. Mixmaster? I have to place the motor. Yes. It's the mixmaster!

CRISSIE. Not the mixmaster, B.A.! Oh not that.

B.A. It's coming toward you from behind that last ash can.

CRISSIE. Please turn it off. Pull out the plug, B.A.

B.A. Will you get the wine?

CRISSIE. Anything. I'll do anything! I can't stand to be whipped into an angel food—not twice in one morning.

B.A. (*taking a cane from its fitting on the carriage side, she strides to the last ash can and lifts the cane to strike the can*). I, Beatrice Anderson Mayhew, am in command of this street. I hereby turn off all electric current. (*Bangs on the can and* CRISSIE *relaxes.*)

CRISSIE. Oh, thank you, B.A.

B.A. You can prove your thanks by obeying me.

COPPER QUEEN. If you don't want wine, I'll share my goofballs—pop, pop. (*Looks in box*) All gone. All gone, where'd . . . I can't last . . . got to get to work . . . got to connect . . . where is he? Why didn't he meet me. Oh God, it'll go away . . . it'll go away if I can just . . . it'll go away if I can

just hold the baby, only for a little while . . .

CRISSIE. B.A., the poor little thing . . . what shall we do?

B.A. A moment, a moment till I plan our day. Now let's see? We've covered the *Green-witch* Village area; the mid-East Side, we have three avenues left to go. However, if we fortify ourselves with the wine, we might get ourselves up to Gramercy Park, and that would be good, because there's a *slightly* better class of garbage in that area, and we'd be well ahead of the Sanitation Department. I say we deserve refreshments. We've been out since three.

CRISSIE. But the baby? . . .

B.A. String her along. She'll forget baby . . . she doesn't even know her own name.

CRISSIE (*crossing to* COPPER QUEEN). I want to thank you for your kind offer. We've had an extremely busy morning and we'd certainly enjoy a refreshing pause.

COPPER QUEEN. Sit right down here beside me, little lady from San Fran and Santa Fe. You're like my friend Lucy. She takes care of me. She's a honey. She's comfortable. She comforts me. When I really feel bad she sits on my lap and kisses my new and oncoming wrinkles away . . . only you're prettier . . . you were . . . yes, you are.

CRISSIE. B.A., did you hear? The little whore thinks I'm pretty?

B.A. Crissie, "whore" isn't exactly a term of affection.

CRISSIE. B.A., did you hear? She says I'm pretty.

B.A. Pretty broken down and out!

COPPER QUEEN. It's a pleasure to tell you so. They ain't enough pretty people in this universe. Did you ever see such an ugly city? The streets are flooded with uglies. But you, you're pretty. I'm much obliged.

B.A. Is there wine or is there not, "pretty"? I can't waste precious business time with this bum. Bring that wine here if there is any.

CRISSIE. Of course there's wine. (*Handing the bottle to* B.A.) You take the first sip, B.A.

B.A. Don't mind if I do.

COPPER QUEEN (*the pills are beginning to work*). Ah . . . Yeah, yeah, yeah. That's what I was waiting for. Slow. Don't go by fast this time. Quiet. Make it quiet this time, baby, let me float right off the street and get to work. Oh yeah. Stoning it! Make the ce-ment sidewalk jealous—yeah! Mount Rushmore—that's me!

B.A. What'll we drink to? We did beat our best time record this morning.

COPPER QUEEN. Pop, Pop . . . fly . . .

CRISSIE. Don't waste our toast.

B.A. Yep, that's the only reason I'm allowing a change of schedule. We'll make it up tomorrow. But only because we're ahead of ourselves anyway. Your turn.

CRISSIE (*toasting heroically*). To Beatrice Anderson Mayhew who is in command of this street.

COPPER QUEEN. Drink up, friends, and friends of friends, the end is soon in sight. Everybody drinks. Everybody wins. You're hard to find in this town. I dug you the first I saw you dancing out on the dancing floor.

CRISSIE. Was it a waltz or a mazurka?

COPPER QUEEN. You're like the cute little doll that got left in the rain. Like that doll I had when I lived in the big house with them . . . you know them? . . . That man and that woman that lived there where I did . . . and they, you know, just hardly wouldn't talk to me.

CRISSIE. They wouldn't talk to you either?

COPPER QUEEN. Nope. Not word, one. That whole mountain of copper could have melted into gold and they wouldn't of said a word to me.

CRISSIE. I lived on Nob Hill, and no one spoke to me either, except the ice cream man, and the foghorns in the Golden Bay under the Gateway to the Orient. Sometimes B.A. won't say a word to me, not even if I say—please.

B.A. (*the wine is beginning to hit her*). Another belt, Crissie?

CRISSIE. I would care for one more swallow, B.A., thank you. This used to be Papa's favorite wine. (*Gracefully takes a long swallow.*)

COPPER QUEEN. Somebody got a stick? Give me a drag. I can't go that liquor no more. You sip it up, little women, and I'll sing you a little old western song, like they sung it to me in the West. (*Sings to the tune of "Streets of Laredo".*)

And this and the forenoon comes
To lean against time

When Gary rides into the West
Of the High down because we ain't ready
For the lowdown—
It is too far to stoop.
So come a ty yi yo—git along little
     girlies
I'll sing you a song that is not of my own
Lie down beside me my fine little girlies
And I'll sing you to heaven that's not
     of my own
But I'll love you and hug you
And pull off your dresses
And curl your hair
And paint your nails
And soothe you and sing you
And kiss all your questions
And I'll save you from nothing—
     no less!

CRISSIE. What a sweet, sweet song . . . You have a very nice-sounding voice . . . not operatic mind you, but the sound . . .

COPPER QUEEN. It was a sound that won me a prize in the talent part of the quest . . . O little woman O . . . took me a set of pills. I'm stoned out of my head. I feel so cold in this city. Give me some more . . . I need a new set . . . find me the little black and white ones and the red heart ones and we'll cap it all with a yellow jack. Look down there on that sidewalk. You see any little yellow pills? You do . . . yes . . . lady—find some! I can't go on like this.

CRISSIE (*tries to look some more*). I gave you all I found. (*Sipping her wine wonderingly.*) B.A., what's a set of pills?

B.A. Just a new kind of hophead. I read in the *New York Post* that these types take sleeping pills and wake-up pills all at the same time, and maybe a Benzedrine chaser. She don't know where she is.

CRISSIE. I'll help find her. Nobody will talk to *her*, either.

B.A. Can't say as I blame them. Is this all the wine? Hey, what's the fur she's wearing? That looks like, yes, it's civet cat . . . maybe she has some money . . . Let's sit beside her. No, not here. You're right, Crissie, maybe we *can* find her. (*They go to* COPPER QUEEN *and sit one on each side and help her to sit up.*)

COPPER QUEEN (*welcoming them, she pulls herself up by flinging an arm around each shoulder*). Hey, that's better, I like warm space. I don't know what it is . . . I give them all my money, and still they hurt me. Still they walk out on me. Why do my friends do that? I'm not talking about men, I mean my friends, too. You expect it of men. But friends are supposed to be friendly. I want to help people. But that's the way I am; I'd give away everything I had, only I already did, I already gave it away . . . I think I did . . . you feel warm . . . you're so . . . so warm . . .

CRISSIE. Poor little thing.

B.A. (*feeling the coat*). Nice coat . . . once!

COPPER QUEEN. I won the contest when I was only seventeen, did you know that?

CRISSIE. A contest? How lovely. Where was it?

COPPER QUEEN. Why it was in Butte. Butte, Montana. Where else?

CRISSIE. Where else? Of course, it was in Montana!

COPPER QUEEN. Of course.

B.A. (*drinking more wine*). Oh, my God. If it wasn't in New York—why it had to be Montana.

COPPER QUEEN (*painfully, but bravely, trying to figure it out*). But why do they take my things. I let them stay at my place, and they steal my suitcases. I got nothing left to pack anything in, even if I did get up the guts to go back home. They sleep in my bed and take my watch that I got for graduation from the eighth grade. I didn't graduate the high school. I came to New York for another queen contest, but I didn't win that one. Why do I give money away? I need money. Miss Copper Queen—1949.

CRISSIE. I'm glad I don't have to worry about money any more. Terrible responsibility! B.A. is a good business woman. I had lots of money once, and all the machines they bought, those machines had me and they told me they wanted more and more and I fed them until I just ran out of feed.

B.A. (*disgusted*). You don't have any money, eh?

COPPER QUEEN. 'Course I got money. They wouldn't let me starve.

CRISSIE. They wouldn't let you starve, and neither would we.

COPPER QUEEN. They send me lots of money. And I need it. I got a hell of a habit to support. Where is he? Oh, but this is good. I work, too. I work as hard as you two do, that's what hung me about you two, seeing you prospect like a couple of Mountain Men looking through those litter baskets and garbage pans, placer miners, panning a rich stream.

B.A. Send you money, eh? What is it? They pay you to *stay* away?

COPPER QUEEN. They's generous. They don't want me to come home like this. They don't want him to see me like this. Yeah, you need money in this town. Hell, the pioneers had it easy. I got a hundred from hustling and I picked up fifty for posing in m'birthday suit. And I got my month's allowance from Mom.

B.A. Who'd give you an allowance? You don't even have a mailbox.

COPPER QUEEN. Hell, I don't want to be like this. But you want to know a secret?

CRISSIE. Yes, yes.

COPPER QUEEN (*to B.A.*). And do you want to know a secret? (B.A. *nods.*) I'm a pushover. I guess I like it. I like to be dominated. I . . . CRAVE . . . being . . . dominated!

B.A. You poor little girl. You better let me keep your money for you; somebody would rob it from you the state you're in.

COPPER QUEEN. It's in this here bag. You keep it for a while. I wouldn't have it all in one place like that. It's bad. (*Angry.*) You give some of the money to her to hold. (*Gestures toward* CRISSIE, *and* B.A. *gives* CRISSIE *some money.*)

CRISSIE. Now it's safe, dear. It's in two places.

COPPER QUEEN. Yes. I'll tell you something, if you'll bring me the baby to hold . . .

B.A. You tell first.

COPPER QUEEN. It's something you won't believe; it's stranger than anything. I loved him since I loved anyone. No matter wherever I am . . . that boy knows . . . before I do. Do you know that he can find me within five minutes when I hit that Butte town. No more'n five minutes, and he knows where. I look around, I just might turn around, and there he is . . . But you can't take a pimp home to yer father and mother. Don't never try it.

B.A. What a mess.

COPPER QUEEN. Can you imagine how I could take him home? But that tender boy, he can find me no matter what day or hour or where, when I roll into Butte. We find each other. I've loved him for ten years, and he's loved me. Yes, he has!

B.A. Your people, do they know where you are?

COPPER QUEEN. They think they know. But they don't know, really. Fact is, they have never even been able to find me. You know why?

CRISSIE. Why?

COPPER QUEEN. Because they don't know how to look! (*Laughs.*)

B.A. Where do you live, girl?

COPPER QUEEN. Butte, Montana.

B.A. I mean in New York.

COPPER QUEEN. I live here and there, mostly there. (*Giggles.*) I'm a transient. (*Looks at* CRISSIE.) You know, you have 'em in Cal. Them transient workers that follow the harvests and live in tents, like the Okies used to be. I'm a Montana Okie. But dammit I can still work—if I could just walk.

B.A. You work every day?

COPPER QUEEN. I always work, no matter how stoned or hung up I am. I come from a long line of workers. Don't matter how much bread you store in the box, everybody works in the West. You couldn'ta stayed alive in the West in the old days if you didn't work . . . Do you work?

B.A. Of course, you just seen us. We don't even take Sundays off. We start work while it's still dark to beat the Bowery bums to the pickings. However, we're better organized; we're business women, and we have a warm place to sleep.

COPPER QUEEN. I need that . . . warm place . . . a warm place . . . to sleep.

CRISSIE. Let's take her home with us, B.A., the lonely little thing.

B.A. No room.

CRISSIE. Please, B.A. We could have at last someone to talk to, she and I.

B.A. Her people would have us picked up for kidnapping.

CRISSIE. Why, she's a grown woman, and besides, they don't know our address. We're unlisted!

B.A. Definitely we cannot take her.

CRISSIE. But someone to talk to—you don't know what that means!

B.A. I talk to you, don't I? Who pulls out the plugs—who beats up the mixmaster—who

holds you in the night when the brocade starts to fly?

CRISSIE. Oh, B.A., I'm sorry. I didn't mean to say it that way. I didn't mean to hurt you . . . I . . .

B.A. (*indignant*). I resent that! I've never been hurt in my life.

CRISSIE. She needs rest, poor thing. Look at the circles under her eyes. Please let's take her to our basement and put her to bed, and then finish our picking. I'll work twice as fast. I promise.

B.A. She probably can't move. We can't afford any unmovable items taking space. Be months to get her into a decent salable condition.

COPPER QUEEN. Think and see if you could know and maybe you could tell me why my mother just sat there on her needlepoint chair with her eyelids heavy like the Virgin Mary? She knew I was drunk? Didn't she! I tell you she knew it! She saw me all sloppy and come staggering in higher than anyone can be, and she just sat there and pretended nothing was wrong.

CRISSIE. Our sitting room had needlepoint chairs.

COPPER QUEEN. How could she do that? She sat there so holy and looking like an innocent lamb, looking with her eyes from one side of the room to the other like she didn't see me. She thought I was the wall . . . and the stairs going up. But it was me all right! I crawled past that wall. I was drunk; I *knew* I was drunk . . . and I called to her . . . and I couldn't see . . . but she wouldn't touch me . . . I just wanted to go upstairs and talk to my baby before he went to sleep. But she took him, and called him "Brother." It ain't legal. He's *my* son!

CRISSIE. Don't you worry. We'll find you a baby again. We find new things every day. Don't we, B.A.? You can push the carriage all the way home if you want to. (COPPER QUEEN *nods and takes* CRISSIE'S *hands.*)

COPPER QUEEN. They were so good to me. We went down to Arizona to have the baby in a nice resort home. The best in the Southwest. Daddy came, too. It was the first vacation we'd ever had, all of us together. Then they said I could come to New York and stay as long as I wanted. Forever, even . . . and not have to live in a dumb small town . . .

they're raising him like their own son . . . they're so good to him . . . and they send me my money every month . . . every liver-squeezing month . . . She just sat there the whole time like the Virgin Mary . . . She thinks he came straight to her from God . . . She pretended I had nothing to do with it . . . just between her and God . . . Is ten years a long time to love someone . . . ?

B.A. No time—hardly a turn in the litter basket. We have to go back to work now. Thank you for the wine. It was clean and good. (*Pockets the money.*)

COPPER QUEEN. Help me up now. I got to see that baby.

CRISSIE (*pleading*). B.A. . . .

B.A. Some other time. We got a schedule to meet.

COPPER QUEEN. You drank my wine. You promised . . . you promised I could see that boy!

B.A. And you can, too. Just as soon as we get back here. Tomorrow morning at the same time.

COPPER QUEEN (*struggling to her feet*). I've got to see that boy. (*Lurches—but regains her balance.*)

B.A. Tomorrow, it's too late now.

CRISSIE (*can't bear to see* COPPER QUEEN *disappointed*). Stop her, B.A.

COPPER QUEEN (*staggers to the carriage, looks in, sees her own child there among the rags*). Oh . . . yeah . . . O yeah . . . baby. Hi lover! Hi fat boy! God you've grown so. Me—I've shrunk . . . You don't have enough covers . . . She should cover you more . . . God knows she's got money to do it with . . . (*She takes off her fur coat and painfully manages to get the coat tucked around the carriage. B.A. casts a satisfied glance toward* CRISSIE. *The coat is an unexpected bonus.*) Here, my honey boy. It's cold in this city. That's better, huh. Don't look at me like that. Take me back. You know me? You want me? Take me back. You're new enough to give me another chance. I'll be good. I'll go straight. I'll be such a good Mommie. See how I love you—see . . .

B.A. (*coming over to the carriage*). He's a fine-looking boy.

COPPER QUEEN. Baby baby boy. Pretty baby boy . . . nobody could have talked me out of having you. (*Shudders; the pills are wearing off.*)

B.A. Crissie. It's nearly six A.M. Get her away. Talk her back to the stoop. We have to get down to the next street. The bloody Bowery bums will beat us to it.

CRISSIE. But she's found her baby, B.A., and we've found this—(*Holds her share of money.*)

COPPER QUEEN (*rocking the carriage*). Rock that boy, boy, rock-a-bye boy and a rock, and a rock, and a rickity boy rock . . .

B.A. (*taking* COPPER QUEEN *by the arm*). I have an idea. It's an orderly one, and fits in with the morning program. You station yourself here, while we run down to pick Avenue D. When we finish at six-thirteen we'll hurry back and pick you up. And then you know what?

COPPER QUEEN. No. What?

B.A. When we get back here, we'll let *you* wheel the buggy all the way down to Avenue B.

COPPER QUEEN. Me? You would trust me? You would trust me to do that? And you don't even know me?

B.A. (*solemnly*). I would trust you.

COPPER QUEEN. Much obliged. I sure do thank you.

CRISSIE (*wanting to believe* B.A.). And when we get all finished with work, maybe you and I could sit in the East River Park and just talk . . . and take the baby for some river air . . . and just do as we please . . .

COPPER QUEEN. I'd like that. Oh, I would like that, little lady.

CRISSIE. I'll work fast. So fast. I can hardly wait.

B.A. Come on, Crissie. If we march, we'll just make the next stoplight.

COPPER QUEEN. You swear now, you'll meet me right here! Right here! You like me, right? I never took anything in my life. I give it away. I gave the clothes off my back and the skin off my face.

B.A. (*pulling the carriage away from* COPPER QUEEN). Come on. We've got to make the light. They've just finished putting out the cans on the next street.

COPPER QUEEN (*without the carriage to support her, she falls back toward the stairs*). And then you'll meet me?

CRISSIE (*catching* COPPER QUEEN). We can't leave her!

B.A. (*grabbing* CRISSIE *by the arm*). Come on, Crissie, or I'll turn the electric current back on.

CRISSIE (*quickly*). Good-bye, Miss Copper Queen. Remember, I meant what I said—if you ever come out to San Francisco . . .

B.A. (*almost offstage, pushing the buggy before her*). Crissie!

CRISSIE. I'm coming . . . thank you Miss Queen . . . for thinking me pretty . . . (*They're gone.*)

COPPER QUEEN (*waving after them with all her strength*). I'll wait here, little lady. I be right here till you come pick me up. I get to wheel him all the way down to Avenue B . . . you said! All the way home to . . . Avenue . . . B . . . Avenue . . . B . . . All the way . . .

 (*As the lights go down the curtain closes slowly.* COPPER QUEEN *sings as she lies back down on the stoop.*)

Ty yi yo git along little girlies
You knew that Montana was yer old home—

You walked and you talked and you
Showed off yer asses

Now you got to find you a
New—old home—

And we'll take the fat baby
To Avenue B—
And take my baby to
Avenue B—

All the way down to—
All the way—
All the way down to Avenue B—

B . . . B . . B . . .

 (*Her voice fades out and she is rigid.*)

CURTAIN

SKYWRITING

by **Rosalyn Drexler**

The characters are a MAN *and a* WOMAN. *The time is the everpresent.*

> *When the curtain rises the stage is divided down the middle by a partition. On one side of the partition there is a blue-white neon light on the diagonal; on the other side of the partition there is a purple neon light on the diagonal, both reaching from corner to corner of their respective partition sides. Heavy black curtains line the entire stage. Stage left the* WOMAN *is seated, and stage right the* MAN *is seated. They must move around and act when they speak. The picture postcard which they are sparring for is a projection of a picture postcard, which can jump to either wall, over the partition, left or right, as the director decides. At no time may the actors cross the barrier or touch, but at the end they each go to the wall as if holding up the enormous card together. Also, each must act to a phantom partner as if the phantom were the person in the adjoining section, and also pretend to be handling the card when necessary. (Perhaps an interesting effect and an irritating one would be to have a continual mechanical humming sound heard throughout, but very low, so as to be able to hear the lines.) This play should be stylized—coordinated—and choreographed.*

> *The scene begins with the* MAN *and* WOMAN *struggling for the picture postcard.*

WOMAN. It's mine.

MAN. What makes it yours?

WOMAN. I look at it and I've been there.

MAN. It's a picture of clouds. You don't need a picture of clouds.

WOMAN. I've been under them by foot and through them by plane. When I watch clouds I think of my picture postcard, and I look at it and it's pretty.

MAN. I bought it for you; you once said we could share it.

WOMAN. Transfer of property.

MAN. It belongs to both of us.

WOMAN. What do you want it for? You don't need a picture of clouds.

MAN. I see things in the clouds . . . gigantic female nudes with fluffy floating breasts, their Venus Mounds dripping with rain . . . I sold my umbrella.

WOMAN. And you lost your hair! How does it feel to be dripped on?

MAN. Absolutely, gloriously, radioactive! My brain is eaten into . . . my skull is a well of piss from the heavens . . . Ah, the outdoors!

WOMAN. You are disgusting. I know what you really want to do with this card!

MAN. What? . . . if anything.

WOMAN. You want to pick your teeth with its sharp edges, or put it under an ashtray, or squash a bug with it, or drop it behind the couch . . . nothing has value for you beyond its immediate use . . . nothing . . . because you don't believe in private property. Because you believe in replacement after defacement.

MAN. you save all kinds of shit. So save it! But you're not going to keep me from holding that card in my hands and viewing it! No woman can do that to me. Nozir!

WOMAN. Nozir is an Oriental name, is it not? Like Fawzier. Why are you calling Nozir? Is there someone in the house called Nozir?

MAN. You haven't told me why you won't give me the card . . . the real reason . . . the difficult reason . . . the filigreed reason, decorative but full of holes . . . the full-

ROSALYN DREXLER (1927–   )

Toward the end of the 1950's, rising production costs Off-Broadway as well as on caused some of the more experimental playwrights, such as Rosalyn Drexler, to look to yet another outlet for their work. Places of worship such as the Judson Memorial Church, coffeehouses such as Café Cino and La Mama, and second-story lofts became the focal points for the latest avant-garde theatre in New York. In 1960 critic Jerry Tallmer, then of the *Village Voice,* coined the name Off-Off-Broadway for these dramatic activities.

By 1964 Off-Off-Broadway was receiving serious critical attention. In that year Drexler's play *Home Movies* won the Obie Award, thus establishing her as one of the first of that astonishing group of women dramatists who were to dominate the avant-garde theatre of the 1960's.

Playwriting, however, is only one of Rosalyn Drexler's talents. Indeed, it is not far-fetched to say that she resembles a Renaissance man—with a bit of Horatio Alger thrown in. Born in the Bronx, Drexler dropped out of high school to pursue a brief career as Rosa Carlo, The Mexican Spitfire—a woman wrestler. This experience was to become the basis of her third novel, *To Smithereens,* which was published in 1972.

In 1946 Rosalyn Bronzhick married painter Sherman Drexler. They have two children. So, in addition to her varied career as a playwright, painter, wrestler, novelist, and film critic, Rosalyn Drexler adds that of wife and mother.

Perhaps the most notable feature of her

PHOTO BY ALIX JEFFRY

Rosalyn Drexler

work is that rare quality that identifies her as a comic artist in the most profound sense of the term. *Skywriting,* first produced at the Cafe à Go Go, is a good introduction to Drexler's often scatalogical cosmos.

Critical terms like "pop" and "camp" help to place her within the contemporary avant garde. Her literary output includes nine novels, among them the best seller *I Am the Beautiful Stranger* (1965), and more than a dozen plays, the latest of which is *He Who Was Shih* (1976). She is also a regular contributor to such leading publications as *Ms., Sports Illustrated, Village Voice, Madamoiselle, Harper's Bazaar* and *The Paris Review.*

Drexler's life and work display the exuberance and zest that characterized the 1960's.

of-holes reason, into which you are afraid you will fall endlessly . . . without your skyscape, which belongs to me as well as you.

WOMAN. I know what you really want to do with this card; you want to sail it across the room, you want to prop it up on the window sill and peek at it, you want to obliterate

the cumulus perfection of a blue day, you want to fuck it!

MAN. Fuck you and fuck your picture!

WOMAN. I knew it! You do want to fuck it! You long to gloss over it. Slippery slidery all over it. Gook and puke on it. And you won't tell me why you really and truly want to.

MAN (*singing*). "Blue skies, shining at me . . ."

(*He continues singing "Blue Skies."*)

WOMAN. Yes, if I fall endlessly into a hole that is endless it will be endlessly dark, and the sky will become, no the sky will not become, and the sky will *seem* to become a heavy cesspool cover, an obstacle dragged into place by you, preventing my escape. But you, once you have trapped me, will be able to walk back and forth over it, safely; because you believe in immediate value, immediate use of an object after emplacement, that's why you'd walk on it. No man can do that to me.

MAN. No man can do that to you and live, with the picture of it still in his mind or on his window sill.

WOMAN. Which reminds me . . . the window sills have to be dusted. The city is sifting in; its ashes are piling up. Cremation may be a sunny bright way to lay waste to waste, but the Sanitation Department is scattering the dearly departed at our doorstep.

MAN. The footsteps on the rug are ashes. The fertilizer in the plants, ashes. The dandruff in my hair, ashes. The pillows are stuffed with ashes. My coffee is sweetened artificially with ashes. The soft gray dawn wipes off on my hand and washes off in thick black streaks of reconstituted ashes. Our ancestors, our garbage, our mortuary is with us, hiding like golden flecks of sunlight in the clouds!

WOMAN. Whose clouds?

MAN. Your clouds! Your clouds, heavy with dirt.

WOMAN. And Venus Mounds dripping with golden piss, you pisspot!

MAN (*singing*).

Would I were a pisspot round,
Lying on the cold, cold ground,
Who would make a tinkling sound,
Love the pisspot they have found?

WOMAN. Sentimentalist!

MAN. We used to attend functions together. Accept every invitation. Now that you stay at home gazing at your piece of sky, I take your place. That's not sentimental.

WOMAN. Social butterfly.

MAN. What do you think about when I am flitting aimlessly from one thing to another?

WOMAN. I think you're getting laid . . . and I think wouldn't it be nice if he never came back . . . and I never had to think he was getting laid . . . I wake up every morning trying to think back day by day to the time that I was born, and when I am there, squalling and covered with bloody wax, I think myself back here, day by day, to the morning I wake up.

MAN. Why?

WOMAN. Every day I save thirty years. I remain fixed at thirty years. My age is thirty years of age. I always come back to the same day, thirty years from the day of my birth. I can do it. There are some years along the way I skip. Those are the bad years. The ones that add up. The ones that would age me, bring me to death's door, the ones that create powdered footsteps across a vacuumed rug. I look at the dirt you bring in on the soles of your shoes, and I thank God for my system. For letting me discover what makes time stand still.

MAN. Only an alien would say a thing like that. Why don't you go back to where you came from? Dust to dust . . .

WOMAN. I wanted to create a dust-free life for us.

MAN. If only I could remember *Ode to a Grecian Urn,* that might convince you. A Grecian urn is a receptacle of great beauty. Many have been laid to rest in the cooled baked clay. A work of God in a work of art. It can be sealed, too . . . waterproofed . . . protected from vermin . . . protected from the wiggling vermicelli worm which burrows its way out of any Chinese puzzle . . . sealed against the wind that wants to whip you into the tearing eye of God and make it burn!

WOMAN. What's that called?

MAN. Conjunctivitis.

WOMAN. Shit on you! Shit on you for talking dirty!

MAN. Give me that French postcard. I want to post it.

WOMAN. *Merde! Merde au bas, et merde en haut! La carte postale,* she is belong to me, Inspector.

MAN. I didn't mean to make you mad.

(*He pronounces this as "merde."*)

WOMAN. But you demand custody of the card! You want to send it far away, where I'll never see it again. You don't care whether it will be thumbed, torn, read by everyone along the route. Marked for life. Why should it have to depend on you for its very existence? Why should it have to depend on your whim for its final destination?

MAN. Jesus Christ, it's just a card! It cost a nickel. There were fifteen others just like it in the store. There are thousands of other stores that carry the same line. I don't have to have your card! Your card is a duplicate, baby. A repeat! A reasonable facsimile of a reasonable facsimile. One of a long line of cardboard farts that cut the asshole which ejected it. Now tell me the real reason why you don't trust me.

WOMAN. I don't trust you.

MAN. How long has it been since you rode through a cloud in an airplane?

WOMAN. Thirty years.

MAN. Would you like me to take you along on my next business trip?

WOMAN. What business?

MAN. Cloud inspector. You did call me inspector a while back there. You called me inspector. I'd like to take you along.

WOMAN. You dare to suggest *that* to me? You dare to ask *me* to *witness* the *act* of *you* entering the clouds! I'll kill you first. I'll kill you. I'll kill you! (*She pauses.*) I'll kill you with love. What an exciting idea . . . skimming above the earth . . . fastened into my seat . . . forced to *witness,* watching you melt like a stick of butter shoved into a five-pound hill of mashed potatoes . . . meshing and grinding, groaning and whining, shoving and loving, aboving . . . asking the stewardess for seconds. What an appetite!

MAN. I'm hungry.

WOMAN. I'm Felice Mignon. Eat me.

MAN. Your initials, *F.M.,* shine on me with a glowing germfree fluorescence. I've lost my appetite!

WOMAN. I know why you want the card.

MAN. Because I have holes in the soles of my shoes, and want to stuff cardboard in them?

WOMAN. No. And don't think you'll gain my sympathy. You'll never gain it.

MAN. Why do you think I want the earbent, messageless, skycard? Tell me. Tell me before I take my things and get out of here.

WOMAN. You want it because it's mine.

Plain and simple, because it belongs to me. And you think that I belong to you too, and that's why you want me. You want me and my art reproduction. You want my art reproduction and my entire reproduction system. You hate both my systems. The *HOW TO LIVE FOREVER* system, and the *HOW TO LIVE HARMONIOUSLY AS A WOMAN* system. And I hate you in turn, for selling your umbrella and losing your hair, and getting excited at French postcards, and pretending to be dependable just because you attend all natural functions you are invited to without me, just to show me up! Do you dance there? Are you always cutting in? How do the ladies function at the functions? I'll surprise you one day, I'll accompany you, and then you'll dance with me . . . you'll dance to *my* tune!

MAN. Ladies and gentlemen: the band is now taking requests! You, Madame, what is your tune? Ah yes, "Change Partners." The band will now play and I will now sing one of the all-time favorites of yesteryear . . . a tuneful standard by Irving Berlin . . . now let us stray down memory lane . . . (*He begins to sing.*) "Must you dance, every dance . . ."

WOMAN (*applauding*). Bravo! Bravo! Now let us come back from memory lane; let us step out on the concrete walk of life and break our arches on it! You fool, I'll never, never, never, ever, ever, ever, give it up . . . my sublime, my magnificent, frame of reference! Never!

MAN. I know why you won't share. Why you have to go to your own corner to look at your own picture with your own two eyes. I KNOW! First of all, there is no longer any sky left out there. Don't be shocked. It's true. The sky has been falling on people's heads for years, tiny infinitesimal pieces that were taken to be pigeon droppings, circulars, petitions, balloons, a baseball, snow, sleet, a pair of wet panties fallen from a clothesline; piece by piece the sky fell in clever disguise, clothing the earth with its own fallout; removing the vital blue dome of its protection. And that is why you, obeying a sixth sense, covet, crave, collect to your bosom a holy relic: the sky-blue, cloudlined cradle of galaxies.

WOMAN. Oh God! Oh God—I knew it! I

knew something was wrong when it was always night and never day, and dark as a cesspool with the cover tightly closed, even though I never saw a cesspool. And really, you didn't buy me that card, it came in the mail. Remember? But here . . . I want you to hold this end of it and look at it with me . . . it's absolutely holy, and miraculous . . . look!

MAN. I see things in the clouds . . . gigantic female nudes with stormy heaving breasts, their pores oozing domestic cheese . . . and crackers bearing them away.

(*Stage dark—special black lights on, the kind that make white glow phosphorescently. From each side of the darkened partition, hand-folded paper airplanes rain in steady profusion— back and forth, glowing like falling stars—until the theatre empties or the house lights go on.*)

THE END

DR. KHEAL

by **Maria Irene Fornes**

There is a reading stand, a small table with a jug of water and two glasses, a blackboard, and a stand with various charts. PROFESSOR KHEAL *enters.* HE *is small, or else the furniture is large.*

DR. KHEAL. The professor picks up the chalk,

> (DR. KHEAL *picks up the chalk.*)

and writes.

> (DR. KHEAL *writes* The Outline *on the blackboard.* HE *looks at what he wrote and decides to draw a line along the edges of the blackboard.*)

He looks at the class with an air of superiority and counts to three, demanding their attention. One, two, and three. He asks his first question.

> (HE *mouths a question and then puts his hand to his ear as if listening to the answer.*)

Wrong.

> (*Pointing in different directions.*)

Wrong. Wrong. Wrong. Wrong. Then, suddenly, someone shouts his answer from the back. Others join him. They all shout at once. It becomes a loud and fast thing. The teacher speaks rapidly, trying to reply to each. Wrong, wrong, wrong, wrong, wrong, wrong, wrong. Damn it! You're wrong.

> (*Suggesting a voice from the distance.*)

"Dear professor, perhaps you have the wrong answer."

> (HE *looks at the audience fiercely.*)

My answer wrong? It couldn't be that my answer is wrong. I am the master. Let us proceed.

> (HE *looks among his papers, then talks to himself.*)

How could my answer be wrong? . . . Hmmm Did I have an answer?

> (HE *thinks.*)

Nonsense, I don't need an answer. I am the master. . . . Let me see. . . . Let me see. . . . I'll find an answer. Hmmm . . . Hmmm . . . How is that possible? I don't even remember the question. Was there a question?

> (*To the audience.*)

Was there?

> (*To himself:*)

Hmm. Of course there was. There's always a question, and who knows what the answer is?

> (*To the audience:*)

Raise your hand if you know the answer. . . . Ha ha. There you are! There are many of you, but the multitude is often wrong.

> (HE *starts to erase the blackboard.*)

Is it not?

> (HE *looks to see if someone replies.* HE *then erases the blackboard and writes* On Poetry.)

Now, poetry is for the most part a waste of time, and so is politics . . . and history . . . and philosophy. . . . Nothing concrete. Nothing like a well-made box. Which is concrete and beautiful and you can put things in it. But what can you do with poems? Tell me. And with politics, and with history, and with philosophy?—You can wrap them up, shove them up your ass, and what do you have?

> (HE *moves his hands as if he were doing a magic trick which ends with the middle finger up.*)

. . . Nothing. . . . Ha ha ha ha ha ha.

> (*Invaded by an immense poetic feeling.*)

But if you can make a box, think, have you not made a lyrical thing?

> (HE *thinks he hears someone speak.* HE *squints, and looks over his glasses, then ignores the possible speaker.*)

Poetry, on the other hand, is just a few words put together. Just a few. Just words. There is poetry. . . . And then they say there are

MARIA IRENE FORNES (1930–   )

Chief planner for the New York Theatre Strategy is the group's president, Maria Irene Fornes, whose Greenwich Village apartment serves as its headquarters and gathering place.

Fornes herself has had little formal education and even less dramatic training. Born in Havana, Cuba, she attended school only through the sixth grade before moving to New York with her mother and sister. This was followed by years of eking out a living at an assortment of odd jobs. Fornes' first love was painting, and she eventually left New York for a brief period to study with the Abstract Expressionist Hans Hoffman at the Provincetown School.

In 1960 she turned to playwriting and quickly established herself as a major figure in what has come to be known as "alternative" theatre. Critic Richard Gilman has described Fornes as "a dramatist of almost pure imagination." In addition to *Dr. Kheal*, her plays include *Tango Palace* (1965), *The Office* (1966), *Promenade* (1969), and *Fefu and Her Friends* (1976).

She has won numerous awards for her plays, including two Obies. Productions of her plays, many of which she has directed and designed, have appeared not only in New York but across the United States, as well as in Europe and South America.

PHOTO BY SANDY UNDERWOOD

Maria Irene Fornes

Dr. Kheal premiered at two simultaneous productions in 1968—one at the Village Gate Theatre, and the other at the New Dramatists Workshop.

---

poets . . . poets of this sort, poets of that sort, and poets of the other sort. . . . But who, tell me, understands the poetry of space in a box? I do. . . . Abysmal and concrete at the same time. Four walls, a top, and a bottom . . . and yet a void. . . . Who understands that? I, Professor Kheal, I understand it clearly and expound it well.

(*Memory holds his attention.*)

And then, there is the smell of wood, that sober smell.

(HE *takes a deep breath, then goes to the blackboard and writes* On Balance. *Then he draws the following figure:*)

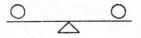

(HE *moves away, looks at the blackboard, looks for his glasses in his pocket, puts them on, and points to the blackboard.*)

Balance can save your life. Imbalance can destroy it.

(*Lost in his thoughts.*)

. . . What is balance? . . . Balance is a state of equilibrium between opposing forces. The harmonious proportions of elements in design. Balance is keeping my pants up. My groin in place.

(HE *looks around with raised eyebrows for a moment.*)

Any more questions?

(HE *goes to the blackboard, erases, and writes* On Ambition.)

Then, of course, there is the question of will. Oh, will, will, will, will. Always will. Tell me, does anyone here know the evil of will?

(HE *waits for an answer.*)

Does anyone know the nature of will?

(HE *waits for an answer.*)

Does the thing happen, or does one do it? . . . Through will. Does the thing happen, or does one do it? Of course, sometimes it happens and other times one does it. I don't mean . . . just anything . . . ordinarily. . . . I mean how . . . what . . . which . . . Is *it* made. . . . Can *it* be made. . . . What? Life! Of course life. Do you know the difference between will and appetite? Can life be made? No, I don't mean birth. I mean life. The life you lead. Can I make my own life . . . Construct my own life? . . . Through will? Of course not, you fool. Of course you can. But then, a well-planned life is pitiful. Doesn't it seem richer if the firmament puts its silvery hands in it? In your life?

(HE *puts his hand to his ear.*)

What?

(HE *listens.*)

An old-fashioned thought?

(HE *listens again.*)

Modern thought has what? . . . Modern? . . . Mo-dern? . . .

(HE *scrutinizes the speaker.*)

You scum, you turd, you stale refuse. Worse than that! Plastic face!

(HE *blows air through his mouth.*)

That is what I think of you. . . . I'll take your will and chew on it, like a little oyster, or a clam. Chew, chew, chew, chew, chew your little will, yum yum . . . I'll chew your little entrails.

(HE *darts his tongue like a satyr. Then HE puts his hands over his groin with a scared look. HE looks around the audience.*)

What would you like? A show of hands? All right. Let's have a show of hands. Those in favor of the firmament leading you by the hand, raise your hands.

(HE *counts.*)

Those in favor of making your own life raise your hands.

(HE *counts.*)

All I can do is peepee before you.

(HE *raises his leg like a dog and then shakes it.*)

And the rest, those who did not raise your hands—what do you think? Is there another alternative? Either you do it, or else it does itself. Life, that is. What other way is there? None.

(HE *looks suspiciously at a few.*)

None. There is no other way. All right.

(HE *erases the blackboard and writes On Energy. HE goes to the chart stand.*)

Here is the next question.

(HE *unrolls a chart that reads: "How does one do a million little things?"*)

How does one do a million little things? . . . What is the answer? How does one do a million little things?

(HE *waits a moment for the answer.*)

One at a time.

(HE *is pleased with the incisiveness of his answer.*)

Now.

(HE *unrolls the next chart. It reads: "How does one do a million big things?"*)

How does one do a million big things? . . . Hmmm . . . Does anyone know the answer?

(HE *waits a moment.*)

One at a time. Ha ha ha ha ha . . . What a surprise. . . . Surprised, everyone? Now, the last of the three.

(HE *unrolls the next chart. It reads: "How does one do one big thing?"*)

How does one do one big thing? . . . Ha ha ha ha ha ha ha. Extraordinary question, isn't it? I'll answer it.

(HE *goes to the blackboard and makes this drawing:*)

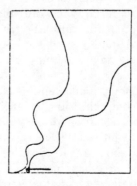

(*Pointing to where the arrow indicates:*)
Start here.

(HE *fills in the space indicated as follows:*)

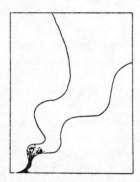

(HE *darts his tongue like a satyr.*)
Would you have guessed? Never.

(HE *erases the blackboard and writes* On Speech.)

Now . . . words change the nature of things. A thing not named and the same thing named are two different things. Ha ha ha ha . . . The ways of the Devil . . . that son of a gun. . . . Someone once said, "In the beginning was the word." Guess who? The Devil . . . clever bastard. He'd say anything. In the beginning was not the word. He names things to make them other than what we know them to be. Then he renames them. So the name he first gave them becomes separate from the thing, and we are left without the word or the thing, the new word having none of the spirit of the first. Think of the word "sin." The Devil first named sin to make the thing we did other than what we knew it to be. Then, once we understood what sin was and learned to sin and repent, and sin and repent again, and we had a clear understanding of what sin was, the Devil, in order to deprive us of this knowledge, decided to declare the word void. Today you say the word "sin," and little frigid minds (the Devil's assistants) snub you. So you recoil and quickly say something accepted by these frigid little minds. "Guilt." And their expression of smug condescension changes to one of smug comprehension. In their minds, the word "sin" has been dispossessed of its meaning and "guilt" has been sanctioned by reason. Today who dares to speak of freedom . . . goodness . . . happiness? . . . Happiness . . Who dares to say the word without

some kind of (*Mocking their manner*) "Intellectual hesitation." (*Still mockingly*) "Happiness . . . happiness. . . . What do you mean by happiness?" (*Back to himself*) And I show them my teeth.

(HE *opens his mouth wide, then puts his fingers in his mouth.*)

And I say to them, here is happiness. My teeth are good. That makes me happy.

(*Forcing his hand in the mouth of an imaginary person.*)

And I put my whole hand in their mouths and I call them every name in the book. Violent! I am. I get angry. But it doesn't matter. I am always right. You see, we who speak must not let words turn upside down on us and turn us into fools.

(HE *goes to the blackboard, erases, and writes* On Truth.)

Most people believe that truth is the order in which they live. Others, the bright ones, believe that there is no truth at all but only an arrangement. Both are mistaken. Ha ha ha ha ha ha. Now, truth is not at all the way we understand things to be. Why? The moment you name it, it is gone. A chair. You name it: "Chair," and there it is, still a chair. A dog. You name it: "Dog," and it comes. But truth . . . you name it and it vanishes. What is truth then? Anyone know?

(HE *stands like a bullfighter and makes three rapid passes.*)

There is truth. Three quick passes. Name it here, here, and here. Surround it, and you'll have it. Never touch it. It will vanish. That is truth . . . elusive.

(HE *goes to the blackboard and erases. Then* HE *writes* Anecdote.)

On my way here this evening someone said to me . . . "Dr. Kheal, is being poor a sign of stinginess?"

(HE *opens his mouth as if to laugh, but makes no sound.*)

I said, no, it isn't. (*Pause*) But of course it is. (*Pause*) Ha ha ha ha.

(HE *erases the blackboard and writes* On Beauty and Love.)

The morning was fine. I cleaned the bathroom, then the kitchen. What else is there but cleanliness?

(HE *looks over his glasses expecting objections.*)

And then, I lay down to rest with my head on

a high pillow. "Gee, look at my belly going up and down. I must be alive." Well . . . in that case . . . I go to my dresser, I look in the mirror. "Gee, look how pleasant my face is in the mirror, I must be beautiful." Ha ha ha. Well, we each have our way. I know that we can only do what is possible. I know that. We can only do what is possible for us to do. But still it is good to know what the impossible is.

(*There is a pause.* HE *is looking at the impossible.*)

Beauty is . . . the impossible. . . . Beauty . . . beauty . . . Crissanda, thou art the impossible. . . . Beauty . . . what art thou that drives me out of my mind? Beauty . . . Shall I tell you?

(HE *sees Crissanda in front of him.*)

She speaks in riddles, like the gods. "ksjdn-hyidfgesles." She says:

(HE *chants the following.*)

"I am the supreme lover. I bring you bliss. . . . Listen to me. . . . Listen. . . . I know . . ."

(*Back to his own voice.*)

The fool, she knows nothing. I just love the way she talks. She chants in riddles, like the gods. "ksjdudyehrs." She says:

(*Chanting again.*)

"Don't move your hands when you talk. It tickles me. From the distance, the movements of your hands tickle me."

(*Back to himself.*)

And I laugh. . . . And I move my hands. Ha ha ha ha.

(HE *pauses.* HE *looks at* CRISSANDA.)

And she looked at me surprised, and her little eye wandered and was lost.

(HE *watches her vanish.*)

"Where are you?" I said, "my little one . . . Crissanda . . . don't go . . . I didn't mean to laugh." And she appeared in the distance . . . just for a moment . . . just to say: "Crazy people are fools.

(*Making his voice faint.*)

You fool . . . you fool . . . you fool. . . ."

(*His eyes are open very wide. They are filled with tears.*)

And she left. "Crissanda, Crissanda," I called after her. . . . She was gone. . . . What happened? What happened . . . I know what happened and yet I cannot say. I do not know the words to speak of beauty and of love. I,

who know everything. . . . Some things are impossible. . . .

(HE *goes to the blackboard.*)

Love, as we know it, increases daily. Let us say the average level of love is 100 degrees. We add a daily increase of 10. We subtract 7 for daily wear and tear and we have a daily increase of 3 which is cumulative. In 10 days we have an increase of 30 which has raised the level to 130. We have a big fight which reduces the level by 50, leaving love at a low level of 80. However, the daily increase of 10 minus daily wear and tear of 7 continues . . . producing a true increase of 3 which is cumulative. After 7 days we have an increase of 3 times 7 which is 21. Added to the low level of 80 we have 101. Back to normal.

(HE *has written the following:*)

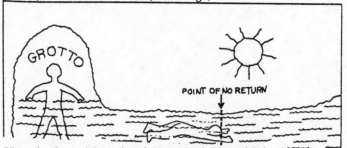

Here is the arithmetic of love. Ha! You think that is contradictory? Love and mathematics? Don't you know that you can take a yes and a no and push them together, squeeze them together, compress them so they are one? That in fact that is what reality is? Opposites, contradictions compressed so that you don't know where one stops and the other begins? . . . Let us proceed.

(HE *erases, and writes* On Hope.)

And here, is a picture of hope.

(HE *draws the following picture as He describes it.*)

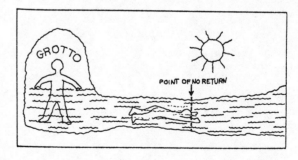

Man stands in his life, "Grotto." Always with a sense of being enclosed. He thinks of freedom, open space, air, sun. The only way out is always narrow, always arduous and frightening to cross. He dares. He fills his lungs with air. He swims. He is courageous. He reaches the point where, if he goes any further, he won't be able to return. "Point of no return." If he continues he might find the exit, if there is an exit . . . if the exit is within reach of his endurance. That is the point. Does he continue? Does he return? There, is the picture of hope.

(HE *erases and writes* On Cooking.) Have you ever cooked brussels sprouts? The miniature cabbage? Toy vegetable? Have you ever seen how beautiful they are?

(HE *erases and writes* Summing Up.) And now, to conclude, I'll sing you a song.

The other day,
Looking at a weird-looking spider,
With legs ten times longer than its body,
Who moved in the most senseless and
Insane manner,
I said, "Spider, you are spastic and I am
A superior beast."

There! That is what it is all about.
Man is the rational animal.

(HE *exits.*)

SLAM THE DOOR SOFTLY

by Clare Boothe Luce

CHARACTERS

THAW WALD
NORA WALD

SCENE: *The* THAW WALDS' *cheerfully furnished middle-class living room in New York's suburbia. There are a front door and hall, a door to the kitchen area, and a staircase to the bedroom floor. Two easy chairs and two low hassocks with toys on them, grouped around a television set, indicate a family of four. Drinks are on a bar cart at one end of a comfortable sofa, and an end table at the other. There are slightly more than the average number of bookshelves. The lamps are on, but as we don't hear the children, we know it is the Parents' Hour.*

THAW WALD, *a good-looking fellow, about thirty-five, is sitting in one of the easy chairs, smoking and watching TV. His back is to the sofa and staircase, so he does not see his wife coming down the stairs.* NORA WALD *is a rather pretty woman of about thirty-two. She is carrying a suitcase, handbag and an armful of books.*

THAW *switches channels, and lands in the middle of a panel show. During the TV dialogue that follows,* NORA *somewhat furtively deposits her suitcase in the hall, takes her coat out of the hall closet, and comes back to the sofa carrying coat, purse and books. She lays her coat on the sofa and the books on the end table. The books are full*

of little paper slips—bookmarkers. All of the above actions are unobserved by THAW. *We cannot see the TV screen, but we hear the voices of four women, all talking excitedly at once.*

THAW (*to the screen and the world in general*). God, these Liberation gals! Still at it.

MALE MODERATOR'S VOICE (*full of paternal patience wearing a bit thin*). Ladies! Lay-deez! Can't we switch now from the question of the sex-typing of jobs to what the Women's Liberation Movement thinks about . . .

OLDER WOMAN'S VOICE. May I finish! In the Soviet Union 83 percent of the dentists, 75 percent of the doctors and 37 percent of the lawyers are women. In Poland and Denmark . . .

MODERATOR. I think you have already amply made your point, Mrs. Epstein—anything men can do, women can do better!

YOUNG WOMAN'S VOICE (*angrily*). That was *not* her point and you know it! What she said was, there are very few professional jobs men are doing that women couldn't do, if only . . .

THAW. Well, for God's sake then, shuddup, and go do 'em!

BLACK WOMAN'S VOICE. What she's been saying, what we've all been saying, and you men just don't want to hear us, is things are the same for women as they are for us black people. We try to get up, you just sit down on us, like a big elephant sits down on a bunch of poor little mice.

MODERATOR. Well, sometimes moderators have to play the elephant and sit down on one subject in order to develop another. As I was about to say, ladies, there *is one thing* a woman can do, no man can do—(*in his best holy-night-all-is-bright voice*) give birth to a *child*.

YOUNG WOMAN'S VOICE. So what else is new?

CLARE BOOTHE LUCE (1903–)

Slam the Door Softly first appeared in *Life* Magazine under the title *A Doll's House 1970*. Its author, Clare Boothe Luce, was admittedly rendering a modern version of Henrik Ibsen's century-old classic. *Life* described her as "an outspoken defender of Women's Lib before it became fashionable." It was altogether appropriate, therefore, that she provide us with an updated Nora-Torvald struggle.

Luce was born in New York City and attended the Clare Tree Major School of Theatre. While still a child, she understudied Mary Pickford in *A Good Little Devil*. Luce's mother, a former chorus girl, urged her daughter to give her luck a try in the then infant motion picture industry located in nearby Fort Lee, New Jersey. She appeared in a minor role or two before marrying George Brokaw. They were divorced in 1929. The couple had one child, Ann, who was killed in an auto accident in 1944.

The theatre had always been Luce's first love; however, before finding her place in it as a playwright, she enjoyed a lucrative career in journalism. By 1931 she was associate editor of *Vanity Fair* Magazine. Two years later she became its managing editor at an annual salary of $10,000, which was a considerable amount of money at that time.

Her first Broadway play, *Abide with Me* (1935) was a failure, but the success of *The Women* in 1936 established Luce as a major comic dramatist. *The Women* continues the tradition of dark satire in this country, at which (since Anna Cora Mowatt) only women have succeeded in portraying their sisters with such pointed cynicism. *The Women* was followed by *Kiss the Boys Goodbye* (1939) and *Margin for Error* (1939).

PHOTO BY CARL MYDANS

Clare Boothe Luce

Like another legendary woman playwright, Aphra Behn, Luce became involved with politics as well as the theatre. Unlike Behn, however, Luce enjoyed a most successful career. In 1943 she was elected to the first of two terms as a United States Representative from Connecticut. Her subsequent appointment as Ambassador to Italy in 1953 made Luce only the second woman in U.S. history to hold so high a diplomatic post.

Clare Boothe married publisher Henry Robinson Luce in 1935. In a Gallup poll conducted in the early 1950's, her background as a playwright, politician, diplomat, author, and war correspondent (1940–42) placed Clare Boothe Luce fourth in line for the title of the World's Most Admired Woman. She followed only Eleanor Roosevelt, Queen Elizabeth II, and Mamie Eisenhower.

THAW. One gets you ten, she's a Lesbo.

MODERATOR (*forcefully*). And *that* brings us to marriage! Now, if *I* may be permitted to get in just *one* statistic, edgewise: two thirds of all adult American females are married women. And now! (*At last he's got them where he wants them.*) What *is* the Women's Lib view of Woman's Number One job—Occupation Housewife?

THAW. Ha! That's the one none of 'em can handle!

YOUNG WOMAN'S VOICE (*loud and clear*). Marriage, as an institution, is as thoroughly corrupt as prostitution. It is, in fact, legalized and romanticized prostitution. A woman who marries is selling her sexual services and domestic services for permanent bed and board.

BLACK WOMAN'S VOICE. There's no human being a man can buy anymore—except a woman.

THAW (*snapping off the TV*). Crrr-ap! Boy, what a bunch of battle-axes! (*He goes back to studying his TV listings.*)

NORA (*raising her voice*). Thaw! I'd like to say something about what they just said about marriage.

THAW (*in a warning voice*). Uh-uh, Nora! We both agreed months ago, you'd lay off the feminist bit, if I'd lay off watching Saturday football.

NORA. And do something with the children. But Thaw, there's something, maybe, I ought to try to tell you myself. (THAW *is not listening.* NORA *makes a "what's the use" gesture, then opens her purse, takes out three envelopes, carefully inserts two of them under the covers of the top two books.*)

THAW. Like to hear Senators Smithers, Smethers and Smothers on "How Fast Can We Get Out of Vietnam?"

NORA (*cool mockery*). That bunch of pot-bellied, baldheaded old goats! Not one of them could get a woman—well, yes, maybe for two dollars.

THAW. You don't look at Senators, Nora. You listen to them.

NORA (*nodding*). Women are only to look at. Men are to listen to. Got it.

> (THAW *is now neither looking at her nor listening to her, as he methodically turns pages of the magazine he has picked up.*)

THAW. Finished reading to the kids?

NORA. I haven't been reading to the children. I've been reading to myself—and talking to myself—for a long time now.

THAW. That's good. (*She passes him, carrying the third envelope, and goes into kitchen. Then, unenthusiastically.*) Want some help with the dishes?

NORA (*from kitchen*). I'm not doing the dishes.

THAW (*enthusiastically*). Say, Nora, this is quite an ad we've got in *Life* for Stone Mountain Life Insurance.

NORA. Yes, I saw it. Great. (*She comes back and goes to sofa.*)

THAW. It's the kind of ad that grabs you. This sad-faced, nice looking woman of fifty, sitting on a bench with a lot of discouraged old biddies, in an employment agency. Great caption!

NORA AND THAW (*together*). "Could this happen to *your* wife?"

NORA. I'll let you know the answer very shortly. (*A pause*) You really don't hear me anymore, do you? (*He really doesn't. She buttons herself into her coat, pulls on her gloves.*) Well, there are enough groceries for a week. All the telephone numbers you'll need and menus for the children are in the envelope on the spindle. A girl will come in to take care of them after school—until your mother gets here.

THAW. Uh-huh . . .

NORA (*Looks around sadly*). Well, goodby dear little doll house. Good-by dear husband. You've had the best ten years of my life. (*She goes to the staircase, blows two deep kisses upstairs just as THAW glances up briefly at her, but returns automatically to his magazine. NORA picks up suitcase, opens the door, goes out, closing it quietly.*)

THAW (*like a man suddenly snapping out of a hypnotic trance*). Nora? Nora? *Nor-ra!* (*He is out of the door in two seconds.*)

THAW'S AND NORA'S VOICES. Nora, where're you going?—I'll miss my train—I don't understand—It's all in my letter—Let me go!—You come back! (*They return. He is pulling her by the arm. He yanks the suitcase away from her, drops it in the hall.*)

NORA. Ouch! You're hurting me!

THAW. Now what is this all about? (*He shoves her into the room, then stands between her and door.*) Why the hell . . . ? What're you sneaking out of the house . . . ? What's that suitcase for?

NORA. I wasn't sneaking. I told you. But you weren't listening.

THAW. I was listening—it just didn't register. You said you were reading to yourself. Then you started yakking about the kids and the groceries and the doll house mother sent . . . (*Flabbergasted.*) Good-by? What do you mean, *good-by?*

NORA. Just that. I'm leaving you. (*Pointing to books.*) My letter will explain everything.

THAW. Have you blown your mind?

NORA. Thaw, I've got to scoot, or I'll miss the eight-o-nine.

THAW. You'll miss it. (*He backs her to the sofa, pushes her onto it, goes and slams the door and strides back.*) Now, my girl, explain this.

NORA. You mean what's just happened now?

THAW. Yes. What's happened now.

NORA. Oh, that's easy. Muscle. You've made with the muscle—like a typical male. The heavier musculature of the male is a secondary sexual characteristic. Although that's not certain. It could be just the result of selective breeding. In primitive times, of course, the heavier musculature of the male was necessary to protect the pregnant female and the immobile young.

THAW (*his anger evaporates*). Nora, are you sick?

NORA. But what's just happened now shows that nothing has changed—I mean, fundamentally changed—in centuries, in the relations between the sexes. *You* still Tarzan, *me* still Jane.

THAW (*sits on sofa beside her, feels her head*). I've noticed you've been, well, acting funny lately.

NORA. Funny?

THAW. Like there was something on your mind. Tell me, what's wrong, sweetheart? Where does it hurt?

NORA. It hurts (*taps head*) here. Isn't that where thinking hurts *you?* No. You're used to it. I was, too, when I was at Wellesley. But I sort of stopped when I left. It's really hard to think of anything else when you're having babies.

THAW. Nora, isn't it about time for your period?

NORA. But if God had wanted us to think just with our wombs, why did He give us a brain? No matter what men say, Thaw, the female brain is not a vestigial organ, like a vermiform appendix.

THAW. Nora . . .

NORA. Thaw, I can just about make my train. I'll leave the car and keys in the usual place at the station. Now, I have a very important appointment in the morning. (*She starts to rise.*)

THAW. Appointment? (*Grabs her shoulders.*) Nora, look at me! You weren't sneaking out of the house to . . . get an abortion?

NORA. When a man can't explain a woman's actions, the first thing he thinks about is the condition of her uterus. Thaw, if you were leaving me and I didn't know why, would I ask, first thing, if you were having prostate trouble?

THAW. Don't try to throw me off the track, sweetie! Now, if you want another baby . . .

NORA. Thaw, don't you remember, we both agreed about the overpopulation problem.

THAW. To hell with the overpopulation problem. Let Nixon solve that. Nora, I can swing another baby.

NORA. Maybe you can. I can't. For me there are no more splendid, new truths to be learned from scanning the contents of babies' diapers. Thaw, I *am* pregnant. But not in a feminine way. In the way only men are supposed to get pregnant.

THAW. Men, pregnant?

NORA (*nodding*). With ideas. Pregnancies there (*taps his head*) are masculine. And a very superior form of labor. Pregnancies here (*taps her tummy*) are feminine—a very inferior form of labor. That's an example of male linguistic chauvinism. Mary Ellmann is *great* on that. You'll enjoy her *Thinking about Women.*

THAW (*going to telephone near bookshelf*). I'm getting the doctor. (NORA *makes a dash for the door, he drops the phone.*) Oh, no, you don't! (*He reaches for her as she passes, misses. Grabs her ponytail and hauls her back by it and shoves her into the easy chair.*)

NORA. Brother, Millett sure had you taped.

THAW. Milly *who?* (*A new thought comes to him.*) Has one of your goddam gossipy female friends been trying to break up our marriage? (*He suddenly checks his conscience. It is not altogether pure.*) What did she tell you? That she saw me having lunch, uh, dinner, with some girl?

NORA (*nodding to herself*). Right on the button!

THAW. Now, Nora, I can explain about that girl!

NORA. You don't have to. Let's face it. Monogamy is not natural to the male.

THAW. You know I'm not in love with anybody but you.

NORA. Monogamy is not natural to the female, either. Making women think it is, is the man's most successful form of brainwashing the female.

THAW. Nora, I swear, that girl means nothing to me . . .

NORA. And you probably mean nothing to her. So whose skin is off whose nose?

THAW (*relieved, but puzzled*). Well, uh, I'm glad you feel that way about—uh—things.

NORA. Oh, it's not the way I *feel*. It's the way things really are. What with the general collapse of the mores, and now the Pill, women are becoming as promiscuous as men. It figures. We're educated from birth to think of ourselves just as man-traps. Of course, in my mother's day, good women thought of themselves as private man-traps. Only bad women were public man-traps. Now we've all gone public. (*Looks at watch.*) I'll have to take the eight-forty. (*She gets out of her coat, lays it, ready to slip into, on back of sofa.*)

THAW (*a gathering suspicion*). Nora, are you trying to tell me that *you* . . .

NORA. Of course, a lot of it, today, is the fault of the advertising industry. Making women think they're failures in life if they don't make like sex pots around the clock. We're even supposed to wear false eyelashes when we're vacuuming. Betty Friedan's great on that. She says many lonely suburban housewives, unable to identify their real problem, think more sex is the answer. So they sleep with the milkman, or the delivery boy. If I felt like sleeping with anybody like that, I'd pick the plumber. When you need *him,* boy, you *need* him!

THAW (*the unpleasant thought he has been wrestling with has now jelled*). Nora . . . are you . . . trying to tell me you are leaving me for someone else?

NORA. Why, Thaw Wald! How could you even *think* such a thing? (*To herself.*) Now, how naïve can I be? What else do men think about, in connection with women, *but* sex? He is saying to himself, she's not having her period, she's not pregnant, she's not jealous: it's *got* to be another man.

THAW. Stop muttering to yourself, and answer my question.

NORA. I forgot what it was. Oh, yes. *No.*

THAW. No what?

NORA. No, I'm not in love with anybody else. I was a virgin when I married you. And

intacta. And that wasn't par for the course—even at Wellesley. And I've never slept with anybody else, partly because I never wanted to. And partly because, I suppose, of our family's Presbyterian hangup. So, now that all the vital statistics are out of the way, I'll just drive around until . . . (*Begins to slip her arms into coat. He grabs coat, throws it on easy chair.*)

THAW. You're not leaving until you tell me *why.*

NORA. But it's all in my letter. (*Points.*) The fat one sticking out of Simone de Beauvoir's *Second Sex.*

THAW. If you have a bill of particulars against me, I want it *straight.* From you.

NORA. Oh, darling, I have no bill of particulars. By all the standards of our present-day society, you are a very good husband. And, mark me, you'll be president of Stone Mountain Life Insurance Company before you're fifty. The point is, what will I be when I'm fifty?

THAW. You'll be my wife, if I have anything to say. Okay. So you're not leaving me because I'm a bad husband, or because my financial future is dim.

NORA. No. Oh, Thaw, you just wouldn't understand.

THAW (*patiently*). I might, if you would try, for just one minute, to talk logically.

NORA. Thaw, women aren't trained to talk logically. Men don't like women who talk logically. They find them unfeminine—aggressive.

THAW. Dammit, Nora, will you talk sense!

NORA. But boy! does a man get sore when a woman won't talk logically when *he* wants her to, and (*Snaps fingers.*) like that! And *that* isn't illogical? What women men are! Now, if you will step aside . . .

THAW (*grabbing her and shaking her*). You're going to tell me why you're walking out on me, if I have to *sock* you!

NORA. Thaw, eyeball to eyeball, *I am leaving you*—and not for a man. For reasons of my own I just don't think you *can* understand. And if you mean to stop me, you'll have to beat me to a pulp. But I'm black and blue already.

THAW (*seizes her tenderly in his arms, kisses her.*) Nora, sweetheart! You know I couldn't really hurt you. (*Kisses, kisses.*) Ba-aaby, what do you say we call it a night? (*Scoops her up in his arms.*) You can tell me *all* about it in bed.

NORA. The classical male one-two. Sock 'em and screw 'em.

THAW (*dumping her on sofa.*) Well, it's been known to work on a lot of occasions. Something tells me this isn't one of them. (*Pours a drink.*)

NORA. I guess I need one, too. (*He mixes them.*) Thaw?

THAW. Yes.

NORA. I couldn't help being a *little* pleased when you made like a caveman. It shows you really do value my sexual services.

THAW. Geez!

NORA. Well, it can't be my domestic services —you don't realize, yet, what they're worth. (*Drinks.*) Thaw, you do have a problem with me. But you can't solve it with force. And *I* do have a problem. But I can't solve it with sex.

THAW. Could you, would you, *try* to tell me what my-your-our problem is?

NORA. Friedan's *Feminine Mystique* is very good on The Problem. I've marked all the relevant passages. And I've personalized them in my letter. (*He goes to book. Yanks out letter, starts to tear it up.* NORA *groans. He changes his mind, and stuffs it in his pocket.*)

THAW. Look, Nora, there's one thing I've always said about you. For a woman, you're pretty damn honest. Don't you think you owe it to me to level and give me a chance to defend myself?

NORA. The trouble is, *you* would have to listen to *me*. And that's hard for you. I *understand why!* Not listening to women is a habit that's been passed on from father to son for generations. You could almost say, tuning out on women is another secondary sexual male characteristic.

THAW. So our problem is that *I* don't listen?

NORA. Thaw, you always go on talking, no matter how hard I'm interrupting.

THAW. Okay. You have the floor.

NORA. Well, let's begin where this started tonight. When you oppressed me and treated me as an inferior.

THAW. I oppressed . . . (*Hesitates.*) Lay on, MacDuff.

NORA. You honestly don't think that yank-ing me around by my hair and threatening to sock me are not the oppressive gestures of a superior male toward an inferior female?

THAW. For Chrissake, Nora, a man isn't going to let the woman he loves leave him if he can stop her!

NORA. Exactly. Domination of the insubordinate female is an almost instinctive male reflex. *In extremis,* Thaw, it is *rape.* Now, would I like it if you should say you were going to leave me? No. But could I drag you back?

THAW. You'd just have to crook your little finger.

NORA. Flattery will get you nowhere this evening. So, where was I?

THAW. I am a born rapist.

NORA. Wasn't that what you had in mind when you tried to adjourn this to our bedroom? But that's just your primitive side. There's your civilized side, too. You are a patriarchal *paterfamilias.*

THAW. What am I now?

NORA. Thaw, you do realize we all live in a patriarchy, where men govern women by playing sexual politics?

THAW. Look, you're not still sore because I talked you into voting for Nixon? (*She gives him a withering look.*) Okay. So we all live in a patriarchy.

NORA. Our little family, the Walds, are just one nuclear patriarchal unit among the millions in our patriarchal male-dominated civilization, which is worldwide. It's all in that book.

THAW. Look, Nora, I promise I'll read the damn book—but . . .

NORA. So who's interrupting? Well, Thaw, all history shows that the hand that cradles the *rock* has ruled the world, *not* the hand that rocks the cradle! Do you know what brutal things men have done to women? Bought and sold them like cattle. Bound their feet at birth to deform them—so they couldn't run away— like in China. Made widows throw themselves on the funeral pyres of their husbands, like in India. And men who committed adultery were almost never punished. But women were always brutally punished. Why, in many countries unfaithful wives were *stoned* to death!

THAW. This is America, 1970, Nora. And here, when wives are unfaithful, *husbands* get stoned. (*Drinks.*) Mind if *I* do?

NORA. Be your guest. Oh, there's no doubt

that relations between the sexes have been greatly ameliorated.

THAW. Now, about *our* relations, Nora. You're not holding it against *me* that men, the dirty bastards, have done a lot of foul things to women in the past?

NORA (*indignant*). What do you mean, in the *past?*

THAW (*determined to be patient*). Past, present, future—what has what other men have done to other women got to do with us?

NORA. Quite a lot. We *are* a male and a female.

THAW. That's the supposition I've always gone on. But Nora, we are a *particular* male and a *particular* female: Thaw Wald and his wife, Nora.

NORA. Yes. That's why it's so shattering when you find out you are such a typical husband and . . .

THAW (*a new effort to take command*). Nora, how many men do you know who are still in love with their wives after ten years?

NORA. Not many. And, Thaw, listen, maybe the reason is . . .

THAW. So you agree that's not typical? Okay. Now, do I ever grumble about paying the bills? So that's not typical. I liked my mother-in-law, even when she was alive. And God knows that's not typical. And don't I do every damn thing I can to keep *my* mother off your back? And that's not typical. I'm even thoughtful about the little things. You said so yourself, remember, when I bought you that black see-through nightgown for Mother's Day. That I went out and chose myself. And which *you* never wear.

NORA. I had to return it. It was too small. And do you know what the saleswoman said? She said, "Men who buy their wives things in this department are in love with them. But why do they all seem to think they are married to midgets?" That's it, Thaw, that's *it!* Men "think little"—like "thinking thin"—even about women they love. They don't think at all about women they don't love or want to sleep with. Now, I can't help it if you think of me as a midget. But don't you see, I've got to stop thinking of myself as one. Thaw, *listen* . . .

THAW. Why the devil should *you* think of yourself as a midget? *I* think you're a great woman. A *real* woman! Why, you're the dear-est, sweetest, most understanding little wife—most of the time—a man ever had. And the most intelligent and wonderful little mother. Dammit, those kids are the smartest, best-behaved, most self-reliant little kids . . .

NORA. Oh, I've been pretty good at Occupation Housewife, if I do say so myself. But, Thaw, *listen.* Can't you even imagine that there might be something *more* a woman needs and wants?

THAW. My God, Nora, what more can a woman want than a nice home, fine children and a husband who adores her?

NORA (*discouraged*). You sound like old Dr. Freud, in person.

THAW. I sound like Freud? I wish I were. Then I'd know why you're so uptight.

NORA. Oh, no you wouldn't. Know what Freud wrote in his diary when he was seventy-seven? "What do women want? My God, what do they want?" Fifty years this giant brain spends analyzing women. And he still can't find out what they want. So this makes him the world's greatest expert on feminine psychology? (*She starts to look at her watch.*) To think I bought him, in college.

THAW. You've got plenty of time. You were saying about Freud . . . (*He lights a ciga-rette, hands it to her, determined to stick with it to the end.*)

NORA. History is full of ironies! Freud was the foremost exponent of the theory of the natural inferiority of women. You know, "anatomy is destiny"?

THAW. I was in the School of Business, remember?

NORA. Well, old Freud died in 1939. He didn't live to see what happened when Hitler adopted his theory that "anatomy is destiny." Six millions of his own people went to the gas chambers. One reason, Hitler said, that the Jews were *naturally* inferior was because they were effeminate people with a slave mentality. He said they were full of those vices which men always identify with women—when they're feeling hostile. You know, sneakiness and deception, scheming and wheedling, whin-ing and pushiness, oh, and materialism, sensu-ousness and sexuality. Thaw, what's *your* favorite feminine vice?

THAW. At this moment, feminine mono-logues.

NORA. I didn't think you'd have the nerve to say sneakiness. I saw you sneak a look at your watch and egg me on to talk about Freud, hoping I'll miss my train. I won't.

THAW. So nothing I've said—what little I've had a chance to say . . . (*She shakes her head.*) You still intend to divorce me?

NORA. Oh, I never said I was divorcing you. I'm deserting you. So you can divorce me.

THAW. You do realize, Nora, that if a wife deserts her husband he doesn't have to pay her alimony?

NORA. I don't want alimony. But I do want severance pay. (*Points to books.*) There's my bill, rendered for ten years of domestic services—the thing sticking in *Woman's Place* by Cynthia Fuchs Epstein. I figured it at the going agency rates for a full-time cook, cleaning woman, handyman, laundress, seamstress, and part-time gardener and chauffeur. I've worked an average ten-hour day. So I've charged for overtime. Of course, you've paid my rent, taxes, clothing, medical expenses and food. So I've deducted those. Even though as a housewife I've had no fringe benefits. Just the same, the bill . . . well, I'm afraid you're going to be staggered. I was. It comes to over $53,000. I'd like to be paid in ten installments.

THAW (*he is staggered*). Mathematics isn't really your bag, Nora.

NORA. I did it on that little calculating machine you gave me at Christmas. If you think it's not really fair, I'll be glad to negotiate. And, please notice, I haven't charged anything for sleeping with you!

THAW. Wow! (*He is really punch drunk.*)

NORA. I'm not a prostitute. And *this* is what I wanted to say about the Lib girls. They're right about women who marry *just* for money. But they're wrong about women who marry for love. It's love makes all the difference.

THAW (*dispirited*). Well, *vive la différence.*

NORA. And, of course, I haven't charged anything for being a nurse. I've adored taking care of the children, especially when they were babies. I'm going to miss them—*awfully.*

THAW (*on his feet, with outrage*). You're deserting the children, too? My God, Nora, what kind of woman *are* you? You're going to leave those poor little kids alone in this house . . .

NORA. You're here. And I told you, your mother is coming. I wired her that her son needed her. She'll be happy again—and be needed again—for the first time in years.

THAW (*this is a real blow*). My *mother!* Oh, migod, you *can't,* Nora. You know how she— swarms over me! She thinks I'm still twelve years old! (*His head is now in his hands.*) You know she drives me out of my cotton-picking mind.

NORA. Yes. But you never said so before.

THAW. I love my mother. She's been a good mother and wife. But, Nora, she's a *very* limited woman! Yak, yak—food, shopping, the kids . . .

NORA. Thaw, the children love this house, and I don't want to take them out of school. And I can't give them another home. Women, you know, can't borrow money to buy a house. Besides, legally this house and everything in it, except my mother's few things and my wedding presents, are yours. All the worldly goods with which thou didst me endow seem to be in that suitcase.

THAW. Nora, you know damn well that all my life insurance is in your name. If I died tomorrow—and I'll probably blow my brains out tonight—everything would go to you and the kids.

NORA. Widowhood is one of the few fringe benefits of marriage. But, today, all the money I have is what I've saved in the past year out of my clothes allowance—$260.33. But I hope you will give me my severance pay.

THAW. And if I don't—you know legally I don't have to—how do you propose to support yourself?

NORA. Well, if I can't get a job right away —sell my engagement ring. That's why they say diamonds are a gal's best friend. What else do most women *have* they can turn into ready cash—except their bodies?

THAW. What kind of job do you figure on getting?

NORA. Well, I do have a Master's in English. So I'm going to try for a spot in *Time* research. That's the intellectual harem kept by the Time, Inc. editors. The starting pay is good.

THAW. How do you know that?

NORA. From your own research assistant, Molly Peapack. We're both Wellesley, you know. She's a friend of the chief researcher at *Time,* Marylois Vega. Also, Molly says, computer programming is a field that may open to women.

THAW (*indignant*). You told Peapack you were leaving me? Before you even told *me?* How do you like *that* for treating a mate like an inferior!

NORA. Thaw, I've told you at least three times a week for the last year that with the kids both in school, I'd like to get a job. You always laughed at me. You said I was too old to be a Playboy Bunny and that the only job an inexperienced woman my age could get would be as a saleswoman.

THAW. Okay. Where are you going to live?

NORA. Peapack's offered to let me stay with her until I find something.

THAW. I'm going to have a word with Miss Molly Peapack tomorrow. She's been too damned aggressive lately, anyway!

NORA. She's going to have a word with you, too. *She's* leaving.

THAW. Peapack is leaving? Leaving *me?*

NORA. When you got her from Prudential, you promised her, remember, you'd recommend her for promotion to office manager. So, last week you took on a man. A new man. Now she's got a job offer where she's sure she's got a forty to sixty chance for advancement to management. So you've lost your home wife and your office wife, too.

THAW. And *this* is a male-dominated world?

NORA. Thaw, I've got just five minutes.

THAW. You've still not told me *why*—

NORA. Oh, Thaw darling! You poor—*man.* I have told you why. I'm leaving because I want a job. I want to do some share, however small, of the world's work and be paid for it. Isn't the work you do in the world—and the salary *you* get—what makes you respect yourself, and other men respect *you?* Women have begun to want to respect themselves a little, too!

THAW. You mean, the real reason you are leaving is that you want a *paying* job?

NORA. Yes.

THAW. God, Nora, why didn't you say that in the beginning? All right, go get a job, if it's that important to you. But that doesn't mean you have to leave me and the kids.

NORA. I'm afraid it does. Otherwise, I'd

have to do two jobs. Out there. And here.

THAW. Look, Nora, I heard some of the Lib gals say there are millions of working wives and mothers who are doing two jobs. Housework can't be all that rough.

NORA. Scrubbing floors, walls. Cleaning pots, pans, windows, ovens. Messes—dog messes, toilet messes, children's messes. Garbage. Laundry. Shopping for pounds of stuff. Loading them into the car, out of the car—(*A pause.*) Not all of it hard. But all of it routine. All of it *boring.*

THAW. Listen, Nora, what say, you work, I work. And we split the housework? How's that for a deal?

NORA. It's a deal you are not quite free to make, Thaw. You sometimes *can't* get home until very late. And you have to travel a lot, you know. Oh, it might work for a little while. But not for long. After ten years, you still won't empty an ashtray or pick up after yourself in the bathroom. No. I don't have the physical or moral strength to swing two jobs. So I've got to choose the one, before it's too late, that's most important for me—oh, not for me just now, but for when *I'm fifty*—

THAW. When you're fifty, Nora, if you don't leave me, you'll be the wife of the president of Stone Mountain Life Insurance Company. Sharing my wealth, sharing whatever status I have in the community. And with servants of your own. Now you listen to *me,* Nora. It's a man's world out there. It's a man's world where there are a lot of women working. I see them every day. What are most of them really doing? Marking time and looking, always looking, for a man who will offer them a woman's world—the world you have here. Marriage is still the best deal that the world has to offer women. And most women know it. It's always been like that. And it's going to be like that for a long, long time.

NORA. Just now I feel that the best deal I, Nora Wald, can hope to get out of life is to learn to esteem myself as a person—to stop feeling that every day a little bit more of my mind—and heart—is being washed down the drain with the soapsuds. Thaw—listen. If I don't stop shrinking, I'll end up secretly hating you and trying to cut you—and *your* son—down to my size. The way your swarmy mommie does you and your dad. And you'll become like your father, the typical henpecked husband. Thinking of his old wife as the Ball and Chain. You know he has 'a mistress? (THAW *knows. He belts down a stiff drink.*) A smart gal who owns her own shop—a woman who doesn't bore him.

THAW. Well, Nora . . . (*Pours another drink.*) One for the road?

NORA. Right. For the road.

THAW. Nora . . . I'll wait. But I don't know how long.

NORA. I've thought of that, too . . . that you might remarry . . . that girl, maybe, who means nothing . . .

THAW. Dammit, a man needs a woman of his own.

NORA (*nodding*). I know. A sleep-in, sleep-with body servant of his very own. Well, that's your problem. Just now, I have to wrestle with my problem. (*Goes to door, picks up suitcase.*) I'm not bursting with self-confidence, Thaw. I do love you. And I also need . . . a man. So I'm not slamming the door. I'm closing it . . . very . . . softly. (*She leaves.*)

CURTAIN

THE INDEPENDENT FEMALE

by **Joan Holden**

CHARACTERS

MATILDA PENNYBANK, *53, mother of two*
GLORIA, *22, her daughter, engaged to John*
JOHN HEARTRIGHT, *27, junior executive*
SARAH BULLITT, *25, feminist*
WALTER PENNYBANK, *58, president of the Chamber of Commerce, Matilda's former husband, long-lost father of Gloria*
THE BARKER

INTRODUCTION

BARKER. Ladies and gentlemen. The San Francisco Mime Troupe proudly welcomes you to this evening's performance of *The Independent Female, or, A Man Has His Pride.* We humbly introduce you to the characters and the themes of this tender but passionate drama. Our heroine (*characters enter as they are introduced*)—the beautiful, innocent, but impressionable *Gloria.* Will this fragile creature be led down the road to ruin, and parted forever from the manly, promising, and courageous *John?* Or will our hero save her in time? Will this young couple know the bliss that Gloria's *Mom*—to her eternal regret—willfully denied to herself and her patient, long-suffering *Walter?* Will this honest capitalist be reunited with the daughter he has never known? Or will the mad lust for power and the devilish plotting of the unspeakable *Sarah Bullitt* push everyone—even the city of San Francisco—

The San Francisco Mime Troupe is a self-supporting collectively run theater company whose aim is to make art serve the people. *The Independent Female* was the Troupe's first production to be written, directed, and designed by women. In the course of working on it, the company eliminated the position of secretary (but not the woman who had held it) and instituted women's and men's meetings. The play was performed free in Bay Area parks throughout the summer of 1970, toured the midwest and southern California in winter 1970–71, and the southeast in fall 1971.

Performance rights reserved: Contact San Francisco Mime Troupe, 855 Treat Street, San Francisco, Calif. 94110. Copyright © 1970 by the San Francisco Mime Troupe, Inc.

over the brink of destruction? We hope all present find our story instructive, and are especially pleased that so many of the fair sex could be with us this evening, as it is in their interest —above all—to be reminded that:

In perfect trust, and mutual fondness twine
The mighty oak tree, and the clinging vine.

(*Music.*)

ACT I
THE PENNYBANK HOME

SCENE I: MOM, GLORIA

MOM (*enters*). Today must be the happiest day of my life—except the day Walter asked me to marry him—and the day little Walter graduated from college. My daughter Gloria just got engaged—and this engagement is extra special. Gloria sometimes acts a bit . . . independent; I often feared she might not have a future. But now it's all settled—and old Mom hasn't lived in vain! (*Gloria enters.*) Darling —do you want the bridesmaids in aqua or salmon?

GLORIA. There may be no bridesmaids (*sobs*)—we just had our first fight!

MOM. Today? (*Aside.*) A bad sign. (*Aloud.*) But why?

GLORIA. John doesn't want me to work.

MOM. The sweetheart! But what did you fight about?

GLORIA. I *like* working.

MOM. Gloria! What are you getting married for?

GLORIA. Because John is the most wonderful man in the world—deeply intelligent—and serious, and commanding, and tall. But Mom, must a woman devote all her time to her marriage?

MOM. What else could she do? Oh, this might never have happened, had tragedy not obliged you to support us . . .

GLORIA. But Mom . . .

JOAN HOLDEN (1939–   )

The Independent Female was written in 1970, at the height of the Radical Feminist Movement. As Joan Holden described it, the play expresses her "new awareness and the self-discovery of women in the [San Francisco] Mime Troupe, which was then reorganizing itself as a collective following the departure of its male founder-director."

The Mime Troupe grew out of the activities of R. G. Davis, a Paris-trained mime, who by 1958 had taken up residence in San Francisco. Employing agitprop dramas, coupled with the performance techniques of the commedia dell'arte, the San Francisco Mime Troupe toured the city's parks with its radical political messages.

Holden herself was active in the antiwar movement of the 1960's. When in 1967 the Mime Troupe needed a play about Vietnam, she offered her adaptation of Goldoni's 18th-century comedy *L'Amant Militaire.*

The Independent Female was one of the first plays to be performed by the Mime Troupe after collective creation became the dominant production method following the ouster of R. G. Davis. The altered version is included here. Holden rewrote the play (with reluctance, she admits) to bring it more into line with the relatively positive-minded ideology of the Bay Area Feminist Council. In doing so, she also made it more palatable to a general audience. The play is something of a cultural phenomenon, being one of the few early feminist works written in a popular form (i.e., melodrama) —and one of even fewer comedies to come out of the Woman's Movement at all.

Despite her political awareness, Holden believes that her education at Reed College and the University of California at Berkeley prove that "social concerns were antithetical

Joan Holden

to politics." So she sought her inspiration in the Left Bank cafes of Paris. Upon her return to this country, she took a job as a school teacher and joined the antiwar movement. Her former husband's involvement with the Mime Troupe led her, in turn, to political theatre.

Holden lives in San Francisco with her two small daughters and is an active participant in the work of the Mime Troupe. Her move from the New Left to the Feminist Left is typical of many women of her generation.

MOM. I know. I know who keeps putting these wild ideas in your head—it's that ugly Sarah Bullitt—that career woman you've grown so fond of! She knows she'll never find a husband, so she can't bear to see you happy with a young prince like John!

GLORIA. Well, at least Sarah's nice to me! And John was so mean! Oh, Mommy—he yelled at me! He called me a . . .

MOM. Don't cry, dear—you'll get used to it.

You see, darling, there is one thing education and modern home appliances and the pill can't change, and that's the basic difference between a man and a woman. A man has his pride. We may not be slaves in our homes any longer, but our main job is still to help our man feel strong.

GLORIA. Is that what you did with Dad?

MOM. I *failed* as a woman. And I don't want to see you make the same mistake, Gloria!

You children didn't know this, but—I used to criticize Walter.

GLORIA. You don't think he just left because you got old?

MOM. No, darling—he *had* to leave, because I *threatened* him. Don't suffer as I have! Tell John you've decided to give up your job. Be a woman, darling, before it's too late! Oh, my shame! (*Exit.*)

GLORIA. Poor Mom! Can I be headed down the same road? And is it true what she said about Sarah? Oh, I mustn't be so headstrong and selfish—I love John, and I want us to be happy—but this crazy independence (*karate movements*)—sometimes it's stronger than I am!

SCENE II: GLORIA, JOHN

(JOHN *enters and she hits him inadvertently.*)

JOHN. Do you still think I don't make enough money?

GLORIA. I never said $50 wasn't enough! But my salary would help—but it's not just the money.

JOHN. I told you I would give you an allowance. Am I not enough for you, Gloria?

GLORIA. Darling, you're everything! But what about the job?

JOHN. What about it?

GLORIA. Mr. Peabody says he doesn't know how they'll replace me. He's sweet—do you know what he said about our engagement? "I hope this doesn't mean you'll be breaking up the team."

JOHN. Gloria. Once upon a time, not so long ago, man roamed the woods, hunting food, while woman stayed home and tended the fire. On the surface, things have changed since; but in his heart, man is still a hunter—at least I am; and I still want a woman in my cave!

GLORIA. Oh, John!

JOHN. I thought you were a real woman, Gloria—that's why I chose you for my wife. If you want a career, I won't stand in your way—but I want a wife, not a business partner. Goodbye.

GLORIA. No!

JOHN. A man has his pride.

GLORIA (*aside*). Mom was right! (*To* JOHN.) Wait, John—I'll do it—I'll quit! I'm going to make being your wife my full-time job!

JOHN. Little girl!

GLORIA. Forgive me, darling—I want us to have a good marriage—it's just that I've got the—independence habit. (*Hits him again.*)

JOHN. I'll help you get over it. Lean on me, Gloria—I'm going to treat you the way my Dad said every woman ought to be treated—like the most precious thing a man owns!

SCENE III: GLORIA, JOHN, SARAH, MOM

SARAH (*enters*) (*aside*). Beauty—and the beast! (*Aloud.*) Am I intruding? (MOM *peers around curtain, sees* SARAH.)

JOHN (*aside*). Sarah Bullitt—the company malcontent! I fear her ill influence on Gloria!

GLORIA. Sarah! We're going to be married!

SARAH. This is quite a surprise.

JOHN. Miss Bullitt has some news of her own, I believe.

SARAH. I've been fired. (*She's happy.* MOM *checks and finds* SARAH *still there.*)

JOHN. Terminated, I understand, for insubordination.

SARAH. I said if they refused to promote me, I'd have to put a hex on the company.

GLORIA. It seems so unfair. Why, Sarah was the best accountant the company had! And the cheapest. Don't feel too bad, dear—I guess a woman can't win. And you won't be all alone—I've decided to quit!

SARAH (*aside*). Disaster—for her life and our plot! (*Aloud.*) Only last week you said you'd never been so happy at work.

GLORIA. I know, but John would prefer I stayed home.

SARAH. So you're signing over your independence.

JOHN. You girls were made for the lighter work—washing, cooking, raising children.

SARAH. And you for the heavy stuff eight hours a day. Why, men are so strong, they get paid for work we do; promoted for ideas we have; they get their names on books we write.

JOHN. This bitterness is what makes your life difficult. If men have privileges—it's because we've earned them. After all, *males* are responsible for every major achievement of our civilization.

SARAH. War, waste, competition, pollution, inflation . . .

GLORIA. What have we done?

JOHN. Take Gloria, forever prattling about the way things should be; she needs me to stand between herself and reality. Why aren't you girls content to be what we need? Competent secretaries . . . thrifty housewives . . .

SARAH (*to* GLORIA). What did you want to be?

GLORIA. A forest ranger.

JOHN. Ha, ha, ha.

GLORIA. What's so funny?

MOM (*enters*). Why, Miss Bullitt. What a surprise!

SARAH (*aside*). Uncle Mom!

MOM. A lovely dress—I believe I admired it at the Polish Emporium.

SARAH. Yes, didn't I see you there with Lawrence Welk?

MOM. Well . . . three's a crowd, don't you all think? So John, you'll let Gloria help her Mom with the tea?

JOHN. It's my pleasure.

MOM. Come dear. (*To* SARAH.) I'm sorry you have to run off!

(GLORIA *and* MOM *exit*.)

JOHN. You're wasting your time trying to convert Gloria, Miss Bullitt. She's a normal girl.

SARAH. Anyone can see she's going to be very happy.

JOHN. She will be if I can help it! But this must be painful for you—I doubt there can be any happiness for a woman who wishes she were a man.

SARAH. I doubt it myself—after all, what sort of woman *would* wish to be oversized and underdeveloped—a vain, childish, life-hating under-sexed clod? It's true that some women want justice!

GLORIA. Darling—lemon or cream?

JOHN. My hat! The only justice a woman needs is a man to shut her mouth. (*Grabs* GLORIA *and kisses her*.) I'll call when you have time to see me. (*To* SARAH.) Do you know what the trouble with you is? You're frustrated. (*Exit*.)

SCENE IV: GLORIA, SARAH

GLORIA. How can I hate the man I love?

SARAH. How can you marry that swine?

GLORIA. We're engaged! And you can just save your breath—I've accepted my role as a woman.

SARAH. To gratify, amuse, cushion, flatter, and serve.

GLORIA. We should let men be boss, since it means so much more to them.

SARAH. To be seen as a piece of meat by every man who walks by?

GLORIA. That's the price we pay for being attractive.

SARAH. You're preparing to spend your days as personal property. You'll end up with no life.

GLORIA. What's the choice—to end up lost —the way you are?

SARAH. You could have a choice—if women demanded their rights.

GLORIA. What rights?

SARAH. All the ones men have—plus a few of our own. What do you think would happen if all the women in our office went on strike?

GLORIA. Oh, Sarah—don't be silly; a strike in the *office*? That's impossible—they don't even know how to type! I mean the machines —the correspondence—the phones—well, I just can't imag—why, the whole thing would stop!

SARAH. Divine vision—and women would be fighting back. You've got to take my place— bring every woman at Amalgamated out on strike for equal work *with* men, equal work *by* men, equal pay for equal work . . .

GLORIA. Equal pay? But wouldn't that be wrong? Are you sure the company can afford it?

SARAH. Are you kidding? They own Argentina!

GLORIA. I could talk to the other girls— there's 100 of us in the department—then 200 downstairs—then the whole seventh floor— golly, there must be 500 women in the company!

SARAH. How many men?

GLORIA. Maybe 50 . . . Let's do it!

SARAH. Don't you think you'd better ask John?

GLORIA. Oh, I don't have to—he's bound to find out—what mad passion stirs in me?

SARAH. The righteous rage of female rebellion!

(*Exeunt*.)

ACT II

SCENE I: *Outside the Office*—SARAH AND GLORIA

SARAH (*enters*). "In education, in marriage, in everything, disappointment is the lot of woman. It shall be the business of my life to deepen this disappointment in every woman's heart till she bows down to it no longer."— Lucy Stone, 1855. Lucy was a revolutionary history has made anonymous. In history, the slaves never rebelled, the Indians died of shame, and all women ever wanted was the vote. But black resistance is as old as slavery and there have been women fighting in this country since men first established it; and what now is smoldering between the lines will soon break out and cover the page. Our work proceeds swiftly—in a week Gloria had every woman in her office on fire—in two weeks the fever was sweeping the city. Today any laundromat may harbor an agitator—every steno pool may be a dangerous cell. (GLORIA *music.*) But Gloria still wants her freedom and her fiancé—at any moment that balancing act could topple our plans. (*More* GLORIA *music.*)

GLORIA (*enters*). Equal pay! Equal power!

SARAH. Smash men! Let's hear your report.

GLORIA. Here's how the different departments line up. Accounting and billing are eager to move. Marketing only needs one more push to get started. The cafeteria girls are with us to a man. (*Pauses.*) But I'm having a little trouble in—Personnel.

SARAH. Personnel? But that's your own department!

GLORIA. And—John's.

SARAH (*aside*). Gadzooks—just what I feared! (*Aloud.*) He knows nothing?

GLORIA. Nothing—he still thinks I'm planning to quit; he thinks—oh, this makes me feel awful—he thinks we're planning a surprise for his birthday!

SARAH. He'll get one! If you want your independence, you'll have to sacrifice your chains.

GLORIA. But what about love? To serve our cause can't mean I mustn't love John!

SARAH. That's not love—that's penal servitude. If you want your independence you'll have to sacrifice your chains. Very soon now you'll have to make a choice.

GLORIA. No! I'll tell John everything! I'll make him understand!

SARAH. Tell him—but not until after tonight.

GLORIA. Our first open all-women's meeting.

SARAH. Seize the time—this very night we will call for a strike.

GLORIA. Strike!

SARAH. And it won't end at Amalgamated Corporate Life: Business in San Francisco will grind to a halt—and it won't start up again until we change everything!

GLORIA. *Everything?* Oh, Sarah—you frighten me!

SARAH. "We've tried peaceful education for 1900 years—now let's try revolution and see what it can do."—Helen Keller, 1916. Call in sick and go to work on your speech. And remember—at all costs our plans must be secret.

GLORIA. At all costs . . . (*Music.*)

SARAH. Hairy race of tyrants—your doom is nigh! (*Music.*)

SCENE II: *The Pennybank Home*—MOM *and* JOHN

MOM (*offstage*). Coming! Another paper! What can Gloria be up to? The way she banged in and out of here . . . (*Another knock.*) Come in! (JOHN *enters.*) Why, John!

JOHN. Good afternoon, Mrs. Pennybank. Is Gloria in? (*He is feigning calm.*)

MOM (*feigns surprise*). Ah, no! Shouldn't she be at work?

JOHN. She telephoned and said she was sick.

MOM. There must be some mistake. Why, I just can't imagine—

JOHN. Well, I can! Gloria's been acting very strange lately. She avoids me in the office. She's always whispering with the other girls. Today she—missed my birthday. Her mind's not on me. There's only one explanation. Mrs. Pennybank, *who is the other man?*

MOM. No . . .

JOHN. Your attempt to protect Gloria is shortsighted. Don't you see that her interest lies in my knowing everything?

MOM. Gloria doesn't confide in her Mom anymore! I admit she's preoccupied—seems driven, sometimes; makes phone calls at all hours; comes and goes without warning . . .

JOHN. That's enough—farewell, Mrs. Pennybank. (*Going.*)

MOM. Wait—perhaps there's another explanation! (*She stretches out her hands and* JOHN *sees the paper.*)

JOHN. What's that? It's in Gloria's hand!

MOM. Oh, yes—she dropped this just now.

JOHN (*grabs it, reads*). "Are women human? Adored and ignored—last hired and first fired." (*Looks accusingly at* MRS. P.)

MOM. I don't understand.

JOHN. I'm afraid I'm beginning to. "When will women break the chains of slavery and assume their rightful place beside men in the life of the world?"

MOM. It doesn't sound like a love letter.

JOHN. It's much worse. Have you heard of "Women's Liberation," Mrs. Pennybank?

MOM. You mean "menstruation."

JOHN. Liberation.

MOM. Menstruation.

JOHN. Liberation.

MOM. Menstruation. I've heard of it.

JOHN. "Liberation" is the high-sounding term with which a clique of unwomanly, power-mad females masks its plot to destroy the family and enslave the male sex.

MOM. Gloria's a good girl. (MOM *kicks* JOHN *and* JOHN *gets hat.*)

JOHN. I know it (*returns hat*)—but one gone far astray.

MOM. I know who's at the bottom of this—it's Sarah Bullitt!

JOHN. Good thinking (*receives hat*)—there's no villainy of which she's incapable! Here's another line—"We meet here tonight"—zounds. This makes it sound like a speech! Poor deluded Gloria is serving them as a carrier of the disease!

MOM. We must stop her.

JOHN. I mean to stop her—and when I bring her back she'll need your constant attention. (*Kisses her hand.*) (*Going.*) Permit me to say, Mrs. Pennybank—this is what can happen when female "independence" is not nipped in the bud! (*Exit.*)

MOM. Oh, I've failed again! Failed as a mother!

(*Exit.*)

SCENE III: *Back at the Office* (*"Ladies Lounge"*)—JOHN, GLORIA, SARAH

(*Enter* SARAH *and* GLORIA)

SARAH. At last the stage is set for our all-female revolution! It's taken only 10,000 years. Now to reach the meeting hall without being seen.

GLORIA. What we're about to do sets me tingling all over—my heavens, in a single month, how I have changed!

JOHN (*enters without being seen*). Something's afoot—(*Sees them.*) Aha!

SARAH. Remember—no one must see us.

JOHN. Feeling better, Gloria?

GLORIA. No, I feel worse.

SARAH (*aside*). Meddling lout!

JOHN. You needn't sneak and lie anymore—I know all.

GLORIA. All? You know about the—

SARAH. Let him tell us what he knows.

JOHN. I know what a fool I was to allow you near Gloria—know what poison you've ad-ministered to her innocent mind—how you've provoked her to dissatisfaction; intoxicated her with insane ambition; hypnotized her into stirring up discontent!

SARAH (*to* GLORIA). We're safe—he doesn't know about the strike!

JOHN. Thank God this is not going to go any further. (*Seizes* GLORIA.) Listen, darling—it's all a lie! It's a plot against our happiness! Don't you want children?

GLORIA. Oh John—happy birthday.

SARAH (*takes* GLORIA's *arm*). Yes, happy returns—now you'll have to excuse us.

JOHN. Don't touch her!

SARAH. Gloria's not your property yet!

JOHN. Be very careful. There are laws to take care of people like you—new ones every day!

SARAH. "We are not bound to obey laws in which we have no representation."—Abigail Adams, 1776.

JOHN. Darling, forget this woman—let me take you home now!

GLORIA. I can't—tomorrow I'll explain!

JOHN. Tomorrow! Do you think I could live through the night?

GLORIA. Please, John—what I'm doing is for us! It's for all men and women!

JOHN. Gloria, the male spirit shrivels when deprived of the confidence, the trust, of the female. I tell you this thing is wrong you scoff at my words! Of course, you can't know how you're hurting me—but I'll have to break off our engagement.

GLORIA. No!

JOHN. Then come home with me now!

GLORIA. Oh!

SARAH. Gloria!

JOHN. My darling, my angel, my sweet—is this the end, or only the beginning?

GLORIA. It's—the beginning.

SARAH. And the end of your independence!

(GLORIA *is seized with a terrible fit.*)

JOHN. My God! It can't be hopeless?

SARAH. Precisely—it's hopeless for you! Women will soon be moving as one, and man will either move over—or go under, and learn for yourselves what it is to be kept for pleasure and breeding.

(*Exit, helping* GLORIA.)

JOHN. Hideous affliction! But if it's too late to save Gloria, what must I do to spare others the same fate?

SCENE IV: MOM *and the Above*

MOM (*enters*). John!

JOHN. Mrs. Pennybank! You—here!

MOM. I've found another paper! (*Hands it to him.*)

JOHN. "Strike meeting, 8 o'clock." Strike meeting—oh no! What hellish vision rises before me?

MOM. It's ten to eight now!

JOHN. After you—we haven't a moment to lose!

(*Exeunt. Chase scene.*)

SCENE V: *A Hall in San Francisco*

SARAH. Welcome to our first all-women's meeting. I'm glad to see so many of you here. And now I'd like to introduce our speaker, our sister from Amalgamated Corporate Life—Gloria Pennybank.

GLORIA. My sisters! We're here to decide whether women are human. Men struggle to make themselves more than they are—women struggle to make themselves less. Masculinity is a cloak to cover up men's faults, and femininity is a drug to make slaves out of women. And when I say we're slaves, I'm not just talking about the housewife who works a sixteen-hour day for what she can beg from her husband. I'm talking about every woman who assumes she's worth less than a man—and we all know that's every woman here, regardless of how she's paid, or how many token privileges separate her from her sisters.

SARAH. Women aren't the only slaves in this country—a few men own all the others. But all men oppress women—even modern husbands who are happy to let their wives work, so long as they do the housework at night—even you hip ones who don't insist your old ladies be faithful so long as they take care of the kids—and how many women know the simple facts of our plain economic oppression? Our average wage is 50 percent of men's. Our relative salaries have been steadily *declining* for the past twenty years!

GLORIA. They tell us to get an education—a woman with a college degree earns less than the average male high school dropout! The only group that earns less than white women is women who aren't white.

SARAH. A world where women are really equal would be a world with nobody on the bottom—because our egos don't die if we're not on the top! But men aren't going to give us equality—(*enter* JOHN *and* MOM)—so it's up to us—we've got to show the men that drive this machine where the power is that runs it!

JOHN. Gloria!

GLORIA. That means—Strike!

SARAH. That means women say no! Stop typing, stop filing, stop taking orders, stop serving, stop spending—start moving—until we have a new society where no one needs to be dependent on one, because all are equally dependent on all!

GLORIA. Free our sisters!

SARAH. Free ourselves!

TOGETHER. Free our sisters! Free ourselves!

(*They exit.*)

JOHN. My worst nightmare come true . . .

MOM. Shrill voices! Raised fists! Anger is so unbecoming! For the first time in my life I'm ashamed of my sex. What would Gloria's father say if he knew about this . . .

ACT III

SCENE I: *Office of the Chamber of Commerce, Not Long After.*

(*Chanting offstage:* "Strike!" "Strike!" "Strike!" WALTER *enters.*)

WALTER. Will they never stop? This is the worst pressure I've known in 35 years in management! (*Bell rings.*) Miss Jones, get the door. Money that could have been spent on poverty programs—money we could have used to clean our polluted environment! (*Bell rings again.*) Miss Jones! Perhaps that's someone with the answer. (*It rings again.*) Miss Jones! (*Again.*) Miss Jo—Et tu, Miss Jones? Come in!

(JOHN *enters, disheveled and desperate.*)

JOHN. Mr. President, sir? Forgive my appearance—I had to come through the sewers.

WALTER. What do you want?

JOHN. My name is John Heartright. Amalgamated Corporate Life. (*They shake hands.*) I—I know something that may help you deal with the strike. (*Aside.*) Gloria, forgive me—this is for your own good.

WALTER. Out with it, man!

JOHN. First—my idea is so extreme—I must know your plans.

WALTER. What harm is there, after all? Might as well have it out. They've got 100,000 women on strike. Business is paralyzed. Money's rotting in the banks—we can't move it. For the first time in my life, I can't make anything happen. Now you can't put men in those jobs.

JOHN. Men wouldn't take them. This can't mean you're going to give in?

WALTER. Of course not. After all, we still own everything. "Equal work" of course is out of the question—we'd end up without a clerical force. And "free nurseries"—"free transportation"—"free phones"—pretty soon they'll be crying "Free Bobby!" "Free Ericka!"* But that means we can't get around equal pay. We'll have to cut men's salaries.

JOHN. You couldn't cut—profits?

WALTER. You mean capital expansion? Are you suggesting we castrate the American eagle?

JOHN. Oh, no sir—I wasn't thinking. (*Squares his shoulders.*) All right—I'm resolved.

WALTER. Let's hear it fast—their bargaining committee will be here any minute!

> (JOHN *whispers to* WALTER, *who likes what he hears. Bell rings.*)

Step into my inner office! (JOHN *exits.*) Come in.

SCENE II: SARAH, GLORIA, WALTER, JOHN
> (*Music.* SARAH *and* GLORIA *enter.* WALTER *steps out.*)

WALTER. Good morning. Are you girls looking for work?

GLORIA. Equal work!

WALTER. So this is the bargaining committee. (*He bows. They hold out their hands, obliging him to shake hands.*) It's a pleasure to meet two such dedicated ladies. (*To* GLORIA.) You look like a very dangerous adversary. (*Aside.*) She would be, if we were alone!

SARAH. Spare us your compliments—you know our demands.

WALTER. Yes: "free everything." I find them excessive. Management is prepared to make a very generous offer. (*Aside.*) I wouldn't care to be alone with *this* one!

GLORIA. Pretty generous, giving us what we've won!

WALTER. Spunky—I like that. Our offer is prompted by concern for the families. (*Aside.*)

---

* Bobby Seale and Ericka Huggins of the Black Panther Party, who were tried for murder in New Haven in 1971 (and acquitted).

Where have I seen a face like that before?

SARAH (*to* GLORIA). It seems your appeal has reached management.

GLORIA. Ugh—I hate older men!

WALTER. Who's tidying the home? Who is washing the clothes, who is taking care of Junior, while women are out parading in the streets? Management doesn't think any man should have to hold down two jobs, so it is acting fast to bring working women back to their posts.

GLORIA. We are waiting for your offer!

WALTER. I'm confident we can work out an agreement. But first meet the other half of management's team. (*He lifts curtain, revealing* JOHN *with pistol to temple.*)

GLORIA. Oh, no!

SARAH. Curses—foiled again by this idiot!

JOHN. Gloria, please renounce your demands.

GLORIA. What does this mean?

WALTER. It means that at least one American boy is not a curly-haired crybaby Communist!

SARAH. It means male supremacy is the pillar of capitalism.

JOHN. It means a man has his pride. I took a lot from you, Gloria. You challenged my masculine roles—I forgave you; you flaunted your disregard for my will—I still loved you. Had you been content to attack me alone, God help me, you might have destroyed me; but when you threaten every red-blooded man in this country, when you would sap the very life-force of American business, that's when I come out fighting like a man. Either you sign this contract (*holds out paper*), or I blow my brains out.

SARAH. Tear it up. The gun's probably not loaded.

WALTER. Does she want to find out?

GLORIA (*reads*). "The San Francisco Women's Union hereby acknowledges its previous error in proclaiming the equality of the sexes. Henceforth our organization recognizes the superiority of the male. In addition its members agree to return to work at previous rates of pay." Why don't you shoot *me*?

JOHN. I couldn't.

GLORIA. But you're asking me to betray 100,000 women out there!

WALTER. What's 100,000 women against one brave man who loves you? By God, if there were still some lead in my pencil I'd do the same!

SARAH. Love—the tender trap to pacify women!

WALTER (*to* JOHN). If you live I'll see you get a raise to start a good life with her.

JOHN (*to* GLORIA). I couldn't look you in the face if I weren't man enough to do this.

GLORIA. The man I love—or everything I've worked for!

SARAH. Choose—your master or your independence. (*All look to* GLORIA.) Tear it up!

GLORIA. I can't—love is stronger. (JOHN *lowers gun.*)

WALTER. Thank God—just sign here.

SARAH. Not so fast! (*She has them covered with a .38.*) Now—tear it up. (JOHN *starts to raise gun.*) Drop that or I'll blow your hand off! (*He drops it.* WALTER *tears paper.*) Now, we're going to write a new statement—one that puts the workers at the head of every company in San Francisco: equal work, equal pay, and equal power.

WALTER (*clutches chest*). Ugh, my wallet—I think it's my heart . . .

SARAH. But first, we must arm our troops. Call the commander of the National Guard. Tell him you're sending 100,000 women over. Tell him they're strike-breakers—ha, ha, ha—and tell him you want them armed. Dare to win! Thus do we accomplish in minutes what I thought would take years to achieve. Go on—call.

JOHN. You can't do it, sir—it will mean revolution!

WALTER. The woman is crazy—she'll kill us!

SARAH. "Where the broom does not reach, the dust will not vanish of itself."—Mao Tse-tung.

WALTER. "I don't understand these young people."—Pat Nixon.

SARAH. Make that call!

SCENE III: MOM *and the Above*
  (*Music.*)

MOM (*offstage, calls*). Gloria!

GLORIA. Mom?

MOM (*enters*). I have something to say.

WALTER. *Matilda?* (*Looks at* GLORIA)—oh, no!

MOM. Walter.

WALTER. Matilda. (*Clutches his heart.*)

MOM. Walter!

WALTER. Matilda! (*Staggers.*)

MOM (*ferociously*). Walter—Walter—Walter!

WALTER. Aargh! (*Dies elaborately of a heart attack.*)

  (*Music.*)

GLORIA. *Dad?*

MOM. I thought if you two knew each other, things might work out.

GLORIA. Now there's no one to sign anything!

SARAH (*who has turned her back in disgust*). Even death's a male chauvinist!

JOHN (*picking up his gun*). Truer than you think! (*He shoots her.*)

GLORIA (*catching* SARAH *as she falls*). Sarah, darling! Say something!

SARAH. My last curse—their own works will destroy them. And my epitaph: "Shot in her back for refusing to live on it." (*Dies.*)

JOHN. There's no fair play with pure evil.

MOM. I'm just glad it's all over. (*They move toward* GLORIA.)

GLORIA (*grabs* SARAH'S *gun*). Don't you come near me!

MOM. She's very upset.

JOHN. Darling! Don't you love me?

GLORIA. I love my sisters! And my brothers, if I meet any. I'm going out to find everyone who wants to turn your prison homes, and your frozen minds, and your whole profit, progress, power monster male system over. And we *will* turn it over. And when we all have our independence, then we can all have our pride. (*Exit and return.*) Coming, Mom?

  (MOM *looks at men, then at* GLORIA, *and exits with upraised fist. Freeze at curtain. Finale music.*)

BARKER (*enters*). Will headstrong youth's impetuous course be halted? (*Indicates* GLORIA. *Milks response from audience.*) Will manhood recover its pride? (*Indicates* JOHN.) Will responsible leadership withstand this assault? (WALTER *gets up. If answer is no, falls down again.*) Or does the implacable rebellious spirit of *independent females* portend this society's ultimate collapse? Young ladies and gentlemen, the future lies in your hands.

  (*All bow.*)

A LAMENT FOR THREE WOMEN

by Karen Malpede

For my mother

CHARACTERS

RACHEL
RUTH
NAOMI

Three characters. RACHEL, a young woman, the age of a daughter of the middle-aged woman if the middle-aged woman had had children in her early twenties. RUTH, a middle-aged woman. NAOMI, a woman near seventy. They are just three generations. The young woman's father, the middle-aged woman's husband, the elderly woman's son are dying of cancer in rooms close by.

The three women have been sharing one another's grief for the past six months. They have been set apart by the length of their grief, and anyone who watches them does so from a distance.

The three women are present at an extended predeath wake made possible by modern science and medical research. There is no ritual, there is not even the empty outline of one, to prescribe how to handle this situation. They are inventing their responses.

The women are not filling time. They are obsessed with its passage. Each second brings them closer to the death of the men who have been at the center of their lives.

This is what happens in their play: First, they tell stories, the same stories they have been telling each other for months. Then, RACHEL returns like a messenger from the sight of the dying. And finally, the three women turn to each other. They ask one another for support and they grow strong together.

RUTH. I saw the doctor walking down the hall. I thought, my husband has died in the operating room. The doctor walked directly to me and without a word to prepare me said, "The ulcer we were looking for is cancer." The cancer had already spread from the stomach where it started to the throat, to the small intestine and maybe to the colon. He told me I should let my husband die. It would take three months at most. But at a cancer research hospital he would have a chance for a longer life. I couldn't let him die without a fight. He'd be afraid to die. I decided not to tell him. I moved him here a year ago.

RACHEL. For so long there has been only this routine. Up in the morning. Into the car. Onto the highway. Through these halls. Into his room. The conversation . . . I end up here. These two women and I eat lunch together. I tell Ruth not to take the meat and scold Naomi about the fried foods and the sweets. We eat too much every day and we come away hungry. We who will be mourners make a life for ourselves around the rhythms of their dying.

NAOMI. The last weekend they let me take him home I made honey cake for him and lentil soup. Favorite foods from when he was a boy. His aunt and uncle came and we drank wine together. I would have lit the candles but I was so busy in the kitchen, I missed the sunset. The three of them were talking in the living room and they forgot. It's been so long. I consoled myself as I used to console myself when he was young. "How can I keep the Sabbath when there's washing and mending and cleaning to be done. When the work is shared the Sabbath can be kept. But a woman alone with a growing son keeps the day holy in her heart or not at all."

When I sit with him I pretend he has another fever. I sing to him. A grown man. I sing to him and stroke his forehead. Sitting

KAREN MALPEDE (1945–)

With the tone of high seriousness that marks so many like-minded feminists, Karen Malpede sees her work as an attempt to break "the silence which keeps us complicit in our own destruction." Verse, she suggests, is "the language of insightful feeling and can forge a true, ennobling connection between our inner needs and the shape of the social world we make."

Malpede began to see the possibilities of social action and political protest in the theatre by observing the work of the Living Theatre and, later, the Open Theatre. These two major experimental groups of the 1960's were to become the cornerstone of her own particular blend of aesthetic and critical reasoning. She published *Peoples Theatre in Amerika* in 1972 and *Three from the Open Theatre* in 1974. These two books represent her analysis of the importance of radical theatre in this country.

Born in Wichita Falls, Texas, Malpede attended the University of Wisconsin before coming East to do graduate work at Columbia University. *A Lament for Three Women*, begun in 1973, is her first play.

In writing *Lament* Malpede broke an 11-year creative silence that she had imposed on her "poetic voice." She isolated herself in a one-room tenement apartment on the Lower East Side of Manhattan, where, by exploring her own feelings—feelings born out of a troubled life—she eventually came to look "far into the source of women's sorrow and rage."

About that time, too, Malpede began meeting with a group of writers and directors who were looking for a new direction for the nonverbal theatre of protest with which they had been involved during the 1960's. Two of these people, Eleanor John-

PHOTO BY LAURA W. PETTIBONE

Karen Malpede

son and Judah Kataloni, agreed to create a production around Malpede's drama.

A Lament for Three Women was first presented at the Cummington Community of the Arts in Massachusetts and later at the Open Mind Theatre Off-Off-Broadway. Her next play, *Rebeccah* (1975), premiered at Playwrights Horizons in New York.

With director Burl Hash, Malpede founded the New Cycle Theater in Brooklyn. It opened with a production of her latest play, *The End of War,* in 1977. Of her current venture, Malpede says, "We intend to create a repertory of poetic language, feminist plays, and to develop an acting company skilled in their presentation."

by his bed I half forget and half expect the fever to break suddenly and his eyes to open clear and out of pain.

RACHEL. Not long before my father's operation he came to me. Or maybe I was looking for him there. We were in the front seat of the car, parked in the driveway. He was behind the steering wheel. I was next to him. He took me in his arms and he cried and cried on my shoulder. He held me in his arms and he stroked my hair. He kissed my neck, my ear lobes and my lips. I thought I should run from the car. I thought it was bad to kiss that way unless you were married and it was even worse if the man you wanted was married to your mother. We kissed a long time in the car. We were both crying when we parted.

Some of the sadness he faced along with his

sickness was that I was growing older and would leave him for another man and part of my anguish is that in his pain he turned from me back to my mother. And soon we'll be separated for the last time. Without ever having been together we'll be kept apart forever.

RUTH. My father was a late bloomer. He had never been excited by my mother. But he became excited by me. When I was twelve he began to hug and kiss me in the warmest, most affectionate way. Then, slowly, what he was doing dawned on him. He turned on me with such contempt. He stopped talking to me. He accused me of sins that seemed so vile when he said them. When I was hurt. When I was doubled up inside my stomach like an animal cowering in the corner of some cage, he would come to me and ask forgiveness.

I learned to love like this. One minute I was in the midst of it, the next I was shut off from it like a half-wild creature kept tied outside the door. I met my husband the year my father died. I used to wait outside the window, shivering in the cold, counting the minutes till he came. I waited for him until he told me that he loved me. After we were married he would often wake up crying in the middle of the night and hit his head against the wall and sob until I comforted him. Holding his head against my chest his mouth would find the nipple on my breast.

The night before his operation I put my head on his naked stomach. I traced around the mound of flesh with my fingers as it rose and dipped softly into the damp creases of his groin. I said, "Tomorrow your beautiful stomach will be scarred and sore." I pointed out the faded stretch marks from when I bore him children. "Your stomach will be imperfect then like mine."

NAOMI. My father, who every day thanked god he was not born a woman, naturally wanted a son. Instead god blessed him with a daughter so brutal to her mother during childbirth that the wife could not conceive again. My father's love turned angry like his god's. He never spoke except to humble me.

When I found out my baby was a boy it was as though my sin had been atoned for. I had never been a blessing but now I had been blessed by love. My husband didn't care about the baby. He wouldn't look at me or at the child. He wouldn't touch me. He never picked the baby up. He wanted all my time and when I couldn't give it, he sulked.

When my husband died my old boss took me back. I did fine stitching work on hats. I sewed most of the night. During the day I cleaned and cooked and watched my son grow. The nights passed almost without my knowing. He would find me asleep in the chair some mornings and tugging at my arm would get me up to light the fire and make the breakfast, pack his lunch, get him off to school. What a flurry we would make in the kitchen. He would pull on his trousers standing by the stove, hopping from one foot to the other. I would stir the oatmeal over his jumping head. Sweeten it with jam or honey, pour in rich milk. And bread, big slices of black bread with cheese between them, I packed for his lunch. And cookies and some fruit. "Save the bag," I said. And sometimes he would.

RACHEL (*she has come from a visit to her father's room*). He is sitting up in a chair with a metal bed table pulled around in front of him like a school desk. He's working on a puzzle. Last month someone brought him a thousand piece puzzle. It took up hours of his time.

And today someone has given him a new puzzle. He's sitting in a chair engrossed. Someone has given him a puzzle of a duck. A wooden puzzle with just ten pieces. A duck with a smile on its face. I stood in the door and watched him for awhile. He was putting down the pieces one by one, taking a long time to find the shape that fit the space he'd made. He stopped when I moved closer and looked up at me. He almost remembered who I am, or almost didn't remember. He looked at me as though he thought he knew me and then he looked down at the puzzle piece and then up again at my face in the door. We stayed like that.

A minute more we stared. I could see the recognition come across his face. He let go of the piece of the puzzle in his hand and said, "hello, babe." Said, "hello, babe," to his daughter. Said, "hello, babe," to me, the woman standing in the door. The woman who saw that the puzzle piece he had just let go of was not the one that would fit next in place.

I thought I might meet him over that puzzle. We could have finished it off together. I could have given him my opinion. His fingers might have picked out the pieces I selected.

He's sitting in a chair propped up by pillows. His anus is too diseased to take his weight directly. His narrow hip bones would scrape against the leatheret. He weighs 98 pounds. There's not an ounce of flesh left on his frame. The skin on his face is stretched across pure bone.

Next to my father's chair on a stand is the intravenous feeder connected to his left arm by a clear plastic tube. Through that tube drip the fluids that let him continue putting together a wooden puzzle of a duck.

The doctors look in hourly to marvel that this obsolete frame is still, technically speaking, in working order. They have hacked out the way to death past all our previous knowing. The journey to death. Here I am watching my father move down it. What are the words I'll remember when he's dead. Here he comes now past own locomotion, past eating, past hunger and voluntary excretion, rounding the corner past mind.

He's living officially. He's alive according to the fine measurements of our fine scientific establishment.

What are the words I'll remember when he's dead.

The mind has gone away. The light of the eyes has long been out. And the flesh is left alone . . . in a chair.

(*Silence.*)

He should be dead.

RUTH (*comes to her*). Rachel. Be quiet now for awhile. Let the suffering inside you settle. You'll grow accustomed to the suffering. You'll learn to wear it like you might wear an old coat. In awhile the covering that seems so heavy to you now will stretch and you'll be moving free again within it. Time makes all things bearable.

RACHEL. It doesn't help to know that in a year or two the distance between me and this grief will have grown greater. If it's so it's because each grief is one bead on a string upon which other, heavier beads are being strung.

RUTH. Once you were happy together. There were many times when you were a pleasure to him. Accept it as a mercy that he lived to see you grown.

RACHEL. Lies . . . from a person who has seen what I've seen, who knows, or might know, what I know.

RUTH. My husband is terrified of dying. He wants to go on living.

RACHEL. It's exactly what he wants that he's not getting.

RUTH. When he shakes in my arms what do you want me to answer? "Though I walk through the valley of the shadow of death, I will fear no evil: for thou art with me: thy rod and thy staff comfort me." As I read him the words of the Bible I also begin to tremble.

NAOMI (*chants in Hebrew*). Shema Israel/ Adoni eloeinou/ Adoni ehahd. (Hear, Oh Israel/ The Lord our God/ The Lord is One.)

RACHEL. Naomi, as much as your son needed you when he was young, I need you now. Or more than that. When he was a baby sucking at your breast. No. More. When he was a fetus breathing your blood, taking his form from your flesh. I need you that much. I give up my father as I have to. Come with me now. Give up your son since you must, but don't give up your struggling daughters.

NAOMI. My son is the only one I ever cared for.

RACHEL. And who will you care for when he's dead.

NAOMI. He's still dying. What gives you the right . . .

RACHEL. I take the right because my father's dying faster. I'm a woman and I'm good at suffering silently. But I have not been good at living. And now think how out of my fear, I have become good at killing. Because I stand and watch his torture does not make me any less a partner in it. There is evil in not doing and I feel that evil alive inside myself. I feel it growing in me like a poison vine that winds around the healthy stalk. I am burdened by a parasite so ugly yet so well-disguised it feeds off my will without my knowing; it has filled itself off my hunger.

NAOMI. You blame yourself too much and then unable to bear it by yourself you blame us. Accept that things cannot be other than they are. However you explain it, they would still be dying and we would still be staring at it: daughter to father, wife to husband, mother to son.

RACHEL. We are just shadows of ourselves and they in their deathbeds are shadows of shadows. Men without muscles, without wills, without minds. Unable to talk, to reason, to imagine. Not shadows even, but dark spots. Dark spots left on life.

NAOMI. I'm an old woman and I see my only son is dying. I need all my strength to stand steady enough to let him pass. I can't consider what could have been. I'm an old woman and I've prayed to god to end my life instead of his. But with every pain he suffers I am stronger. Every time he cries my determination grows. The joke of motherhood. When her child needs her, she endures. Joke again. The child never feels more abandoned, never turns against her with more bitter rage than he does now, watching his own mother watch him die.

RACHEL. You shouldn't have to feel your grief alone for then the will to prolong it strengthens. If grief is all I know of life I cannot help hold onto grief. Until it seems impossible to end the grief by ending the hold on me of the one who makes me grieve. Ending it I would be left without it. Without it, I don't know who I am.

NAOMI. My life is almost over. I cannot question it the way you do. My life is a pattern and no matter what that pattern has been based on it's a pattern in the cloth itself. Not a fashion that can be put on or taken off at will. One doesn't change the way the threads have come together without unraveling the entire piece of cloth. I understand what you are saying, I can't participate. I can't continue to exist if everything is taken from me.

RACHEL. The pattern that you make extends its shape from you through Ruth to me. I know I have the right to change it in my life. Do I have that right still if changing my life demands that you change yours.

NAOMI. Let me be. Let me spend my energy mothering my dying son. The thought sounds strange to me even as I say it. Of all a mother's functions my son's illness has already fully stripped me. My son moans in his bed. He moans from deep inside his throat. "How do you feel," I ask him. Drugged, he feels nothing except he has been betrayed by me. And perhaps he has been. Only how could I have known it. How could I have born the hardship of his early years and education if I had thought there was this one lesson I should teach him. I didn't bring him up to watch him die. What mother does this?

RACHEL. Some must have. Why do some people but not others put on their finest qualities like brilliant colors and flaunt their living beauty in the face of death?

RUTH. One of you is old, the other young.

One's life is nearly over, the other's just begun. But I'm in the middle of my life. Who am I if I'm not my husband's wife? My children have grown up and gone away. My husband's dying. And I who thought I had a position, have none. Once he's dead I might as well never have existed. I'm nothing. Who am I?

RACHEL. Fear of death keeps him living. Fear of life keeps you clinging to him. It's not unnatural to be frightened, living is a frightening occupation. But remember, you made children from the center of you where eating, feeling, loving are united. Find the healthy breath inside you that allows you to still his heavy breathing. Take life for yourself from the one who is dying.

RUTH. I can't do it. If I did it it would be murder. It must happen slowly and I must show grief openly. Don't push me. A man is dying who has hit me, who has called me whore, who has ridiculed me before my children, and convinced me I am nothing. The same man who sought my bed and showed off my stylish beauty to his friends.

RACHEL. Letting him live won't quiet the wish to kill inside you. But there's a human limit to hate, the limit love puts on it. Love is a changing emotion and they are past changing. Everyday they are less than they were. So we let them go for love's sake or we let ourselves go on hating.

RUTH. The person who is dying had a body whose love I wanted and whose love I thought I needed. For love's sake I waited while he came into me from behind and I buried my face in the folds of the pillow and clawed the varnished bedstead. For lack of his love I've run screaming from the room. I've thrown plates of food on the floor and crawled after every crumb while he sat tipped back in his chair. I've put my hand through the storm door and walked barefoot on broken glass. Locked myself in the bathroom and spit up blood, straining to hear someone's step in the hall. I've apologized for everything I've ever done.

NAOMI. Ruth, the cycle cannot end unless we end it. My son will die a better death if you reach out to me.

RUTH. I'm the one between you. I must find my strength from my unhappy place in time. What has been passed down has been passed through me. So I can also pass on the new wisdom growing up.

NAOMI. And I'll receive it and return it modified with age. We three. Three generations. We are all the firsthand knowledge nature lets us have of what's before, what's to come. Past, present, future, embodied by us three. Now we exchange it.

RACHEL. We'll go down the hall together and take the intravenous needle from his arm. I'll hold his hand and watch his passage.

RUTH. Then we'll go on to my husband. I'll hold his hand and watch his passage.

NAOMI. And we'll come to my son at the end of the hall. I'll hold his hand and watch his passage.

RUTH. We plan their deaths together but we stand alone when we stand for the last time in the gaze of son, husband, father. Lonely twice over. Lonely from our need to be alone. Lonely, too, as the murderer is lonely. It is still murder we commit in just a minute. We three women do it. We cannot give an order for it to be done. We will put our hands around the plastic tube and pull the intravenous needle slowly from the swollen arm. And tomorrow and the next day and the next day we will be without this person's presence.

RACHEL. My will grows outward toward my body. The thought steps forward and the human act takes shape. My father's sickness worked the life force in reverse. The will was absent first, then the body shriveled. And the memory of the man who lived there—empty. When I let him die it's the emptiness I murder.

(RUTH's *wail is heard; she has done it.*)

NAOMI. Now we are alone. Alone with our lament. Left alone by our own hands with our sorrow.

The three women (RUTH *returns.* NAOMI *acts. The chant continues.* NAOMI *returns.* RACHEL *acts. The chant continues. It is done. The three women lament together. Their lament is a song. It passes through all shades of grief and brave exaltation.*):
Let our lament go out.
Let us sing of our sorrow.
Let the weight of our deed
fill our words.
Let our lament go out,
Heavy like our heart,
Clear like our sight,
Warm as tears.
Let our lament go out.
Let the song of our sorrow be heard.
Let the weight of our sorrow
be shared
by the world.

PIMP

by **Martha Boesing**

CHARACTERS

Jo, *the Mother*
ADRIAN, *the Daughter*
RUTH, *the Wife*

SCENE *1: The lights come up on* ADRIAN'S *doll, alone. "Bobby Shafto" is played off-stage on a music box or a xylophone.* ADRIAN *comes on and sits with her doll.*

ADRIAN *sings:*
Bobby Shafto's gone to sea
with silver buckles on his knee;
he'll come back and marry me—
pretty Bobby Shafto.

    (RUTH AND JO *enter slowly and join*
        ADRIAN, *singing*):
I have these to sell:
I have to sell
old rags and dust,
my names,
dried-up passions,
wasted hours;
who will buy them?
I have these to sell:
dancing dresses,
pressed corsages,
banished books,
worn-out affections;
I wish to sell them all.
And I will sell
my last week's dream,
broken mirrors,
used-up prayers.
Oh, who will buy
legs that never moved me forward fast
   enough?
Oh, who will buy them?
I have flesh for sale:
flesh and fiber,
fish and foetus.

I have babes,
these babies up for sale:
old promises,
and names
and rags
and used-up prayers,
and all my babies,
all my babes for sale.

SCENE *2:* Jo *is brushing* ADRIAN'S *hair.*

Jo. Such pretty hair, Adrian. (*Pause.*) Who was that boy I saw you with yesterday?
ADRIAN. Oh, Eddie.
Jo (*mimicking*). Oh, Eddie.
ADRIAN. He's O.K. He's kind of dirty.
Jo. He doesn't take a bath?
ADRIAN. He talks about . . .
Jo. You must remember to wash your brush when you shampoo your hair, dear.
ADRIAN. I let him kiss me, Mama.
Jo. Why did you do that, Adrian?
ADRIAN. It felt good.
Jo. Felt good?
ADRIAN. Well, no, it didn't feel good.
Jo. Well, did it or didn't it?
ADRIAN. Mama, can you get pregnant if a boy touches your tongue . . . with his tongue?
Jo. No, dear. Whatever gave you that idea?
ADRIAN. Well, Margaret said . . .
Jo. Well, you can't. (*Pause.*) Your ends are splitting, dear. We must get them trimmed.
ADRIAN. Does it feel good?
Jo. Does what feel good?
ADRIAN. Getting pregnant.
Jo. Not before you're married it doesn't. Only whores like it before they get married.
ADRIAN. Margaret said . . .
Jo. Do I have to make myself clearer?
ADRIAN. No.
Jo. After you're married it will feel good. Then he'll stay with you and love you. I wish you'd let me curl your hair—not tight curls, just soft little waves, all around your face.

MARTHA BOESING (1936–)

The Minneapolis-based At-the-Foot-of-the-Mountain is a feminist theatre ensemble. Through consciousness-raising workshops in vocal and body awareness and the exploration of various improvisational and gestalt disciplines, "we are in the process of developing our company work and radicalizing our collective vision."

Martha Boesing is a member of this seven-woman company. She is, moreover, responsible for much of the material that it uses in its productions. *Pimp* and its companion piece, *The Gelding*, were the first offerings of this feminist collective when it opened in 1974.

Accent of Fools was Boesing's first play, written while she was still a student at the Connecticut College for Women. She temporarily abandoned the theatre while pursuing first a master's degree from the University of Wisconsin and, afterwards, postgraduate work at the University of Minnesota.

Eventually, Boesing dropped out of academic life to work with the Minneapolis Repertory Theater. With John Donahue, she also helped to found and codirect the Moppet Players, which evolved into the famous Children's Theatre Company.

After three years at the Firehouse Theatre as "an actress, fund-raiser and closet dramatist," she and her husband, Paul

Martha Boesing

Boesing, began to collaborate on songs and dialogues, which they took on tour around the country. Their operas *The Wanderer* (1969) and *Earth Song* (1970) were commissioned by the Minnesota Opera Company and the American Friends Service Committee respectively.

Among her most recent plays is *Raped* (1976), a feminist adaptation of Brecht's *The Exception and the Rule*, and *Mad Emma* (1977), a portrait of anarchist Emma Goldman. Boesing lives in Minneapolis with her three children and director Phyllis Wagner.

(ADRIAN *moves away.* JO *lights up a cigarette.*)

ADRIAN. Mama, why do you smoke?

JO. Because I didn't have the good sense to listen to my mama when I was your age.

ADRIAN. Did Daddy smoke?

JO. A pipe.

ADRIAN. Did you like that?

JO. Uh-huh.

ADRIAN. Sometimes I think that I can still smell him.

JO. Well, you can't.

ADRIAN. Did you walk around the house nakid when Daddy was here? Emily Packard's parents do.

JO. I could care less what Emily Packard's parents do!

ADRIAN. Why did Daddy leave?

JO. It's too complex. Have you ever thought of cutting your hair short like Emily's? It would be so pretty.

ADRIAN. I love you, mama.

JO. I love you too, dear.

(*They embrace.* JO *returns to brushing* ADRIAN'S *hair. She puts a bow in it.* JO *places a photograph of a man in* ADRIAN'S *hand.* ADRIAN *becomes a very pretty doll. She whirls out of* JO'S *space into the next scene.*)

SCENE 3: RUTH *is perched high on something.*

RUTH. Are you lost?

ADRIAN. Who said that?

RUTH. I said that.

ADRIAN. Where are you?

RUTH. Up here. Well? Are you?

ADRIAN. Am I what?

RUTH. Lost.

ADRIAN. Oh, that. Well, yes. As a matter of fact I am. Do you by any chance know this man? (*She hands the photo to* RUTH.)

RUTH. I know him very well.

ADRIAN. Then perhaps you can point me in the direction of his house.

RUTH. Why do you want to go there?

ADRIAN. He just bought me.

RUTH. He just what?

ADRIAN. My mother sold me to him for forty thousand dollars. And I'm supposed to go where he lives. I'm also not supposed to tell anyone.

RUTH. That's . . . preposterous!

ADRIAN. Well, you might think it's preposterous, but I think it's awful.

RUTH. He bought you?

ADRIAN. Yes. My mother collected the money yesterday.

RUTH. Forty thousand dollars?

ADRIAN. Forty thousand dollars.

RUTH. Well, I think . . .

(*Pause.*)

Sometimes I actually think. . . .

(*Pause.*)

He really . . . ?

(*Pause.*)

How could he!

ADRIAN. Who?

RUTH. He's my husband!

(ADRIAN *collapses. Whimpers.* RUTH *climbs down and comes to her. Tentatively she soothes* ADRIAN.)

JO (*sings*).

Bobby Shafto's gone to sea
with silver buckles on his knee;
he'll come back and marry me—
pretty Bobby Shafto.

SCENE 4: JO *is talking to someone who is not present. Perhaps through the walls, perhaps on the telephone.*

I told him that he had to come over to see me. I just couldn't handle this kind of thing on the phone. It was so . . . dangerous . . . horrible. And of course I really do care for her. No, I said, I'm not backing out. But couldn't we just sit down and talk for a little while about it? I want to feel sure that you'll be kind to her, I said. She's still a v . . .

baby, you know. I would feel so much easier about the whole thing if we could just talk. You've got to understand how painful this is for me. No, I'm not backing out. After all, I am her mother. When she was little I'd tiptoe into her room late at night and just look at her. She was such a beautiful child—always smiling in her sleep. I'd touch her ever so lightly, tucking the covers up under her chin. I'd lay my hand against her cheek. It was soft. I wanted to take her in my arms, hold her against my breast. I had to resist waking her up and pushing her back inside of me somehow! Don't you understand? She was my flesh! But now she thinks she's separate from me! What does she know of that? She said that I smothered her! That ungrateful little wart! That's when I decided to sell her. She owed me that much at least. Take her! Take her! Good riddance, I say, to bad rubbish! But send me the money first, you fucker! You goddamned bastard—send me the money first!

SCENE 5: JO *sits staring into space.* ADRIAN *is talking to her doll.*

ADRIAN.

Mama, what if I don't like him?
Who will comb my hair?
My hair will get all tangled.
You hate it when it's tangled, mama.
Who will comb it?
I'd sweep the floors, mama.
I'd wash the dishes.
I'd clean my room.
I'd comb your hair, mama.
Your hair's so pretty.
I'd read to you at night.
When you can't sleep at night, mama?
I'd read to you.
And scratch your back.
Like you did when I was seven.
Do you remember, mama?
Don't make me go.
I'm your daughter, mama.
I'll be your sister.
You never had a sister.
I'll be your mama, mama.
I'll take care of you!

(*She goes to* JO *and begins to brush her hair.*)

Last night, mama,
in a dream—

your face:
it was melting!
Suddenly your eye
burst out of its socket
onto the ground
and it became—
it was horrible, mama—
your eye turned into me!
I wouldn't want to hurt you, mama!
I would do anything for you, mama—
anything!

(Jo *turns her head to look at* ADRIAN. ADRIAN *becomes a doll again. She drops the brush into her mother's lap and leaves.*)

SCENE 6: *The three women come together as adolescent girls, sharing fantasies.*

ADRIAN. One upon a time there was a handsome prince. He came riding through the woods one day on his pure white horse. I was scrubbing the flagstones in front of our house, dressed only in rags. I was singing and my song drew him to me.

RUTH. Once upon a time there was a wise yogi. He lived alone in a hut in the woods. I saw him one day when I was out walking by myself. He was sitting cross-legged, deep in meditation.

JO. Once upon a time there was an artist—filled with passion. He had a studio at the very top of a mountain. I traveled for thousands of miles to see him because I had fallen in love with his paintings. When I arrived I threw open the door and saw him standing before his easel, trembling with creativity.

ADRIAN. I had never seen a more handsome man!

RUTH. Never had I seen such a holy man!

JO. I had never before seen such a vital man! I tore off all my clothes and fell down at his feet.

ADRIAN. His doublet was made of velvet. And he had two great ostrich feathers in his broad-brimmed hat. He held a wild cougar in his arms which he had tamed.

RUTH. As I approached, he opened his eyes and smiled at me. I asked him if I could become his student. I said that I would pick wild berries for him and fetch water from the brook for him and attend to his needs.

ADRIAN. He stopped in front of our house and looked down at me.

JO. In a gesture of compassion he swept me into his arms

RUTH. He stood up and came

JO. And took me—

ADRIAN. No word—only a smile—

RUTH. to where I was,

JO. O, thunder in the heavens!—he took me

ADRIAN. And I knew that he saw through the rags and through the dirt on my face

JO. right there on the floor of his studio!

RUTH. and he put his arm around me.

ADRIAN. and I became transformed into beauty.

JO. And the earth heaved.

RUTH. He said that it was not yet time.

ADRIAN. He said that he would return to me one day.

JO. I said that I would come and make love with him, day and night, but he told me that it was not yet time.

RUTH. He told me that the time would come when I was grown that I would be ready to come to him

JO. You will know, he intoned to me, you will know by the fire in your heart when it is time. And then you will come and be my lover and give yourself to me, to my consuming passion, and to my art.

RUTH. and that we would become lovers then and I would serve him and learn wisdom from him and live with him in his hut in the woods.

ADRIAN. and he would take me on his pure white horse back through the woods to his palace where I would become his queen and (*sadly*) we would live happily ever after.

SCENE 7: JO *is smoking a pipe.* RUTH *comes in and sits beside her.*

JO. Can I get you something, Ruth? (*No response.*) Well . . . ? (*Again no response.* JO *offers* RUTH *the pipe. She refuses.* JO *mocks* RUTH, *reading the smoke signs.*) It say here, little cloud—it say you very tight. Tight-lipped, tight-assed. It say you not happy, you volunteer slave, nigger, escapee from great plantation.

RUTH. Jo, I don't find that funny.

JO. Why you stay if life so unfunny?

RUTH. I stay because he needs me.

JO. Bull-shit, little cloud. Bull—shit!

RUTH. I like to be with him.

Jo. You stay because you slave. You scared if you not slave, you be no thing. No thing at all. Poof! A little smoke. No thing more than that. You willing slave: housewife, dishwasher, laundress, foot scratcher, cock sucker.

Ruth. I think you're disgusting.

Jo. Me disgusting? No. Me big chief. You squaw. You not grow up yet into big chief. You make heap big fire. Me go out to kill moose. You make plenty fire-water to warm belly. We roll around on grass together. You like. How long you willing to take orders? Look! (*Jo sees* Ruth's *death standing behind her left shoulder.*)

Ruth. What?

Jo. Behind you.

Ruth. There's nothing there.

Jo. You missed it.

SCENE 8: Adrian *caresses and polishes the pipe. It is a sexual act.* Ruth *enters.*

Ruth. I'll take that.

Adrian. It's mine.

Ruth. It's his.

Adrian. He gave it to me to polish.

Ruth. He gave it to me to polish.

Adrian. He doesn't like the way you polish anymore. He told me to do it instead.

Ruth. I'm not done yet!

Adrian. Perhaps he thinks you are.

Ruth. I came to him of my own free will. I wasn't sold.

Adrian. You're a bitch.

Ruth. You're a whore.

Adrian. Bitch!

Ruth. Whore!

> (*They begin to wrestle. Slowly. They undress down to tank suits. It becomes a real match between two women wrestlers—violent and terrible to watch. They pull at each other's hair and tear at each other's skin. Jo comes out to watch.* Adrian *wins.* Jo *holds her arm up as victor.* Jo *and* Adrian *leave.*)

SCENE 9: Ruth *is alone. She talks to the pipe.*

When I was five we used to go out skating. When he came home from work and the sun was going down, we'd go out skating on the lake. It was cold and we were skating to the other side to buy licorice, singing yankee doodle, turkey in the straw. My skates had double runners. Sometimes I fell behind his long striding gliding out. On the way home it was already dark and the ice began to crack way down its crevices like thunder. O, I hung on to him then! Holding his hand so the giant at the bottom of the lake couldn't reach up through the crevices and pull me down through the ice!

After we came home he lit the fire. I felt safe for a little while.

When I was six, he left. I never said a word about it. It wasn't till much later, when I first began to bleed, I felt the loss. My mother tried to hide the wound with towels and hunks of cotton. She told me not to be concerned, that it was normal; but of course I knew some part of me was cut away. He had taken something when he left; that much was clear.

He left me, and I became a hundred and twenty-nine years old—at six.

SCENE 10: Jo *is again talking to someone who is not present. Perhaps through the walls, perhaps on the telephone.*

Of course I called him to say that I had done it, it was done. I guess I was afraid he might not like it. He was kind of funny that way. Guess what? I said. I have a surprise for you! Don't you want to guess what it is? You'd better pack your bags!—that's what I said. Well . . . where would you like to go? Tanzania? Ceylon? Greece? Maybe our ship came in! That's what I said to him: maybe our ship came in! And we can lie in each other's arms in the sun! Oh, I felt the sun tumbling right down out of the sky and entering my blood and warming me down to my toenails! Oh, yes, my darling! Yes! I said. Warm hair, warm skin, and bird-free! And I want to stay bird-free forever! Forever, I said. Forever!

SCENE 11:

| Adrian (*older, estranged*). Remember the crazy woman who lived next door | Jo (*like a small animal. She curls around* Adrian's *hair and body*). |

to us, Mother? You remember the old yellow barn behind her house? Crazy Susan Fling?

She kept all her old things up there. Rags, pictures, falling out of their frames, old iron tables painted white, wicker cane chairs, and beds. There were beds there, Mother.

We went there and hid up there, Tommy and I, my cousin and I. Hiding. We lay on the beds and talked a lot. He pulled my pants down once and pushed my legs apart and looked at me. He looked at me, Mother, and poked at me. I felt like rubber. He poked at me like a piece of rubber.

It wasn't bad like you said it would be—being with boys. Being looked at.

Being poked on beds. It wasn't good like you said it would be.

(ADRIAN *narrates coldly. Only the screams are real.*) I felt like rubber. That's all. I came home and you were sitting there, Mother. Asleep on your chair. The fire had gone out. I smelled Scotch. In the air, on

I love your hair. It's silky. My fingers caress it. I could wrap my hands through it. It's soft. It feels like me.

I love to wrap my hand and arms through you silky, soft threads. I'm in love with your hair.

I could roll my body through your hair, your young hair, caress it with my arms, my thighs, belly, toes, breasts.

Your hair rubbing against my skin, your hair against my hair, your body against my body. and we could be like two little animals, snuggled in our lair.

We could be like one little animal. One. You and me. Me. Mine. (*Her speech trails off into a hum. She rolls away, into her own stupor, drunk on* ADRIAN'S *smells.*)

your breath. I went upstairs, Mother. To my own room. I pulled the covers over my head. And I screamed out loud, Mother. I screamed out loud. Agh! I screamed out loud, Mother. Agh! I screamed, Mother. Agh! I screamed. Agh! Agh! Screamed, Mother. Screamed. Agh! Agh! Agh!

SCENE *12:* Jo *is sitting, lighting up her pipe.* RUTH *enters.*

JO. Hi.
RUTH. Take that pipe out of your mouth!
JO (*pause*). Ruth wants Jo to take the pipe out of her mouth. Jo hasn't finished lighting it yet. (*She slowly finishes lighting the pipe and then puts it down.*)
RUTH. We have to talk about something.
JO. Something? What something?
RUTH. The situation.
JO. The situation?
RUTH. Look, Jo, Adrian is in my house!
JO. Yes, Adrian is in Ruth's house. Jo put Adrian in Ruth's house.
RUTH. Jo, it's not natural. (*Pause.*) You've done a terrible thing! (*Pause.*) Jo, listen to me!
JO. Jo is listening.
RUTH. I don't understand why you've done this, Jo! I don't understand.
JO. Need. Jo's need. Adrian's need. Needs that Ruth can't understand.
RUTH. Adrian's need?
JO. Adrian's need as seen by Adrian's mother. Adrian's need to get away from her mother, Jo. Jo put Adrian in a safe place.
RUTH. What about me?
JO. Ruth is all grown up. She can take care of herself. Just like Jo.
RUTH. I think you're flipping out, Jo. Don't you knew what it is to love anyone?
JO. What do you know about love?
RUTH. I know this: You don't sell people you love. You don't sell people.

Jo.
O, you're getting smart, Ruth.
You're catching up.
I can see that.
But time's moving, Ruth.
Time's running.
You have to run with it . . .
or you'll be dead!
You have to plunge in, Ruth,
jump into it head first!
Who are you to ask me what I've done?
I'm alive! I'm here!
I took the plunge and I'm here, Ruth!
Right in front of your eyes!
Are you here, Ruth?
Maybe you're somewhere else!
I did it for him, Ruth! Don't you get it?
I am loved, Ruth!
What about you?
(RUTH *is visibly moved. Changed.*)

SCENE *13: The three women meet as successful, perfect women (movie stars, panel experts, Vassar graduates, etc.) sharing their fantasies.*

RUTH. Once upon a time
Jo. Once upon a time
ADRIAN. Once upon a time there was a very wealthy and very handsome bachelor. He collected women as some men collect pottery and phonograph records. He was forever putting his most recent conquest carefully on his shelf and going off in gay pursuit of some new woman whom he had heard about from a friend or a prince.

RUTH. there was a very smart man. He played chess. He could play circles around all the chess players in the world because he was so smart. He was smarter than all the scientists and all the businessmen and all the politicians in the world.

Jo. there was a very powerful king. He was mightier than all the other kings on earth. Nothing terrified him on the battlefield—not on the land, not on the sea. Swords, cannons, rifles, arrows—he had withstood them all, leaving victorious from all encounters. But, strange to say, this mighty king was terrified of women!

RUTH. One day he was challenged to a chess game by a woman! It was said of her that she was so smart that it was almost as if she had the brains of a man. He didn't want to play with her because he thought it wouldn't be any fun. But finally public pressure made him agree to play. They met in the square. Everyone brought lunch with them and lots of beer because they thought the game would go on and on all day long. But she was so smart— that woman was so smart—that in three minutes, she had him checkmated. Not one time, not twenty-six times, but thirty-nine times! And the last time he became so enraged to be beaten by a woman that he flew into a great temper. She said she couldn't help herself;

ADRIAN. One day he met a woman who was so exquisite, so graceful and beautiful that he thought surely she was made of precious crystal. He pursued her for over a year. Ever so delicately, ever so cautiously, not wanting to frighten or to harm her. Finally he won her over—delighting her with gifts of perfume and flowers and the very finest vintage wines. But as he was about to place her on his shelf with the rest of his collection, he suddenly dropped her.

Jo. Whenever he looked at a woman, no matter how frail or petite she might actually be, he saw a great giantess looming down from above him. And her voice came at him like a thundering god no matter how softly she spoke to him. All women made him quake in his boots and he responded to them in the tiny high voice of a child. One night his wee bird of a wife was bathing him in his marble bathtub. She was shaving the hair around his navel, because it itched and bothered him dreadfully. Suddenly her hand slipped. The razor plunged downward. It was an accident. Not really the act of an amazon mother. But simply an accident.

RUTH. it was only an accident, she said.

ADRIAN. It was only an accident. But she shattered into a million tiny pieces of cut glass and two of the smallest fragments from a splinter flew into both of his eyes, blinding him. He lost his sight and never again could he recapture the joy of gazing at his beautiful collection of women during the long lazy hours of his remaining days.

RUTH. But in his fury, the blood vessels stood out from his forehead like cows' tits ready to gush forth. And then suddenly, his head burst open and his brain splattered out on the ground at her feet. Everyone gasped! His brain—that brilliant mind that everyone had been admiring all these many years—was nothing but a great squirming mass of long, white, wiggly worms!

Jo. But before either of them knew what had happened, the water became blotted with blood. And he lay there, this mighty king, metamorphosed into his wife's twin. Poor little bird, lying there without his weapons—open!

SCENE *14:* ADRIAN *is about six years old.*

Jo. You left your doll out in the rain!
ADRIAN. I did?
Jo. You did. It's ruined! Soaked through!
ADRIAN. I didn't mean to. Is she dead?
Jo. Dead? She's a mess! That's what she is. I don't think you really give a damn about her!
ADRIAN. I love her. She's my dolly.
Jo. You left her out in the rain!
ADRIAN. I'm sorry, Mommy. I'm sorry, Dolly.
Jo. Adrian, when are you going to grow up?
ADRIAN. I didn't mean to do it.
Jo. You didn't mean to do it. You never mean to do it. But you do it and you do it and you do it unless I nag and nag at you until I feel like an old crow. Or unless I take care of it myself. We can't go on like this.
ADRIAN. I said I was sorry.
Jo. Being sorry isn't going to straighten out your doll!
ADRIAN. I wish you'd shut up!
Jo. Adrian! Don't you talk to your mother like that!
ADRIAN. Well, I wish you would.
Jo. You go upstairs to your room until you can hold your tongue!
ADRIAN. I hate you! I hate you!
Jo. Get out of here! Right now! Before I swat the living daylights out of you!
(Jo *chases* ADRIAN *out. She grabs* ADRIAN'S *doll and beats it and beats it.*)

SCENE *15:* RUTH *enters and speaks to* Jo.

RUTH. I did wash the dishes, Jo. I washed the bone china dishes when the Wilsons and the Laymans came to dinner. I put out the crystal and I lit the candles. I lit the candles for him. I was his wife. I made the dinner—

croutons on the salad and drawn butter for the crab and hot brandy as we sat around the fire.

And when his friends had left and he said: "Oh, I am an old man; oh, I am dying!" I said: "My dear, my dear, you are pure gold. You are very tall; everyone looks up to you."

Later when I climbed in under the covers beside him in the bed, I kissed his shoulder. I laid my hand against his thigh. My hand was always cold, and he shivered without wanting to be cruel. He shivered and turned over on his side, his back confronting my open body like a wall of steel. And I hated him for that, Jo.

And I have never told this story to anyone before today.
(Jo *exits.*)
(ADRIAN *is perched high on something.
. . . The same thing that* RUTH *was perched on in Scene Three.* RUTH *discards her wedding ring.*)
ADRIAN. Are you lost?
RUTH. Who said that?
ADRIAN. I said that.
RUTH. Where are you?
ADRIAN. Up here. Well, are you?
RUTH. Am I what?
ADRIAN. Lost.
RUTH. Oh, that. Well, yes, as a matter of fact, I am sort of lost. I just left home/him. (*Pause.*) I left him!
(ADRIAN *giggles.*)
RUTH. Do you find that amusing?
ADRIAN. Well, it seems like everything's turned around.
RUTH. It always does. (*Pause.*) It always does!
ADRIAN. Actually it seems like a good idea.
RUTH. What does?
ADRIAN. Your leaving home/him.
RUTH. Oh, that. Yes, I guess it is a good idea. It was time for me to grow up.
(ADRIAN *giggles.*)
ADRIAN. You already seem like a grown-up to me.
RUTH. Well, maybe that's one of the turned-around things.
ADRIAN. Aren't you glad? I mean, doesn't it feel good?
RUTH. What? Being turned around?
ADRIAN. No. Being grown up!
RUTH. No. As a matter of fact, it feels really awful.

(RUTH *collapses. She whimpers.* ADRIAN *comes down to* RUTH. *She soothes her tentatively.*)

ADRIAN (*sings*):
Bobby Shafto's gone to sea
with silver buckles on his knee;
he'll come back and marry me—
pretty Bobby Shafto.

SCENE 16: *"Bobby Shafto" is played off-stage on a xylophone or a music box* ADRIAN *is alone. She gets her doll.*

She was fifteen when it happened. She was very little. I hardly noticed her stomach growing bigger. I didn't really know her at all. She wasn't a friend of mine. She wasn't my kind of person. She was one of the townies. One of them. One time she told me—at recess, at school, it was in the fifth grade—that if a girl ever touched the tip of another girl's tongue with the tip of her tongue that no lies could ever pass between them again. I didn't do that with her. I wasn't that kind of a girl. I knew she was a witch anyway. I knew it before anyone else. After it happened, they found a doll in her room. It had Mr. Prinkle's name pinned on its chest. He was the principal. It had pins stuck in it. All over its body. (*As she speaks she puts pins in her doll's body.*) I knew that about Alice a long time before it happened. That she was a witch, I mean. When the baby got inside her, no one paid any attention for a long time. But everyone knew of course. Crazy Bruce had blatted it all over the school. He was a moron. I mean really. He was demented. It was hard at first to know whether to believe him. About Alice, I mean. But pretty soon she started getting fat. And then of course the cat was really out of the bag. Everyone knew what had happened. Finally Mr. Prinkle had to tell her that she couldn't come back to school. I mean what else could he do? The whole town was talking about it. It was a very awkward situation. That must have been when Alice made the doll. She spent an awful long time alone after that. I was scared of her. She looked more like a witch than ever. Her hair got all matted. And her face just got thinner and thinner while her belly got fatter and fatter. I always crossed the street when I saw her coming. Poor Alice. Poor, poor Alice. (RUTH *and* JO

echo, in whispers, almost soundlessly, like the wind: "Poor Alice!" "Poor, poor Alice!") She did it in the bathroom. She must have been watching herself in the mirror while she did it. (ADRIAN *begins to act out the part of* ALICE *here, even while narrating in the third person.*) She poured a whole bottle of iodine into her Coke. It probably tasted awful. They found the empty bottle afterwards. And the last of the Coke. She must have swallowed it down very fast. Maybe she expected to go right away. Maybe she felt scared when she still saw her face in the bathroom mirror. That's probably why she got the razor blade too. She must have been frantic. To do such a thing. She must have grabbed it, half crazy with the fear, and dug at herself with it, cutting open the wrists in great gashes. Maybe she didn't feel it because of the iodine. Up and down her arm in huge slashes, the blood must have spurted out all over her, even while she was still watching. They found it later on the sink, and on the floor—the blood, I mean—and it was even smeared over the mirror where her face had been—like dried rain, like God crying out for Alice. . . .

SCENE 17: *A ritual in which* RUTH *and* ADRIAN *meet and touch each other, reborn, and* JO, *still possessed by her need, is stuck.*

(JO—*like a wild animal—grabs the doll and runs with it as if to hide. She attacks* ADRIAN'S *body with her words.*)

JO (*crying out, extending the sounds*). Waif! Cast-off! Orphan! Foundling! Leper! Pariah! Poor, poor Alice!

(RUTH *comes to* ADRIAN *and helps her up. They face each other and slowly stick out their tongues and touch the tips of them together.*)

ADRIAN (*sings*). I will cut the roots of all delusive passions.

AD & R. I will cut the roots of all delusive passions.

AD, R, J. I will cut the roots of all delusive passions.

ALL. cut the roots of passion
cut the roots of passion
cut the roots of passion

(JO *gives out. As she is about to flagel-*

late herself with the doll, RUTH *comes and takes the doll away from her, placing it carefully in front of a man in the audience.*)
(RUTH *and* ADRIAN *leave.*)

SCENE *18:* JO *speaks to the audience.* (*It is the first time in the play that the audience has been directly acknowledged.*)

JO. I don't want you to think I'm terrible. All I want is a little comfort. Love. You have to give a little to get a little. You know? I mean, Adrian will be happy. She's well taken care of. And I'll be happy. I gave him all the money. Forty thousand dollars. And he's happy. And now he owes me something. And I'm safe. And everyone is happy.

It's important to me that you don't hate me. I want you to like me. Women are creatures born to be liked.

I want someone to say he loves me.
I want to be the most important person in
   someone's life.
I want someone to speak all the languages of
   love to me:
Je t'aime!
Io te adore!
Ich liebe dich!
Se ago po!
I want someone to call me his petite chou.
His darling, his precious. . . .
I want someone to say
he would sail the seven seas for me,
that he would rather die a silent death of
   despair
under the stars
for me
than forgo one more touch,
one more moment with me.
I want someone to tremble when he touches
   me, and say:
"O, your skin is so soft!
Your eyes are burning with love!
Your thighs are stronger than my father's
   arms!
Hold me!
Hold me!
Never let me go!
I will stay with you forever!"

It is so much to ask?

(*All three women freeze.*)
(RUTH *and* ADRIAN *break the freeze to scream, cry, or make whatever noise will express the pent-up feelings of the play.*)
(*Again they freeze. A silence.*)

SCENE *19: The three women come together.*

ADRIAN. Once upon a time there was a young concubine. She was very pretty, and very obedient to her lord and master, the Sheik.

RUTH. One upon a time there was a barren queen. She served her king graciously, guiding him in all domestic matters of the kingdom. Being someone's queen was a very serious business to her, and she had put away all her childish toys and dreams.

JO. Once upon a time there was a crotchety old woman. She lived in the coldest region of the north, inside a house made of ice. She hated the coldness and she would bundle herself into whatever blankets and old rags she could find to try to stop the shivering.

RUTH. One day she met a large spider who said to her: "How useless you are. You work only for others, and do nothing for yourself. Why aren't you more like me—a spinner of beautiful webs?" And the barren queen saw that it was true.

ADRIAN. One day a small beggar girl went running past the window of the Sheik's palace, screeching and hollering at the top of her voice—whether in joy or in sadness, no one knew. Suddenly, as if possessed, the concubine raced to the great window, and flinging herself against the bars, she started screaming herself, joining in the ragged child's strange, exultant chorus. The Sheik, of course, placed her in the dungeon as a punishment for making such a ruckus. But it was too late. The concubine had felt her pain.

JO. Every night she dreamed that a stranger had come to her home and built a huge fire all around the outside of her ice house and that he had melted down the walls. But instead of simply warming her, the fire would leap onto her clothes, burning her hair and her flesh. And she woke up each night screaming from the heat, terrified of dying in the flames.

ADRIAN. On the very first day that she was again allowed into the upstairs rooms, she found a way to escape from the palace. And following one of the servant girls down to the well in the center of the village, she threw off the fine harem silks which the Sheik had given her and cried out to the people gathered there: "Look at me! I don't belong to anyone! I'm free!"

(ADRIAN *exits*.)

RUTH. And so she left the castle. At first she was frightened, not knowing in which direction to travel. She thought of the spider and wanted desperately to curl up inside of her strong and comfortable web. But then the queen remembered that spiders often trap the creatures they lure into their nets—and eat them. And so she decided to leave all that was familiar to her, and to walk alone up and down the highways of her kingdom until she found out who she was.

(RUTH *exits*.)

JO. The days passed, and the stranger in her dreams never came. She just sat waiting and growing older and older, colder and colder. One night the stranger did not appear in her dream. Instead, she dreamt that she herself built a fire inside her house, just big enough to warm her, to take away the cold. When the fire went out, she woke up.

(JO *exits*.)

SUPPLEMENTAL READINGS

1900–1909
- *Katy Did* — Rachel Crothers
- *A Man's World* — " "
- *The Rector* — " "
- *Diana of Dobson's* — Cicely Hamilton
- *Lady Geraldine's Speech* — Beatrice Harraden
- *Cranford: A Play* — Marguerite Merrington
- *Her Lord and Master* — Martha Morton
- *Mice and Men* — Madeleine Lucette Ryley

1910–1919
- *The Arrow Maker* — Mary Austin
- *Melinda and Her Sisters* — Mrs. O. H. P. Belmont
- *Two Sons* — Neith Boyce
- *Children of the Earth* — Alice Brown
- *They That Sit in Darkness* — Mary Burrill
- *He and She* — Rachel Crothers
- *Little Mother of the Slums* — Emily Herey Denison
- *Mine Eyes Have Seen* — Alice Dunbar-Nelson
- *The Pixy* — Edith Ellis
- *The Subjection of Kezia* — " "
- *The Neighbors* — Zona Gale
- *Overtones* — Alice Gerstenberg
- *The Patroness* — " "
- *Bernice* — Susan Glaspell
- *Close the Book* — " "
- *Rachel* — Angelina Weld Grimke
- *Jack and Jill and a Friend* — Cicely Hamilton
- *Just to Get Married* — " "
- *Enter the Hero* — Theresa Helburn
- *Good Gracious, Annabelle* — Clare Kummer
- *The Piper* — Josephine Preston Peabody
- *The Girl from Colorado* — Selina Solomons
- *The Woman Who Wouldn't* — Rose Pastor Stokes
- *Funiculi, Funicula* — Rita Wellman
- *The Flower Shop* — Marian Craig Wentworth
- *War Brides* — " " "

1920–1929
- *An Irish Triangle* — Djuna Barnes
- *She Tells Her Daughter* — " "
- *Exit an Illusion* — Marita O. Bonner
- *In the Morgue* — Sada Cowan

221

Expressing Willie	Rachel Crothers
Nice People	" "
What They Think	" "
The Death Dance	Thelma Duncan
Miss Lulu Bett	Zona Gale
Mr. Pitt	" "
The Verge	Susan Glaspell
Color Struck	Zora Neale Hurston
Blue Blood	Georgia Douglas Johnson
*In Review	Ruby Livingston
The Conflict	Clarice Vallette McCauley
Aria da Capo	Edna St. Vincent Millay
The Lamp and the Bell	" " " "
Graven Images	May Miller
Portrait of Mrs. W.	Josephine Preston Peabody
Days End	Alice Pieratt
The Hunch	Eulalie Spence
The Starter	" "
Four Saints in Three Acts	Gertrude Stein
Machinal	Sophie Treadwell
Sun-Up	Lula Vollmer
Wreckage	Mary Heaton Vorse
Sex	Mae West

1930–1939

The Old Maid	Zoë Akins
Mourners to Glory	Rietta Winn Bailey
Kiss the Boys Good-bye	Clare Boothe
Margin for Error	" "
The Women	" "
When Ladies Meet	Rachel Crothers
Susan and God	" "
Take My Stand	Elizabeth England
*Yesterday, Today and Tomorrow	Ada Reed Ferguson
Another Language	Rose Franken
Alison's House	Susan Glaspell
The Children's Hour	Lillian Hellman
Days to Come	" "
Here We Are	Dorothy Parker
Lawd, Does You Undahstan'	Ann Seymour
Dr. Faustus Lights the Lights	Gertrude Stein
Mighty Wind A'Blowin'	Alice Holdship Ware

1940–1949

*Filmy-Cooperation	Maude M. Aldrich
The Antiphon	Djuna Barnes
Claudia	Rose Franken
Soldier's Wife	" "
Watch on the Rhine	Lillian Hellman
The Member of the Wedding	Carson McCullers
Pickup Girl	Elsa Shelley
Yes Is for a Very Young Man	Gertrude Stein

Hope for a Harvest   Sophie Treadwell
On Whitman Avenue   Maxine Wood

1950–1959
  In the Summer House   Jane Bowles
  Trouble in Mind   Alice Childress
  A Raisin in the Sun   Lorraine Hansberry
  The Autumn Garden   Lillian Hellman
  Glory Day   Goldie Lake
  Incident at a Grave   "   "
  Ladies of the Corridor   Dorothy Parker and Arnaud d'Usseau
  The Happy Housewife   Hedda Rosten
  Let's Get Out of Here   Rae Welch

1960–1969
  Gloria and Esperanza   Julie Bovasso
  Wine in the Wilderness   Alice Childress
  Home Movies   Rosalyn Drexler
  Promenade   Maria Irene Fornes
  Tango Palace   "   "   "
  Funnyhouse of the Negro   Adrienne Kennedy
  The Owl Answers   "   "
  But What Have You Done for Me Lately?   Myrna Lamb
  Futz   Rochelle Owens
  Homo   "   "
  Calm Down Mother   Megan Terry
  Viet Rock   "   "

1970–
  Medea   Gloria Albee
  The Gelding   Martha Boesing
  Love Song for an Amazon   "   "
  A Late Snow   Jane Chambers
  The Confessions of Clara   Gwendolyn Gunn
  In Defense of Lou Andreas Salome   Barbara Kraft
  Mod Donna   Myrna Lamb
  Rebeccah   Karen Malpede
  Mourning Pictures   Honor Moore
  Family, Family   Sally Ordway
  Approaching Simone   Megan Terry

---

* These titles were published by the Signal Press or by
its predecessor, the Women's Christian Temperance Union
Publishing House. None of them show a copyright, so
the plays have to be dated on the basis of internal evidence.